THE COSMIC PLAY OF POWER

Goddess, Tantra and Women

THE COSMIC PLAY OF POWER

Goddess, Tantra and Women

Sanjukta Gupta

MOTILAL BANARSIDASS PUBLISHERS
PRIVATE LIMITED • DELHI

First Edition: Delhi, 2013

ISBN: 978-81-208-3542-9

MOTILAL BANARSIDASS
41 U.A. Bungalow Road, Jawahar Nagar, Delhi 110007
8 Mahalaxmi Chamber, 22 Bhulabhai Desai Road, Mumbai 400026
203 Royapettah High Road, Mylapore, Chennai 400026
236, 9th Main III Block, Jayanagar, Bangalore 560011
Sanas Plaza, 1302 Baji Rao Road, Pune 411002
8 Camac Street Kolkata 700017
Ashok Rajpath, Patna 800004
Chow, Varanasi 221001

Printed in India
by RP Jain at NAB Printing Unit,
A-44, Naraina Industrial Area, Phase I, New Delhi–110028
and published by JP Jain for Motilal Banarsidass Publishers (P) Ltd,
41 U.A. Bungalow Road, Jawahar Nagar, Delhi-110007

Contents

Introduction

Over the length and breadth of South Asia countless South Asians - Hindus, Buddhists, Jains - worship goddesses. Muslims do so too. For instance, in the early nineties I went to the south of Kolkata to visit a shrine of the Tiger god, Dakṣiṇarāya (the king of the south) at Dhabdhabi, a small village in the 24 parganas(S), West Bengal. In a village near Dhabdhabi I came across a little shrine with an image of a mother goddess surrounded by tiny clinging babies. I came to know that the local Muslims managed this shrine and a Muslim boy fetched the key from the caretaker so that I could go in and have a good look at the image. Unfortunately, I could not find any name of the goddess. Another goddess who is very popular amongst some middle class Bengali Hindu women in Kolkata is called Āsān Bībī, an obviously Muslim name [*āsān* may indicate that she removes all problems of life, *muśkil āsān*].

However, in this collection of essays, we are interested only in the Hindu Goddess Śakti and goddesses śaktis.[1] Śakti subsumes all śaktis who are but aspects of herself. In Hindu theology one is constantly confronted by this contradiction: it incorporates both monotheism and polytheism within its concept of God(dess). We have to either accept it or find a way around it. I shall come back to this topic and try to explain the Tantric and Purāṇic ways of solving this problem.

The second problem is to find a fixed character for the goddess. She can be either terrifyingly destructive (*ugra*), or compassionate and motherly (*saumya*). She can have anthropomorphic or theriomorphic forms or even can be represented in an aniconic form, such as a black triangular pebble. The most famous of her theriomorphic forms is Vārāhī or Vārtāḷī (boar-faced) goddess. She can be depicted naked, can even appear loathsome, Cāmuṇḍā, or can be exquisitely beautiful and bedecked as a queen. Her rituals can be public or esoteric. Finally, she may be both ferociously demoniac and irresistibly seductive as the repository of erotic enjoyment (*rasātmikā*). Goddesses like Kālī, Tārā, Cāmuṇḍā, are fierce and ugly to loathsome in appearance, and yet for countless Hindus they are the ultimate refuge to escape the trials and tribulations of life – the results of one's own acts in one's previous lives. The Goddess is the cosmic mother and only a mother's love has sufficient indulgence for her children, her loyal devotees to forgive their sins.

On the other hand, even though majestically beautiful, Durgā appears totally ruthless and invincible in any battle against powerful and majestic demons (*asura*) like the Buffalo demon and the royal demon-brothers Śumbha and Niśumbha. She is the concentrated fighting energy of the gods, emanating as the embodiment of divine righteous fury. In the cosmic struggles between the gods, the upholders of cosmic law and order, and the demons, the powers of chaos, Durgā destroys the creatures of chaos and re-establishes cosmic order. The same is true of Kauśikī, a much more complicated goddess incorporating various strands of Purāṇic and Tantric ideas. She does not hesitate to use war tactics such as showering taunts on her enemies and challenging them in a roundabout way, misguiding them into thinking of her as a seductive woman who can easily be won over. But when real battle starts, her furious battle stance appears in the front line and she destroys the demons. This is a display of her *māyā*.

By contrast, Vāgdevī/Sarasvatī, the goddess of knowledge and art, is serene, beautiful and compassionate. She represents divine wisdom/knowledge, the primal movement of the creative urge of the Creator, and is identified with divine Speech. Even so, the same Goddess can appear in a dark form and present a formidable figure. I shall come back to this while describing the Goddess Kālī.

Yet another aspect of the great Goddess is manifest in Lalitā/Tripurasundarī and Mīnākṣī. They are exquisitely beautiful and are very seductive goddesses. They often manifest a tension for supremacy between the male godhead and its female counterpart. In their mythology and theology they show the autonomous character of the supreme Goddess and often the male creator God recedes into the background.

In other contexts, where a male God Śiva is supreme, Umā/Pārvatī epitomizes motherhood. Her sons Gaṇeśa and Skanda, inspite of their many acts of valour and protection, remain her little children. Pārvatī, together with Lakṣmī, also is the model of wifely perfection.

Whatever her appearance may be, for the devotee the Goddess is the adorable mother who is full of affection and is instinctively protective towards her devotees, who are indeed her children. She is also the supreme cosmic Power (Parā-śakti), the indomitable and omnipotent divine Śakti from whom even a chance glance directed at the praying devotee is enough to remove all fear of existential problems. In fact devotees propitiate and invite her attention because of her natural compassion and her supreme cosmic power, which can intervene between their karma and its fruition. Only the devotees' total dependence, trust and loyal devotion activate her grace. Her compassionate attention is seen in her glance. The supreme Goddess at Kāñcī in south India is called Kāmākṣī; the name is interpreted as 'She whose glance fulfils all a devotee desires'.

The concept of the Goddess is intimately related to the theories and practices of the Tantric religions. The Goddess here primarily is the divine cosmic Power, which is autonomous, adamantine and indomitable. The Goddess theology is multifaceted and full of mysticism. Hence her characteristics are full of contradictions. In recent years several western and Indian scholars have been studying the theology of the Goddess and her religious ideology and practices. S.B. Das Gupta, Gopinath Kaviraj, Vraj Vallabh Dviveda, N.N. Bhattacharya, Wendel Beane, Ernest Payne, Alexis Sanderson, André Padoux, Cheevar M. Brown, Thomas Coburn, David White, David Kinsley, Cynthia Hume and Rachel MacDermott, to name just a few, have done great work on this subject and have revealed its complexity.

My personal encounter with Mm Gopinath Kaviraj was the great starting point of my studies in the theology of Divine Śakti. I was further helped and my Śakti understanding was enormously enhanced by my long and intimate study of the subject with V.V. Dviveda. He is the unchallenged authority in the traditional learning of the subject with his vast firsthand knowledge of the various systems of the Śakti cult. This is enhanced by his long and deep acquaintance with rituals practised by the followers of these varied systems, though he himself is a *smārta* (non-sectarian and orthodox high caste Hindu), pundit. I must specially mention Mackenzie Brown and Thomas Coburn for their excellent studies in the Devī theology. I have borrowed many of their discerning observations on the nature of the Goddess as revealed in the *Devī-Bhāgavata Purāṇa* and the *Devī-māhātmya* and other relevant Purāṇa materials.

The corpus of Tantric religious texts is vast and is written in many Indian languages - classical, medieval and modern. There are the Āgamas (technically canonical literature), commentaries, ritual manuals, eulogies, and most importantly the Epics and Purāṇas. Amongst these texts by far the most popular is the *Devīmāhātmya*, which is appended to the *Mārkaṇḍeya Purāṇa.*[2] It is also the earliest Purāṇa to present the Goddess as supreme Divine Power, as well as the source and locus of the entire creation. Another seminal Purāṇa celebrating the Goddess is the *Devībhāgavata Purāṇa.*[3]

Because of the popularity of these two texts among the majority of Goddess-worshipping traditional Hindus, I think a brief analysis of the earlier of the two Goddess Purāṇas will give me an opportunity to discuss various aspects of the Goddess cult.

The canonical texts concerning the goddess are in a general way referred to as Tantra. There are countless Tantras, originating from the north, south, west, central, east and far northeast regions of India. Each Indian region abounds with local powerful protecting goddesses. These deities often have a very long and continuous presence. The popularity of the *Devīmāhātmya* lies in its successfully subsuming many of these goddesses within the Supreme Goddess: for example, Cāmuṇḍā, the group of war goddess called Mātṛkā, and Śivadūtī.

It is now well known to the scholars of ancient Indian religions that, from the Kushana period, the sovereign Divine power Durgā and the war goddesses called the seven Mātṛkās started appearing prominently. The novel religious attitude towards the Goddess as the cosmic sovereign, controller and protector of the divine world order found expression in the concept of Durgā. Her ascendance continued throughout the early Gupta period.[4] Thus the *Devīmāhātmaya* must belong to this period. The celebration of the goddess Durgā as the embodiment of supreme power in warfare and victory, albeit at the cosmic level, together with her ethical stance for establishing the divine system of law and order, *Ṛta,* against the sudden upsurge of chaotic power of the Asuras, reflect the view of the period of the great Kushana and Gupta dynasties. This political ideology continued throughout the subsequent political history of the Hindu kingdoms.[5]

The rise of the great monotheistic religions, at about the same time, must have had a reciprocal impetus and helped the rise of the theology of the all-powerful divine Śakti. The concept of Śakti in this theology is absolutely central to Tantra. Not only is this Śakti the divine indomitable Will (*icchā*),[6] divine ominscience (*jñāna*), and divine omnipotence (*kriyā*), but also the divine sovereign power to control the creation (*aiśvarya*).

It is very difficult to find an overarching definition of Tantra that includes all its various forms and ideologies. Very generally speaking, "Tantra is a form of religion in which worldly, temporal goods and theology are perfectly integrated. It advocates the worship of power for the attainment of power".... "Tantra supported neither meekness nor passivity. Tantra is undertaken for salvation, *mukti*, as well as for personal gain and power, *bhukti*. *Bhukti*, literally 'enjoyment', is realised through power."[7] Thus power, Śakti, is central to the Tantric religious ideology and that power is based on Śakti's possessing *aiśvarya*, i.e. total control of the universe.

This Tantric ideology, giving full sanction to both these goals of *bhukti* and *mukti* as being of equal value, is demonstrated in the two major actors of the framing legend of the *Devīmāhātmya*, i.e. King Suratha and the *vaiśya* (a merchant?) Samādhi. To propitiate the Goddess the former practised the worship and meditation of the Goddess for *bhukti*, whereas the latter did so for *mukti*. Their performance of worship and meditation is termed *tapas*, voluntary observance of severe austerities. They restricted their food intake and often went without any food. They offered the Goddess flowers, incense, fire-sacrifices and libation of water. They deeply meditated on the Goddess and offered her *bali* (mainly non-vegetarian food), sprinkled with blood extracted from their own bodies; this they did to an earthen image of the Goddess, which they made themselves. Samādhi also muttered (*japa*) the Vedic hymn on the Goddess (the *Devī-sūkta*). The succinct description of the method of propitiation of the Goddess leaves no doubt that the King and the Vaiśya followed Tantric ritual worship of the Goddess.[8]

An interesting point to note is that many of the Goddess Purāṇas provide a brief, or sometimes not so brief, description of the mode of Śakti's worship and meditation (*sādhanā*), revealing its innovative nature. In fact the *Devīmāhātmya* text was soon appended by three secret *sādhanā.*[9] Another important feature of the text is that it specifically instructs the devotees of the Goddess to recite the DM while performing a brief ritual worship of the Goddess. It is also efficacious in dire necessity if a devotee just recites the DM while mentally worshipping her. The closeness of its theology and philosophy to the Trika system of Tantra is indeed considerable and may throw light on the date and provenance of the text, especially of its third legend (*carita*). In the Trika and the Yoginī Kaula Tantras the Goddess soared above all other divinities, celebrating Her power, omniscience and omnipotence. All other goddesses are but emanations from Her.[10]

Of the three episodes in the *Devīmāhātmya,* the first one relates the creation myth, where Viṣṇu is sleeping afloat on the chaotic primeval waters. From this the orderly cosmos would emerge through the activating of Viṣṇu's sovereign Energy, a positive miraculous power, viz. Viṣṇu-māyā. The task of creating a well-organized cosmos out of the primordial chaos is not an easy one. The creator must somehow transform the chaos of the primordial waters into a thoroughly regulated cosmos.[11] The burden of this fell on Brahmā, who appeared on the lotus that rested on Viṣṇu's navel. Brahmā embodies the Vedas, the storehouse of divine wisdom, and by means of that concentrated wisdom the cosmos was to emerge.

All went well until the moment when from Viṣṇu's earwax there emerged two demons, called Madhu and Kaiṭabha, who were the embodiment of the power of the primordial chaos. As they prepared to destroy Brahmā, the latter propitiated the supreme power Viṣṇu-māyā, present there as the sleep of Viṣṇu. At Brahmā's humble request she left Viṣṇu. Viṣṇu woke up and attacked the demons but failed to subdue them until Viṣṇu-māyā deluded them into agreeing to be slain by Viṣṇu. Brahmā's attitude to the Goddess was utter self-surrendering devotion.[12] He propitiated Her with epithets that clearly put her in the position of the supreme divinity who creates all and controls all. The overtone of *bhakti* is unmistakable, and it is *bhakti* to the Great Goddess, the one and only object of the devotee's adoration.

At this point I would like to compare an early Vaiṣṇava (Pāñcarātra) Āgama's presentation of the same myth. While it has more or less the same overtone of *bhakti*, the *Jayākhya Saṁhitā* presents the story quite differently. At the dawn of the new creation Viṣṇu encircled himself with his Power, transforming it into water. He creates Brahmā, who is the embodiment of knowledge (*vidyā*). Brahmā started creating the world, but for this he needed to be conscious of his ego as the creative energy. But his ego grew and overwhelmed his pure brilliance of knowledge. Enfeebled by his ego, Brahmā could no longer hold the burden of the creation. Therefore Viṣṇu assumed a divine form and lay floating in the primordial waters, covered by his own power in the form of *māyā*. While being created, Brahmā shed a couple of sweat drops. Those drops produced two demons called Madhu and Kaiṭabha. They then conquered the world and stole the Vedas, thereby plunging the world in darkness, and Brahmā too was covered with ignorance. After that the two Asuras disappeared under the water.

In this cosmic crisis the sages and gods persuaded Brahmā to propitiate Viṣṇu to save the creation. God took pity on Brahmā and agreed to remedy the situation. He took up two forms, one consisting of knowledge and one of *māyā*. In the former form, which is *Śabdabrahman*, Viṣṇu encapsulated all knowledge in the mantra *Oṃ* and with it, having entered Brahmā's person, replenished him with all knowledge.

In his *māyā* form God fought the demons fruitlessly for thousands of years. Finally realising that it was futile to fight with them just by means of *māyā* Viṣṇu discarded it and took up the form that embodies all mantras, the *mantramūrti*. After that he effortlessly destroyed the demons, Madhu and Kaiṭabha.[13]

It is important to note that these two mighty Asuras were subdued only by *mantraśakti*, which is a manifestation of the divine power of grace (*anugrahaśakti*) which supersedes all other cosmic laws. In the *bhakti* ideology, divine grace overrules the karmic cyclical existence of a person and brings about his or her release from *saṃsāra*. *Mantraśakti* exists for releasing individuals from worldly suffering through divine grace. This power of grace is supreme and may act with total authority over all divine laws. The power of *mantraśakti* is based on the concept of *bhakti* and its theory of divine grace in the sectarian religions of Śaivism, Vaiṣṇavism and Śāktism.[14] The power of *anugrahaśakti* in the theology of the Āgama and Tantra śāstras is immense. It is autonomous and supersedes all other powers functioning in creation. In the *bhakti* theology of the inclusive monotheism of the Tantra, the five cosmic acts of the Godhead are disappearance, creation, sustenance, dissolution and grace (*tirodhāna, sṛṣṭi, sthiti, laya* and *anugraha*). By 'inclusive monotheism' I mean that in this ideology the supreme godhead is one but it subsumes many other divine beings, which function as the supreme God's various manifestations. It is a matter of hierarchy and not exclusion. Each of the five functions is a *śakti*. The first one is *māyā* or, in the context of DM, Mahāmāyā, the Great power which deludes the individual, keeping him from understanding the real nature of his own identity and the identity of Godhead; this is how the creation (*sarga*) starts. But boundless divine compassion also keeps the line of escape clear by having the *anugrahaśakti*, in the form of the *mantraśāstra*, waiting to help a desperate seeker gain release from karmic limitation (*mukti*). The primary sign of God's grace is to find a really knowing preceptor (*guru*) who is willing to initiate the seeker; the second is when the seeker is properly initiated. These signs are called *śaktipāta*, advent of grace. Therefore, God's *mantramūrti* is the irresistible power that can remove all evils and problems of life.

Reading these two versions of the same myth clearly shows that the position of Śakti in the DM is higher than Viṣṇu, while in the JS it is a power of Viṣṇu, viz. *anugrahaśakti* or *mantraśakti*. In the DM Viṣṇu had to be helped by the supreme power Mahāmāyā to delude the Asuras into false bravado and handing Viṣṇu the opportunity to kill them. In this connection one should note that the Śakti's power to delude manifests itself through the creation of desire (*kāma*), hence her name Kāmeśvarī (goddess of desire). This aspect of her is underscored by her eroticism, which comes into play in DM's third episode.

In the second episode of the Goddess, DM describes the battle with the Asura Mahiṣa (buffalo). In former times gods and Asuras fought great battles. Indra, the king of the gods. was challenged by the Buffalo demon, the king of the demons. The demons defeated the gods and drove them out of the heaven. The latter approached Brahmā, the creator, to report their fall. Brahmā took them to Viṣṇu and Śiva. The three cosmic divinities grew furious at the demons' misconduct and their fury, combined with the heat of anger of the rest of the gods, produced a mass of brilliance covering the universe. Gradually that brilliance took the shape of an exquisitely beautiful woman who showed irresistible valour. All the gods provided her with their divine weapons and her steed, the mountain lion. Standing on her lion, the Goddess emitted her ferocious war cry in the form of an unbearably loud laugh, which shook the earth, whereupon all the sages offered their devotion to her and wished her perpetual victory. The

Buffalo demon, disturbed by the earthquake, came and saw her filling the world with her heroic body, consisting of a thousand arms, etc. poised for battle. The enraged Buffalo attacked her with his huge army. Fighting all of them alone, the Goddess grew hot and from that heat generated countless divine hosts who also fought the demon army. Finally the Goddess destroyed the Demon. The gods, headed by Indra, sang a great eulogy to her and when she offered to give them fulfillment of a wish they asked her to be always ready to come to their rescue whenever they faced calamity and prayed for her aid.

What is important to note is that the Goddess fought the demons alone until from her body-heat the host of an army (*gaṇa*) automatically appeared. She fought the battle alone, depending on her own power and energy. She is the supreme protector, as she represents the totality of divine power. No gods or goddesses are mentioned joining her as allies. This is the triumph of *bhakti.* A devotee needs only to surrender to the divine mercy without any other effort besides his/her absolute faith in the efficacy of divine grace (*prasāda*).

The third story of DM is also a triumph of the Goddess as the supreme Godhead. It too is firmly rooted in the ideology of *bhakti.* In another cosmic crisis of fighting between gods and demons, Indra and other gods were defeated and driven out of their abode and privileges. In dire privation they approached the Goddess, remembering her promise of help, and sang her praise as they prostrated themselves before her.

This famous eulogy of total surrender by the gods to her protection is treated even today as a separate mantra, applied to propitiate the Goddess when a person is in great danger of losing everything to an adversary. The scene is also set in the region of the Himalayas, where the Goddess Pārvatī resides with her spouse Śiva. Pārvatī arrives near the assembled gods and sages who are eulogising the Goddess, and asks them whom they are propitiating. At that moment the supreme Goddess emerges out of the sheath of Pārvatī's body and answers that she herself is the object of their propitiation. The brilliantly beautiful Goddess, the cosmic Mother, is called Kauśikī because she emerged from Pārvatī's body-sheath (*kośa*). Strangely, Pārvatī herself at that moment underwent an amazing disfiguration and became dark, like a shadow, and thereafter confined herself within the Himalayan mountains.[15]

In this third story of the Goddess and her cosmic fight with the twin demon royal brothers Śumbha and Niśumbha is totally different from the previous two myths. The Goddesss Kauśikī, who is exquisitely beautiful, young and utterly desirable, in her first encounter with the demon emissary takes up a fun-loving, playful and even apparently impudent stance. To the proposal of marriage with the demon king she answers coyly that she has made a thoughtless vow to be wed only to the person who can defeat her in battle.[16] Until the real battle begins the Goddess shows tremendous erotic attractiveness. DM hardly describes Kauśikī, the supreme Goddess, in a warlike form. No weapons are described; before the real battle even her steed is not described. Unlike the case of the Goddess in the second myth, Kauśikī in the fight with powerful demon generals first creates Kālī from her own terrifying wrath. Kālī appears as demoniac as the demons, and devours the demon army as well as slaying the powerful demon generals Caṇḍa and Muṇḍa. The Goddess then bestows on Kālī the name Cāmuṇḍā. When the royal demon brothers first send their most powerful and tricky general, the cloning demon Raktabīja,[17] to attack the Goddess Kauśikī, Śiva and other gods come to her aid by manifesting their energies in the form of divine female warriors–matṛkās[18]– to fight the demon warriors. Mātṛkās are the powers of great gods and bear the same attributes as do those gods. Besides them, the Goddess created from her own energy a fierce goddess called Śivadūtī. These eight divine energies, Mātṛkās, together with Śivadūti fight Raktabīja and his armies of ferocious demons. The fall of Raktabīja signals the final stage of the battle when both Śumbha and Niśumbha challenge Kauśikī. Niśumbha first falls in the battle and desperately angry Śumbha challenges the Goddess to a duel. The Goddess takes it up by re-absorbing the Matṛkās and other warrior goddess within herself. After a terrifying fight between the Goddess Kauśikī, fighting alone, and the demon king, Śumbha, the latter finally is killed. The Goddess triumphs again, bringing back peace and order to the creation. Only then do the gods come back to her and, as at the end of the second episode, offer their unrestrained loyal adoration, propitiating her with a great eulogy and total surrender to her protection. The *bhakti* ideal has triumphed.

This third episode, of the struggle between the divine king Indra and the demon kings who usurp his divine kingdom, in which the Goddess comes to rescue the gods, throws a special light on the Goddess. In the first episode She worked in the background, leaving Viṣṇu in charge of the demons' annihilation. In the second She alone fought the Buffalo demon as Durgā, the concentration of divine energy, riding on her lion. The fight between gods and demons condensed to the fight between Durgā, the combined Energy and prowess of the gods, and the Buffalo demon, the chief demon foe of Indra. In the third episode, however, there are three battles. Various terrifying warrior goddesses are introduced as the supreme Goddess's fighting companions.[19] The character of Kālī as an ogress, licking Raktabīja's blood and devouring the demon army, recalls the same goddess described in the Mahābhārata. The Mātṛkās include three Vaiṣṇava forms: Viṣṇu, Varāha and Narasiṃha. The story of naming Kālī Cāmuṇḍā, and the character of Śivadūtī, howling like packs of jackals, certainly shows both the lateness of the text and also the tendency to attach various strands of the fierce goddess cults to the central figure of the supreme Goddess, who has much more affinity to the Goddess Tripurasundarī and her cult. The theology of this system follows the Trika and the Kaula systems. The supreme godhead here is the supreme (*parā*) Goddess and her emanations carry out the cosmic functions.[20] In this Śākta sectarian theology the male divinities are not in evidence. In the following analysis of the DM episodes, this point will become clearer.

In the first battle, Kauśikī fights the demon general Dhūmralocana. The attitude of the Goddess appears to be more playful. Dhūmralocana has been sent to fetch the Goddess as a prisoner because she refused the demon king Śumbha's proposal of marriage. The Goddess taunts the demon commander and then destroys him and his army single-handed, aided just by her mount the lion.

In the second, the Goddess confronts two ferocious demon generals Caṇḍa and Muṇḍa, who are attended by a formidable army of demons. The apparent erotic personality of the Goddess and her playfulness now give way to anger. From her angry frown springs forth a most terrifying goddess, huge and dark and demonic. In the ensuing battle this dark goddess simply devours the demon soldiers and eventually beheads Caṇḍa and Muṇḍa. The battle over, the Goddess praises the dark goddess and gives her the name Cāmuṇḍā. There must be a connection between the two words Caṇḍa and Muṇḍa and the word Cāmuṇḍā, but it is not transparent.

In the third battle, the royal brothers Śumbha and Niśumbha mobilise all demon warriors and attack the Goddess. The Goddess also produces her army of Mātṛkās, Cāmuṇḍā and a hideous goddess representing the cremation ground, Śivadūtī. Her appearance is like the fearsome form of Śiva Bhairava and the text almost identifies her with Śiva. She howls like hosts of jackals (*śivā*) and has smoke-coloured hair. In a significant gesture, the

Goddess orders Śivadūtī to go to the demon kings as her messenger and demand their surrender. Thereupon the final battle starts. In it all the horrific demon commanders, including the king's brother Niśumbha, are killed. Finally, the Goddess and the demon king Śumbha come face to face. The latter challenges the Goddess to a duel without the other śaktis. The Goddess takes up the challenge, retracting her *śaktis*, i.e., her different aspects, back into herself and thus proving that she is herself the supreme divine Energy and the others are just emanations from her, like rays of the sun. The Goddess confronts the demon Śumbha, the king of chaos, alone, as the primal power of protection of the regulated creation, the cosmos. In that duel, the demon king is killed and the Goddess saves the creation.

Even though they are same supreme Goddess, the contrast between Durgā and Kauśikī could not be more stark. In both the second and third episodes in the DM, the Goddess fights the demons without the active aid of the gods' king Indra and his army, or of the divine cosmic triad. In the case of the Buffalo demon, a host of creatures born of the Goddess' fury assisted her in her struggle with the demons. The beautiful Goddess, beautifully adorned, is nevertheless an extremely capable protector of her devotees and formidable to her adversary. Her fury encompasses the enemies of gods and any threat to the cosmic pattern of law and order. In all righteous warfare, Goddess Durgā is victory itself (Vijayā). Her demeanour is heroic, and like the Vedic Indra she drinks alcohol before battling the enemy to his death.

The goddess Kauśikī, on the other hand, is eulogised by the gods, who address her as Ambikā, the mother, and as the epitome of feminine perfection. At the same time her erotic character is quite pronounced in her preliminary conversations with the Demon Śumbha's emissaries. Moreover, she is also knowledge (*jñāna/vidyā*).[21] The

Goddess on this battlefield is surrounded by *śaktis* emanating from her own self. The emanation of the dark and ferocious goddess Cāmuṇḍā and Śivādūtī and the seven Matṛkās clearly links this text with the description of the supreme divine Power/Energy (Parā/śakti) of the old Trika cult of the *Siddhayogeśvarīmātā Tantra* and other Trika texts. Kauśikī is the Parā-śakti. Calling her the goddess Vidyā, DM keeps up the Vedic tradition that the supreme creating divinity is Vāc, i.e. Speech. She is transcendent consciousness. Right at the beginning of Kauśikī's story, her close connection with Śaivism is established by identifying her with Pārvatī. DM briefly describes her iconography as three-eyed Kātyāyanī, but in her warring form the luminescent Goddess holds, amongst other objects, a trident, a bell and a sword. The bell may symbolize her identity with Vāc or Śabdabrahman.[22] As the furious Goddess in the battlefield she has arms and faces all over so that she can tackle the army of demons and their leaders by herself.[23]

Her close affinity with Tripurasundarī or Lalitā is very clear. Goddess Tripurasundarī or simply Sundarī is the Godhead in the Yoginī-Kaula cult. There are two most important canonical works, viz. the *Nityasoḍaśikārṇava* and the *Yoginīhṛdaya Tantra*. The commentators of these two texts hailed from Kashmir and from the west and south of India. Scholars like Vraja Vallabha Dviveda already in 1988 said that from the textual evidence it is clear that the cult travelled from west and central India to Kashmir and then again travelled back to south India, where it has flourished ever since.[24] In the *Saundaryalaharī*, ascribed to Śaṅkara, the Goddess bestow on her devotees not only śāstric knowledge but also poetic and musical genius. In the *Lalitopākhyāna*, an appendix to the *Brahmāṇḍa Purāṇa*, Indra and his gods invoke Goddess Lalitā to annihilate the fraud (Bhāṇḍa) demon. In the ensuing battle one of her two chief assisting śaktis is called Saṅgītamātā, the Mother

Music, who is goddess Sarasvatī. This dark śakti is there depicted as the presiding goddess of music.

This identity of the Goddess Kauśikī with Tripurasundarī, or Goddess Kāmeśvarī, became much pronounced in the *Devībhāgavata Purāṇa,* where the erotic aspect became prominent even for Durgā. The Buffalo demon was smitten and he offered the Goddess marriage instead of battle though in vain. DB also makes an interesting innovation in the Kauśikī myth by letting her take Kālī along with her to destroy Śumbha and Niśumbha. This text addresses Kauśikī as Parā-śakti and Kālī as the Goddess's terrifying aspect known as Kālarātrī. As Kauśikī and Kālī approached the city of the demons the former started singing sweetly and enchantingly to attract and confuse the demons.[25] The most interesting point in the Kauśikī myth in the DB is that in order to invoke the Goddess the gods performed the Tantric form of meditation by muttering the seed mantra of Tripurasundarī (*hrīṃ*), before singing the hymn of prayer.[26] The Goddess' erotic nature becomes increasingly emphasised. The story of the goddess Lalitā appended to the *Brahmāṇḍa Purāṇa* clearly equates her with the great Goddess Tripurasundarī and also connects her with the goddess Kāmākṣī and with the cult of Śrīcakra as she is worshipped in the famous temple of Kāmākṣī at Kāñcīpuram in south India.[27] I shall come back to the Sundarī cult.

Thus it is clear that the most popular and renowned Purāṇas about the great Goddess drew their inspiration from the Tantras and Tantric traditions, in the case of Kauśikī from the Kaula and Trika traditions of the North. The latter are ritual based, and esoteric, whereas Purāṇas about the Goddess are exoteric though rituals form an essential part of their narratives. It is interesting to note that the DM emphatically teaches the recitation of the entire DM in connection with the ritual worship of the Goddess. Such a recitation of the relevant deity's eulogy is indeed prescribed in the Tantric system of ritual worship of a Goddess; it has to occur towards the end of the programme of worship (See Tantric Sādhanā, p. 123). This is done regularly in all forms of *Tāntrikī/Paurāṇikī* ritual.

The canonical texts of Tantra religion make it clear that the technical teaching of the system of mantras and the rituals connected to them along with their esoteric meaning are to be revealed only to initiates. Tantric initiation is the prerogative of specially trained and spiritually gifted teachers, gurus. There are several stages in an initiate's training both technical and spiritual.[28] This training lasts for years. It is also a deep and sustained intellectual efforts for the trainee, who gradually absorbs the theological and philosophical implications of his/her specific cult's ideology. This training is expressed by the term *sādhanā*, an absorbing tireless effort to understand and acquire competence in Tantric rituals, and become concentrated on his/her goal. That goal is to relate to the deity of the trainee with emotional attachment and total loyalty, *bhakti*. This is the higher goal of *mukti*. There is also the goal of acquiring supernatural power, *bhukti*. But a true guru eschews that selfish goal. The frame story of the DM neatly shows this by relating how king Suratha wanted *bhukti* and Samādhi *mukti*.[29]

Now I turn back to the intriguing connection of Kauśikī with Lalitā. The cult of Tripurasundarī or just Sundarī, the beautiful lady of three cities, is an old Tantric form of religion within the broad sect of the Kaulas. The original followers worshipped the goddess for such worldly rewards as winning the favour of one's desired woman as is evident in the earliest extant complete scripture of the sect, viz. *Nityaṣoḍasikārṇava Tantra*. But in the hands of the Kaulas, and possibly being influenced by the *pratyabhijñā* doctrine of the Kashmiri Śaivas, the sect reached much deeper spirituality (Cf. *Yoginīhṛdaya Tantra*). I shall deal with two minor scriptures of the Tripurā cult mainly of South Indian provenance. These are the *Lalitā Upākhyāna* (LU) appended to the rather late text the *Brahmāṇḍa Purāṇa* and the *Saundaryalaharī* (SL) ascribed to Śaṅkarācārya. Its most important commentary is by Lolla Lakṣmīdhara. The commentary is also called Lakṣmīdhara. Goddess Tripurasundarī is also known as Kāmeśvarī, the goddess of love. However, in the latter Purāṇic and other related literature she is more famous as Lalitā, Sundarī and Kamalā/ Śrī. (Cf. *Lalitāsahasranāmam*).

The object of worship in this cult is indeed the sacred formula known as Śrīvidyā. Vidyā here means the secret knowledge encapsulated in the syllables of a mantra. Śrīvidyā is the knowledge of Śrī, i.e. Tripurā, which when realized empowers one with various powers and even brings about release from recurring transient existence (*saṃsāra*).[30] In esoteric Tantric practice, Śrīvidyā, Śrīcakra and the Goddess Śrī/Tripurā are held to be the same unique entity, the Śakti, who is the supreme reality.[31]

Śrividyā consists of fifteen syllables (ka e ī la hrīṃ' ha sa ka ha la hrīṃ; sa ka la hrīm;). [32] The arrangement of these syllables varies according to different traditions. There are three important traditions of the form of this *vidyā*, namely, the *hādimata*, the *kādimata* and the *kālimata* or *kahādimata*.[33] Different traditions use the basic *vidyā* in different sequences of the syllables. In the LU *kādimata* is followed. As Sanderson remarks, in Tantric ritual tradition, mantras are the most important factor to determine its deity's identity as the mantra-Power. Therefore any minor or major difference in any important mantra gives rise to difference in ritual exegesis. Thus the matras mentioned above though refer to the same mantra, slight changes in the sequence of the letters gave rise to very different systems and ritual exegesis in the Śrīvidyā cult.[34] The youngest of these systems is called the Samaya mata. I shall describe it in a moment.

In the Śrīvidyā cult the object of worship is Śrīcakra or, Śrīyantra. It is a cosmogram, the *cakra* (circle) representing the cosmos. The Goddess here is seen both consisting of the entire cosmos projecting it from herself in the form of śaktis represented by triangles and at the same time she is in its centre represented by a *bindu* (dot/point), the unmoving centre/essence of the cosmos. Śrīcakra consists of a diagram made of nine intersecting triangles which produce nine concentric enclosure or circles with a point in the middle enclosed by a triangle. A triangle represents a source or womb, *prakṛti.* The cosmos is created by the supreme Power from herself through a series of projected śaktis also wombs or prakṛtis who appear as the universe. Thus the universe is an abstract idea while a Śrī-yantra is its physical representation in cloth, metal, rock or, crystal.

SL is a long hymn consisting of one hundred verses eulogizing various aspects of the Goddess Tripurasundarī. The poet devotee totally surrenders himself to the Supreme Goddess who is the ultimate resort for one's salvation. While describing Her iconography the poet mentions Her carrying a sugarcane bow and five flower-arrows, usually the distinctive weapons of the god Kāma, the god Eros. This clearly supports the theory that the Goddess Tripurasundarī is indeed Kāmeśvarī, Goddess Eros. SL also identifies the Goddess with Kuṇḍalinī-śakti, the supreme divine power that lies dormant in all individual beings. Kuṇḍalinī-śakti is the focal point of the Tantric yoga practice.[35] These two descriptions of the Goddess reveal her basic nature: firstly, she fits perfectly in the Vedic idea of cosmogony, which says the original creating Divine was alone and then he became self-conscious and felt lonely. He experienced desire (*kāma*) and that lead to the creation of the universe.[36] She is the Goddess desire Kāmeśvarī. Secondly, the Goddess as the Kuṇḍalinī abides in every individual person (jīva), as the essential reality of a person. SL is written with excellent poetic diction. It identifies the supreme creating reality in terms of a couple eternally united who create through their ecstatic enjoyment of the act of creation.[37] There appears a strong influence of the Trika system of Śakti meditation, leading to the adept's identity with the Goddess, which is the system's soteriological goal.

This hymn emphasizes the Kuṇḍalinī yoga as the path to realization of the Goddess who is depicted in the Śrīcakra and who is called Kāmakalā. Kalā here means śakti. The realization is bliss, but this is equated with erotic bliss. At the same time, once this realization is achieved the adept instantly acquires perfection in poetic power.[38] This special power to bestow creative artistic capacity runs through many a Goddess myth where she is equated with the primal Vāc. Thus she is associated not only with poetic genius but also with music and dance. The poet also credits the Goddess with complete mastery of classical music by identifying three creases on her throat with the three pitches or gamut's (*grāma*) used in the classical Indian music system.[39] It is a sophisticated literary creation written with excellent poetic diction.

The tradition of the Samaya-mata is very interesting.[40] It certainly developed in south India. It takes the two abovementioned texts LU and SL as its main āgama. It propagates a special type of inclusive monistic vedānta, which is iconographically depicted in Tantra as '*ardhanārīśvara*'. Interestingly, though, this cosmographic iconology is described in the ritual texts more graphically as the divine couple in coitus. Above all, the tradition firmly believes itself to be directly linked with the Vedic tradition. The earliest proponent of the school was Lolla Lakṣmīdhara, who belonged to the court of the Gajapati kings of Orissa. In his commentary called Lakṣmīdhara on SL he propagates this Samaya-mata. Lakṣmīdhara believed that Śaṃkara, the composer of SL, belonged to the Samaya school, and therefore he composed the hymn to praise Samayā, otherwise called Candrakalā.[41]

Lakṣmīdhara's commentary elaborates on the system of the Kuṇḍalinī yoga followed in SL and successfully argues the specific points of this yoga hall marking the Samaya-mata. There appears to be a strong influence of the Trika system of Śakti meditation, leading to the adept's identity with the Goddess, which is the system's soteriological goal. It propagates a type of monistic Vedānta and firmly believes itself to be directly linked with the Vedic tradition. His date can be fixed between the late thirteenth and early fourteenth century C.E. In his commentary, he accepts Śaṅkarācārya as the composer of SL and argues that SL belongs to the Samaya school, which bases its religious practices on meditation without putting emphasis on external forms of worship. Internal evidence proves that the poet hailed from Tamil country.[42] Samaya-mata became more powerful in the later development of the Lalitā cult.

The *Lalitopākhyāna* (the story of Lalitā) is unique in its character. It narrates a legend about the Goddess Lalitā or Kāmākṣī, the unique Mother, i.e. the creatrix and the concentrated divine power and sovereignty. Without going into the text in detail I can just point out that it is written by a single author and its focal point is the Goddess Kāmākṣī of the temple in the sacred city of Kāñcī. It is a late text. In order to establish the supremacy of Goddess Kāmākṣī/Lalitā it not only presents a new version of DM, but also narrates all the myths of the Epics and other Purāṇas in modified forms favouring the position of the Goddess. It establishes Her transcendental nature, albeit in readiness to create. It also establishes the total identity between Lalitā and Kāmeśvara Śiva, even though they appear ever engaged in the act of creation depicted as the act of sexual intercourse. This mode of the supreme Reality, which posits the concepts of two-in-one, transcends Sadāśiva, the supreme Reality in the Śaiva Siddhānta system. LU advocates theistic non-dualism and establishes Lalitā as the supreme godhead. It follows the Tripurasundarī cult as depicted in the *Paraśurāma-kalpa-sūtra* and the *Śrīvidyārṇava Tantra.* An important appendix to LU is the famous hymn to the Goddess, *Lalitāsahasranāmam* (*The Thousand Names of Lalitā*). For the devotees of Goddess Lalitā, who often recite the text daily, LS is as important as the DM is for the worshippers of the Goddess Durgā/Caṇḍī.

Lalitā's origin is slightly different from that of Durgā, in that she appeared from the fire and smoke of the Vedic sacrifices performed incessantly by Indra and other gods in order to get back their kingdom of heaven, which had been conquered by the demon Bhaṇḍa. Thus the Goddess not only represents the divine power but also the Power of the Vedic sacrifices. It is interesting to note that in the hymn of Lalitā's thousands names constituting LU's final section the goddess is addressed as she who emerged from the fire of Consciousness (*cidagnisambhūtā*). Describing the heaven where Lalitā resides, LU describes "There, in an enormous fire-pit, the fire of consciousness burns fed by hundreds of flows of nector (perhaps here equated with ghee?). This sacrificial fire burns in great flames only by the fuel of nectar poured by the two sacrificers, viz. the great goddess (i.e. Kāmeśvarī) and the Lord of desire (Kāmeśvara). These two incessantly perform the sacrifice in order to protect the creation." (LU 36.1-5).

The character of the demon Bhaṇḍa is also interesting. He is the fake Manmatha, the god of sexual desire. When Śiva's meditation was disturbed by Manmatha, Śiva in his anger burned him to ashes. Citrakarṇa, one member of Śiva's hosts, made an effigy of Manmatha from that ash. Being in front of Śiva, the effigy instantly became alive. Citrakarṇa advised him to worship Śiva by chanting the Vedic hymn *Śatarudrīya*. This lookalike Manmatha successfully propitiated Śiva and became the most powerful in the creation. One of the gods tried to warn Śiva by saying 'It is a fake', (bhaṇḍa), hence the curious being got the name Bhaṇḍa. In her great battle with Bhaṇḍa Goddess Lalitā is helped by her chief minister (mantranātha), the goddess

Śyāmalā also known as Saṃgītamātā (the goddess of music), and by her chief commander (daṇḍanātha), the goddess Vārāhī. Notably, Lalitā refused Śiva's help.[43]

The history of the connection between the Kashmir Trika/Kaula system of worshipping Goddess as the supreme divinity Parā or even the transcendental Anuttarā with the south and west Indian Tantric Śrīvidyā cult of Lalitā/Tripurasundarī is still not very clear. Already in the thirteenth century C.E., as is evidenced by the writings of Śivānanda, the Tripurā cult was popular in the south of India. The pupilary tradition of Śivānanda clearly shows the cult's close relationship with the Kashmirian Trika system greatly elaborated by Abhinavagupta and his circle.[44] The tradition here is predominantly Kaula esoteric practices. The ritual system elaborated in the works of Śivānanda clearly establishes this fact.[45] Śivānanda followed the hādimata tradition. He and his followers were great authors and a large literature grew within that tradition.[46]

However, Śivānanda's tradition was only one of the many esoteric traditions that grew around the Tripurā cult. The two most prestigious scriptures of the cult, the Tantras *Nityaṣoḍaśikārṇava* and *Yoginīhṛdaya*, do not always support identical concepts of the nature of the Goddess Tripurā. The latter firmly depicts an ideology, which is rooted in the Pratyabhijñā system of non-dualism. Śivānanda himself was based on this system and followed the sectarian tradition called the 'hādi-mata'. The *Nityaṣoḍaśikārṇava* (NṢA), on the other hand, followed the Trika tradition, which conceived the Goddess in three hierarchically arranged levels of existence, namely, aparā, parāparā and parā (dual, dual and nondual, and nondual). But running through all these three levels, the Goddess exists as their essence, which is known as 'anuttarā' or the Supreme/Transcendental. The ritual tradition of NṢĀ too is esoteric and probably older than that of YH. Amṛtānanda and others seem to have followed this tradition of NṢĀ though the former practised both

Trika and Kaula traditions.[47] The esoteric Lalitā cult came to south India at the beginning of the second millennium C.E. It then reached Maharashtra, and the great Tantric exponent Bhāskararāya of the 17th century enlivened the tradition with many commentaries and monographs on the exegesis of the esoteric rituals of the cult.[48]

In the LU, the ancient Kashmiri Trika ideology finds ample support. Goddess Tripurā is not only manifest from the fire of consciousness but also is the 'ādi-kāraṇa'. It establishes identity of the three: parā, aparā and parāparā states. (3,4,39. 5-8). The tripartite division of parā, etc. of the goddess is pervaded by the supreme (anuttarā state of the goddess) which also transcends them. LU seems to have made a supreme effort to unify all śakti tradition in the anuttarā identity of the goddess (43.15; this is the thousands syllabled vidya of Śrī). Similarly, SL refers to this supreme goddess above her tripartite division which the text equates with Sarasvatī, Lakṣmī and Pārvatī, who is wife of the supreme reality (parabrahman).[49]

It is impossible to fix the exact date of these texts. The Sanskrit is highly literary with very fancy alaṃkāras (literary embellishment) used skilfully. The Goddess is eulogized in her own right as a supreme sovereign deity without losing sight of her being the spouse of the Supreme god Śiva. The pre-eminence of the betel leaf as a means of showing favour to a favourite courier certainly seems to be a late motif.

However, it is clear from the above discussion that Goddess Lalitā, the supreme Cosmic Goddess, is mainly characterized by her erotic nature. She is the source and agent of creation and indeed is the Supreme Mother. This core concept overarches the Goddess cult both in her beautiful form and the dark even hideous form.

Here I would like to turn my attention to the great Mother Goddess, Kālī, the Dark Goddess and thereby approach the Tāntric dimension that affected the eastern parts of India. Although the DM does not really touch on her, she is one of the earliest forms of the cosmic sovereign Goddess. On the broad canvas of a pan-Indian divine Power, the most important Goddess in the Tantric systems is Kālī, the dark Goddess. She figures in many cults and sects, one of them is the system of Krama. The Krama system became very important in Kashmir and the Himalayan region, spreading all the way to Nepal, Mithila (Bihar) and Bengal. Sanderson already in 1988 published a short history of the early development of the Kālī cult in Kashmir.[50] These different streams of the Kālī cult spread also in Nepal and Mithila.[51] In this region a very early form of this Goddess called Kubjikā flourished for a long time. But at present hardly any living tradition of this cult can be found.

The nature of Kubjikā as representing the (Sanskrit) phonemes is similar to the nature of the goddess Mālinī of the *Mālinīvijayottara Tantra.* As identified with these phonemes, albeit not in the usual Sanskrit alphabetical order, the goddess represents all mantras. This characteristic feature makes her encompass, through the phonemes, the entire creation, as the phonemes are the bricks and mortar of the creation. Thus she is the autonomous creatrix of the universe. At the same time, as these specially arranged phonemes being the root of all mantras and *vidyās,* Goddess Kubjikā or Malinī is the divine grace who provides the discerning and devoted Tantra practitioner with the appropriate mantra or vidyā to pursue the yogic path that leads to release the yogin from the bondage of *saṃsāra.*

The dark Goddess Kālī was mentioned in the epic *Mahābhārata,* once each in the *Virāṭa Parvan* (4.67-12) and in the *Bhiṣma Parvan* (6/23 4-16).[52] In both places the Goddess is identified with goddesses Yoganidrā, Durgā, Kātyāyanī, Kauśikī, etc. It is difficult to decide whether these two sections are interpolations or not. But Nīlakaṇṭha certainly commented on them, and he was a very careful editor of the *Mahābhārata:* hence one can accept that in

Bengal and other eastern parts of India the Goddess became an important cult. Nīlakaṇṭha belonged to the latter part of the seventeenth century C.E. but he collected an amazing number of MSS., to edit a fairly critical version of the text and to write his commentary, the *Mahābhāratabhāvadīpa*. It is fair to assume that many of those MSS must have been copied earlier than in Nīlakaṇṭha's own time.[53]

In Bengal Kālī is worshipped as the dark Goddess of the cremation ground, surrounded by corpses and howling jackals and abandoned cremation pyres. She is addressed, perhaps euphemistically, as Dakṣiṇā (compassionate) Kālī. Kālī can be regarded as the main form of the supreme Goddess worshipped in the region designated as Gauḍa, i.e. the east and north-east of India plus Nepal.

A separate stream of the cult of the Dark supreme Goddess seems to have appeared from the north-east of India, viz. the cult of Tārā or Ekajaṭā or Nīlasarasvatī. This cult also became dominant in the region of Mithila (Bihar) and in Bengal, along with the Krama cult of Goddess Kālī.[54] The system of ritual worship of the Goddess follows the methods of Mahācīnācāra. This Buddhist Goddess became very popular in eastern India and a cult of ten *vidyās* (esoteric spell) and their goddesses totally captivated the Kālī Tantrics and deeply influenced their practices. This combinations of the two fierce goddesses Kālī and Tārā gave rise to the cult of the ten great mantras/*vidyās*. The iconographies of these two goddesses are very close. The late *Śakti-saṃgama* Tantra produces a good overall picture of the spread of the cults of Kāli and the ten great *vidyās*. The *Kālikā Purāṇa* too, mentions more than one such group of *vidyās*. It is undoubtedly a late medieval phenomenon. Though very many Tantras include their names, there is no certainty whether or not these are late inclusions. Among the important Tantras are the *Mahākāla Tantra*, the *Kālī Tantra*, the *Phetkāriṇī Tantra* and the

Tārābhaktisudhārṇava. Although the *vidyā* of goddess Kālī is deemed to be the most important one and she is designated as the Primary One (*ādyā*), the importance of Tārā is almost as great. Many important scholars have presented their views on this subject and still there is much research to be done.[55]

There are two points I should like to underscore in the worship of Tārā. One of them is the importance of women in that system of worship. The special position of women in this cult had a wide influence in the pre-modern as well as the early modern extension of Goddess cults and their systems of worship. The Tārā cult has always been the most important in the great centre (*mahāpīṭha*) of the goddess Kāmākhyā in the region of Kamrup in Assam. It is also important in Nepal.[56] The other important feature of the Tārā cult is the centrality of its sexually oriented rituals and Yoga system.

Finally, I should introduce the role of the Cosmic Goddess Śakti in the oldest sectarian Vaiṣṇava theology of the Pāñcarātra sect.[57] Antiquity of this theology is well established. There is archaeological evidence of the temples and monuments built to worship the deities of the cult of Caturvyūha, a four-fold emanation of God Vāsudeva, about two centuries before the common Era.[58] The early canonical Pāñcarātra texts, viz. the Saṃhitās Jayākhya, Pauṣkara and Sāttvata emphasize the role of Śakti as the active or cognitive consciousness (saṃvit) of the supreme God. In the theology, cosmogony and soteriology presented in these texts, Śakti takes the central role. This is especially evident in the old Pāñcarātra soteriology of gnosis. This salvific gnosis is obtained through contemplation and meditation on the gradual emergence of the primal cosmic categories based on the primal diversification of the Śakti, viz. Saṃvit, the divine cognitive consciousness. The practitioner must at the beginning learn this cosmogonic system, and then meditate on the process in reverse order, experiencing and realizing the process of unity of all phenomena in Saṃvit, which diversifies through five śaktis as the empirically experienced creation. This system of yoga is called Laya yoga.[59] The Pāñcarātra religion was present in Kashmir from an early period. The Jayākhya Saṃhitā most probably existed there and had its followers even before the Kashmir Śaiva system Pratyabhijñā was introduced. Vāmanadāsa's Saṃvit-vimarśa deeply influenced Utpala Vaiṣṇava, who was respectfully mentioned by Abhinavagupta.

This rather brief introduction to the Supreme Goddess is designed to prepare the reader for the articles that follow. They are mainly on various aspects of the Cosmic Sovereign Goddess, including Her local manifestations. An important question may be asked: does the gradual superseding of the cosmic gods by the Goddess reflect any social reality? In other words, did the women in society become more powerful and earn any freedom of action? A few of my articles tackle this problem. A major enquiry in this regard is to what extent the supremacy of the Goddess affects the non-Sanskritic segments of the society, including those from other religions..

In the following articles I have confined myself mainly to the great cosmic Goddess and her ritual worship, Tantric theology and praxis in a wider sense, the attitude of her devotees towards her authority and the social character of the Tantric practitioners, and the position of Bhakti. I have also tried to figure out the position of women inside the Tantric and non-Tantric Hindu religious milieu. The Goddess symbolizes the supreme divine authority that activates the creation, protection and governance and necessary dissolution of the world in accordance with the ancient Indian concept of cyclical Time. But She also discharges the divine sovereign privilege of punishing evildoers and rewarding true devotees.

Finally, the relevant forms of the Cosmic Goddess in

these articles are Śrī/Tripurasundarī/Lalitā; Goddess Kalī and Her various emanations; and Lakṣmī and Her powers in the Pāñcarātra canonical texts.

Goddess Sarasvatī/Vāc, discussed in the first article *Sarasvatī/Vāc : The Sacral Word and the Supreme Cosmic Goddess,* is the oldest cosmic form of the Goddess. She is the primary Divine Power to bring the regulated cosmos out of the primal Chaos, often represented as the primordial Waters. The second article, *Śakti the Supreme Divine Power: The Role of Lakṣmī in Pāñcarātra Sotereology,* discusses Lakṣmī as the prime Cosmic Divine Power as presented in the Pāñcarātra theology. In the third article, *Hindu Tāntrism : Sādhanā, Pūjā,* the method of worshipping Tripurasundarī has been discussed. The fourth article, *The Worship of Kālī according to the Toḍala Tantra,* deals mainly with the worship of Kālī as the Primal (ādyā) Goddess but also briefly touches on the system of worship of the other goddesses belonging to the group of ten goddesses worshipped with ten great mantras (daśamahāvidyā). The fifth article, *Maṇḍala as an Image of Man,* deals with the Tantric cosmogram but discusses the position of the Tantric worshipper. In the sixth article *The Religious and Literary Background of the Navāvaraṇa-kīrtana: Dikṣtār's Cycle of Nine Hymns to Goddess Tripurāsundarī/Śrī-cakra* Dikṣitār, the famous South Indian poet devotee, expresses in this cycle of hymns the Tāntric theology and cosmology of the Tripurasundarī cult. The seventh article, *The Domestication of a Goddess: Caraṇa-tīrtha Kālighāt, the Mahāpītha of Goddess Kālī,* focusses on the Goddess Kali of Kalighat. It mainly discusses the attitude of the worshippers to this originally local Goddess – both the priests who own the temple and the countless pilgrims. The eighth article, the only one besides my Introduction, deals with the Goddess Durgā. It is mainly a socio-religious study of the Goddess and Her relation to the local kings and landlords, which I wrote together with Richard

Gombrich.

The ninth article, *Hindu Tantric and Śākta Literature in Modern Indian Languages*, moves to the literary output of the devotees from many parts of India who pour out their devotion to and dependence on to the cosmic Supreme Power, Śakti, appearing in various forms and revealing Her diverse aspects to Her loyal loving worshippers.

The tenth and eleventh articles again make a shift to the socio-religious studies but mainly focused on the position of the Hindu women in the religious context, in relation to the Hindu attitude towards the supreme Goddess. *Women in the Śaiva/Śākta Ethos* deals with the lives of three women Śaiva-poet-saints of medieval India and contrasts these with three women Vaiṣṇava-poet-saints of the same period, discussing their lives and literary output. *The Goddess, Women, and Their Rituals in Hinduism* throws light on intimate domestic rites and rituals followed exclusively by women in Hindu families.

The last article, *Lālan Fakir – The Confluence of Islam and Hindu Popular Mysticism,* is an excursion into the Tantra and its influence on a different dimension of the Indian religions, namely, the Folk Religion of the Bāuls. This sect has followers from miscellaneous religious traditions in Eastern India. The Bāuls have an itinerant mode of life and hence have very wide influence on the society. The centre of their religious belief is the 'Person' who resides in the innermost recess of the Bāul's heart (maner Mānuṣ). A Bāul is a self-contained individual, who himself and the beloved god, the microcosm and the macrocosm are completely fused together. As a result he has nothing outside his self to venerate. The only exception is his religious teacher – his preceptor. A Bāul is regulated by no system of religious tradition, nor any cultic rules and regulations. He is guided only by the inner 'Person' and feels completely one with nature. He is a free individual and blended with the God's creation.

NOTES

1 Some of the essays are published and some are papers read in various conferences.

2 *Devīmāhātmya* constitutes chapters 81-93 of the *Mākaṇḍeya Purāṇa*. See also Thomas B. Coburn, *Devī-Māhātmya: The Crystallization of the Goddess Tradition,* Delhi: Motilal Banarsidas, 1984; *Encountering the Goddess: A Translation of the Devī-Māhātmya and a Study of its Interpretation.* SUNY, 1991.

3 See Lalye, P.G. *Studies in Devī Bhāgavata,* Popular Prakashan Private Ltd., Bombay, 1973. Brown, C. Mackenzie, *The Triumph of the Goddess: The Canonical Models and Theological Visions of the Devī-Bhāgavata Purāṇa,* SUNY, Albany, 1990.

4 See V.S. Agarwal, *Devī-Māhātmyam: The Glorification of the Great Goddess,* All-India Kashiraj Trust, Ramnagar Varanasi, 1963, pp. iv-xi.

5 See Gupta, Sanjukta and Richard Gombrich, *Kings, Power and the Goddess,* in *South Asia Research,* Vol. 6, No. 2, November 1986, pp. 123-138.

6 Cf. *Śvetāśvatara Upaniṣad vi.* 8.

7 Gupta, 1986, p. 125.

8 See Gupta, 1979, *Tantric Sādhanā,* pp. 124-129; 165-169.

9 Cf. Coburn, 2002, pp. 80ff; and Coburn 1991, pp. 109-117. Cf. also *Brahmāṇḍa P.* Appendix, *Lalitopākhyāna.*

10 These *śaktis* are called *kalā* or *yoginī* or *nityā.* Cf. *Nityaṣoḍaśikārṇava,* Introduction; Sanderson (90), pp. 31-88 and Padoux, *Le Coeur du la Yoginī. Yoginīhṛdaya, avec le commentaire Dipika d'Amṛtānanda,* Introduction, pp. 5-22.

11 See the first article *Sarasvatī/Vāc.* in this book.

12 The *Kālikā Puraṇa* (13th or 14th century C.E.) describes the same myth in a more or less similar text. KP 62. 4-47. Cf. Karel van Kooy, pp. 131-134. Cf DBP I. 6-7. In this text we find more or less the same story as in DM and KP but characteristically

the goddess shows her erotic side more emphatically. DBP I. 9. 61-83.

13 Cf. *The Jayākhya Saṃhitā*, ch. 2.

14 See the Introduction to the *Lakṣmītantra: A Pāñcarātra text*, pp. XIV-XXV and XXXi-XXXII; JS. 3.17-22.

15 I wonder if this part of the story is added to the story in order to reconcile the story of Pārvatī's peeve at Śiva's addressing her as the dark (ugly?) lady. A story mentioned in various Tantras and temple legends. Cf. Ekāmreśvara temple at Tanjore. In the Himalayan region Pārvatī is Gauḍī, i.e. the fair one. On the other hand, in many temples of the south Indian region, she is dark.

16 DM, 5. 65-70, 75-76.

17 Every drop of blood shed from Raktabīja's body produced countless clones of himself. At the biding of the Goddess, Cāmuṇḍā/Kālī licked up every single drop of Raktabīja's blood to prevent the automatic creation of his innumerable clones, DM 8, 51-61.

18 Mātṛkās are eight viz. Brahmāṇī, Māheśvarī, Kaumārī, Aindrī, Vaiṣnavī, Vārāhī, Nārasiṃhī and Cāmuṇḍā. Excepting the last, others are the divine powers of Brahmā, Śiva, Maheśvara, Kumāra-skanda, Indra, Viṣṇu, Varāha and Narasiṃha. This last may vary in different cult systems.

19 Harper, Katherine Anne, *The Warring Śaktis*, in Harper, Katherine Anne and Robert L Brown (ed.), *The Roots of Tantra*, pp. 115-131.

20 Paroux, André, op. cit. Sanderson, *Śaivism;* Sanderson, *The Visualization of the Deities of the Trika*, pp. 31-88; Dupuche, John R., *Abhinavagupta: The Kula Ritual*, pp. 8-22.

21 Cf. DM, 11.5, *vidyā samastās tava devi bhedāḥ striyaḥ samastāḥ sakalā jagastsu.* "All vidyās and all women in the entire world are parts of you."

22 Cf. *Pauṣkara Saṃhitā*, 34. 56, *śabdabrahmasvarūpaṃ ca ghaṇṭāvigrahalakṣaṇā*, "the bell symbolises the form of śabdabrahman".

23 DM, ch. 11.

24 *Yoginīhṛdaya*, p. 13.

25 DB 5.23.1-16.

26 DB 5.22.23-24, ...*devīdhyānaparāyaṇāh//māyābījaṃ hṛdā nityaṃ japantaḥ sarva eva hi/*, see Brown, *The Triumph of the Goddess.*

27 For a short and detailed study of this goddess see Sylvia Schwarz Linder, *The Lady of the Island of Jewels and the Polarity of Her Peaceful and Warring Aspects,* pp. 105-122; and Annette Wilke, *Śaṃkara and the Taming of the Wild Goddesses,* pp. 123-178; in Axel Michaels, Cornelia Vogelsänger, Annette Wilke (eds), *Wild Goddesses in India and Nepal.*

28 See Brunner.

29 DM, 23. 11-16.

30 See LU Ch. 39.37-40.

31 Vide Laksmidhara's commentary on the SL 41-43 and 98-99.

32 Cf. *Navāvaraṇa Kīrtanam.*

33 There are various opinions on this name inside the Tripurā tradition.

34 Cf. Sanderson '90; 78. See Khanna, op. cit

35 See Somadeva Vasudeva, *The Yoga of the Mālinīvijayottaratantra;* also Śrī Bhāskararāya Makhin, *Varivasyārahasya,* 82-110.

36 *Ṛgveda* 10.129; *Bṛhadāraṇyaka Upaniṣad,* I. 4

37 SL. 41, 57. The poet also identifies her with all eight distinctive aesthetic enjoyments (*rasa*), SL 51.

38 SL. 12, 13; cf. Lakṣmīdhara's commentary on SL 99: *ṣaṭkamalabhedamate sukhasvarūpaiva muktiḥ/sukhaṃ tu laukikadṛṣṭāntena strīsambhogātmakameva/loke'pi strīsammelanāt param sukham nāsti/;* "In the system of piercing the six lotuses, (i.e. the six yogic centres of the microcosm, the individual), salvation (*mukti*) is identical with bliss. This bliss is, according to the pragmatic experience, same as the sexual enjoyment. In this world one cannot experience any greater bliss than sexual bliss." Lakṣmīdhara elaborates on the Samaya-mata in his commentary on SL 31 and 32. It quotes various Āgamas and Tantras and some also are named. But the most interesting quotation for us is from the *Nityaṣoḍaśkārṇava Tantra* depicting the worship of sixteen Nityās. *Lakṣmīdhara on* SL 31-32, pp. 73-78.

39 SL. 69, 74.

40 See the elaborate colophon at the end of Lakṣmīdhara's commentary and his own short lyric, quoted by the editor Vidvan N.S. Venkaṭanāthācārya of the *Saundaryalaharī* Mysore Oriental Research Institute No. 114.

41 See Lakṣmīdhara's Introduction to his commentary on SL 1, p. 2.

42 Lakṣmīdhara commentary on SL 41-43 and 99.

43 LU. chs., 11-29. See also Dikṣitār's Cycle of Hymns to the Goddess Kamalā.

44 Padoux, 1994, pp. 7-10; 15-22.

45 Thesis Khanna, Alexis '90 Śivānanda's tradition allegedly belonged to the tradition of a monastery/seminary (*maṭhikā*) connected with a certain Tryambaka. The daughter of Tryambaka established a separate *maṭhikā* as an annex to her father's where kaula mysticism to be practised. (*Tantrāloka* 36, 16.) Madhu Khanna, Thesis 26.

46 Cf. Vraja Vallabha Dviveda, *Nityaṣoḍaśikārṇava*, Introduction.

47 Sanderson '90.

48 Ibid 80ff.

49 SL 97.

50 Sanderson, *Śaivism and the Tantric Tradition*, pp. 138-157, 164-167.

51 Schoterman, J.A. *The Ṣaṭsahasra Saṃhitā*, Ch. 1-5, Edited, Translated and Annotated, Leiden, 1982, pp. 5-8.

52 These sections are omitted by the B.O.R.I. critical edition but Nīlakaṇtha has commented on them and hence they cannot be totally ignored. See Upendrakumar Das, *Śāstramūlak Bhāratīya Śaktisādhanā*, Part 1, pp. 98-108. For excellent translations of these two eulogies of the Goddess see *Mahābhārata Book Four, Virāṭa* (tr.) by Kathleen Garbutt, pp. 57-63; and *Mahābhārata Book Six, Bhiṣma*, Vol. 1, (tr.) Alex Cherniak, pp. 163-197.

53 Minkowski, Christopher, *Nīlakaṇṭha's Vedic Readings in the Harivaṃśa Commentary. Epics, Khilas, and Purāṇas: Continuities and Ruptures*, pp. 411-415.

54 See Meisig, Marion, *Die "Chinas-Lehre" Des Śaktismus:*

Mahācināčāra Tantra: Kritisch ediert nebst Uebersetzung und Glossar. Otto Harraassowitz, Wiesbaden, 1988, pp. 1-12.

55 Cf. Prabodh Chandra Bagchi, *Foreign Elements in Tantra,* in *Studies in Tantras,* part I, pp-45-60. Meisig, op. cit.

56 The general frame story of the Tāra Tantras such as the Mahācīnācāra,, Nīlasarasvatī etc. connects the name of the sage Vasiṣṭha with the popularization of the Tārā cult and its central theme of sexo-yogic and antinomian practices. This must have affected the later folk cults of Bengal. See the article on Lālan Fakir.

57 Gupta, Sanjukta, *Lakṣmī Tantra: A Pañcarātra Text,* Indian Edition, Delhi, 2000, pp. XXI-XXXIX.

58 Gupta, Sanjukta. *The Caturvyūha and the Viśākha-yūpa.*

57 Gupta, S. *Lakṣmī Tantra,* pp. 129-130, 223-226.

1. Sarasvatī/Vāc, the Sacral Word and the Supreme Cosmic Goddess[1]

One of the oldest and continuously revered and adored Hindu goddess is Sarasvatī, the personification of Word/ Speech (Vāc). She is also the deity of poetic genius, of musical skill and of other artistic abilities, though she is not the divine inspiration for crafts or such skills as archery. In the earliest scripture of India, viz. the Ṛgveda a fascinating history of the early development of these originally two separate goddesses Sarasvatī, a river goddess and Vāc, the sacred magical speech and their fusion as Sarasvatī/Vāc, is recorded. In the later Vedic literature we find the unfolding of the final development of this deity. A brief survey of that history will throw considerable light on the post-Vedic development of the Brahmanical concept of the philosophy of language and grammar developed by Bhartṛhari, on the one hand, and astonishing position of this deity in the Śaiva, Vaiṣṇava and Śākta Āgamic theology, on the other.

This earliest literature of Brahmanical south Asia (the Ṛgveda goes back to circa 1500 B.C. E.)[2] was composed of verses called Ṛk or hymns. All Vedic texts are regarded as revealed to some Vedic poet or poetess called Ṛṣi. These visionary poets, seers, composed them in praise of deities like Fire, Sun, Dawn and so forth and they are meant for recitation accompanying sacrificial rites. Not only the early poets used wonderful metaphors and similes and other literary figures but also showed great felicity in describing the beauty of these deities in marvelously apt description. Therefore it is no wonder that the Vedic poets were concerned with Sarasvatī/Vāc, the sacred Speech and the divine poetic inspiration, analogous to a Greek muse.[3]

Gonda has emphasized the point that Sarasvatī was originally the name of a river of the North-West region of the subcontinent. I quote "That Sarasvati primarily was a river is beyond dispute".[4] Ṛg Veda (ṚV) 10.64.9 mentions Sarasvatī together with Sarayu and Sindhu. ṚV 10.75.5 mentions Sarasvatī with Gaṅgā, Yamunā and Śutudrī. ṚV

1.3.10-12, invokes Sarasvatī both as a river rewarding the sacrificier with plenty of grains. But she also is praised for stimulating the intelligent people. These two identity of the goddess Sarasvatī caught the attention of Vedic scholars like Professor Gonda. In his monograph *Pūṣan and Sarasvatī* he particularly addressed this problem. I shall use this work quite extensively.

André Padoux has dealt with this material in his monumental work Vāc, etc. Its recent translation has made this work available to English-speaking scholars. This monumental work has very neatly treated the later development of Vāc, the goddess of Speech, mainly in later Tāntric texts. I shall come to that aspect of the goddess in the second half of this paper.

ṚV 8.100.10-13 tell us that the gods created goddess *Vāc* (Sacral Speech). She is here envisaged as a milch cow (*dhenu*) which is agreeable and gives abundance of goods. The image of a cow in connection with Sacral Speech needs some explanation. In the Ṛg Veda as well as in other Vedic texts the cow symbolizes an almost inexhaustible source of sustenance and riches. J. Gonda writes "In view of this 'imagery' the application of the word for milch cow to the almost inexhaustible source of inspiration and imagination on which all those that had the gift of speech could draw freely and copiously and to the psychological stratum in which all processes connected with verbal expression and poetic art have their origin is not so strange as it would seem to be at first sight."[5] By means of the symbolism of the cow, the Vedic sage poet conveyed the concept of abstract Speech (*Vāc*) as the seminal entity from which all verbal wisdom flows. ṚV 1.164 41-42, describes her, again recalling the cow imagery, as the creator of the primal cosmic waters while she who (appears as verses consisting of) a single foot, two feet, four feet, eight feet or nine feet, (in fact) exists in this supreme heaven as infinite and eternal. "From her (Vāc) the clouds shed abundant rain and thence (the people of) the four quarters live; thence the moisture spreads and the universe exists."[6] Further on, verse 45 of the same hymn says: "Four are the definite grades of Speech: those Brāhmaṇas who are wise know them: three, deposited in secret these never manifest themselves, men speak the fourth grade of Speech."[7] This verse is of immense importance for the later development of the concept of Vāc which developed into a fully fledged philosophy of language and grammar.[8] I shall come back to this later.

Although some verses of the ṚV relate a homology between Sarasvatī, primarily the goddess of a river on the bank of which the early Indo-Aryan-speaking people resided and prospered, and the conceptual divinity Vāc, the ṚV also records their independent existence. Gonda really believes that Sarasvatī as the most important and life-saving local river grew enormously in importance to the early Vedic poets who praised her as the source of life and food.[9] But the distinction between them became blurred and their homogeneity got more emphasis from the Vedic sages. In many Vedic texts later than the ṚV, Sarasvatī is addressed as Sarasvatī Vāc,[10] and towards the end of the Vedic period Sarasvatī's integration with Vāc becomes complete when she is addressed as the goddess Speech (Vāgdevī, Gīrdevī and Brahmāṇī).[11] These early texts also tell us that if a person has some speech defect or is unable to speak properly this person should offer an ewe to Sarasvatī.[12] Thus Sarasvatī is Vāc, the sacred Word or Speech who is full of magical power and sometimes deemed as the great divine capacity that activates all other divinities. For she as the great Vedic sacral Word which, according to the Vedic poet-sages, when uttered properly by the sacrificer, can move the other divine power as well. Thus the power of Vedic Sacral Word is the supreme one.

The *Bṛhaddevatā* by Śaunaka, an index of Vedic goddesses and gods, says that divinities should be praised by recalling their names, their forms, their acts and their allies, which implies that each verse and hymn of the Vedas is envisioned by a sage who propitiated some divinity.[13] But there are some hymns which are self-laudatory; the hymn (RV X. 125) to the goddess Vāc, the sacral Word, is one of them. Its sage is Vāc, Āmbhṛṇī, i.e. the daughter of Ambhṛṇa. One may imagine that the poet was Ambhṛṇa, and that he visualized and praised his own muse, the divine force underlying the sacred speech of the hymn. If this is accepted then there is no hymn or verse addressed to Vāc visioned by any woman sage.

Whatever that may be, ṚV 10.125 witnessed the crystallization of the supreme power of the sacral Word. I quote:

1. I move with the Rudras, with the Vasus, with the Ādityas and all other gods. I carry both Mitra and Varuṇa, both Indra and Agni, and both the Aśvins.
2. I carry the swelling Soma and Tvastṛ, and Pūṣan and Bhaga. I bestow wealth on the pious sacrificer who presses the Soma and offers oblation.
3. I am the queen, the confluence of riches, the skillful one who is first among those worthy of sacrifice. The gods divided me up into various parts, for I dwell in many places and enter into many forms.
4. The one who eats food, who truly sees, who breathes, who hears what is said, does so through me. Though they do not realize it, they dwell in me. Listen, you whom they have heard; what I tell you should be believed.
5. I am the one who says, by myself, what gives joy to gods and men. Whom I love I make awesome; I make him a sage, a wise man, a Brahmā (a depositary of sacred Prayer).
6. I stretch the bow for Rudra, so that his arrow will strike down the hater of prayer. I incite the contest for the people. [It may mean verbal contest]. I have pervaded sky and earth.

7. I gave birth to the father on the head of this world. (i.e. the sky, *dyaus*). My womb is in the (cosmic) waters, within the ocean. From there I spread out over all creatures and touch the very sky with the crown of my head.
8. I am the one who blows the wind, embracing all creatures. Beyond the sky, beyond this earth, so much have I become in my greatness.[14]

This short hymns shows how, early in the Vedic religion, Vāc attained great power. She accompanies all gods and supports them. Originating in the primal cosmic waters she was the power behind all phenomena and thus was the queen of all. As the immediately preceding source of the creation she pervaded it. Vāc came to mean the abstract power of magic that inheres in the Vedic hymns when they are applied to sacrifices offered to various gods for the attainment of various goals.[15]

In ṚV.10.71, the nature of Vāc comes out more clearly. This hymns is addressed to the god Bṛhaspati (the lord of speech) and it describes the origin of Vāc differently.

1. Bṛhaspati! When they [the first poets and sages] set in motion the first beginning of Speech, giving names, their most pure and perfectly guarded secret was revealed through love.
2. When the wise ones fashioned speech with their own thought, sifting it as grain is sifted through a sieve, then friends recognized their friendships. A good sign was placed on their speech.
3. Through the sacrifice they traced the path of speech and found it inside the sages. They held it and portioned it out to many; together the seven singers praised it.

....

8. When the intuitions of the mind are shaped in the heart, when Brahmins perform sacrifices together as friends,

some are left behind for lack of knowledge, while others surpass them with the power of praise.[16]

Thus, as Norman Brown has said, "the close relation between ritual and magic leads to what is essentially an ascription of creative action to the power of words or sound. That is the potency of words is considered to be the effective creative force. When the gods utter the names of things, at the time of the first sacrifice, these things come into existence (ṚV 10.71.1; 10.82.3). In the self-praise hymn to Vāc, who is as said above, a deification of the sounds of the sacrifice, she claims control of the universe for herself, and tells us her birth place was in the waters, the ocean, as is elsewhere that of Hiraṇyagarbha (the primal Being and Creator. 10.121.1), whence she spread out on all sides over the world and reached the sky. We may possibly be justified in thinking that Vāc is conceived as being the creative force of the universe, though there is no explicit statement to that effect. If this is meant, then we have the apotheosis of the spell, the final exaltation of the magic sound."[17]

This apotheosis of Sarasvatī/Vāc should be understood in the light of the sacrificial religion of the early Vedic period. The deity of a mantra (formula or spell) was identified with the underlying magic force of the mantra. Making an offering to Sarasvatī/Vāc while reciting her mantra activates or stimulates the power inherent in sacred Speech. To quote Gonda again: "Sacred word or words uttered in a ritual context as well as the names of the deities that represent them are not empty things; they have life and a highly characteristic power of their own, a decisive power, and the one who utters such words, or the divine name, sets power in motion."[18]

Sarasvatī/Vāc is also connected with mind (manas) as a vital principle of gods and men. This can be described as the principle of existence (Daseinsmacht), and is essentially a form of creative force.[19]

In this way in the ṚV there seemed to be two lines of thought regarding her origin. Either those who possess *dhi* (creative inspiration) deliberately create her ṚV10.71; ṚV 1.164.24), or, she is identical with the primal waters from which the creation emerged (ṚV 10.125.7). However, Vāc, although a goddess, seems in the Ṛgveda to remain a conceptual divinity, a mere personification, devoid of any mythology.

This situation changes in the later Vedic literature. In the *Śatapatha-Brāhmaṇa*[19] we are told that the creator god Prajāpati performed *tapas*, i.e. austerity, and emanated Brahman, and then likewise created waters out of the world of Vāc or Brahman, which here means the three oldest Vedas. This Brahman served the creator as his foundation. It is significant that in cosmogonic hymns the primal water is equated with chaos, from which the regular creation is brought forth. Probably because her original identity was the river Sarasvatī, Sarasvatī/Vāc is somehow equated with these cosmic waters, which in their turn became the Creator's support or foundation. She then as identified with Brahman created the world out of that water. Thus in effect she became both the creatrix and the substance of the creation. The post- Ṛgvedic connection of Vāc/Sarasvatī with Prajāpati, the creator might have created the theology of goddess Vāc the primieval active principle, the creating divine power of the Tantra religions. To quote Gonda "according to the sāmavedic tradition handed down in PB 20.14.2 and JB 2.244, Vāc, the Sacral Word, was Prajāpati's only own (*svam*), when in the beginning (*agre*), he was alone here. He emitted (*vyasṛjata*) it and it pervaded the whole universe (*idaṃ sarvaṃ vibhantyait*) rising upwards as a continuous stream of water. By means of this (Vāc) Prajāpati then created the tripartite universe: he cut off three sounds which became the earth, the intermediate region and the heavens. A later commentator observed that the tripartite universe consists of words (names) and objects (*Śabda and artha*)."[21]

In the post-Vedic period this homology between Brahman and Vāc became a very creative idea. The school of grammarian philosophers posited the Word-principle (*Śabdabrahman*) as the seminal source of creation. They argued that Word evolved and existed on four levels or stages (Cf. ṚV 1.164). The highest of the four is the Primal Word, the first cosmic principle. The second state is cosmogony, when the first principle creates all things by the utterance of their names (Cf. ṚV 10.71. 1; p. 3 above). Thus ideal speech is fashioned before the creation of the objects it refers to. The third stage of speech is the ideal-language inherited by every person. The fourth is the actual, audible speech used for religious and social transactions.

In this way both the philosophical speculation on the Word principle and the theology of important gods and goddesses of the later Brahmanical religious tradition continuously drew on the Vedic literature. The early abstract idea of Vāc/Sarasvatī was hypostatized in the post-Ṛgvedic period as the Goddess of sacred Speech and the muse or poetic genius (*dhi*) of the Vedic sages.[22] By the time we arrive in the post-Vedic period her deification is complete. Yāska's *Nirukta* (c. 6 B.C.E.) records the important deity Sarasvatī/ Vāc with various important aspects and powers.[23]

When we turn our attention to the development of Sarasvatī/Vāc in the Āgamic, Purāṇic and Tāntric literature we must keep in mind the importance of the above discussed Vedic concept of the close relationship between Sarasvatī/ Vāc and the Creator god Prajāpati. As seen above, this goddess is conceived of as the first creation of the creator God, born in the cosmic waters or homogeneous with them. The primordial waters represent the chaos from which the cosmos, the organized creation emerged regulated by a settled standard of law and morality, *ṛta*. As such she became the creative force which supported the creator. One may be reminded of the Vaiṣṇava Āgamic concept of Viṣṇumāyā, the divine creative force of the primal deity

Nārāyaṇa, transformed as the primal waters on which Nārāyaṇa floats, sleeping just before the creation.[24]

Another close connection between the Āgamic and the Ṛgvedic cosmogony is to be found in the cosmogonic hymn 10, 129. As Gonda points out there are several links between the two on the speculations of cosmogony. The word *āvarivaḥ* he takes to mean moved (Donigar: stirred) and this he thinks is linked with the Āgamic *spanda* theory. The second important link is the mention of desire (kāma).

Building on that line of thought, in the Tantric religion Vāc became the active aspect (Parā Śakti; parā cit, etc.), of God thereby not compromising God's transcendence and changelessness. God remained passive. She is God's creative urge (*icchā*), his creative thought, omniscience (jñāna śakti, *vimarśa, saṃvit-śakti, parā, pratibhā* or *sudarśana,* etc. in the Śaiva and Vaiṣṇava Āgamic texts and in the philosophy of the Grammarians) as well as active creative power (*kriyā śakti*). She is the foundation (*bhitti*) which is but the divine self (*sva*) in which the creation is reflected as in a mirror. Here is the unmistakable echo of the Brāhmaṇa passages mentioned above.[25] In other words the supreme god, although the prime mover remains passive in the process of creation. He remains transcendent and immutable and, at least in theory, impersonal. What constitutes his inner and outer divine personality is conceived as his Power, Śakti. She is hypostatized as the sovereign goddess encapsuling the concepts of the indomitable divine Will, divine omniscience and divine omnipotence.[26]

In the Vedic cosmogony there exists quite a lot of the erotic imagery concerning Prajāpati, the first creator, and his depression at being alone, which led to his urge to create. Therefore it is not surprising that in the post-Vedic mythological literature this Śakti, the goddess, became the Creator's spouse. The Śaiva Tantric religion emphasized the passivity of the creator and his lack of involvement in the world by presenting the Supreme God as a renouncer.

The goddess, divine Śakti as the active sovereign divinity, is the real creatrix. As Vāc she is the divine vision, and fashions the universe according to that vision. This creative vision is the second stage of sacred Speech; in it are reflected all the phenomena of creation before they come into existence. It is called Vāc's all-seeing stage or she is designated the divine genius or inspiration (*pratibhā*).

It is easy to see that this Tantric theology was inspired by the Vedic concept that Vāc homologous with the thought or inspiration (*dhi*; *manīṣā*) of the Vedic sages who envisioned the magically potent hymns, mantras. In Tantric theology the goddess Vāc not only envisioned the creation as *pratibhā*, but also fashioned it out of herself (Cf. above pp. 5-6). Thus the creation is a projection of her active force which also is the ultimate controller.

Vāc, sacred Speech, in her third stage represents ideal language, which in ancient India was not seen as separate from knowledge. This knowledge in the form of language every human being inherits and further adds to. But a special felicity in handling language is only a grace given by the goddess Vāc. Some are blessed with that grace from birth while others may acquire it through active propitiation of the goddess. Even those who possess it should constantly propitiate her and be full of gratitude for the blessing. The image of the goddess in the capacity is called Sarasvatī. Other homonyms are Vagīśvarī, Vāṇī, Bhāratī, Brahmāṇī, etc. She is the beautiful embodiment of aesthetic pleasure (Sundarī, Lalitā).[27]

The most important aspect of Vāc for worshippers, Tantric and others, directly links her to the Ṛg Vedic Vāc, Sacral Word or Speech. She is the abstract force underlying the mantras, spells, and formulas. In Tantric parlance these are called *vidyās*, sacred wisdom. They are special manifestations of Vāc, the goddess, as embodiments of her divine grace. The devotee receives one of these *vidyās* at his or her initiation and ritually worships and meditates on this *vidyā* as the sonic embodiment of some special aspect of goddess. If the devotee is successful in this religious endeavour he or she receives her grace and is identified with his/her *vidyā*. That grace may be part of her supreme sovereign power appropriate for the personal need and capacity of the devotee or it can take the form of final release from the bondage of recurrent life and death. In any case the proper realization of one's received *vidyā* opens up the path of realizing the cosmic knowledge and wisdom of Vāc. The Vedic sages possessed this wisdom and so were described as *Kavi* (inspired and skilful) and *manīṣī* (possessors of supreme wisdom). Her grace can bestow the same vision of the cosmic Truth on her devotee.

As inspiration, Vāc in the post-Vedic period not only became the goddess of Speech, eloquence and wisdom, but also the goddess of music. Music as an art is closely related to poetry in the Sanskrit tradition. Therefore in late Tāntric tradition the goddess is also designated as the mother of music (*saṅgītamātā*) and melody. Thus in the visual representation of the goddess since the medieval period she not only holds a text but also carries a *vinā*, the Indian lute. In another form the goddess is holding a parrot or myna reminding one of her Vedic connection with these talking birds.[28]

I do not intend here to expatiate on the later Tāntric development of the goddess Vāc. I have dealt with it in another paper on Tripurasundarī.[29] In a long article Alexis Sanderson has traced the iconographic development of the Trika deities in the Śaiva tantric sects and shown how their supreme deity iconographically is an ectype of Sarasvatī/ Vāc, the goddess of learning.[30] The influence of the Trika system displayed in the Mālinivijayottara Tantra and developed by Abhinavagupta equated the grammarian school's supreme sound-reality, Śabdabrahman,, with the supreme speech, parā Vāc. Her iconography retains the Purāṇic iconography of Gāyatrī, the deity representing the Vedas and the Vedic knowledge. She follows some traits of the iconography of Brahmā, riding a goose, holding the rosary and the Vedas in her hands, and so forth.[31] As pure knowledge she has a very fair complexion. She has four arms but in the Tantric iconography her other two hands are held in the gesture of granting wishes, vara and promising protection, abhaya. Daṇdin began his *Kāvyādarśa* with a prayer to Sarasvatī: "Let Sarasvatī, who is completely white, play in my mind as she always does like a goose in the lotus garden of the four (lotus) faces (of Brahmā)."[32] Here Sarasvatī is indeed identified with the four Vedas spontaneously uttered by Brahmā.

In Vedic literature the river Sarasvatī, identified with Vāc,[33] was associated with Prajāpati the creator. The creation began by arranging the primal waters into a cosmic system, in which function Prajāpati was aided by Sarasvatī/Vāc (see above). In the Purāṇas the four - faced Brahmā is the creator; he created with the aid of the Vedas which became personified as the goddess Sarasvatī, who is Brahma's spouse and Śakti. In the Tantras she became the supreme divine power, combining in herself the divine creative impulse, cognition and action. In some later period she became not only poetic inspiration and the embodiment of aesthetic pleasure but also the embodiment of music.[34] In the last role she is called Saṃgītamātā and in South India is identified with the goddess of the famous temple of Madurai. Her association with music is symbolized in iconography by her holding the viṇā, the Indian lute. She is goddess Vāgīśvarī worshipped by countless Hindus on the fifth lunar day of the bright fortnight in spring.

What the later Purāṇas did to underscore the total identity between Kālī and Durgā as well as between the erotic beautiful goddess Lalitā and the aggressive (*ugra*) forms of the Goddess in their own idiom, was achieved more explicitly in the late Tantras like the *Prapañcasāra* and the *Śaktisaṅgama.* To illustrate this let me summarize ŚsT's account of the cosmic creation. In this Tantra Kālī is the supreme Goddess. She is in spite of her awesome iconography, called the compassionate Kālī(*dakṣinākāli*). She is the primeval Goddess and she was dancing the dance of dissolution and the destroyed world including the Vedas lay about at her feet like so many corpses. Then she returns to her true nature of pure consciousness and subsumes both Śiva and Śakti. At a certain primordial moment she beholds within herself her own mirror image or shadow, which is indeed delusion, Māyā. In that Māyā, Kālī created the imagined form of Śiva who became the primeval God and Kālī's spouse. Then Kālī created empty space and she engaged in sexual intercourse with Śiva, taking the reverse position and the active role. The result of this coitus was a beautiful girl whom Kālī called simply Sunadarī, i.e. the beautiful one. Her beauty completely deluded Śiva, who wanted to express his emotion. Śiva's longing for self-expression produced Speech which from its central unity developed into the system of sounds, letters and language and became all pervasive. Śiva, however on creating Speech, first addressed the goddess Sundarī as his heart's desire, the loveliest in three worlds, the exquisite sovereign goddess and the ocean of nectar-like compassion. Next he addressed Kālī as most terrifying, howling frightening roar. As soon as Śiva uttered these two sentences addressing the two goddesses, as if offended, Goddess Kālī suddenly disappeared, leaving Śiva with Sundarī, the product of delusion, while she got on with her task of creation. Kālī, who is transcendent and the essence of creation, transformed herself into the abstract cosmic dynamic power. Loss of Kālī made Śiva utterly despondent and confused and he started lamenting for her desperately urging her to take pity on him and return. The compassionate goddess Kālī then removed Śiva's confusion by infusing him with unimpeded cognitive knowledge and desire to procreate and gave him Sundarī as his partner. Sundarī is most of all, Ambikā, the cosmic creatrix (ŚsT I.I.22-45).

Śakti Tantras further amalgamated other important goddesses from other cults and developed the cult of supreme spell or mystical formulas vidyās. There are many clusters of them. But a group of ten became more important cult which continues even today. One final remark I want to make and that is Kālikā as she appears in her iconography is far from an erotic figure. Destructive she is and being both the original supreme being from whom everything emerged and essentially compassionate, she is the supreme mother Ambikā but her erotic manifestation is Tripurāsundarī, the loveliest lady in the three-worlds.

NOTES

1 An earlier version of this paper was presented to the Fifth Biennial Conference of the European Society of Women in Theological Research. University of Leuven/Louvain, 1993.

2 See Gonda, *A History of Vedic Literature: A History of Indian Literature*, Vol. I, Otto Harrassowit, Wiesbaden, 1975, pp 60-76. I have also extensively used Professor Gond's two other works, viz., *Puṣan and Sarasvatī* and *De Kosmogonie Van Ṛgveda 10. 129.*

3 Gonda (85); p. 7.

4 Ibid; 31.

5 H.H. Wilson; *Ṛig-Veda,* Vol 2; 78. ṚV. 1.164.41-42 and 46.

6 Ibid; 78. RV. 1.164. 45.

7 Cf. Bhartṛhari, *Vākyapadīya* Canto I, 131, 133, 138 and 143. See *Mind, Language and World: The Collected Essays of Bimal Krishna Matilal,* Edited by Jonardon Ganeri, OUP, New Delhi, 2002, pp. 339-341.

8 Gonda (85), pp. 9-10.

9 Gonda (85), pp. 31-33.

10 Gonda; 160, footnote.... "This (ritual) importance came to be enhanced by her association and 'identification' with Vac, the sacral Word, the potency and healing function of which is more than once (e.g. Tait Br. 1, 8.5.56) referred to."

11 Brāhmanī from the word brahma, in early Vedic literature it means sacred utterance, prayer etc. Cf. ṚV 1.164. 35. "*brahmāyaṃ vācaḥ paramaṃ vyoma.*" This sacrificial prayer is the supreme heaven of Speech.

12 *Taittirīya Saṃhitā,* 2. 1. 2. 6; 3.4.3.6.

13 BD 1. 2-4.

14 Wendy Doniger O'Flaherty, *The Rig Veda: An Anthology,* Penguin Classics, 1981.

15 Gonda (85), p. 64.

16. O'Flaherty, pp. 61-62.

17 Norman Brown, p. 27.

18 Gonda (85), p. 34.

19 Ibid, p. 37.

20 *Śatapatha-Brāmaṇa;* 6. 1. 1. 8ff;

21 Gonda (85), p. 65. *Pañcaviṃśa-Brāhmaṇa* 20. 14. 2, and the commentary thereon; *Jaiminīya-Brāhmaṇa* 2. 244.

22 Gonda (75), pp. 65-73.

23 Yāska, *Nirukta,* 11. 25. 607; 11. 27. 1-3; 11. 27. 1-5; 11. 28. 1-3; and 11. 29. 1-2.

24 JS, 2.34-75; 3. 14-28; 4. 14-25.

25 JS, 4, 82-85; LT, 6.38; 18. 14-37; 22, 7-10; Sanderson '90; 50.

26 Gupta (72), Introduction, XXIV-XXVI. Sanderson, opus citum.

27 Cf Saundaryalaharī by Saṇkarācārya. Gupta, (87), 10-19.

28 Vājasaneyi-Saṃhitā, 24. 33; Gonda 37.

29 Gupta (87), 11-19.

30 Sanderson (90); 50ff.

31 The goose as Sarasvatī's carrier (*vāhana*) grew from the Vedic concept of the mind being the carrier of Sarasvatī, i.e. Speech. Cf. Gonda (85) 37; "The psychological process is briefly described in ŚB [Śatapatha-Brāhmaṇa] 12, 9, 1, 13 "whatever one thinks with one's mind that one says with one's speech", and while Sarasvatī is *vāc*, Indra is declared to be *manas*. It is metaphorically suggested in RV 10, 177, 2: "the bird, i.e. the internal light of visionary and spiritual illumination, bears speech with its *manas*".

32 Kāvyādarśa 1, 1.

33 Gonda (85), 60-64.

34 Saundaryalaharī, verses 16, 17, 64 and 66.

2. Śakti the Supreme Divine Power: The Role of Lakṣmī in Pāñcarātra Sotereology

The principle *śakti* - inscrutable power and autonomous dynamism - has been used by Indian theologians to explain the concept of the supreme divine, the creator and the saviour. Indeed, late Upaniṣadic thinker accepted Brahman as their supreme God. But they confronted with a contradiction, which was hard to overcome. Early Upaniṣadic Brahman is not only the unique Reality but is also totally transcendent. Nothing can be predicated to it. Moreover, this Reality is totally identified with *ātman*, the individual self. For the monotheists these contradictions begged for a new definition. These theologians tackled this problem by introducing the concept of *śakti*. In the *Śvetāśvatara Upaniṣad* (1.10.4.1 & 5.5.14.) the creating God created through His multifaceted *śakti*, which in the theistic cosmogony has dual functions, viz. evolving as the ultimate source, *prakṛti*, as well as obscuring the true identity of death and rebirth (4.9-10). *Śakti* is called *māyā*. *Māyā* is not just illusion that affects individual beings, it is in fact, God's incomprehensible power. *Śakti* is variegated, which enables God to create the diversified universe.[1] In this paper I want to deal with the Pāñcarātra view on *śakti*, which in the system's early period occupied the central position as the divine personality as well as the essential source of conscious individuals. However, in the system's long history especially in the theology of the Śrī Vaiṣṇava sect, *śakti's* centrality in its cosmogony started to become obscure, until in the 14th century C.E. she became the centre of a major controversy in the system. Then a schism took place amongst the adherents of this system, dividing them into a northern group and a southern group.[2]

I shall later discuss that this divine *śakti* is the same goddess as Lakṣmī/Śrī– the innate power/energy of God, hypostatized as goddess and mythologized as the supreme God's divine spouse. This last development most probably took place early in the Christian era, reaching its peak in the Imperial Gupta period. The *Mahābhārata* yields ample examples of the association of Lakṣmī with Nārāyaṇa[3] and the various Gupta coins and other evidence confirm this mythology of Lakṣmī-Nārāyaṇa.[4] However, in the narrow sectarian theology of the Śrī Vaiṣṇavas established by Rāmānuja, becoming Nārāyaṇa's wife proved to be somewhat problematic for goddess Lakṣmī and as a result she gradually lost her cosmic autonomy since the very strict Śrī-vaiṣṇavas believed that their position as *ekāntin,* i.e. loyal devotees of only one supreme Divine. Hence she is accepted as the perfect wife of the great godhead and perfect devotee who has made herself totally subservient to her lord and protector spouse. Her autonomy turned into her power of intercession (*puruṣakāra*). This power is absolutely necessary for a devotee to receive God's redemption and grace which is the only way for him to salvation (*mukti*).

I shall now briefly give an account of the concept of *śakti* in the Pāñcarātra system of theology in order to make it clear how important is *śakti* in that system's cosmogony and soteriology. The Pāñcarātra soteriology closely follows the gnostic way of the Vedāntic/Upaniṣadic soteriology, i.e. one reaches salvation through the realization of one's self as essentially not different from God's *śakti.*[5] This soteriology follows the yogic method of analysing the nature of an individual being in his/her quest for understanding this essential person, eliminating all grossness, diversity and opacity that obscures that essence. This is achieved by understanding the process of creation which evolves from and through *śakti,* which is innate in God, coexistent and consubstantial with Him.

At the first polarization of God's unity there appeared in God, speech, *vāc,* which is also considered in the sect's philosophy to be the divine cognition or awareness, *jñatva.* In the Pāñcarātra system this consciousness is called *saṃvit,* which is the eternally immutable divine power (*acyuta śakti*). *Saṃvit* is both pure consciousness and the reflective consciousness. The latter is stated to be the "I-ness" (*ahaṃtā*) of the primal supreme Person, Nārāyaṇa or Vāsudeva.[6] Thus *saṃvit* or consciousness is in this case awareness of the supreme Person as self, *ātman.* In other words it is the primal moment of self-consciousness of the supreme Person, the end of His indeterminate and quiescent state, heralding His creative will and agency. Being aware of Himself starts the subject-object, cognitive polarization although at this point both are the same. The polarity in God and his awareness or self-reflection is expressed by the term *vāc,* speech or language, the vehicle of reflection.[7] Yet this is still integral to the supreme Person. From this self-awareness and reflection (the thinking) of Nārāyaṇa there develops the divine will (*icchā*) to create and the supreme divine *śakti* which is the active *saṃvit,* the supreme Person's "I-ness", i.e. the divine personality which projects the embodied beings. The power, *śakti* that creates is variously called *vidyā, prakṛti, māyā,* etc. and is thus the divine creativity. Therefore to know one's own true self is to know one's identity with *śakti.* Each individual's personality emanates from the divine personality. The relation between Brahman and the word or speech is very clearly put forward by Bhartṛhari (c. 6th century C.E.).[8] The Kashmiri philosopher Vāmandatta who wrote a clear exposition of the position of *saṃvit* in Pāñcarātra soteriology and cosmogony,[9] also supported the early Pāñcarātra system's idea that speech, *vāc,* was identified with *śakti,* i.e. *saṃvit śakti* and was the active principle in the act of creation.

The concept of *saṃvit śakti* is central in early Pāñcarātra soteriology. In Pāñcarātra the final phase of the yogic practice leading to emancipation, is known as the yoga of *tattvajaya,* i.e. removing the yogin's association with the empirical categories which created his individual identity differentiating it from the supreme being.[10] He does it by identifying himself with the primal group of *śaktis* who emanated successively from the original *saṃvit śakti.* The yogin of course does it in the reverse order, fixing his mind on the *mantra* of each of them. While concentrating on the supreme *śakti,* who represents in Pāñcarātra the totality of the six divine qualities, viz. *jñāna, aiśvarya, śakti, bala, vīrya* and *tejas* which are integral for the concept of a personal godhead, the yogin understands her to be the divine personality and also realizes that the primary divine quality is indeed *jñāna,* i.e. consciousness, both pure and static consciousness and potentially dynamic awareness; the remaining five qualities are merely refractions of the first.[11]

To make *śakti's* centrality in this soteriology clear let me now briefly explain the nature of the *tattvajaya* yoga. In 1992 I published an article on the yogic practice described in the three early Pāñcarātra Saṃhitās namely, the *Sāttvata* (SS), the *Jayākhya* (JS) and the *Pauṣkara* (PS), as well as in two late texts of the schools, the *Lakṣmī Tantra* (LT)[12] and the *Ahirbudhnya Saṃhitā* (AS).[13] There I mainly concentrated on the yoga in which one meditates on the basic Pāñcarātra four-fold divinity, i.e. Vyūha-Vāsudeva.[14] The *śakti,* inherent and active in Vyūha-Vāsudeva, remained in the background. In this paper I shall concentrate on the divine *śakti* and *śaktis* and Pāñcarātra soteriological practice (*sādhanā*), dealing with their place in the cosmology and ontology of that system with some remarks on their iconography.

In his *Yoga: Immortality and Freedom* Mercia Eliade remarks: "In tantric *sādhanā,* iconography plays a role that, though of greatest importance, is difficult to define in a few words."[15] Further he writes, "Tantric iconography represents a 'religious' universe that must be entered and assimilated.

This 'entrance' and 'assimilation' are to be understood in the direct meaning of the terms: in meditating on an icon, one must first 'transport' oneself to the cosmic plane ruled by the respective divinity, and then assimilate it, incorporate into oneself the sacred force by which that particular plane is 'sustained' or, as it were, 'created'.[16] Eliade's observations show his deep understanding of the system of meditation involved. He further remarks, "When a tantric text describes the way to construct a mental image of a divinity we seem to be reading a treatise on iconography."[17] The description he is referring to is what is known as *dhyāna* – the point of focus where the yogi is to fix his mind in one-pointed meditation. It is a fact that tāntric iconography is based on these *dhyānas*. Thus the yoga system of the Pāñcarātra too extensively uses the mantras and the iconography of their divine forms – forms on which the yogis practice the assimilation and absorption of their individual selves into different planes of the cosmogonic moments (tattvas), albeit in reverse order. The *tattvajaya* system of meditation described in the *Pauṣkara Saṃhitā* gives a clear depiction of these *śaktis*. It should be noted that in the Pāñcarātra parlance these *śaktis* are called *kalā*, while the four Vyūhas are called *tattvas*, and essentially the two groups are not different.[18]

The Pāñcarātra sacred texts describe these *dhyānas* as the divine forms of the deities of the mantras which are their sonic counterparts. On these forms the yogin who follows the gnostic path should focus his mind and achieve stasis of his naturally dynamic thought process. Yogic meditation, both in its differentiated (*savikalpa*) and non-differentiated (*nirvikalpa*) states, uses threefold system of meditation *dhyāna, dhāraṇā* and *samādhi*. When the yogin achieves the knowledge that is truth in itself, *ṛtambharā prajñā*, and the idea that he is totally unrelated to any form of diversity, *kaivalya*, his final stage of meditative process starts leading to salvation, *mukti*.

In theistic systems God is responsible for creating not only the empirical world but also the world of mantras and their deities – the means to escape the transient existence of the empirical individual. Like the act of creation, which is in fact an expression of the actively creative *śakti*, the mantras and their deities are also expressions of the same *śakti* which embodies God's compassion and grace providing the yogin with a system or way to achieve salvation.[19] As the *ṛtambharā prajñā* or *viveka buddhi*, i.e. the real discriminating knowledge, dawns in the yogin's awareness, he finally realizes the nature and functions of divine *śakti* and her various aspects, also called *śaktis*. He recognizes the four redemptive (*upāya*) aspects of *śakti*, viz. *jñāna, kriyā, icchā* and *prāṇa*, i.e. divine omniscience, omnipotence, will and primal dynamic flux. These four are, in the reverse order, the pure forms of *śakti* symbolized in the fourfold divine image of the four Vyūha deities, viz. Vāsudeva, Saṃkarṣaṇa, Pradyumna and Aniruddha.[20] He also realizes the true nature of creative aspects of the same *śaktis* plus an extra one called *kāla* or time which heralds the moment of transience. He understands that in their creative aspects these *śaktis* are arranged hierarchically. In the creative order they move from top to bottom as *prāṇa*, then *icchā, jñāna, kriyā* and finally *kāla*.[21] In the salvific schema the effect of time disappears through practice of *savikalpa samādhi* and when the yogin's *viveka buddhi* is awakened. For the yogin the next step is to practise *nirvikalpa* meditation. In this practice he identifies himself with the relevant *śakti* at each step of his spiritual stance, and realizes his identification consecutively with the remaining four *śaktis* ending with *prāṇa* which is pure dynamism, *spanda*, symbolized as Vyūha-Vāsudeva.[22] But all the time he also is aware of the fact that all four are present simultaneously through each step. At this stage the Pāñcarātra yogin realizes the identity of *śakti* as not just flux (*spanda*) but the active divine consciousness *saṃvit* which symbolizes the unity of all other *śaktis*. Now these meditations are conducted by utilizing all three components of the process, viz. *dhāraṇā, dhyāna* and *samādhi,* i.e. concentration, meditation and undisturbed stasis of mind in the object of meditation respectively.[23] Therefore each *śakti* has a *dhyāna*-form for fixing the yogin's mind, as the *mantraśāstra* explains. This constitutes the Pāñcarātra iconography. The early images of deities must have been made to facilitate a yogin's meditation on them. The text I shall use extensively is the PS. It is an early text. The text is not properly edited and some parts of it are clearly late. But the yogic system it teaches is certainly old. As the name *tattvajaya* expresses, the four *śaktis* are equated with the ontological realities that make up the top most stages of the Pañcarātra cosmogony.[24] In order to facilitate their practice of *dhyāna, dhāraṇā* and *samādhi* the yogins depended on the images built according to the *dhyāna* texts of their scripture. Thus the images or icons began to be constructed. It seems during the period between second century BCE and fifth century CE a great number of icons and images of Brahmanical deities were in existence, many of them Vaiṣṇavite.[25] For private worship and meditation a practitioner needed a quiet and secluded place even at his home. These private icons were in the round, showing the deity from all four sides. In Pāñcarātra Vaiṣṇava religion images and icons acquired a very important position at a very early stage. As the *mantras* became the definite focal point of meditation, i.e. *dhāraṇī,* their visual forms too acquire the same status as the manifestation of the power, *śakti,* of that mantra.[26]

I deal now with an early image of these primordial *śaktis,*[27] small but completely in the round and preserving enough features to identify it as a *dhāraṇī.* This will prove how the early Pāñcarātra yogin meditated on the primordial *śakti/śaktis* to attain salvation. In T.S. Maxwell's book *Viśvarūpa,*[28] I came across two diagrams of very important and rare Pāñcarātra cosmogonic icons of composite figures, preserved in the Mathura Museum.[29] They belong to the

Kuṣāṇa period, i.e. first or second century C.E. One of these (Fig. 1) is a composite goddess figure containing a central columnal goddess who is surrounded by five other goddesses.[30] One of these emerges from behind the central figure's head vertically positioned. The four others appear two on each side of the central goddess, growing somewhat obliquely from behind her shoulders and sides of her head. The central columnal figure is the largest form of the group. On the rear of the icon a tree is sculpted. The similarity of this image of the other diagram (Fig. 2), a Caturvyūha image, is striking.[31] The only problem is that there are six goddesses instead of four. Maxwell has discussed the problem quite extensively. As he says, the Caturvyūha form of Viṣṇu/ Nārāyaṇa is cosmogonic. The curved tree behind the multiple-imaged goddess-icon too, having such close similarity to the Caturvyūha icon, must be cosmogonic. Here I suggest that this multiple-imaged icon must have been used as a *dhāraṇī* for the *tattvajaya* meditation which aimed to reach unconditional yogic statis (*nirvikalpa samadhi*).[32]

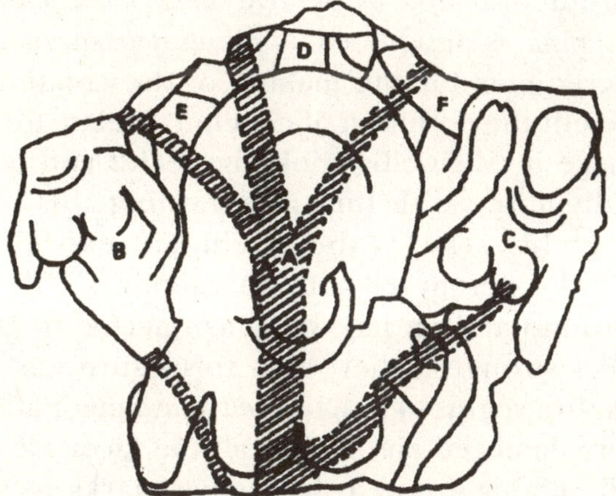

Fig. 1: A diagram of a rare Pāñcarātra cosmogonic icon, depicting a central columnal goddess surrounded by five other goddesses. Kuṣāṇa period, *c.* first or second century CE. Mathura Museum. From T.S. Maxwell, *Viśvarūpa* (Bombay: Oxford University Press, 1988), fig. 1.2, p. 36.

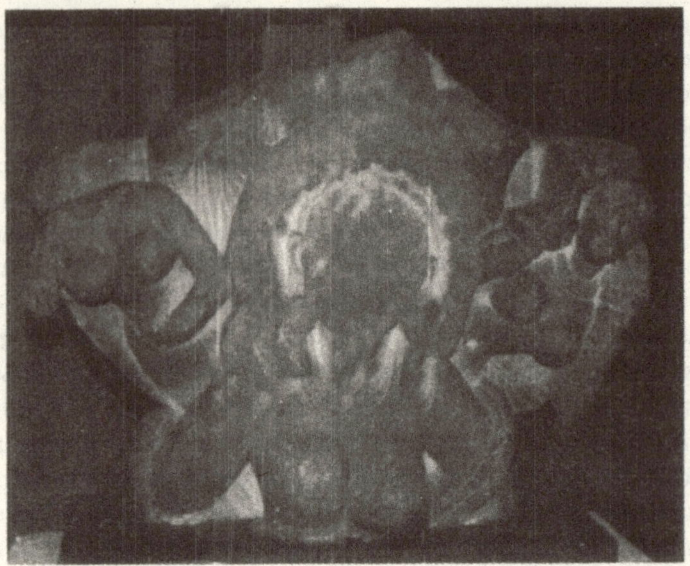

Fig. 2: Photograph of the image in Figure 1. From T.S. Maxwell, *Viśvarūpa* (Bombay: Oxford University Press, 1988), pl. 14

The group of *śaktis*, viz. the five *śaktis, kāla, jñāna, icchā, kriyā* and *prāṇa*, is designated as the *divyopakaraṇa*, i.e. the divine ingredients for the making of the creation,[33] and they represent the evolution of creation. I relate these *śaktis* to the image in Maxwell's book, figure 1.2 and plates 14-16. I totally agree with him in regarding this image of multiple goddesses, "as the intelligent expressions of complex and coherent religious philosophy...".[34] The figure is in the round and on its own, unconnected to any male deity, and I strongly believe that this figure was used by the Pāñcarātra yogins to practise *tattvajaya* meditation. This icon is very damaged and almost all the faces are broken, yet it still retains enough distinctive marks to show its religious affinity to the image of the fourfold cosmic emanations (*caturvyūha mūrti*) of transcendental Vāsudeva, the supreme godhead of the Pāñcarātra Vaiṣṇava sect. I am accepting Maxwell's conclusive identification because I have not seen it myself. From his description it is clear that the central figure is the main object of concentration, i.e. the supreme *Śakti* manifest as *śabda* or *vāc*. This is *saṃvit*, the first emergence of divine awareness, the first moment of polarity within the supreme Being who becomes aware of himself; his cognition of that is the beginning of creative process.[35] The state of quiescence and plenum is passive. The reflexive awareness of the Unique One starts the cognitive activity of the subject and needs to fill up the gap of object, i.e. the content of that cognition, in this case the Unique one's own self, *ātman*. Such cognition needs the speech to illuminate the nature of this cognition, depending on the categories of indicator (*vedaka*), i.e. name, and indicated (*vedya*), i.e. content. Thus the very first moment of disturbance in the unity of the supreme Being is an act of cognition which simultaneously requires speech, the primal manifestation of *śakti*, both as speech, *vāc*, and as active awareness, *saṃvit*.[36] In a recent paper Dr. Joanna Jurewicz, while interpreting ṚV.10.129, i.e. the *Nāsadīya sūkta*, points out that the first creative act of the single creator was a cognitive act. The passage from a total lack of cognition to the awareness of the creator's own self is depicted through the metaphor of his breathing without air through his power (*svadhā*).[37] This hymn mentions the divine power, manifest as breathing (*prāṇa*) and as desire (*icchā*), which is described as the first seed of mind, i.e. the cognitive faculty, here identified with cognition, *jñāna*. The sequence of these three leaves no doubt about the next two emanations of *śakti* viz., dynamism (*kriyā*) and then Time (*kāla*), the beginning of empirical creation. Thus the Pāñcarātra cosmogony can be traced back to the Vedic cosmogony. These cosmic *śakti*-emanations are the five cosmic ingredients, *divyopakaraṇa,* viz. *prāṇa, icchā, jñāna, kṛiyā* and *kāla* mentioned above. Once we see the composition of this primary creation, i.e. *śakti*, and her five emanations, we can appreciate the skilfull location of these *śakti* images. Of these *prāṇa* and *icchā* are depicted closer to the main deity, both being integral to the Unique One's self-awareness and the cognitive process involved, whereas *jñāna, kriyā* and *kāla* are positioned further away, incorporating definitive processes of creative action though all five being clustered together to underscore the fact that they all are equally primary cosmogonic *śaktis.*[38]

As PS says,[39] when the yogin starts on the practice of *nirvikalpa samādhi* he has already moved beyond the range of *kāla* and hence deals with only the four *śaktis,* viz. the *prāṇa,* etc. Thus PS shows that in the creative sequence *prāṇa, icchā, jñāna* and *kriyā* become manifest in that order and kāla, Time, appears last, heralding the empirical world. Although God as Brahman is unconditionally transcendent and immutable, His *śakti,* which is intrinsic in and inseparable from Him, paradoxically can and does change, that is, it evolves into multitudinous pragmatic phenomena. Moreover, God as brahman is a plenum and thus free from any form of action; it is passive and still, whereas His *śakti* is active and even vibrating. Here PS hastens to assert that *śakti* is also immutable, *acyutā.* God is the uncompromisingly transcendent Brahman, but His *śakti,* because of the oppositions in her, is immutable, yet she evolves; she is pure consciousness (*saṃvit*) yet she deludes individuals; hence she is the essential concept to explain creation and cosmogony. Thus *śakti* is a central concept in monotheistic Pāñcarāta theology. It is crucial for the practice of *nirvikalpa samādhi* to understand the relationship between the essential *śakti,* i.e. *saṃvit,* and the four primordial *śaktis.* The *dhyāna* imagery of them, as PS (and also JS) described, is envisaging them as a central mass of illumination with rays surrounding it.[40] This description shows the simultaneity of *saṃvit,* the clear light of consciousness, and its emanations *jñāna, kriyā, icchā* and *prāṇa* experienced by the yogin, as he identifies himself with each of these *śaktis* step by step. Before entering and being assimilated into the central mass of illumination, *saṃvit śakti,* the yogin is aware of his individual self which consists of his mind, intelligence and ego. These are intrinsic part of his personality. In yoga he identifies these group of inner categories with the three *Vyūhas*, viz. Saṃkarṣaṇa, Pradyumna and Aniruddha in this context designated *tattvas*. This idea is expressed in the *Mahābhārata*, and Śaṃkara in his refutation of the Pāñcarātra position in his commentary on the *Brahmasūtra* mentions this notion.[41] The four *Vyūhas* are related to each other in the mythology of Kṛṣṇa/Vāsudeva and are separate personalities. But in the context of Pāñcarātra soteriology the images show minimum iconographic difference, which emphasizes their closeness to their source. The yogin uses the mythology to focus on their relatedness. Then, rising from the realm of mythology to the metaphysical level, he plunges in deep meditation on them. Once realizing his identity with them the yogin concentrates on their essential nature as *śaktis* known as *kalās*, parts of the supreme *saṃvit śakti*. To indicate how the *kalā śakti* are related to *saṃvit śakti*, texts use the analogy of the sun and its rays. Finally, he concentrates on his final gnosis of *saṃvit*, in which experience and its content are totally the same. As I have mentioned in my paper on *The Caturvyūha and the Viśākha-yūpa*, the central *śakti* represented by the columnal icon of a pillar, i.e. *Viśākha-yūpa*, represented in the image as a tree connecting all images, is the essential consciousness, *saṃvit*, and is identical with *śabdabrahman*. The yogin thus experiences in following the *tattvajaya* meditation all three meditative ways of *varṇa*, *kalā* and *tattva*.[42] In Pāñcarātra system, this last yogic practice spanning the ways of *varṇa*, *kalā* and *tattva*, should be repeated again and again until the yogin reaches his final realization of identity of his self with *saṃvit śakti*, the supreme source (*prakṛti*) of all. The five divine ingredient *śaktis* are hierarchically envisaged during the creative process. In the downward motion every later *śakti* is emanated from the previous one and hence every later *śakti* can be merged into her preceding *śakti*, her source.[43] Therefore the yogin in his endeavour to rise above the *tattvas* must start concentrating on the lowest or latest *śakti* emerging at the primordial moment of creation. It is also the grossest. Now the iconography of the object depicted in Fig. 1 clearly shows six figures three definitely female and the rest might as well be same. I agree with Maxwell that this object belongs to the Pāñcarātra sect and is closely connected with the Caturvyūha image of the same period. I shall go further and identify the female image with the upakaraṇa *śaktis*. The farthest yet central figure represents the relatively gross *kāla-śakti* and the main goddess is *saṃvit*. Obviously this was used for *tattvajaya* meditation. Accepting that both the images discussed by Maxwell were used for the same *tattvajaya* meditation I think they were used for two steps of that meditation. Between these steps the first was to meditate on the Vyūha image where the distinct diversification of *śakti* is emphasized and hence is called *tattva* or categories. The second step is the meditation on the *kalā śaktis* together with *samvit*. The *kalās* are still in the potential state of creation.[44] At the last stage the yogin must concentrate on *saṃvit* as his self[45] (*ādhyātmika*) and assimilate his self with it. In the early Pāñcarātra system this was the goal of the followers of the sect.[46]

I have talked about divine *śakti* of Nārāyaṇa, the Supreme Godhead of the Pāñcarātra canon. Although identified with speech (*vāc*) the *śakti* associated with this Godhead is named Lakṣmī or Śrī and not Sarasvatī. Śrī is prominent in early Indian religions as the goddess of wealth and prosperity as well as fertility. Goddess Śrī dominates early female divinities represented in sculpture. She is highly eulogized in the apocryphal *Ṛgvedic* hymn, *Śrī-sūkta*. The *Mahābhārata* records a legend of her abandoning the Asura monarch Bali in favour of Indra. She also left Indra due to the curse of Durvāsās and hid herself under the ocean until the famous cosmic event of the churning of the ocean. She emerged from the ocean and unhesitatingly went into Viṣṇu's arms.[47]

Both the *Mantra-mahodadhi* and the *Śāradātilakam* describe the combined icon of Lakṣmī and Vāsudeva as the primal two-in-one divinity.[48] In early Pāñcarātra texts too Nārāyaṇa/Vāsudeva is associated with Lakṣmī.[49] The Lakṣmī Tantra clearly says that all divine *śaktis* emanated from Lakṣmī.[50]

Lakṣmī being the goddess of beauty, prosperity and royal fortune, it is not surprising that she is associated with the divine sovereigns like Indra and Viṣṇu.[51] When the latter became revered as the supreme sovereign divinity, Lakṣmī naturally became his spouse.[52] Both Raychaudhuri and Jitendra Nath Banerjea recorded that during the early centuries of the C.E. till the decline of the Gupta dynasty[53] Bhāgavata religion[54] drew a lot of attention and appreciation from the imperial Guptas. Not only inscriptions of that period refer to Viṣṇu but also quite a few of the Gupta coins bear the image of both Viṣṇu and Lakṣmī.[55] Although both Bhūmi, the Earth-goddess and Sarasvatī, the goddess of learning, are sometimes regarded as Viṣṇu's second wife and iconographically are shown at the side of Viṣṇu, Lakṣmī remains always on Viṣṇu's right side as his main wife. Banerjea believed that the huge image found at Besnagar belonging to the 3rd to 2nd century B.C.E. represents goddess Śrī, who was already worshipped by the Pāñcarātra cult as the "active energic principle – the chief consort of the Para-Vāsudeva".[56]

Thus Lakṣmī/Śrī the inseparable *śakti* of the supreme Lord Viṣṇu/Nārāyāṇa is revered by the devotees as the Supreme Goddess being the active aspect of the Nārāyaṇa, i.e. *Saṃvit,* God's awareness and the source of the entire creation. Moreover, as the goddess of bounty and prosperity, beauty and grace, fertility and good harvest she is universally worshipped by the traditional Hindus irrespective of sectarian or non-sectarian adherence.

So why was it that in late medieval south India amongst the orthodox Śrī-vaiṣṇavas Lakṣmī's divinity was seriously questioned? Puspendra Kumar has quite exhaustively tackled the position of Lakṣmī in south India.[57] Therefore I shall just discuss a few points. Firstly, both Yāmuna and Rāmānuja the founding teachers of the Śrī-vaiṣṇava sect, followed the Pāñcarātra concept of Lakṣmī: that as Vāsudeva's *śakti* she was essentially homogeneous (*sāmarasya*) with the godhead.[58] Rāmānuja in the *Vedārtha-samgraha* acknowledges Lakṣmī's co-existence with Viṣṇu.[59] Rāmānuja also calls her non-transient (*anapāyinī*), an epithet often used to qualify Lakṣmī in the *Lakṣmī Tantra.* Parāśara Bhattar, a disciple of Rāmānuja, speaks of Lakṣmī as Viṣṇu's *śakti.* He also refers to her as the source of mantras as well as the source of the universe. All *śaktis* emanated from Lakṣmī and she is the life-breath (*prāṇa*) of Viṣṇu. Obviously he was aware of the Pañcarātric idea of the primary polarization of *śakti* as *saṃvīt, vāc* and *prāṇa.*[60]

Secondly, the problem of Lakṣmī's identity as a superior but non-divine person arose during the lifetimes of great Śrī-vaiṣṇava teachers who emphasized on their specific interpretations of bhakti as the doctrine of an *ekāntin,* i.e. devotee of exclusively a single Divine Being, Nārāyaṇa. From the time of Yāmuṇa, Rāmānuja, Parāśarabhaṭṭar and their contemporaries, theologians of the sect started developing the concept of Śrī/Lakṣmī in her role as the supreme intercessor (*puruṣakāra*). This concept is linked with the concept of surrendering to God's will, i.e. *prapatti,* and the uniqueness of God, who is the supreme of the three categories. These three categories are *cit, acit* and *Īśvara,* i.e. the sentient, insentient and God. Early teachers who developed the Śrīvaiṣṇava theology wrote extensively on the nature of these three real categories.[61] As Dasgupta puts it, "...there are on the one side, the self-conscious souls, and, on the other, the omniscient and all powerful Īśvara and the manifold external world. These three categories are real".[62] Inspite of the acceptance of Lakṣmī, being the inseparable divine power of Nārāyaṇa, later teachers encountered difficulty in placing Lakṣmī in either of the sentient categories, viz. *cit* or *Īśvara.* Rāmānuja's theories of God's relationship with individuals, viz. *śeṣa-śeṣī-bhāva* and *śarīra-śarīrī-bhāva,* posed more problems for the sectarians to categories Lakṣmī. The first establishes that individuals belong to God, the final authority. They are entirely under the control of God and God alone. Self-conscious selves exist only for Him. The latter idea posits that the creation, both sentient and insentient objects form God's body and hence is external to Him who is the essence of all. Also, as our inner self controls our body's function so does God control all individuals and insensate objects. The problem of Lakṣmī is whether she is external to God (Nārāyaṇa) or internal. Rāmānuja makes her a special mode (*prakāra*) of God in which He enacts the function of being the source (*prakṛti*) of all. The more conservative adherents of the sect who are uncompromisingly *ekāntin,* do not include Lakṣmī within the category *Īśvara* and hence must include her within the category of *cit,* i.e. individual selves, albeit as the supreme one. Her supermacy is because she is God's spouse and is His most beloved and charming companion. Because of her great beauty and charm and because of supreme wisdom and compassion she cleverly and wisely influences God to pardon His true devotees, even when they have committed sins.

Two great Śrī-vaiṣṇava philosophers and theologians, namely, Piḷḷai Lokācārya and Vedānta Deśika, finally addressed this problem and presented two different characterizations of the Goddess. Both flourished in a period spanning the last part of the 13th and the first part of the 14th century C.E.[63] Without going further into the problem I shall just point out that Vedānta Deśika regards Lakṣmī inseparably within the category of God (*Īśvara*) and hence eternal and all-pervasive, as a divinity integral to Nārāyaṇa who voluntarily accepts dependence on Him, being His spouse. But Piḷḷai Lokācarya strictly regards her as in the category of the sentient individuals, totally different from the *Īśvara* category and hence neither pervasive (*aṇu*) nor eternal; Nārāyaṇa chose her as His spouse because of her countless excellent qualities and her wisdom, devotion and beauty but not her divinity. She is supremely powerful yet she chose to become totally subservient to her husband and completely dependant on Him. Even when she has the power to punish a sinner she lets God do it. She only influences God to exercise His grace to pardon such a sinner because she is the mother of the world and is full of compassion. It is only through her intercessory activities that a mere mortal individual can aspire divine grace.[64] Therefore whenever Lakṣmī is prayed to with great devotions it is to move her to intercede with Nārāyaṇa to fulfil the devotee's prayer. Lakṣmī can only intercede so that God's grace touches a devotee; she cannot grant grace herself.

Salvation only comes through the practice of *prapatti,* i.e. unconditional surrender to God's authority as the total controller, *śeṣa* (the final one), and by no other means whatsoever. The method of *bhakti-upāsanā* advocated by Rāmānuja and by Vedānta Deśika as another means to *mukti* is rejected in this conservative tradition and relegated to the position of self-purificatory practice. Unflinching faith in God's protection has been ranked above meditation on God and His power, both creative and redemptive.

Thus it is that Śrī/Lakṣmī, who began as an independent Goddess of wealth, prosperity, beauty and fertility, worshipped on her own or in conjunction with Kubera, Indra and finally Viṣṇu, progressed in Pāñcarātra religion to become the supreme power of Viṣṇu/Nārāyaṇa and the source of all creation, the divine potency, potentiality and energy and then mythicized as His spouse. But for the southern Śrīvaiṣṇavas her identity as Viṣṇu's wife, an individual separate from her husband, lost her divinity. She is adored as the epitome of wifely virtues and motherly love and compassion, as the perfection of beauty, wisdom and conjugal love and tact. But divine she is not.

I started with the position of divine power in the Pāñcarātra and its supremacy as the means to achieve salvation. This power was early equated with Lakṣmī and mythologized as Viṣṇu's wife.[65] The primary manifestation of the creative urge of the divine is equated with the Goddess *vāc* and her primary manifestations, viz. *icchā, jñāna, kriyā, prāṇa* and *kāla. Vāc* and these five emanations form the primal group of divine power with *vāc/saṃvit* as the active divine awareness, the central cosmogonic power. The soteriological goal of the Pāñcarātra adherents is to realize their true nature as identified with the individual self. This is achieved by one-pointed meditation as one's self identity with these śaktis following the method of meditation prescribed by the Pāñcarātra canons. It is a gnostic method based on a yogic method of progressive spirituality accepted by the early Pāñcarātra system. To facilitate this meditation early meditators used images, a few fragments of which have come down to our time. As Maxwell has reconstructed these fragments, we get the six powers with *saṃvit* in the middle and it is clear that these images were used as objects of mental fixation by yogins desirous of release from the bondage of transient existence. As the fragments date from the 2nd-1st century B.C.E. the Pāñcarātra soteriology can also be dated to about that period. It is possible that the paramount power of Nārāyaṇa was by then identified with Lakṣmī. Her position rose steadily amongst her devotees and other cults of her grew up alongside the Pāñcarātra. But among the strict Vaiṣṇavas certain south Indian groups later demoted her from her divine identity, making her a special category of super human being.

What is the situation at present? Well most Śrīvaiṣṇavas are not aware of the subtle theological distinction between Viṣṇu/Nārāyaṇa and the goddess Lakṣmī. Kanchipuram is said to be a very important northern Tamilnad centre. The

Lakṣmī temple attached to the Varadarāja (Nārāyaṇa) temple seems to be equally important as the latter. The intercessory power of Lakṣmī has put her in a unique position of power. Devotees may reach Nārayaṇa only through her recommendation. Both Śrīvaiṣṇava sub-sects Vadgalai and Tangalai look upon Lakṣmī as the great goddess, the ideal mother and an epitome of womanly modesty and other virtues. As an indulgent mother she grants all her devotees their wishes.[66]

Chart 1

The Pāñcarātra cosmogonic emanations

Transcendent Vāsudeva with dormant śakti

Vāsudeva + Vāc śakti/active consciousness Saṃvit and her integrated six parts (kalā)

Caturvyūha	**Saṃvit*	*Śakti-vyūha.*
1. Vāsudeva	1. Parā	1+2. Vāc + Icchāśakti
2. Saṃkarṣaṇa	2. Paśyantī	3+4. Jñāna-śakti + Prāṇa-śakti
3. Pradyumna	3. Madhyamā	5. Kriyāśakti
4. Aniruddha	1. Vaikharī	6. Kālaśakti

*Saṃvit as Speech (Vāc) also follows the process of gradual cosmic manifestation of emanation — from transcendence via subtlety to grossness, from unity to diversity and from simplicity to complexity. Subtle Vāc is the state of "nāma and rūpa", i.e. the referent (vācaka = nāma). Language is the gross form of Saṃvit.

See Gupta, *Yoga and Antaryāga in Pāñcarātra*, p. 189.

Chart 2

The six trajectories in which Cosmos is refracted.

The yogic ṣaḍadhvā, L.T. 22,7-27.

1. *Varṇa* stands for active Saṃvit or Speech (vāc).
2. *Kalā* stands for six parts (kalā) of Saṃvit, viz. Jñāna (knowledge/consciousness), Aiśvarya (divine glory) Śakti (power), Bala (strength), Vīrya (heroism), and Tejas (splendor).
3. *Tattva* stands for the Caturvyūha and Śaktivyūha.
4. *Mantra* stands for the great corpus of mantras (religious formulas) along with the performance of rituals and repetition of mantra attached to them.
5. *Pada* stands for the individual selves. Every individual passes through three stages of consciousness, viz. when it is awake and having empirical experiences; when it is dreaming; and when it is deeply asleep and experiencing nothing. But the yogins by means of meditation reaches a sublime state when they experience only the essential reality when they experience no diversity at all. This is called the fourth stage of individual awareness (turīya).
6. *Bhuvana* stands for the world with its diversity that forms the content of ones empirical experiences.

There exists a spiritual hierarchy in these trajectories. Obviously the last two form the gross creation. But the individuals being conscious and having the potential for experiencing their true source should be above the sixth. The *Mantra* is the great *bhakti*-path of achieving salvation. Divine Will out of compassion for the individuals, created this trajectory.

The last three trajectories are mainly for the yogins. The *tattvas* describe the process of creation. It is a process of the emanations going from transcendence to gross creation. *Kāla* and *Varṇa* show the polarization of the primal power of the active consciousness, Saṃvit, separately and then Saṃvitśakti as the aggregate of the kalās.

NOTES

1 *parāsya śakti-r-vividhaiva śrūyate svābhāvikī jñāna kriyābalāni ca.. Śv. U. vi. 8.*

2 See K.K.A. Venkatachari, pp. 134-155.

This North-South division is within the then boundary of Tamil Nad. The term vaḍ also means the Northern language, i.e. Sanskrit while ten denotes Tamil language. See Jagadeesan, Dr. N. *History of Sri Vaishnavism* (Post Ramanuja), Kendal Publishers, Madurai, India, 1977, pp. 182-183.

3 MBh. 1.7.61, 92; 5.54. 99-103, 114-117.

4 Hemchandra Raychaudhury, *Materials for the Study of the Early History of the Vaishnava Sect,* University of Calcutta, 1936, pp. 176-177. See also Jitendra Nath Banerjea, *The Development of Hindu Iconography,* University of Calcutta, 1941, pp. 206-214.

5 Cf. Śv. U.I. 14-16.

6 LT. 1 1-29; cf the important Pāñcaratra mantra: *jitante puṇḍarīkākṣa namaste viśvabhāvana/namaste'stu hṛṣikeśa mahāpuruṣa pūrvaja//. VP I.1.1.*

7 In Kashmir Śaivism, this is known as *vimarśa* and is identified with the supreme goddess.

8 See Wilhelm Halbfass, pp. 4-5 and 37-38.

9 Saṃvitprakāśa ch. I. LT quotes the entire first chapter from this text.

10 PS 33,.90.

11 LT, 2 23 ff. Cf. Gupta 1971

12 The lateness of this work does not take away its authority since a well-known Śrīvaiṣṇava commentator on Pāñcarātra scriptures, Alaśiṃha Bhaṭṭa (early 19th century C.E.) extensively quotes it as authority. Its special feature is its close following of early Pāñcarātra concept of transcendent consciousness, *saṃvit.* In the process it quotes a chapter of Vāmanadatta's *Saṃvitpeakāśa.* The latter, clearly a Vaiṣṇava, wrote about *saṃvit* as propounded in the early Pāñcarātra. He extensively quoted from Pañcarātra scriptures. Since the *Kāṣmīrāgama-prāmāṇya* by Yāmuṇācarya is lost we do not know whether or not the Northern development of the Pāñcarātra theology was widely known in the south.

However, as a representative of that Northern tradition and its concept of supreme *saṃvit śakti*, LT is of unique interest. See *Āgamaprāmāṇyam* by Yāmunamuni. Ed. Dr. M. Narasimhachary, Introductory Study, p. 4.

13 Narasimhacharya, Dr. M, *Contribution of Yāmunācārya to Viśiṣṭādvaita*, pp. 26-29.

14 S. Gupta, 1992, pp. 184-187.

15 Mircea Eliade, p. 207.

16 Ibid. loc. cit.

17 Ibid, p. 208.

18 The cosmogony, as a Pāñcarātra yogin knows it, emanates from *śakti* and is refracted in six trajectories, viz. speech, *varṇa, śakti*, as real world ingredients or building bricks (*kalā*); the multiple emanations of Vāsudeva and the other three Vyūhas embodying the cosmic process of the emergence of the universe (*tattva*); mantras and their deities; then the individual person (*pada*) and the empirical world (*bhuvana*). The last two are the subjects and their contents of experience registered in their mind as names and their corresponding forms, *nāma* and *rūpa*. The highly accomplished yogin starts from the *tattvas* and then finally arrives at the *kalā* level, his last stage of soteriological practice which brings about his salvific realization of his identity with the primal *śakti, vāc.* who is the aggregate of these *kalās*. See Gupta, 1992, pp. 184-187.

19 JS 4. 30-33.

20 See Gupta '92, pp. 181-187

21 JS refers to these five *śaktis* in connection with the yoga system which a Pāñcarātra practitioner should follow as part of his religious practice aiming at salvation, *mukti*. Mukti, salvation is the release from being born again. JS 10. 58-59. *Caitanyaṃ jīvabhūtaṃ yatprasphurattārakopamam/bhāvanīyaṃ tu viśrāntaṃ nissṛtaṃ bhūtapañjarāt// niṣprapañce pare mantre pañcaśaktyākhyavigrahe/*. "Consciousness which became individual should be envisaged as a glowing star which having been released from the cage of five elements has become quiescent in the supreme mantra, in the form called the five *śaktis* who are beyond the multitudinous creation."

22 SS 3. 3, 12-13, 15-16. The supreme Vyūha state is stated to be identical with *śakti,* who is called both *svānandā* and *spanda.*

23 Eliade, p. 76.

24 See S. Gupta, Introduction to LT, pp. XXVIII-XXX.

25 Cf. J.N. Banerjea, ch 3-5.

26 Ibid., pp. 369-37372.

27 The Śv U.V. 14 calls the primary creation made of parts and whole as *kalā-sarga.* This sarga can be equated with the above mentioned *śakti*-emanations from the supreme *śakti,* and parts, *kalā* of it. JS 10. 58-59, explains this process of *mantra-yoga* leading to the total identification of the yogin with *icchāśakti* which is the primordial emanation of the divine *śakti* which is also the divine bliss *sānandā.* The same text in another context explains that the supreme unconditioned divine Nārāyaṇa appears in different form subsuming all *śakti* manifestations. JS 4: 20, 21, 117.

28 pp. 18 and 37; plates, 10-16. This proves the early prevalence of the Pañcaratra sect. Two other images of such multiple cosmogonic emanations of *śakti* are preserved in Berlin, in the Museum Fur Indische Kunst. These are also hailed from Mathura region and belong to second century C.E. MIK I 5924 and MIK I 10196. Although they are identified as goddess Ṣaṣṭhi, I believe it is wrong.

29 pp. 18, fig. 1.1 and fig. 1.2; plates 10-16.

30 Maxwell, p. 36.

31 Ibid, p. 18.

32 Ibid, pp. 8-45; Gupta, 1971 and 1992. in my paper on the Viśākha-yūpa I have extensively discussed the cosmogonic nature of the concept of the Caturvyūha and the Vaiśkha-yūpa and their relevance as icons for the purpose of meditation. Sanjukta Gupta, 1971.

33 PS, 33. 139-140.

34 Maxwell, pp. 36-46.

35 JS. 4. 60-61.

36 SS. 3. 3-4. See Sanjukta Gupta, 1992.

37 *Playing with Fire: The Pratīyasamutpāda from the Perspective of Vedic Thought*, in *Journal of the Pali Text Society*, Vol. XXVI, 2000, pp 77-103. Cf. JS 4. 61-62.

38 PS, 33. 133-170.

39 PS. 33. 113.

40 Cf. JS VI. 73-90.

41 Śaṇkara's commentary on *Brahmasūtra* II. 2; *Mahābhārata* (The *Narāyaṇīya* book of *Śāntiparvan*), 12.218.11-12 and 12.334-51.

42 See note nr. 13; Gupta, 1971, pp. 198-199; and Gupta, 1992, pp. 185-186.

43 JS VI. 221-236.

44 Gupta 92.

45 JS. VI. 82, and 211-212.

46 JS. IV. 51cd- 52ab and 60-81.

47 VP. I. 9. 100-107. Padma Purāṇa III. 9-10.

48 MM. 21. 103-104. ŚT. 6. 42-44.

49 SS. XII, 206. JS. VI. 77-78.

50 LT. Chs. 2-4.

51 J. Gonda, *Aspects of Early Viṣṇuism*, pp. 100, 164-167.

52 Hemchandra Raychaudhuri mentions an inscription from Junagaḍh which says about Viṣṇu "who, for the sake of the happiness of the lord of the gods, seized back from Bali the goddess of wealth and splendour". Obviously the author's reference is the story of the Viṣṇu's Vāmaṇa incarnation and he restored Indra's sovereignty by banishing Bali to the lower region (pātāla). *Materials for the Study of the Early History of the Vaishnava Sect*, University of Calcutta, 1936, p. 174. It is clear then that Lakṣmī represented Royal fortune and prosperity. See also Jan Gonda, *Aspects of Early Viṣṇuism*, V.S. Oosthoek's Uitgevers mij, Utrecht 1954, pp. 100, 164, 166, 172, 176 188, 192, 197, 208-9, 211, 217-8 and 224-5.

53 Banerjea, pp. 142-172, passim; Raychaudhuri, pp. 161-177.

54 The Bhāgavatas (lit those who worship Bhagavān Vāsudeva/ Kṛṣṇa) were a coherent community from at least the second century B.C.E. Śankara in his commentary on the Brahma-sūtra II. 2. 42, calls the followers of the Pāñcarātra doctrine as Bhāgavatas.

55 Parameshwari Lal Gupta, *Coins*, National Book Trust, 3rd edition, 1979, p. 56.

56 Banerjea writes, "Sometimes, though perhaps rarely, the image of the goddess Śrī, his [Viṣṇu's] consort *par excellence*, seemed to have been the central object of worship in the Pāñcarātra shrine, as is proved by one of her earliest stone images fully in the round, discovered at Besnagar. It is interesting that one of the oldest Viṣṇuite image should be none other than that of this goddess with unmistakable Pāñcarātra association". op. cit. pp. 370-371.

57 Pratap Kumar, *The Goddess Lakṣmī: The Divine Consort in South Indian Vaiṣṇava Tradition*, pp. 61-67, 80-84.

58 Dr. M. Narasimhacharya, *Contribution of Yāmunaācārya to Viśiṣṭādvaita*, p. 31.

59 Vedārtha Saṃgraha, 5. 217. "O great brahmin just as Viṣṇu pervades every phenomenon so also does she. She is the essence of the gods and also of the human beings."

60 Śrīguṇaratnakośa.

61 S.N. Dasgupta, *History of India Philosophy*, Vol. IV, pp. 136-164.

62 Ibid, p. 154.

63 K.K.A. Venkatachari, *The Maṇipravāla Literature of the Śrīvaiṣṇava Ācāryas*, pp. 94-107. S.N. Dasgupta, *A History of Indian Philosophy*, Vol. III, 4th edition, Cambridge, 1968, pp. 159-162; M. Narasimhacharya, pp. 32-49.

64 Cf. Sri Satyamurthi Swami, Gwalior, *Srivachana Bhuṣhanam*, by Sri Pillai Lokacharya, aphorisms 5-22; *An English Glossary*, pp. 1-7.

65 *Tattitrīya Āraṇyaka* III. 13. 2, "*hrīśca te lakṣmīśca patnau*". Hrī is a manifestation of Lakṣmī.

66 Jagadeesan, Dr. N *History of Sri Vaishnavism in the Tamil Country*, Kendal Publishers, Madurai, 1977, pp. 171-208.

3. Hindu Tantrism: Sādhanā, Pūjā

Introduction

Tantric sādhanā (religious practice) consists of two parts: ritual worship (*pūjā*)[1] and meditation (*yoga*). Both are of equal importance to every Tantric. Even the *Siddha* or *avadhūta*, recognized to be so highly spiritual that he can afford to disregard rules applicable to ordinary Tantrics, continues to perform his daily *pūjā* along with his yogic practices. The importance of *pūjā* cannot be exaggerated. From the time of his initiation till the end of his life, every Tantric is bound by the duty of performing his daily pūjā. But it is not easy to find a definitive form of Tantric ritual. The only possible criterion for labelling a Tantric ritual that we can suggest is that it is a ritual performed by Tantrics. There are, however, dangers in this because Tantrics may also perform non-Tantric rituals. On the practical level, when Tantrics are engaged in performing their religious activities, a great deal of confusion prevails. The muddle is partly due to their non-exclusive allegiance to various streams of tradition, which may be ancient and/or recorded, or comparatively modern and local. Besides, there is a tendency amongst present-day Tantrics not to establish their exclusive identity, but to take over other religious traditions which approximate to their own.

Admittedly there is nothing strange in that. At any point in the history of a religious system of ritual, new and local elements of practice and interpretation may appear to have been introduced into the main body of the recorded system. There are no means of checking this practice, and it continues to date. Within the last hundred years, for instance, a great many texts have been published in the Tāntric milieu recording a mass of magic practices not found in older texts. A typical example is the *Śāvarī Tantra*—a collection of a vast number of magic rites and formulae used by rural people, especially in North India. These are mostly described in local languages, which the editors have sometimes corrected and/or translated into chaste Hindi or Sanskrit.

Nevertheless in describing Tantric ritual, it is safe for our purpose to adhere as far as possible to well-established texts. Here again difficulties arise: the body of these is vast, diffuse and heterodox. Practising Tantrics themselves follow different texts or group of texts as authoritative, according to the particular stream of tradition prevailing within their own group, e.g. Kaulas, Kāpālikas, etc. In this survey we restrict ourselves to the practice of those who worship the Goddess (Śakti/Devī) in three popular forms: as Tripurā/Śrī/-Lalitā, as Kālī and as Tārā (i.e. the Kāśmīra-krama tradition). The famous ten goddesses (*daśa mahāvidyās*) are direct or indirect manifestations of one or other of these three. Secondly, we confine ourselves mostly to textual references recorded in Sanskrit not later than the middle of the nineteenth century of the Christian era. Later texts are consulted chiefly to clarify ambiguous terminology or to explain performances of Tantric rituals that we have actually witnessed. The main bases for our interpretation of Tantric rituals are, however, the earlier Tantras, exegeses and compendiums (e.g. *Nityāṣoḍaśikārṇava, Yoginīhṛdaya, Kulārṇava, Tantrāloka, Mahākālasaṃhitā, Tantrarāja, Mahānirvāṇa, Śāradātilaka, Tantrasāra* by Kṛṣṇānanda, *Prāṇatoṣiṇī, Varivasyārahasya,* Bhāskararāya's commentaries on NṢT, YHT, *Bhāvanopaniṣad* and *Saundarylaharī*; *Paraśurāmakalpasūtra* with commentary, *Nityotsava,* Rāghavabhaṭṭa's comm. on ŚT, etc.).

The criterion for determining a particular Hindu sect or subject is to pick out which deity it regards as its supreme godhead. But for classifying Tantrics it is important to know the particular *paramparā* or group to which they belong.

To determine the *paramparā*, it is further necessary to know its traditional line of teachers, the special etiquette applicable to the tradition followed, the complicated variations in ritual performances arising from the theological and metaphysical background of the *paramparā*, and the personal attitude and idiosyncrasies of eminent teachers in that line. These factors are responsible for the incredible number of divergencies in Tantric ritual activities. Notwithstanding the divergencies, however, the fundamental structure of Tantric ritualism remains constant, whilst it provides scope for introducing almost infinite variations in the ritual practices. These concern the worship of an equally vast number of deities, belonging somewhat loosely to the Śākta pantheon. A fairly regular pattern in Tantric rituals can be discerned by analysing a simple form of daily Tantric worship of the Goddess, which will be described presently.

Tantric ritualism obviously comprises a conglomerate of rites drawn freely from Vedic and other concurrent religious traditions. Tantric tradition has made use of all these rites with modifications to suit its own ideology. The spiritual practice of Tantrics is based on the idea that their philosophical tenets and religious mandates should find expression in a form that can be experienced also physically, and should not merely function as intellectual exercises. Their metaphysical concepts are worked into their mode of life so that the practitioner may experience them in everyday life. Tantra hardly ever rejects any form of religious ritualism; it juxtaposes its own particular ritual practices to the normative (*smārta*) Hindu rituals. Many Tantric rites are modelled on these normative rituals, e.g. the Hindu sacramental rites (*saṃskāra*), the daily obligatory rites performed by the orthodox caste Hindus, such as the ritual bath, worshipping the sun at special junctures of the day (*sandhyārcanā*), and the water-oblation to gods, ancestors, etc. (*tarpaṇa*). Tantric modifications of these rites are mainly theological. As worshippers of one supreme God,

Tantrics regard their chosen deity (*iṣṭadevatā*) as the most sublime manifestation of the divine. Therefore, when they take over a rite in which some other divinity is invoked, they always envisage their own *iṣṭadevatā* as the central point or essence of that deity. For instance, when worshipping the sun, Tantrics will envisage the Goddess in the centre of Sun's orb. They may even envisage her in different colours to represent the different times of the day (the sun's position in the sky at those times). A striking example of how Tantrics adjust a Vedic *mantra* is the popular Gāyatrī-*mantra*.[2] That *mantra* is of vital importance for every initiated adherent of the normative Hindu religion and is, at least in theory, compulsorily worshipped by all such Hindus. Consequently, Tantrics have taken over a skeleton of it to be worshipped at the beginning of all ritual undertakings, but have replaced the name of the sun by that of their own deity.[3] Hence one comes across numerous forms of the Gāyatrī-mantra. This is just a single example; for Tantrics have adopted many other Vedic *mantras*, often without any change whatsoever, or with only slight modifications. Another important rite modelled on a Vedic rite is the fire-sacrifice (*homa*).

What needs to be stressed is the fact that Tantrics continue to ascribe value to the normative Hindu religious rites and if, as belonging to the higher castes, they are obliged to perform these, they do so alongside performing their own obligatory Tantric duties. What is more, they may even give priority to the normative ritual in preference to their own. For instance, persons who have received the standard sacrament of initiation and the sacred thread (*upavīta*), must first observe *sandhyārcanā*.[3a] Since the Tantric type is obviously a copy of the Smārta, it is difficult to understand the reason for the duble performance. A possible explanation is that the theology of the Goddess-worshipping Tantric religion had already firmly imprinted its precepts, code of religious behaviour and duties on its followers long before these were recorded in Tantric texts. Meanwhile, the synthesizing process of Purāṇic and other mythological and historical influences had also been busy infusing Tantric ritual with the prevalent practices of standard Hinduism. The rites practised by Tantrics today are based on texts recorded not much earlier than the fourteenth century of the Christian era. By that time, Tantrics had quite forgotten the source of some of the rites they were performing, and devoutly adhered to the practices they had been taught to follow as belonging to their *parmparā.* So they performed all the religious duties obligatory for their caste, and at the same time never questioned observing all religious duties imposed by their *paramparā.*

There may be another explanation which is admittedly purely hypothetical. The more sophisticated Goddess-worshipping Tantrics tend to treat all their ritual performances as strictly esoteric, and aim at conforming with the dictum that "one should behave like a vaiṣṇava in court (or company), like a Śaiva in ordinary life, and like a Tantric proper only in strict privacy". "Like a Śaiva" presumably means here that Tantrics should behave in the same way as standard Śaivas following the normative religion. Generally speaking the latter worship the group of five deities: Śiva, Viṣṇu, the Goddess, the Sun and Gaṇeśa, with Śiva as their chosen chief god. But it is perfectly permissible for them to select any of the five as their supreme deity. Since Tantrics are urged to keep their religious beliefs secret, they may well have a motive for openly following the standard religious practices of the worship of the five *(pañcāyatana pūjā)* of their society to conform with caste behaviour.

Classifications

As previously stated, the classical division of Hindu ritual, viz. Vaidikī, Tāntrikī and Miśra (Vedic, Tantric and a synthesized form, see BhāgPur. II.27.7) is purely theoretical and never actually observed in practice. All we can say is that there is the normative Hindu ritual as well as the other forms of it containing a vast amount of variations. Tantric ritualism belongs to the latter category, and henceforth we can ignore the classical classification altogether.

In dealing with Tantric ritualism, once again we see how closely it has been modelled on the normative ritualism. Following the latter's example, Tantrics divide their ritual practices into three groups: *nitya, naimittika* and *kāmya.* Nitya covers the group of rites regarded as being compulsory for a Tantric to perform every day; naimittika rites are observed on particular occasions; and *kāmya* rites are performed to fulfil a special wish, or to avert a great misfortune.

The first group, *nitya-karman,* has two subdivisions: 1. *Āhnika-karman* or activities very much resembling the caste duties of the normative Hindu religion. We discussed them above and shall presently enumerate the Tantric innovations therein. 2. The daily worship of the Goddess. This is actually the important part of *nitya karman* and is termed *nitya-pūjā.* A detailed description of this *pūjā* will enable us to detect the basic structure of Tantric ritualism and at the same time reveal its specifically Tantric features. The performance of *nitya-pūjā* and other daily religious obligations brings no special merit to the performer, nor does it avert any particular bad luck. The Tantric has to observe these rites in order to conform to the religious discipline to which he belongs. *Naimittika-pūjā* on the other hand is an elaborate form of worship, in which all the functions of the daily *pūjā* are observed in greater detail. This is in fact considered to be the complete pūjā whereas *nitya-pūjā* is regarded as an abridgement of it.

Tantrics perform *naimittika-pūjā* only on special occasions known as *parvas,* which are usually the eighth and eleventh of the dark fortnight, the new- and full-moon days, the last or the first day of every month, the deity's special annual festival, the birthday of the Tantric's guru, and the festivals of *pavitrāropaṇa* and *damanārohaṇa* (KT. X. 78; PKS p. 280). We shall describe these later on. All these pūjā have special names such as *tithi-pūjā, māsa-pūjā* and *parva-pūjā,* etc. Unlike *nitya-pūjā, naimittika-pūjā* is invariably performed in the late evening (KT.X.1,8); but the time selected has nothing to do with secrecy. As now practised, one tends to think that the main reason for performing these rites in the evening is that then the Tantric has more time and the peaceful atmosphere needed for performing a long drawn-out series of rites with great care and concentration. One has to remember that every part of the ritual has to be performed without mistake, because only faultless performance brings the desired result. A complete pūjā is regarded as an organic whole, and faulty performance in any part of it is a defect disfiguring the whole pūjā.

Kāmya-pūjā covers a completely different category of rites. A special *pūjā*-programme is undertaken in order to obtain particular benefits, either for the *sādhaka* (practiser) himself, or on behalf of somebody else. These rites are also known as ṣaṭkaṛman (infra pp. 135). They can be performed during the day or during the night, depending on the nature of the purpose envisaged (KT XI.8). It is important to know that only the performer of the daily pūjā is eligible to perform *naimittika-pūjā,* and he who is capable of performing both is entitled to perform *kāmya-pūjā* (e.g. KT. XVI.8f.). The reason is obvious. Only a Tantric firmly embedded in his tradition is entrusted to perform these special rituals that aim at mobilizing the divine power for fulfilment of a specific purpose. These rites verge on magic in the sense that, if performed without a flaw, they will automatically produce the desired result. But their potency is only aroused when they are performed by someone in whom the divine power has been awakened (KT. XVI.8). That means that, at least once in his lifetime, the performer of the rite has had direct experience of absolute illumination, i.e. of the Divine as identified with himself. This experience is obtained only through prolonged practice in performing rituals and by meditating on the mantra of one's *iṣṭadevatā* (YHT I.3-4 and II.1). After a lengthy period of intensive daily practice of *pūjā*, meditation and mantra-japa (repetition of the mantra of the *iṣṭadevatā*, also called *puraścaraṇa*, see below), the Tantric receives[4] the awakening of this divine power within himself, if and when his *iṣṭdevatā* is moved to grant him her grace. By then he is sufficiently self-disciplined to prevent misuse of this cosmic power, which he can now direct at will.

Tantric definitions for these three types of *pūjā*, namely *nitya, naimittika* and *kāmya*, are *sāttvika, rājasa* and *tāmasa* respectively, which clearly reveal the Tantric evaluation of these (Bhāskararāya, comm. on BhāvUp.). *Nitya-pūjā* is a manifestation of the Tantric's devotion to his *iṣṭadevatā* and is performed without any ulterior motive. The deity, whose presence is a living fact for the Tantric, must be treated in the only realistic way he spontaneously thinks of. Therefore, *nitya-pūjā* is classified as the purest form of *pūjā* (*sāttvika*). This spontaneity is somewhat lacking in *naimittika-pūjā*. The Tantric is much more self-conscious while performing it and, besides, other people are often present. This elaborate form of pūjā entails much more dynamism, and that inevitably reduces the performer's tranquillity, which is so vital for awareness of his identity with the deity. Therefore *naimittika-pūjā* is described as *rājasa* — a mixture of purity and impurity. It is pure because it is performed without ulterior motive; at the same time it is impure because it tends to defeat the Tantric's main objective of merging himself in his deity.

Kāmya-pūjā, on the other hand, is frankly classified as obviously impure (*tāmasa*) since it is invariably performed with a finite earthly motivation. *Kāmya-pūjā* undoubtedly posed a problem for Tantric ideology. Its importance in the general pattern of ritual is undeniable; but it stands in glaring opposition to the Tantric objective of the votary's perfection and self-liberation. All the cautionary remarks about who is eligible to perform *kāmya-pūjā* and so forth are signs of this mental uneasiness on the part of the later authors of Tantra texts (e.g. Gandharva Tantra xxii.14), who sought to systematize the conglomerate of Tantric religious phenomena.

Further Tantric classification is based on the various aspects of the deity worshipped. Bhāskararāya has classified pūjā in three groups: *āntara*, *japa* and *bāhya* respectively, meaning internal or mental pūjā, muttering of the mantra, and actual offerings made to the deity, according to the supreme, subtle and gross aspects of the deity (Bhāṣya on the BhāvUp. I). The order of sequence in this classification is somewhat arbitrary, since in actual practice *japa* comes at the end of *āntara-* and *bāhya-pūjā*. Otherwise the classification fits the nature of these three distinct parts of a complete ritual worship of the deity that precede meditation. The main characteristic of *bāhya-pūjā* is that it involves physical acts as well as the use of material objects by the votary. Further analysis reveals that the nature of this form of pūjā takes into account many external factors. The votary needs to take physical measures to be clean and pure; the place of worship needs to be consecrated in order to receive the iconic or aniconic symbol of the deity, which is after all a gross form of the divine; the offerings themselves presuppose some form of the acceptance of material objects by the deity. So here the votary serves the deity with his entire person, with deeds both physical and mental — in Indian terms these would be of three forms, namely efforts of *kāya* (body), *vāk* (speech) and *manas* (mind) — and with all that he holds precious, such as his honour, loyalty, devotion, sensual pleasure, etc.

At the *japa* stage, most of the external physical activities are left behind. The votary uses a rosary or his fingers to keep count; the deity is conceived as identical with the mantra he is repeating, and no symbol is used; only the vocal organ and auditory sense are used. The latter two only function at the beginning of *japa*, when the votary performs his *japa* just audibly to himself. After a while, the repetition takes place only in the mind and hardly any count is kept. Thus the use of external tangible matter has been dispensed with, although the role of the rosary betrays some symbolic representation of Word/Letter (any complete system of letters is called *mālinī* and the rosary is usually referred to as *mālā*). While performing *japa*, the votary interiorizes the deity and envisages her as identified with his own self as well as with the complete set of Sanskrit letters (*mantra-mātṛkā*, or fountainhead of all mantras). Just as the Tantric's *iṣṭadevatā* is a special manifestation of the one and absolute divine Being, so also is his *iṣṭamantra* a manifestation of the *mantra-mātṛkā*. The votary evidently employs far less physical activity in *japa* than he does while performing *bāhya-pūjā*. Therefore this form of adoring the deity is regarded as subtler than *bāhya-pūjā*. The third form of *pūjā*, namely *āntara-pūjā*, is mainly contemplative. The worshipper interiorizes the whole of the external *pūjā* with a strong tendency to idealize its concrete elements by transforming them into ontological abstractions such as the five basic elements, mind, etc.

This mode of adoration calls for a well-developed capacity for vivid visualization and sound philosophical training in the ability to form abstractions out of concrete material objects and physical activities. These faculties demand rigorous concentration and this form of worship is held in higher esteem than any other, so that it is considered to be the supreme form of worship. It is the first stepping-stone to meditation, i.e. the stage that leads to the ecstatic experience of bliss. The idea at the root of this is that the further one progresses in spirituality, the less need there is for elaborate methods of pūjā. The point finally reached being that all ritual actitivities — whether actually performed, or lifted to the contemplative plane and interiorized — simply become unnecessary, and all effort on the part of the votary then becomes a ritual form of worship. As Abhinavagupta puts it (TĀ IV.120cd-121ab) 'whatever sensual pleasure (the Tantric) derives by using any of his senses, he attaches the pleasure to the supreme Being and it becomes an item of offering (to the deity)'. This very assertion that there is no distinction between the votary's own sensation of pleasure and the pleasure of his deity makes the monistic (advaita) standpoint clear to the Tantric. The whole point of performing *āntara-pūjā* is to gradually establish this notion in the mind of the Tantric and keep him constantly aware of it. In a certain sense, he is then worshipping his own self-elevated to the level of, and immersed in, his deity with offerings which are, in reality, not different from that same deity (LT 36.81-85).

A similar type of classification is found in some Tantra texts. Rituals are either divided into group according to the three descriptive states of the deity's gradual secession from indivisible absoluteness: *niṣkala* or undifferentiated, *sakalaniṣkala* or undifferentiated and at the same time differentiated, and *sakala* or differentiated; or they are divided into another group of three that is descriptive of the deity in relation to her ontological position, namely *para* (infinite), *parāpara* (infinite and at the same time finite), and *apara* (finite) (YHT III.2).

It is important to understand that these classifications concern the different forms of rites which go to make up Tantric ritual as a whole. Although Tantrics worship many forms or manifestations of the goddess, the modes of worshipping Ṣoḍaśī (Śrī) on the one hand and Kālī/Tārā on the other are the best documented. Since worship of the first form has received the most efficient and systematic treatment and enjoys the most popularity amongst all Tantrics, excepting in the eastern and possibly extreme south-western regions of India, it is best to deal with that first. It should then be easier to revert to the mode of worshipping Kālī by showing the points of difference.

The texts regarded today — or rather for about the last two hundred years — as being the most important, are the Paraśurāma-kalpasūtra, the Paramānanda Tantra, the Pūjāratna written by Śyāmarāja Dīkṣita, the Parānanda Tantra and the Gandharva Tantra. The first and last mentioned of these are popular in the southern regions of India. The Tantrics of Varanasi generally follow the ritual mode laid down in the Paramānanda Tantra, while the Pūjāratna is popular in the region of Mathura. The Paraśurāma KS is a quasi-aphoristic (*sūtra*) work attempting to codify the modes of Tantric ritualism and the cult of Tripurā, and give them an official status side by side with the vast Vedic literature on ritual, the Kalpasūtras. It deals with the following items: 1. *āhnika-karma*, or the daily routine duties of a Tantric; 2. *saparyā*, or the ritual worship of the goddess; 3. *homa*, or the fire sacrifice; 4. *mudrā* or hand- and body-postures; 5. *nyāsa*; 6. *japa;* and 7. *naimittika-pūjā*. The text also deals with astrology, though very sketchily, in order to determine the most suitable moment for starting a ritual; with different forms of initiation and its various stages; and with the worship of different deities.[5]

Āhnika-karma

At the time of initiation, a Tantric gets complete and detailed instructions about his daily duties. This lays down a regular way of life for him. It should be remembered that his first aim is to arrive at directly experiencing the complete identity of 1) his *iṣṭadevatā*, 2) his *iṣṭta-mantra*, 3) his guru, and 4) his own self. What is strongly impressed on him from the very beginning is the fact that in being accepted by his guru, who is in fact the deity herself manifest on earth as guru, he has obtained his first experience of divine grace.[6] And henceforth all along the Tantric's path towards his ultimate goal his guru comes first. Therefore upon waking and while still in bed, a Tantric should sit up and meditate on his guru in the company of his consort as representing the Two-in-One state of the Divine. While envisaging this celestial state of his guru and his Śakti, he offers the mantra of salutations to them, and then recites the five verses in praise of his guru which are called the *Pādukāpañcakam*. By declaring his total submission and loyalty to his guru, he thus confirms his solidarity with Tantric ideology. He then envisages his guru in the middle of the lotus of a thousand petals (meaning of course innumerable petals), which is situated on top of the crown (*sahasrāra padma* at the *dvādaśānta)*.

His next step is to envisage his own self (*kuṇḍalinī*) — usually situated at the bottom of his spinal column (*mūlādhāra*) near his gentials — as a manifestation of his goddess suddenly rising up like a flash of red lightning through the suṣumṇā channel to reach the *sahasrāra* at the top of his head. This visualization occurs while he practises *prāṇāyāma* (rhythmic method of inhaling, holding the breath, and exhaling). *Sahasrāra* is the centre where the supreme deity and his guru are perpetually situated in union and this short practice of meditation brings to his mind the fundamental unity of his own self with the deity and with his guru. He also envisages the letters of the *bīja* of his *iṣṭta-mantra* engraved in appropriate colours on the first three centres through which the Kuṇḍalinī passes on its lightning flight to the *sahasrāra*. On reaching the *sahasrāra* he imbues the *amṛta* existing there, which is another way of envisaging the bliss inherent in the supreme deity. The whole of this imagery links up with several religious concepts. The lotus is always a symbol of purity. Its thousand petals present its infinite nature which, though depicted as the abode of the deity, is none other than the deity herself. To complete the imagery, the goddess is envisaged in the centre of the pericarp of that lotus and being a flower, the lotus naturally contains honey — in this case *amṛta*. But this *amṛta* has no resemblance whatever to the mythical amṛta of Hindu religion. Here it is bliss indeed, permeating the godhead and in fact identical with the goddess. Thus, being once — however passively — reminded of, or rather having contemplated on this ultimate identity of his own self with bliss, the Tantric indirectly gets a taste of that bliss, which is represented by the more or less actual sensation of being bathed in, or saturated with, *amṛta.* Thus totally redeemed from all impurity, he starts his day in peace and confidence.

Next follows the usual process of scrupulously going through the round of observing hygienic habits that culminates in the ritual bath. Up to this point, each Tantric follows the rules of his own caste. The bath however differs from the usual Hindu bath, in that the Tantric takes several forms of bath, one after another.[7] These are called *mantra-snāna* (mantra-bath), *bhasma-snāna* (ash-bath), and so forth. As a group, these different forms of ritual bathing are called special baths (*viśeṣa-snāna*).

The Tāntric Bath

After the usual ritual bath with oil, riverbed-clay and bathing in deep water, whilst still standing in the water the Tantric takes water in his cupped hand, sips it three times and pours back what remains into the water he stands in. With the appropriate mantras he then purifies his six important limbs (*aṅga*), viz. *śiras* (head), *śikhā* (topknot), *netra* (eyes), *hṛdaya* (heart), *astra* (weapon) and *karatala-pṛṣṭha* (palms and backs of his hands), by touching each in turn with his hands and making the appropriate gestures (*mudrā*). Next, he utters the sacred sound '*kroṃ*' and, hooking the fingers of his right hand in imitation of a goad, he evokes sacred water from the orb of the sun, repeats the bīja-mantra of his *iṣṭa-devatā* ten times, and envisages the transformation of the ordinary water into sacred water followed by throwing that water into the actual water while forming a gesture with his hands to resemble a *yoni* (the female sex-organ). After that, with his hands he first makes the gesture (*mudrā*) of *dhenu* (drawing milk from the udders of the celestial cow, which symbolically transforms the water into *amṛta*), followed by the gesture of *yoni* (symbolizing that the water is primordial water).

Next he consecrates the water with the mantra *'aiṃ'* and repeats it ten times. He then envisages *iṣṭa-devatā* in that water, which has now become blissful *amṛta,* and consecrates this *amṛta* by repeating his *iṣṭa-mantra* ten times (*abhimantraṇa*). He then sprinkles himself seven times with this consecrated water which he envisages to be issuing from the goddess's exquisitely beautiful mouth. Then he repeats his *iṣṭa-mantra* twenty-one times, whilst simultaneously taking three dips in the water which he envisages to be a stream of *amṛta* issuing from the goddess's feet. Thereafter he again anoints himself thrice or seven times with the water, his hand held in the gesture of *yoni.* Emerging from the water, he wraps himself in two pieces of clean cloth (one as loin-cloth, the other as scarf), and decorates his forehead with consecrated ash from the sacrificial fire by making the sacred mark of 'tripuṇḍra' (three horizontal darts).

Tantric Aghamarṣaṇa

The Tantric form of *aghamarṣaṇa* (removal of all sins) differs from the Vedic *aghamarṣaṇa* in that it does not use any Vedic mantra (for Vedic *aghamarṣaṇa* see *Brāhmaṇasarvasva* p. 99ff. and P. V. Kane, *History,* Vol IV, p. 130).

The Tantric takes a handful of water and performs *prāṇāyāma* while visualizing that the water in his hand is being inhaled and passes down through his *iḍā-channel* to reach the far end of the left side of his torso, where apparently sins lurk. He envisages wrenching these out and exhaling them through his *piṅgalā-channel* together with the inhaled water which has turned black, and by returning that water to his palm rids himself of all sins.

Tantric Sandhyā

After observing the ordinary worship of *sandhyā,* the Tantric invokes the goddess who resides in the sun and offers her three libations of water while uttering the Vedic *gāyatrī.* Then he repeats the *gāyatrī-mantra* of his *iṣṭa-devatā* (e.g. Ṣoḍaśī-gāyatrī) for a number of times.

Tantric Tarpaṇa

After *aghamarṣaṇa,* the Tantric resumes his usual routine and starts his *tarpaṇa* (water-libation). He first follows the Vedic form, i.e. to offer *tarpaṇa* to all gods and to one's ancestors.[8] But before offering *tarpaṇa* to the Sun-God (*sūryārghya*), he offers it to his *iṣṭa-devatā* and her entire retinue of āvaraṇadevatās, etc. He does this by tracing on the water the basic yantra. He draws a triangle, puts a circle around it and encloses that within a square boundary and then offers libations to these deities. The final *tarpaṇa* is offered to the Sun-god. Last of all he recalls his identity with the Absolute Reality by uttering the formula '*haṃsaḥ so'haṃ*' and then envisages returning the sacred water to the sun. Thus purified, he proceeds to the actual place of worship in absolute silence.

Comparing these three rites, viz. *snāna, sandhyā* and *tarpaṇa* as prescribed by the Tantra texts with those prescribed by the Vedic tradition, we see that the former introduce elements that are specifically Tantric. In the ritual *snāna* (bath), we noticed that the water has to be envisaged as drawn from the sun, which is but one aspect of the goddess symbolizing her omniscience (see LT XXIX, 7-70 to understand how the goddess is represented as Sūrya, Soma and Agni). The water is consecrated by tracing a *yantra* and showing a few consecratory *mudrās.* The element of vivid imagery is brought in too for the contemplative transformation of ordinary empirical things into spiritual ideas in order to create a separate dimension of existence. And so, through vivid imagination accompained by certain acts, a Tantric effectively lifts his dimension of existence from the ordinary worldly level to the spiritual and achieves the same state of existence as his deity. What is noteworthy is that he does not reject anything, but just transmutes everything by aid of something akin to drama. Although he is the sole actor — provided he has the necessary imagination, propensity and experience — with forceful imagery he is able to create a completely different world (a cosmic existence let us say), which he shares with the goddess. The *aghamarṣaṇ* rite is an instance of this. The water exhaled, carrying away all the Tantric's sins, is conceived to be black; and sometimes sins are collectively envisaged as an anthropomorphic being (*pāpapuruṣa*) who is as black as soot. The intensity of such an imagination enables the Tantric to feel these events to be quite real, and they affect him far more deeply than, say, the Vedic ritual of *aghamarṣaṇa* can ever do. Incidentally, Vedic *aghamarṣaṇa* is always accompanied by a couple of hymns collectively called *aghamarṣaṇa-sūktas* (ṚV.x.190.1-3), and is only performed on certain occasions, not daily (the *Brāhmaṇasarvasva* mentions another rite, *drupada*, which bears close resemblance to Tantric *aghamarṣaṇa*).[9]

In the performance of *sandhyā* and *tarpaṇa*, again we encounter another aspect of Tantric religion, namely its monotheism. That is why the ordinary *sandhyā* is followed by the repetition of the goddess's *Gāyatrī-mantra* and, besides offering *tarpaṇa* to the ordinary Vedic gods, sages and one's ancestors, the Tantric offers it to his *iṣṭa-devatā* and her retinue in exactly the same order as is followed in the daily worship of the goddess. Furthermore, the Tantric finally declares his total identity with the Absolute reality, albeit in a cursory manner.

The Tantric form of *tarpaṇa* makes clear that, in spite of being monotheistic, the Tantric does not consider that his is the only deity that exists, denying thereby the existence of any other. To the contrary, he recognizes the existence of other deities, especially those belonging to the goddess's pantheon which does in fact make it possible to include almost every conceivable divinity. The crucial point is that the existence of these deities is considered to depend entirely on that of the goddess, whose manifestations they are; and it should be remembered that the goddess — in full regalia with all her retinue — is always invoked in formal worship. This is where the *sāmpradāyika* (observing the Tantric sampradāya form of ritual worship) differs from the normative (*smārta*) form. Therefore, even in performing as simple a rite as *tarpaṇa*, a *yantra* has to be drawn to indicate that the specially consecrated and protected area has been made worthy for the descent of the goddess (ŚT p. 154, line 19 comm.),[10] and her attendants, bodyguard, etc. are invoked and treated with the respect due to a sovereign's retinue.

Place of Worship

The criterion for a suitable place for worship is that it should be unpolluted and quiet. Some texts give a list of such places: holy places, banks of rivers, caves, hilltops, place visited by pilgrims, water-resorts, near the confluence of a river, sacred woods, lonely gardens, under a bilva tree (aegle marmelos/ woodapple), on the slope of a hill, in a *tulasī* (sacred basil) grove, cowstall in which there is no ox, Śiva temple, in the shade of such trees as the *aśvattha* (sacred fig tree) or *āmalakī* (emblic myrobalan), a cowherd-village near water, a temple, seashore, one's own house, or the house of one's guru (ŚT 2.138-139). Sites such as cremation-grounds etc. are also recommended for Tantric *pūjā*, especially in Kālī worship. Mostly *pūjās* connected with *puraścaraṇa* and *abhicāra* are performed outside home, while other *pūjās* are generally performed in front of the family altar at home, which is strictly guarded from pollution.

Nitya-pūjā (Preliminary Rites)

The next important daily duty of a Tantric is the worship of his deity. This major ritual act, which reveals the essential character of Tantric worship, is divided into several units. The first of these entails the purification (*śuddhi*) of everything involved in the worship and necessitates performing five consecratory acts (*śuddhi*) concerning 1) the Tantric's self; 2) the place (*sthāna*) of worship; 3) the mantra used; 4) all utensils and objects (*dravya*) used for the offering; and 5) the deity (*devatā*) worshipped (KT VI.16).

Before going into the details of these, it should be pointed out that to understand the method of Tantric ritual it is necessary to classify the rites comprised in a fully developed Tantric *pūja* under three main heads. The first of these is the group of purificatory rites; the second group covers precautionary measures aimed at removing obstacles or preventing interference from malevolent agents; and the third group deals with the actual pūjā ceremony in which gifts are offered to the deity. Now all five of these consecratory acts fall under the first group of rites in a pūjā which deals with the purification of everything used in the worship, whereas some of these acts also fall under the second group of precautionary measures. The remaining ceremonies are listed amongst the rites that concern the offering of gifts to the deity. Of all the consecrations, the first — the consecration of the Tantric's self — is of most interest to us as it illustrates the central attitude of Tantrism. Observance of this rites qualifies the Tantric to invoke the deity to be worshipped, and at the same time it covers a wide range of minor rites concerning the Tantric's daily obligatory religious duties, namely *snāna, aghamarṣaṇa, tarpaṇa* and *sandhyārcana.* Once the Tantric completes this *tarpaṇa,* he proceeds in absolute silence to the place where he performs his daily worship (*Tantrasāra,* p. 230). This is a sign that he has already withdrawn himself from his mundane reality and is seeking to attain that other dimension of reality that he shares with his deity. When about to enter the site of worship, he performs the precautionary rite of invoking and worshipping the guardians of the goddess's abode and gate of her cosmic residence. But even before that, he invokes the Sun-God and worships him with a simple offering of water and a few grains of rice smeared with sandalwood. The Sun is invoked to act as chief witness of the Tantric's performance since that god is universally regarded as the witness of good deeds (*lokasākṣī*). Then guardian-deities such as Gaṇeśa, Durgā, Śrī, Vaṭuka, Kṣetrapāla and the like are invoked in order to safeguard entrance by the door of the place of worship. Hence this should be regarded as one of the precautionary rites. At the same time the Tantric consecrates the door by thrice sprinkling consecrated water on it while uttering his *iṣṭa-mantra.* He consecrates this water by filling a jug with clean water brought from some holy source while pronouncing the *hṛd-mantra* (of the six limbs),[11] and then repeats his *iṣṭa-mantra* a couple of times as prescribed by his guru. This is accompanied by the gesture of the *dhenu-mudrā,* whereby he envisages the changing of the water into *amṛta.* This consecrated water known as *sāmānyarghya* is prepared as soon as the Tantric completes his *tarpaṇa* and is used for purpose of consecration throughout the performance of his *pūjā* (see TanS p. 231 and ŚT pp. 230-231). Here we have an instance of how the three groups of rites mentioned above constantly overlap, and this recurs all through the performance. The traditional divisions of a Tantric pūjā are six, viz. *dhyāna* (meditation), *pūjā* (offering), *japa, homa* (fire-sacrifice), *nyāsa* and *tarpaṇa.*

Ātmaśuddhi[12] has to be performed by every Tantric before he can start his pūjā. Only a minor part of this rite, the *āhnika* section, entails physical acts; the major part involves two of the most important features of Tantric rites, namely *bhūtaśuddhi* (consecrating one's physical body) and *nyāsa* (transmutation and accommodation). These concern the process of the sādhaka's sublimation and spiritual transformation. The worshipper first salutes his teacher (guru) and then Gaṇeśa. Then using his yogic teachnique and his highly developed powers of imagination and concentration, the Tantric practiser envisages all the ontological realities that go to make up his personality. He then proceeds to envisage within himself the process of cosmic creation (evolution) in reverse order (i.e. cosmic involution). He follows every single step, imagining the dissolution of each element into its preceding cause, until in the end he is ultimately dissolved or immersed in his cosmic source. He then envisages his own resurrection, retracing each step of cosmic creation. Only now, having burned away with cosmic fire and blown away with cosmic air all his human imperfections and limitations, he experiences bliss and, permeated with it, remains immersed in the cosmic source. He actually pictures himself as bathed in *amṛta.* He now has a body made of pure substance (*sāttvika*) identical with that of the deity's and he is free to invite her to descend into it — to invoke the divine ego to descend on to his ego.

Needless to say, mantras play a central role in the Tantric procedure of translating ontological realities into ritual acts. Each reality is represented by a seed-(*bijā*) mantra, and visual imagery is also provided for each. Thus, having envisaged the cosmic drama of the final cataclysm followed by cosmic creation, the Tantric ensures his identification with the cosmic goddess (*prāṇapratiṣṭhā*). The next stage of the rite of *ātmaśuddhi* is *nyāsa.* He accommodates the divine form, limb by limb, in his own body.[13]

He then proceeds to house the entire cosmos within his body, by conceiving it to be the divine mansion wherein all the attendant deities and the entire galaxy are present. He also accommodates in his body the *mātṛkā* (letters) mantras, their seers, and ritual application (the latter items are obviously an imitation of Vedic tradition). Each act of *nyāsa* is accompanied by a salutation to the object of the act, and the Tantric pronounces the mystic syllable representing the seedmantra each time he vividly envisages the actual placing of that object on a part of his body.[14] At the end of this process, his body has been lifted into the mystic world of the goddess, in the centre of which, in the lotus-sanctuary within the mysterious bejewelled island, she holds her court (see ŚT. p. 9). The rite of inviting the goddess to descend in the heart of the worshipper, which is envisaged as the lotus-seat and is performed after *bhūtaśuddhi*, has already effected the worshipper's essential transformation into divine personality (ŚT. p. 137-8).

Sthānaśuddhi and *dravyaśuddhi*, on the other hand, mostly contain rites of a precautionary nature to ward off evil spirits and other malevolent agencies. These may try to pollute the site or other ingredients of the pūjā, and thereby rob it of its validity as a whole. Many lesser gods and spirits are invoked and offered gifts to ensure correct and safe performance of the pūjā, to protect the premises and the performer, as well as to safeguard that the merit envisaged shall be duly awarded. Some of these rites are reconciliatory, e.g. invoking the lord of the terain (*kṣetrapāla*) and offering food to the spirits (*bhūta-bali*). There are others in which divine protection is sought by envisaging a material representation of the deity's most terrifying manifestation (Vaṭuka, Yoginīs), or typical weapon (arrows, etc.) In the rite of *digbandhana* (enclosing the site of worship within a fixed boundary), the Tantric envisages a magic boundary, consisting of arrows (*nārāca*) shot by the goddess as surrounding the whole area. Similar acts are casting a glowering look around to disperse aerial spirits, stamping the floor three times to drive away any spirits lurking there, and snapping the fingers — thus making menacing noises to frighten off undesirable elements. There are mantras, too, commanding spirits to disappear on the authority of the deity (*apasarpantu*, etc.) The site and all the objects used in pūjā are sprinkled with consecrated water, and all such acts are accompanied by appropriate hand-gestures (*mudrās*), e.g. *nārāca-mudrā*, *chotikā-mudrā*, *avaguṇṭhana-mudrā*, *paramīkaraṇa-mudrā*, etc.

Needless to say, the actual cleaning and scrubbing of the site and of all the utensils and objects used in the ritual have to be done very thoroughly. Moreover, whenever possible the site should be decorated. But usually all that has been seen to long before starting the precautionary rites. Thus the physical cleaning of *ātman, sthāna* and *dravya* does not take place at the same time as the contemplative and symbolic cleansings are performed. It was completed before the rite of door-worship is observed. After that, the symbolic cleansing is undertaken by sprinkling the consecrated water three times accompanied by recitation of the *iṣṭa-mantra* and the *mantra* of the weapon (*astra*) and, in the case of the practitioner, by his taking three sips of that water from his cupped hand and then touching both his ears and shoulders.

The other two consecrations, viz. *mantraśuddhi* and *devatāśuddhi,* are effected solely by contemplative and symbolic means. The main mantra is consecrated by uttering all fifty letters of the Sanskrit alphabet before and after the mantra. The whole mantra thus protected is repeated twice, once in straightforward order and then in reverse order (KT VI.19).[15] The deity is consecrated more elaborately. After having invoked and welcomed her, she is placed on the sacred seat. When assured that she is comfortable and prepared to accept his offerings, the Tantric draws a magic circle (by tracing a circle around her whilst uttering a mantra: the *avaguṇṭhana-mudrā*).

He then performs the rite of *sakalīkaraṇa* (giving the deity a finite form composed of parts) by uttering the appropriate mantra and displaying the relevant mudrā. Next he performs the *nyāsa* of the deity's six main limbs (*aṅga*). After that, he repeats his *iṣṭa-mantra* three times, the *dīpanī-mantra* once, and the *mātṛkā-mantra* once, shows the *dhenu-mudrā,* and sprinkles *arghya*-water on the deity thus visualized. Although generally speaking this concludes the rites of consecration, sometimes certain other forms of consecration are added to these before starting on the actual offerings. On entering the place of worship, the Tantric lights a lamp and worships it as the lord of lamp (*dīpanātha*).[16] He then requests the earth to permit him to sit on her, and after consecrating his three *tattvas* (*ātman, vidyā* and Śiva *tattva*) and other cosmic realities making up his physical existence (thirty-six in number), he takes a little hemp.[17] Next, he arranges in front of himself all the flowers and utensils, etc. that are to be used in the pūjā (see also Bharati, *Tantric Tradition,* pp. 246-247, 251, 254-456 and the notes thereon).

Pūjā is offered to a deity who is represented by various symbols. These are described as the locus (*ādhāra*) of the pūjā offered. The symbol may be some aniconic form such as a liṅga, or a triangular pebble of black marble found in the bed of the Gaṇḍakī. It can be an image made of stone, terracotta, crystal, any precious gem, or metal. It can be a pitcher full of water decorated with vermilion, leaves and grass. A bowl of water (*viśeṣārghya*) or a cup of alcoholic drink (*śrī-pātra*)[18] may represent the goddess; or a water-resort, books, or a plateful of flowers may be used as symbols for the deity; or a young girl (*kumārī*), a woman (*suvāsinī*) and her sex-organ may be worshipped as symbolizing the goddess.

Bhāskararāya enumerates three forms of the goddess that are worshipped: the gross, the subtle and the absolute.[19] Gross forms are those mentioned above. The mantras are the subtle forms of the goddess, while her absolute form is worshipped in the worship of one's guru and of one's own self as pervaded by the goddess. This last form of worship is found in *āntara-pūjā.* In practice however, images are very popular and are widely worshipped. But in a Tantric pūjā, the yantra of the main deity is always worshipped, while a pitcher full of water plays an almost equally important role as symbol of the goddess. A wide range of iconographic descriptions of various deities are available in Tantric literature in the dhyānas of these deities.[20] These symbols are only venerated when pervaded by the deity; otherwise they are merely physical phenomena. It is only after the Tantric has put life into them through performing special rites (*prāṇapratiṣṭhā*) that they become sacred.

The Pūjā Programme

The various purificatory and consecratory rites have been somewhat elaborately discussed in order to emphasize their importance in the performance of a pūjā. The order in which these rites are performed both by Kaulas and by non-Kaulas in a complete pūjā-programme runs as follows:

1. Approaching the door of the sacred pūjā-area and consecrating it.
2. Precautions against three types of hindrances.
3. Worship of Vāstupuruṣa (guardian of the divine abode) and other rites to safeguard and consecrate the place of worship.
4. Purification of the worshipper's seat (*āsana*).
5. Worship of the *guru-paṅkti* (original line of gurus) and of Gaṇeśa.
6. Pūjā of the sun-god.
7. Drawing the cakra or yantra, symbol of the divine abode.
8. Meditation on the goddess's abode.
9. *Bhūstaśuddhi* and other related rites.
10. *Ātma-prāṇapratiṣṭhā*, or meditating on the replacement of the worshipper's mundane self by his divine self.
11. *Prāṇāyāma,* or practice of controlled breathing exercises.
12. Nyāsa.
13. Dhyāna (meditation on the deity) and the showing of mudrās.

14. *Āntarayāga* (interiorized worship).
15. A. Preparing the viśeṣārghya (water used for special consecration) and
    B. Arranging containers for offering drinks to the deities, etc. This second part of the rite is followed by the Vāma and Kaula Tantrics.
16. *Bāhya-pūjā* (physical worship).
17. *Ṣaḍaṅga-pūjā* (worship of the six parts of the deity's body).[21]
18. Worship of the Nityās.
19. Worship of the three groups (*ogha*) of gurus, namely the divine group (*divyaugha*), the sidha group (*siddhaugha*) and the human group (*mānavaugha*).
20. Worship of the deities of the main goddess's pantheon (*āvaraṇadevatā*).[22]
21. *Prāṇāhuti*,[23] or the offering of cooked and other food to the deity.
22. Offering of the kuladīpa (the kula-lamp).
23. Puṣpāñjali (offering a number of flowers).
24. Meditation on *Kāmakalā*.
25. *Homa* (fire-sacrifice).
26. Offering of *bali* and animal sacrifice.
27. *Pradakṣiṇā* (going round the deity one or more times starting from the deity's right side).
28. *Japa* (repeatedly reciting the main mantra).
29. *Stuti* (chanting eulogies of the deity).
30. *Suvāsinī-* or *dūtī-pūjā* (worshipping a woman).[24]
31. *Cakra-* (or bhairavīcakra) pūjā (an equal number of male and female tantrics observing pūjā collectively).
32. *Visarjana* (leave-taking).
33. *Nirmālya-pūjā*.
34. *Kumārī-pūjā*.

Commentary

1. Approaching the place of worship, the worshipper sprinkles the door (sometimes only in imagination) with water from the sāmānyārghya-jug,[25] whilst uttering the mantra *phaṭ* (of the weapon). He worships Mahālakṣmī and Sarasvatī on the lintel; and Gaṇeśa, Kṣetrapāla, Gaṅgā and Yamunā on the sideposts of the door.
2. He banishes interfering spirits, etc. from the sky by casting a glowering look around; from the atmosphere by sprinkling holy water while uttering the mantra *phaṭ*; and from the earth by striking the ground three times with his heel.
3. Entering the sacred precincts, he worships the guardian-deity of the abode and Brahmā on the north-east corner. He consecrates the entire sacred place, that has already been bedecked and cleaned with pañcagavya[26] and with arghya-water, whilst uttering the astra-mantra (*phaṭ*). He further safeguards the site by casting a glowering look around whilst uttering his main mantra and sprinkling the place with *arghya*-water. He then repeats the astra-mantra and strikes the ground with a bunch of kuśa-grass,[27] whilst uttering the same mantra. He then sprinkles the place thoroughly with consecrated water whilst uttering the *varma* (armour) mantra (*vauṣaṭ*). Finally, he burns incense, scatters popped rice, sesame-seed, sandal-wood-paste, rice, ash, darbha-grass and mustard-seed, and sweeps away all spirits while repeating the *astra-mantra.*[28]
4. He then proceeds to consecrate the place he has chosen for his seat. He envisages and utters the mantras of the three boundaries set up by fire, by Śiva's weapon, the *pāśupata,* and by Viṣṇu's weapon, the *sudarśana*-disc. He sprinkles consecrated water on the place selected for his seat, and salutes the soil as vajra (thunder). Then uttering the mantra for drawing

diagrams,[29] he draws a triangle with sacred water and traces the sacred letter *hsauḥ*. He worships the seat as representing the lotus, the supreme Śakti who is the locus of all (*ādhāraśkti*). He requests permission from the goddess of the earth to be allowed to sit on her and then settles himself on his seat. On sitting down, he places a jug full of water on his left side next to a bowl in which to wash his hands, and all the other items of pūjā-offerings on his right side. He consecrates his three basic principles (tattvas), viz. *Ātmatattva, Vidyātattva* and *Śivatattva.* Then he lights a row of lamps or only one lamp.

5. He salutes his preceptor, grand-preceptor and great-grand-preceptor and requests their permission to commence the ritual.

6-7.He worships the Sun (the supreme witness of all deeds) to witness his present endeavour. The description now given is specially relevant to the pūjā of *Śrī-cakra. Śrī-cakra* is a geometric representation of Goddess Tripurā (Śrī) — a complicated diagram of nine figures and nine triangles intermingled to form a concentric figure, in which the central point is conceived as the seat of Tripurā. This figure can be freshly drawn at each performance of pūjā. Otherwise it is curved out on metal plates or blocks of special stones.[30] The Goddess Tripurā is here worshipped as the source and essence of All, the Universe represented by the diagram. As this yantra of the goddess is most popularly worshipped all over india, and as there is a text in the form of a religious exegesis called Paraśurāma Kalpa Sūtra — dating from at any rate the seventeenth century of the Christian era — in which the ritual worship of Tripurā is handled systematically, this form of pūjā has been chosen by us as a model of Tantric pūjā.

The Śrī-cakra (or any other such diagram representing the deity worshipped) should be drawn with care and exact measurements, and then be consecrated. If a metal or stone Śrī-*yantra*[31] is used, it is bathed with consecrated water and with *pañcāmṛta.*[32] It is then wiped with a clean cloth and sprinkled with red powder. Then the yantra is invested with divine personality by uttering the sacred syllables and formulae declaring that the life, soul, senses, speech and mind of the divine *Śrī-cakra* are entering into this phenomenal *Śrī-cakra.*

8. The worshipper carefully envisages the sacred abode of *Śrī-cakra's* presiding deity Tripurā with all its details. It is conceived as a jewelled island floating in an ocean of amṛta. On this fantastic site surrounded by gardens etc. made of precious stones, the goddess's palace stands. Inside, on a special platform decorated with four gates, is set her couch. Brahmā, Viṣṇu, Rudra and Īśvara hold its four legs; Sadāśiva is the plank on which her bed is spread with soft cushions. The *Śrī-yantra* is then conceived to be set on this bed and the worshipper imagines that a big curtain is drawn across in front to hide the bed. While visualizing each details, he salutes it when mentioning it and offers it arghya (perfumed flowers and rice).
9. Now comes the time to perform the consecration of the worshipper's own self (*bhūtaśuddhi*).
10. After completing *bhuūtaśuddhi*, the worshipper invests his own self with divine personality. He visualizes the deity, his main mantra (*iṣta-* or *mūla-mantra*) and his guru as all being identical. The resplendent, divine personage then enters his heart as his essential self. While thus mentally busy, he thrice utters the formula declaring that his own self is identical with the absolute, divine self. It should be noted that the envisaged identification is not effected in one step. There are in fact a series of identifications. First, the worshipper's guru is identified with Śiva. Then Śiva and the Goddess

are identified as the Two-in-One. Next, the main mantra of the deity is identified with the deity's mystic form. Finally, this form replaces the worshipper's mudane self. Only then is the investment of the worshipper with the divine self accomplished.

11. The worshipper then performs regulated breathing (*prāṇāyāma*) sixteen times.
12. He starts performing the rite of *nyāsa.* First in the series of *nyāsa* comes that of the *mātṛkā* (alphabet) as the essential, mystic form of the Goddess who is the source of all the names and forms in the universe. This is followed by the *nyāsa* to sublimate the worshipper's fingers, palms and back of his hands. Thus consecrated, he uses his hands once again to dispel any lurking evil spirits by snapping his fingers, striking the left palm with two fingers of his right hand, and by glowering around. He also recites certain mantras ordering such spirits to depart forthwith. He then continues with the rite of *nyāsa.* The *nyāsas* performed by the worshipper of the *śrī-cakra* are: *mātṛkā-nyāsa* (to consecrate his hands), *nyāsa* to protect the worshipper, *nyāsa* of the four seats,[33] *nyāsa* of the six main limbs of the goddess Śrī,[34] *nyāsa* of the attendant deities, *nyāsa* of the letters of the main mantra, *ṣoḍhā-nyāsa,*[35] and *cakra-nyāsa.*[36] Finally, he transforms his body into the seat of the deity by means of *pīṭha-nyāsa* (*nyāsa* of Devī's seat). The latter stands on eight legs consisting of holy duties (dharma), knowledge (*jñāna*), divine excellence (*aiśvarya*) and renunciation (*vairāgya*) together with their opposites. These are mentally placed on the Tantric's upper body. The mystical lotus-seat of the deity, with its bulb buried on bliss and stalk consisting of pure consciousness, is envisaged in the worshipper's heart. On the pericarp of this lotus the three luminaries, viz. Sun, Moon and Fire with their parts (kalā or digit), are invoked and also the three constituents of the cosmic source (sattva,

rajas and tamas). Next he performs the nyāsa of *ātman, antarātman, paramātman, jñānātman*,[37] and the *nyāsa* of *Māyātattva, Kalātattva* and *Vidyātattva*. After that he performs *nyāsa* of the seat and at the same time recites its mantra which consists of the mystic sound *hsauḥ*. He then salutes Sadāśiva, the supreme corpse (*mahāpreta*) who is symbolic of the goddess's lotus-seat.

13. Whilst meditating upon the goddess as seated, the worshipper shows a set of mudrās. For Tripurā these are ten, but the number varies for each deity (see TanS, p. 90; ŚT p. 141 comm.). *Mudrās*, or symbolic hand-postures, are in fact distinctive features of all deities. For instance, in the case of Śrī-cakra, each of its nine geometrical fingures has a presiding deity whose distinctive mark is represented by the relevant mudrā.[38] The chief goddess Tripurā's special symbol is *trikhaṇḍā* (having three parts), which refers to the mystical visual representation of the goddess as the sound *īṃ* written as a letter composed of three parts. These parts are imagined as portraying her main characteristics as the cosmic woman: attention is focused on her head, breasts and sex-organ. The visual symbol is used for meditation on Tripurā. The mudrā consists of denoting the number three by joining palms and keeping three of the five pairs of fingers in an upright position whilst bending the other two pairs (*Nityotsava*, p. 72). The worshipper then performs a short meditation on the deity in her full iconographic representation, as well as on her as represented by the mystic sound *īṃ* (Kāmakalā).

14. This short meditation is followed by another form of meditation. The worshipper first performs kuṇḍalinī-yoga and envisages the supreme Goddess as pure knowledge, experienced as a luminous flash illuminating his entire *suṣumṇā nāḍī* from the lowest point where cosmic power usually lies dormant

(*mūlādhāra*) to the crown of his head (*brahmarandhra*). He thus identifies his innermost being with the supreme divinity. In the middle of this *suṣumṇā* is the centre of the heart. There he envisages the śrī-cakra with the Goddess upon it. He then starts offering Her the customary services and gifts presented to a deity in ordinary pūjā. Only, he offers these items mentally, substituting ideas in place of concrete objects. This is called *āntara-yāga* (mental offering) and is highly esteemed amongst Tantrics. Flawless performance of this form of pūjā is dependent upon the worshipper's concentrative powers and experience in *kuṇḍalinī-yoga*. A Tantric at the highest stage of spiritual development may depend almost entirely on this mental pūjā and thereby drastically simplify the more concrete, or physical, form of pūjā. Since all the ingredients used in this pūjā are ideas, one has no need to bother about the availability of gifts, etc. for offerings. The worshipper offers the Goddess a seat which is just his heart. He offers water to wash Her feet, and that water is the *amṛta* oozing from the thousand-petaled lotus above the crown of his head. He offers Her *arghya*, and that is his mind. He gives Her water to rinse Her mouth, and that is the same *amṛta*. The latter is again offered to bathe Her in and the principle of the sky-element to dress Her in. He offers Her the cosmic principle of smell (*gandhatanmātra*) as fragrant unguent, his experience as flowers, his vital air as incense, the cosmic fire as lamp, and *amṛta* as food. He offers Her the ringing of a bell represented by unstruck sound (*anāhatadhvani*); a fly-whisk represented by the cosmic element of air; and entertainment in the form of dance represented by the functioning of his senses and the agility of his mind. Finally, he offers Her fifteen flowers representing non-deception, non-pride, non-attachment, non-conceit, non-ignorance, non-boastfulness, non-hostility, non-perturbation, non-jealousy, non-greed, non-violence, non-indulgence (especially in all forms of sensual pleasure), benevolence, compassion, and experience. Then, instead of sacrificial beasts, he offers his two main vices, desire and anger.

After making these offerings, he envisages the fifty letters of the alphabet, each with the addition of its nasal sound, as forming a rosary strung on the *kuṇḍalinī* as thread. Using this rosary, he repeats his chief mantra both in forward and in reverse order. This performance is also offered to the Goddess. Lastly, he performs the fire-sacrifice. The *kuṇḍa* (pit in which the sacrificial fire is lighted) is the *cakra* said to be situated in the vicinity of the navel. The worshipper envisages his antarātman, paramātman and jñānātman as permeating this *kuṇḍa* and awakening his *kuṇḍalinī*-power, which is pure knowledge. In this fire he sacrifices all the activities of his senses and his duties as well as his non-duties (acts to be refrained from). This emphasizes the worshipper's total sacrifice of all his personal interests in favour of the deity's supreme will. Last of all, he sacrifices his *ahaṃtā* (ego) in the same manner. Thus this mental pūjā contains all the three parts of ordinary pūjā: offering gifts and services; repeating the main mantra; and the fire-sacrifice. This form of pūjā is considered to be the ideal one because of its specially exalted spiritual tone. The deity is invited to take possession of the worshipper's inner consciousness by replacing his ego-consciousness. His physical body, his merits and demerits — everything that goes to make up his separateness as an individual — are vividly recalled and then offered to the deity.

It should be noted that often an abridged form of mental pūjā is performed by the ordinary worshipper (i.e. when the Tantric is not performing daily pūjā as part of his *puraścaraṇa* or primary worship of his deity and mantra, and has not vowed to complete a hundred thousand or multiple thereof, repetitions of the mantra, *japa*, terminating upon his attaining perfection in its performance, *mantra-siddhi* and directly experiencing identity with its deity). This abridged form of mental pūjā consists of offering the five basic gifts to the deity, viz. fragrant unguents, flowers, incense, lamp and food, for which the cosmic elements of earth, sky, air, fire and water in the form of *amṛta* are respectively substituted. Finally with the offering of *tāmbūla* (betel-leaf prepared with other ingredients), the worshipper offers all his abilities and energy. Each of these gifts is offered whilst pronouncing a mystic syllable, making an obeisance to the deity, announcing the name of the offering, and at the same time showing its *mudrā*. After that follows *japa* of the mantra and meditation on the deity as the letter *īṃ*, i.e. as Kāmakalā, the cosmic mother.

15. A. An important rite in Tantric pūjā is the setting up of the receptacle for the water of the special arghya. Usually, a white conch-shell, placed on a stand with three legs, is used for this purpose. The worshipper draws in vermilion a special diagram consisting of single and double triangles enclosed within a circle and a square. He then places the three-legged stand upon it. The diagram is worshipped as the source of power, or locus, of the universe; while the stand is worshipped as the orb (*maṇḍala*) of Fire, composed of ten parts (*kalā*). Next he places the bowl or shell on the stand, and worships it as the orb of the Sun, consisting of twelve parts. Then he pours a little alcohol from the container (*kalaśa*) and scented water from the jug of ordinary *arghya* into the receptacle containing the special *arghya*.[39] This he worships as the orb of the Moon containing *amṛta* and consisting of sixteen parts. He pours some of this liquid into a bowl and sprinkles it over himself

and all the offerings, without moving the container of *viśeṣārghya.*

B. In the Kaula type of pūjā[40] with its five special offerings of alcoholic drink, meat, fish, mudrā (snacks like parched grain)[41] and sexual intercourse, the worshipper ceremonially displays the container (*kalaśa*) of alcoholic drink. He then draws a maṇḍala of triangles and circles and encloses it within a square, using vermilion or red sandalwood-paste for drawing the lines. He salutes this diagram as representing the cosmic source, the Śakti. Then he places a low stand upon it, and on the stand the container with duly uttered mantras and other consecratory rites.

Next, he pours alcoholic drink into the container until it is full, while uttering the mantra of *mātṛka* (alphabet) in reverse order. The liquid is then sanctified by invoking and worshipping the orbs of Fire, Sun and Moon and performing various other consecratory rites.[42] Then he toasts the goddess Ānandabhairavī (the goddess of bliss) and her partner with the alcohol and salutes them. After that he places containers full of meat, fish and tasty snacks and consecrates them in the prescribed manner. These items act as purifying agents to counteract the effect of alcohol and always accompany the drinking which, without them, is considered sinful and pointless.

The next important rite in Kaula-pūjā is the arrangement of the drinking-cups (*pātrasādana*). These are small round cups with a rounded bottom and are always set on little separate stands. This particular rite gains special significance in the case of cakra-pūjā, which is pūjā performed jointly by a group of Tantrics on a special occasion. Theirs is a very intimate circle admitting no stranger. A highly experienced and much revered Tantric guru acts as leader and ensures that strict rules of etiquette are observed. The most important cup is that reserved for the Goddess (*śrīpātra*), which is placed in the centre with elaborate ritual. Then come the cups for the guru, for the worshipper's self, for his śakti (female partner), for the yoginī, for the vīra, and the containers for offering bali, pādya (water for washing the deity's feet) and ācamanīyā. These are placed in a row alongside the cup for the Goddess. Starting with Hers, each cup is three-quarters filled with the alcoholic beverage, into which the meat, etc. are put. Finally, *madhuparka*[43] is placed in a cup by the side of these.[44]

16. Now starts the actual ceremony of offerings, or *bāhyapūjā*. The worshipper first worships his own self by placing a fragrant flower upon his head. Then he mentally invokes his spiritual teacher and the latter's predecessors in the holy order of his *sampradāya*. He worships them with flowers, and pours out an alcoholic libation containing some meat, fish and snack of some kind. With these he purifies the three ultimate realities (*Śivatattva, Vidyātattva,* and *Ātmatattva*). Then he sips the alcohol as prescribed in the ritual.

Thus symbolically identified with his guru and guru's line of predecessors, as well as with the Goddess, he performs the pūjā of Her sacred seat. He envisages and salutes the locus-power (in the form of the Goddess holding two lotuses). On her head is perched the bluish turtle surmounted by the foundation-stone, upon which the white serpent Ananta is seated. On this serpent, Viṣṇu (in the form of a boar) is envisaged holding the goddess Earth aloft. The Earth in turn holds the mystic jewelled island containing marvellous and mysterious gardens and pavillions made of gems. In the centre of these, he visualizes the couch of the Goddess as described before (page 107). But now, instead of Sadāśiva, he first envisages the eight-petaled lotus, the mystical seat of the Goddess. The bulb of thc lotus —

buried in the primordial Māyā and Vidyā[45] — is supreme bliss, its stalk is pure consciousness, and the lotus itself consists of all the cosmic realities. Its petals are the primary material source of the universe. Its pollens are the modifications of that primal source. The fifty letters of the Sanskrit alphabet form its pericarp. The three luminous orbs — Fire, Sun and Moon — are placed in this lotus. The worshipper envisages each of these and offers obeisance to it. Finally he envisages each of the three constituents of the praṇava-mantra (a, u, m) and the three elements of the primal source (sattva, rajas and tamas), and worships them as identified with these three luminous orbs. Then at the four corners of the seat, ātman, antarātman, paramātman, and jñānātman are worshipped. Last of all, eight pīṭha-śaktis (guardian deities of the seat)[46] are worshipped. Only after that is Sadāśiva, the actual seat of the Goddess, worshipped. Thus, having envisaged the seat, the Goddess is invoked to arise from the worshipper's heart and take her place on the *Śrī-yantra.* He meditates on the Goddess and her spouse in his heart while holding in his hand a flower smeared with sandalwood paste. Then, by means of prāṇāyāma, he brings the Goddess up through his nose into the flower in his hand. He salutes Her and mentally utters the mantra: 'O mother, supreme goddess, who resides in the great lotus forest, and whose form is the bliss that is the cosmic source, you who are the embodiment of universal goodness, please come here, come here. O supreme goddess, easy to approach through devotion, I beg you to abide here with all your attendant deities for as long as I am performing this ritual worship'. After uttering this mantra he places the flower on the Śrī-yantra.

Then, the elaborate ritual of welcome starts. The worshipper utters his main mantra and, addressing the Goddess, invites Her to come with Her spouse, settle on the *yantra,* be present, confine Herself to the sacred area and meet the worshipper face to face.[47] Each of these requests is spelled out and accompanied with the suitable gesture (mudrā).

This is followed by the interesting rite of *sakalīkaraṇa*, or setting up parts of the deity. This suggests that in reality the Goddess is formless and hence has no parts (*kalā*) but, for the sake of being able to worship Her, she is conceived as an embodied entity. Her main six parts are saluted as separate deities (i.e. hṛt-śakti, śiras-śakti, śikhā-śakti, kavaca-śakti, netra-śakti, and astra-śakti)[48] After that come the ritual safety-measures, such as enclosing Her within a magic circle and dispersing all evil elements by uttering the *astra-mantra* and snapping fingers. Then the Goddess is turned into *amṛta* and acclaimed supreme (*parama*) by means of mantras and gestures. Finally, the *prāṇapratiṣṭhā* is carried out by showing the gesture of flame (*lelihā-mudrā*) while uttering the mantra: 'Let the five life-breaths of the Goddess Tripurā and Her spouse be here in the yantra; let Her soul be here with that of Her spouse; let all Her sense-organs be here; and let Her speech, mind, sight, faculty of hearing and of smelling, Her life-breath, etc. be here'. This mantra is interspersed with the entire alphabet and other mystic syllables. Then the attributes of the deity are shown in gestures.

Then the worshipper welcomes the deity and proceeds to offer Her gifts (*upācāra*). Although a minimum of five items suffices, in practice sixteen items are usually offered.[49] But one may offer ten, thirty-eight, sixty-four, or up to a thousand items. Rāghavabhaṭṭa explains that the term upāçāra means something that enables one to approach the Goddess with devotion and that ensures Her closeness and favour (loc. cit., p. 156). In other words, the purpose of this pūjā is to serve (*upācarati*), and whatever the worshipper served the deity with is an upācāra. Each item is offered with a mantra consisting of a few mystic syllables, an address to the deity combined with a declaration of what the worshipper is offering and his salutation to Her. This is followed by a libation to the deity. After all the *upācāras* have thus been offered to the main deity, the worshipper shows Her a series of mudrās.

17. The six aṅgas of the Goddess, śikhā, etc. are worshipped at the four corners of the yantra, and in front and at the back of the main deity who is in the centre. This forms a David's star with the six tiny triangles each holding one part or *aṅga*.
18. The most intimate attendants of the Goddess are then worshipped. In the case of Tripurā, these are the fifteen Nityās. The Goddess Herself is also worshipped in the centre as the sum-total of all the Nityās. Each Nityā is identified with one of the fifteen vowels, while the Goddess represents the last vowel (*aḥ*). These Nityās and the vowels with the nasal added are invoked on the central triangle of the yantra, five on each side of it.
19. The worshipper then worships his own *guruparamparā* on the first triangle inside the yantra. This rite covers the worship of three groups; the celestial group, the perfected group, and the human group. The list of names varies according to the Tantric's own tradition.
20. The *āvaraṇa* deities or attendants, who reside in the abode of the Goddess and surround Her in circular tiers, are now worshipped, starting from the inner circle and moving outwards. Reaching the square figures at the outer enclosure of the yantra, the ten guardians of the quarters are worshipped, followed by worship of the weapons and all other objects that in Her many manifestations the Goddess holds in Her hands. Finally Vaṭuka, Yoginī, Gaṇeśa, Kṣetrapāla, etc. chieftains of the Goddess's special hosts are worshipped.

21. This is followed by a short ritual offering of the incense, lamp and libation. Finally the worshipper offers cooked food to the deity, which should preferably include rice cooked with milk. This is done with great care after having duly consecrated the food. He requests the Goddess to accept this food prepared with due care skilfully blended to please all varieties of taste and attractively served. He then performs the *prāṇāgnihotram* by offering the Goddess a small portion of the food five times and uttering mantras, each consisting of a few mystic syllables such as *aiṃ, hrīṃ, śrīṃ,* etc. and the five lifebreaths (*prāṇa, apāna, vyāna, udāna* and *samāna*) respectively mentioned in each mantra. The mantras end with the word *svāhā*, standing for an oblation to the fire of the Goddess's life-breaths. The last mantra mentions Brahman separately.[50] Then he prays that the Goddess who is his main mantra too (in the case of Tripurā the mantra is split into three groups of mystic syllables), and who pervades the three fundamental realities of Ātman, Vidyā and Śiva, may find the food acceptable. Next he meditates on the Goddess by envisaging Her as partaking of the food. He finishes this rite by offering Her drinks. After carefully removing the dish of food and placing it at the north-east corner, he offers Her water for washing and rinsing (*ācamanīya*), elaborately prepared betel,[51] money as dakṣiṇā, and then places a lamp of burning camphor in front of Her.

22. In *kaula-pūjā*, the worshipper now offers the Goddess a kula-lamp. It is made of special metal (sometimes it may be made of dough) and is filled with alcohol. This is lighted and he utters the following mantra while swinging it in a circle around the deity: "I offer you the kaula-lamp representing internal fire as well as external fire which has unlimited lustre and I swing it around you three times'.

23. He concludes this part of the pūjā of offerings by taking a handful of flowers and offering it to the Goddess (*paṣpāñjali*) together with praise and a prayer.
24. He meditates for a while on Her Kāmakalā-form and on the seed-syllable of his *iṣṭa-mantra* as identical with the Goddess's essence.
25. The next step is to perform the fire-sacrifice, which is optional. It is performed when time and money permit. Therefore, it is performed regularly in most temples and in domestic worship on special occasions. At the north-east corner of the pūjā-pavilion, a square platform of sand is erected measuring about one-third of a square metre. On it the worshipper draws three horizontal and three vertical lines crossing each other. On these six lines he worships the six deities of the quarters (Brahmā, Yama, Soma, Rudra, Viṣṇu and Indra). Then performing nyāsa of the Fire-god's six aṅgas on his own body, he worships these in the fire-pit. Next, he worships the nine pīṭha-śaktis (goddesses of the Fire-god's seat). He then salutes the three guṇas (sattva, etc.) and the four ātmans (antarātman, etc.). Above them he envisages the triangle which is the symbol of the universal source. In that triangle he envisages the Goddess Vāgīśvarī in sexual union with Vāgīśvara. Then he places the sacred fire in the pit, conceiving it to be their son. He praises the fire and requests it to rise and destroy, burn and roast everything. He recalls all the sacraments (*saṃskāra*) of this fire's lifetime up to his marriage. Then he performs the usual consecratory rites for the fire-pit, envisages the diagram representing fire and worships the Fire-god in its centre surrounded by attendant deities. After consecrating the clarified butter, he offers as oblation one spoonful for each of the Fire's seven flames conceived as tongues. Then he offers three oblations to the Fire-god. Of the seven flames, the central one is the most sacred, and the

worshipper invokes Goddess Tripurā upon it. She is then offered a brief pūjā with five items, after which the worshipper offers Her oblations (thrice, ten times or more) followed by oblations to the attendant deities. Finally he performs the *Mahāvyāhṛti*-sacrifice by offering oblations with four *vyāhṛti*-mantras (*bhūḥ, bhuvaḥ, svaḥm* and then all these three together). In *puraścaraṇa*, the number of oblations offered to the main deity is always one-tenth of the times the main mantra is repeated in *japa*.

26. After the sacrifice, *bali* (offering) of cooked food is made to the other beings (*bhūtas*). Usually Vaṭuka, Yoginīs, Kṣetrapāla (guardian of the ground), Gaṇeśa and all bhūtas (*sarva-bhūta*) are deities to whom *bali* is offered. A *maṇḍala* containing a triangle, circle and square is drawn on the right side of the main deity (but not on the platform itself where the seat of the icon is set up). The worshipper here invokes the deities (usually Vaṭuka, Yoginīs and sarva-bhūtas) and worships them with a libation of water and arghya. Then he offers them food and drink whilst uttering the appropriate mantras. These beings are regarded as being instigators of hindrances (*vighnakṛt*) and are propitiated together with the leader of the Goddess's host, Vaṭuka and the Yoginīs (the Goddess's supernatural followers). The gesture (mudrā) the worshipper makes is significant: it is the *nārāca-mudrā*, or gesture of the arrows, apparently used to intimidate the *bhūtas*.

Animal-sacrifice as bali: In the case of certain deities, such as Durgā or Kālī, and also in some other special forms of pūjā or in fulfilment of a vow, the Tantric sometimes sacrifices a living animal, fish, bird, or even human being as *bali* (see KālPur, ch. 67). Sacrificing a human being seems however to have been practised only by the most violent Tantric groups like the

Kāpālika and by criminals (cf. Bhavabhūti's *Mālatīmādhava*, act V). The most common animal chosen for sacrifice is the goat, though buffalos are also sometimes sacrificed, especially to Durgā. Animal-sacrifice is performed after the usual *bali*-offering. The sacrificial animal is ritually bathed and consecrated, then worshipped with the five *upācāras* and various mantras, including a special Gāyatrī for a *paśu* (human being). The sword used to sever its head is also consecrated and worshipped, and is envisaged as being the seat of the divine triad of Śiva, Viṣṇu and Brahmā. Then after having dedicated the animal to the Goddess, it is beheaded. The head of the animal, a little of the blood and a bit of raw meat are offered in a metal bowl to the Goddess Durgā, or to Goddess Kauśikī. Then blood and raw meat are offered to Vaṭuka at the south-west corner, to the Yoginīs at the north-west corner, to Kṣetrapāla at the north-east corner, and to Gaṇeśa at the south-east corner (PKS, pp. 516-521).

An animal-sacrifice never figures in private daily pūjā, but only in *naimittika-pūjā*, except in big temples like the Kālī Temple in Calcutta where animal-sacrifice is performed in daily pūjā. Again, it is more common in the worship of Kālī than of Tripurā. Kālī is sometimes offered the blood of a freshly killed animal, or of one's own body (see KālPur, 67, 40 and Kālī Tantra ch. 3).

27. The worshipper now circumambulates around the deity and prostrates himself in complete surrender.

28. *Japa* is one of the most important elements of Tantric ritual. It is in fact part of the meditation known as Tantra-yoga, or Mantra-yoga.[52] The Tantric concentrates on the Goddess in two ways, in ritual pūjā he concentrates chiefly on a visual representation of the Goddess, on Her iconographic or linear (*yantra*) form or some symbolic representation, whereas in japa, Her mantra — as one of Her manifestation — is the

most important element. The only concrete object needed to cary out this ritual repetition of the mantra is the rosary, which is very carefully chosen and consecrated. It is concealed from all eyes and carefully guarded from possible contamination. The beads can be made of various substances, e.g. seeds of certain fruits, gems, crystal, special types of wood or bone. Rosaries contain fifty or a hundred beads, with an extra bead called *meru* to mark the centre. After each round, on reaching the meru, one must not cross over it, but must turn back and retrace the order of the beads. This means that instead of turning the rosary circularwise it is moved forwards and backwards.

The consecration of the mantra is equally elaborate. First, the Tantric offers a handful of flowers to the Goddess whilst uttering the usual mantra of offering. Secondly, he performs a brief *prāṇāyāma*. Thirdly, he performs nyāsa of the different elements of the mantra on various parts of his body, concluding with the nyāsa on his hands and on the six limbs (*ṣaḍaṅga*). Fourthly, he envisages setting up a magic enclosure safe from unwanted interference, and then meditates on the Goddess. He meditates on the rising of Śakti within himself and shows the appropriate mudrā. He then utters a series of preliminary mantras to safeguard the efficacy of the main mantra. These are Kullukā, setu, mahāsetu, nirvāṇa, Kāmeśvarī, Kāmakalā, the collective mantra of all Yoginīs belonging to all exoteric and esoteric Tantric groups, utkīlana, sañjīvinī, prāṇa (life-breath), Diīpanī and the mantra of Cāmuṇḍā (the fierce manifestation of the Goddess) to remove all hindrances.[53]

Next he briefly worships the rosary with five offerings, and follows this up with praise and a prayer for safety and spiritual guidance. Then he starts japa (repeating the mantra for the predetermined number of times). After that, he repeats the mystic syllables ascribed to the Goddess's close attendants followed by the mantras of the attendant goddesses, sometimes adding certain prayers. In concluding, he addresses the Goddess as one who conceals all mysteries, and offers Her his performance of japa, and prays for Her Grace and for his own perfection. He also utters a prayer for the rosary and, thanking it, stores it away in a hidden place. He then utters his guru's mantra with salutations, salutes his guru's guru and lastly the *parameṣṭi* guru (the first guru in the line of his tradition).

29. He terminates the worship of the Goddess by singing eulogies of Her and of other deities in Her pantheon.

30. In *kaula-pūjā,* where the five items of alcohol, etc. are compulsorily used, the worship of a young and handsome woman is included after the worship of the main deity. By means of various consecratory rites and simple meditation, she is purged of her worldly impurities and limitations and is elevated to the status of representing the Goddess Herself. The worshipper effects her transformation by means of initiation and *nyāsa.* Then every part of her glorified person is worshipped by the Tantric. After completing her toilet, he dresses her up, presents her with gifts of ornaments and money, food, drink and betel. He concentrates on giving her pleasure which culminates in sexual union (*Nityotsava,* p. 60). Ritual drinking by the worshipper with this woman, who is called his Śakti, is a very important part of this act (see SL, pp. 182-83). The Tantric offers her the first cup of alcohol together with pieces of cooked meat and fish and, after obtaining his guru's permission, lets the woman drink it while he utters a mantra and envisages the consecration of her three essential realities (*tattvas*). She may drink more if she so wishes. Then the Tantric offers her another

cup of alcohol, and addressing her as the Goddess, requests her to accept the drink with the accompanying meat and fish, and to favour him by granting him fame and the destruction of his enemies. The woman then drinks part of what is offered and returns the rest to him with the words: 'my son, I give you back the rest of the drink in my cup. I shall destroy your enemies and grant you the fulfilment of all your wishes'. He drains the cup and does not drink any more and then, when she has finished her meal and is rested, he has sexual intercourse with her.

31. Kaulas sometimes perform a collective form of worship called *cakra-pūjā.*[54] Pupils of the same guru-paramparā gather together in a closed and small circle, each accompanied by his female partner. The convener conducts the *nitya-pūjā,* including a much simpler form of *suvāsinī-pūjā* or *dūtī-pūjā* (worship of a woman) (see KT X, 102). Each member of the group performs the rite of purifying the tattvas by drinking a little alcoholic drink and eating the cooked meat and fish. If the guru of the chief worshipper (convener) or someone of similar status is present, he is invited to be the guest of honour and offered the drinks first. The rest of the pūjā follows the same pattern as in suvāsinī-pūjā, except that the convener, who is the leader of the circle (*cakra*), offers the cups to his guests who share them with their partners. Strict rules of conduct are observed within the circle; ordinary Tantrics who have not yet reached a high level of spiritual competence and have not received their final form of consecration (*pūrṇābhiṣeka*) are not allowed to get drunk and behave improperly (see KT; chapters VI and VII). The spiritual level attained by a Tantric is referred to as *ullāsa* (ecstacy). There are four stages in which after their first initiation Tantrics of the lowest grade learn the intricacies of pūjā and of yoga (the technique of

meditation). The first stage is called the beginning (*ārambha*), the second is adolescence (*taruṇa*), the third is termed youth (*yauvana*) and the fourth is maturity (*prauḍha*). These terms obviously describe the gradual development towards the mature experience of ecstacy, the realization of identity with the deity (Śakti). The last three stages describe both the degree of intensity and the duration of the ecstatic feeling after that experience. After the stage of maturity comes the post-maturity-stage (*prauḍhānta*). The next stage is that which mental limitations no longer have any hold (*unmanā*). Only Siddhas and Vīras reach these last three states and rise above all mandatory rules and protocols (see KT. VII. 2; *Nityotsava*, p. 61).

32. The ritual worship now draws towards its conclusion. The Tantric begs pardon of the Goddess for all his acts whether good or bad, and offers them all to Her. He then sprinkles water from the viśeṣārghya over those assembled as well as over himself. At the same time he begs the Goddess's pardon for any fault or misbehaviour that he may have wittingly or unwittingly committed. He then envisages the disappearance of the Goddess from the yantra back to his heart, while all attendant deities are envisaged as disappearing in Her. He mentally worships Her there in his heart, but very briefly. That is also accompanied by a suitable mudrā (*visarjana* or leave-taking), indicated by the mudrā of *saṃhāra*, or involution).

33. Concluding cautionary measures: the cups used for offering alcoholic drink to the deity and also by the Tantric themselves must be carefully protected by measures to neutralize their potency. These cups are emptied completely, turned upside down on the ground to drip dry, and are then removed, cleaned and stored in a hidden place. The ground protected by tracing a mystic syllable upon it. The flowers and other items

offered, excepting food, are removed from the place of worship on a plate and placed on the ground on the north side of the place of worship, whereupon a *vyāpaka* (general or comprehensive diagram) has been traced. The vyāpaka consists of a triangle, circle and square with a central point. Here the deity of the left-overs (Ucchiṣta Bhairava) is invoked. He (or she) is conceived as possessing a terrible form — a manifestation of Śiva or of the Goddess — who removes all bad luck. This deity is then worshipped with flowers, etc., and the contents of the aforesaid plate are offered to him with the request that he (or she) should protect the Tantric and ensure his success.

Plate 1: Śrī-cakra — the diagram of nine intersecting figures carved on black rock, the square surface of which is slightly elevated and rounded like the back of a turtle. It is mounted on a silver throne. Behind it the drinking cup dedicated to Śrī (Śrī-pātra) is filled with alcohol.

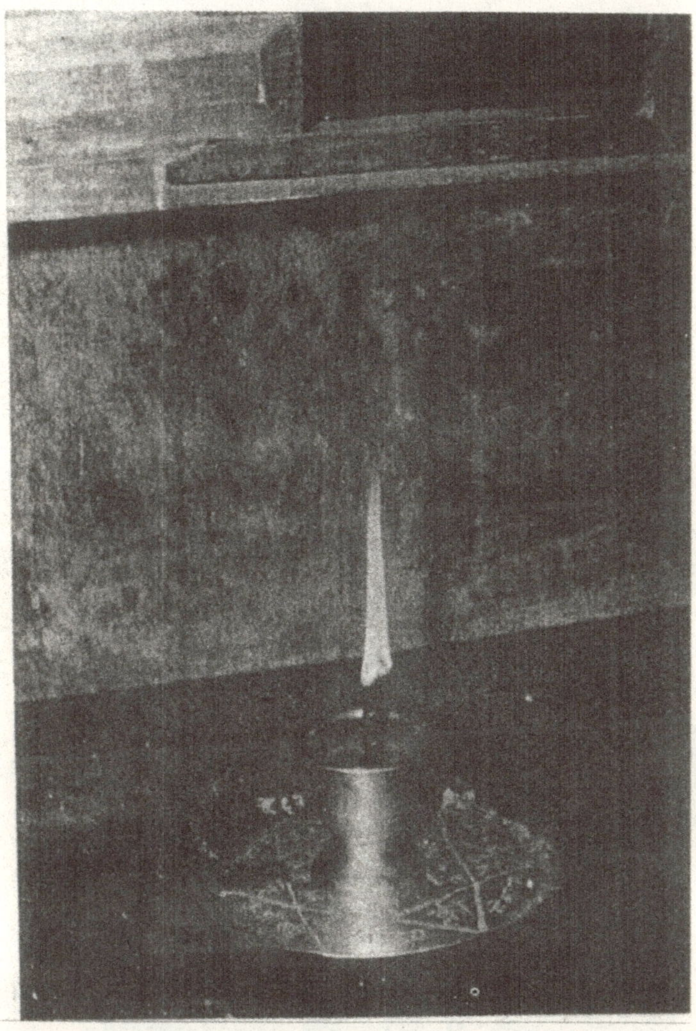

Plate 2: The special lamp is placed on a silver plate on which a diagram (yantra) is painted in vermilion. The wick is fixed in an upright position by securing its bottom end with a little dough.

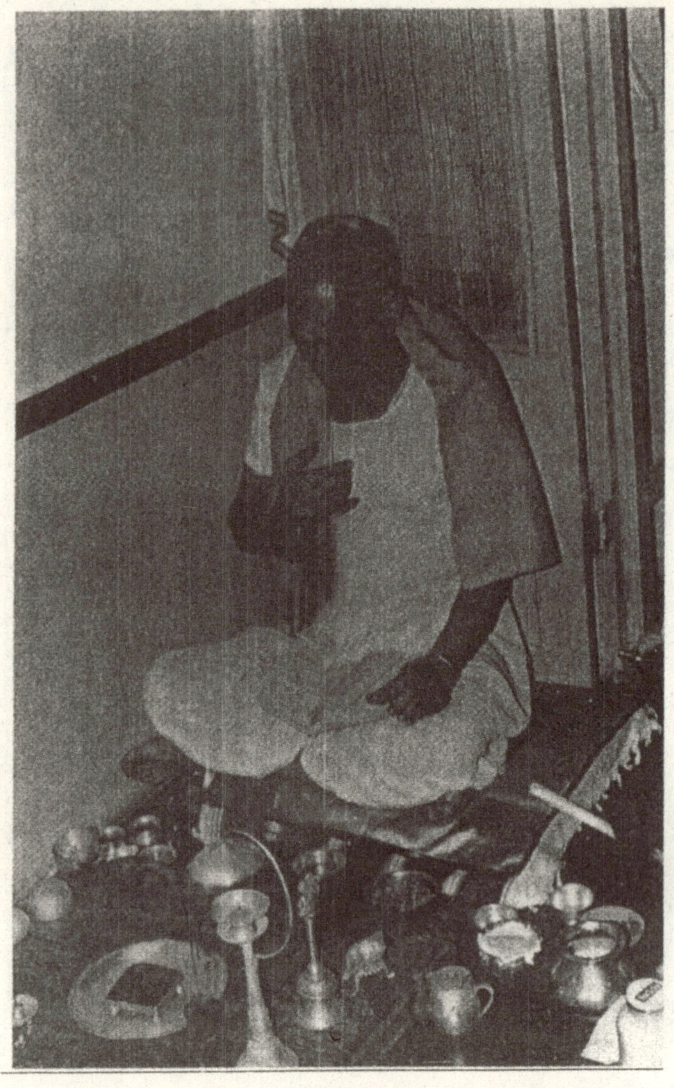

Plate 3: Bhūtaśuddhi — the worshipper is envisaging the deity's descent to his heart.

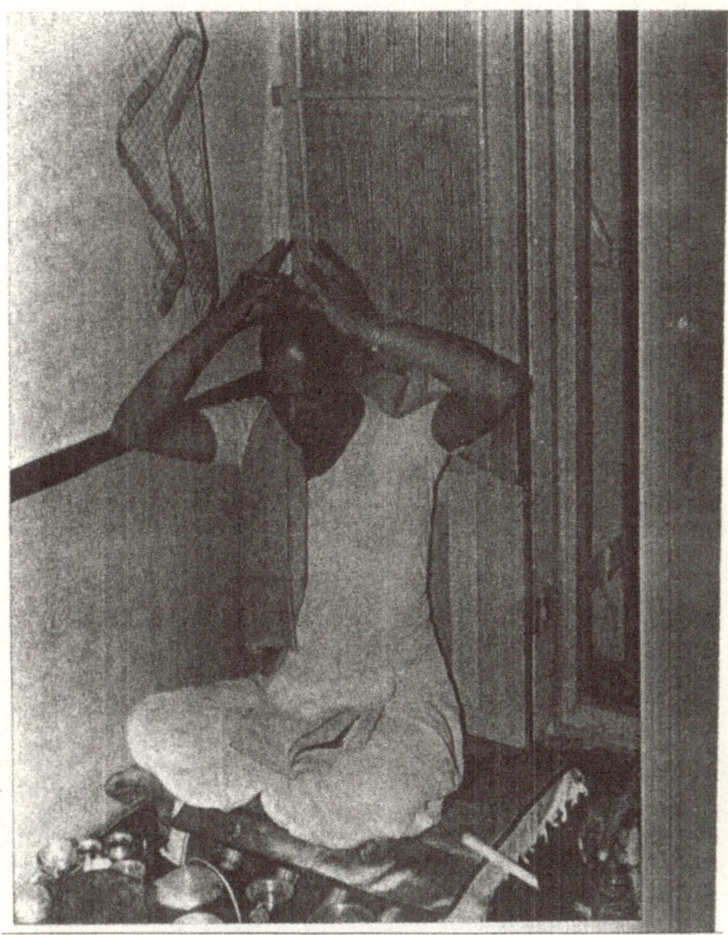

Plate 4: The worshipper is substituting the divine limbs for each part of his physical body (aṅganyāsa). Here he is accomodating the deity's head on his own.

Plate 5: The special jug for alcohol (sudhā kalaśa) is being filled with wine.

Plate 6: The wine jug is being consecrated with a mantra and meditation on the deity as the spirit infusing the alcohol (sudhādevī).

Plate 7: Before utensils are placed on the wooden pedestal, the space allotted to each is consecrated by painting a simple diagram (maṇḍala) upon it.

Plate 8: The jug of alcohol, the jug of special arghya and the cups for offering alcohol to the main deity and attendants are each placed in a row on its own ringstand on the top of a painted diagram. Śrī-pītra is in the centre.

Then the worshipper recites the hymn of well-being (*śānti-stotra*), praying for universal peace and happiness for all. Next he offers a libation to the Sun-god whilst uttering his mantra, and then prays that, by his grace, whatever fault he might have committed while performing the ritual should be condoned (this rite is known as *acchidrāgrahaṇam*). He then takes a flower, sniffs at it and smearing it with the sandalwood paste used for the yantra, utters a curse by saying that whoever he sees first or touches with his foot shall become his slave, even if that person be as powerful as Indra. After that he makes a spot on his forehead with that sandalwoodpaste and does the same to the other Tantrics attending the pūjā. Only now is the worshipper free to eat the food offered to the deity (*naivedya*) after having given some of it to brahmins and other Tantrics.[55]

34. In certain forms of Tantric *kaula-pūjā* after completing the pūjā of the Goddess and Her attendant deities, it is necessary to worship a young, unmarried girl of twelve or under (*kumārī*). The method followed is more or less the same as in *suvāsini-pūjā*, except that no alcohol is offered and sexual intercourse is forbidden (*Nityotsava* p. 27).

This ends the description of the daily worship of the Goddess which is compulsory for every Tantric. Some simplification within the individual rites is permissible. For example, one may reduce the number of attendant deities worshipped after worshipping the main Goddess. It is also possible to use less expensive items as offerings. For instance, it is not always feasible for a poor Tantric to offer alcoholic drink, meat and fish every day, and so substitutes are allowed (e.g. milk instead of alcohol, radish for fish and ginger for meat).

Naimittika-Pūjā

Besides daily worship, a Tantric performs a special pūjā on five particular nights in every month (counted from one new moon to the next). These are the eighth and fourteenth nights of the dark fortnight, the new- and full-moon nights, and the last night of the month (KT X.79).[56] These special pūjās are called naimittika-pūjā and are always performed during the night. The rites of *nyāsa*, internal worship and *japa* are considerably elaborated and the items offered are increased in number and quantity. Otherwise the pattern remains the same. There are also certain occasions in each year that are set aside for special worship. *Damanaka* is an important form of worship performed on the fourteenth night of the bright fortnight of the month of Caitra (spring).[57] That evening the Tantric goes to a garden and cuts a length of the damanaka creeper (artemisia indica). This is then cleaned, placed in a basket, consecrated and worshipped with five *upacāras*. Then, covering it with a piece of fine cloth and placing it in the corner of a temple, he keeps vigil over it throughout that night. This rite is known as *adhivāsa*. Next day, after his daily worship, he performs a special pūjā to the deities in the same manner. He then performs the fire-sacrifice three times in a more elaborate form than usual.

Another special pūjā that is widely regarded as important is *pavitrāropaṇa*. This special worship of the Goddess, observed on the full-moon night in the month of Śrāvaṇa (the rainy season), is an expiatory rite involving the ceremonial offering of a necklace made of thread[58] to the main deity and all Her attendants. This rite is performed to redeem all the accumulated shortcomings of the worshipper on account of mistakes and any other faults on his part during the observance of all the pūjās performed during the past year. The *pavitra* (thread) offered has a certain number of knots in it, each of which is allotted to a particular deity. There are various methods for determining the exact length of the thread, which is made of several strands twined together. It should be noted, however, that this rite is observed by all Hindu sects and is not confined to Tantrics alone.

There are also a few other important dates[59] for observing special pūjās. Besides these, the birthday of the Tantric's guru also counts as one of these special occasions.

Expiatory rites and rites performed on the death of a Tantric (*śrāddha*) also fall within the classification of naimittika-pūjā. The former consists mainly of pūjā and japa of a mantra for a fixed number of times. In the Tantric form of death-rites, the corpse should be specially consecrated with nyāsa, etc. by a Tantric of the same school (*sampradāya*), who then performs the pūjā of the deity and japa of Her mantra for the required number of times before the body is cremated. In case of delay in finding a suitable Tantric, the cremation takes place nevertheless, but within three days the Tantric rite is performed on a tiny replica of the corpse made of grass.[60]

Kāmya-pūjā

The third category of pūjā is known as kāmya-pūjā. These rites are performed in order to achieve a particular aim, or to fulfil a special desire. They are classified in six groups according to the nature of their purpose. However, various texts classify these groups differently. The ŚST names three alternative groups; the TT presents another list; the YogT and the ŚT (23,122f) enumerate śānti, vaśya (subjugation), stambhana (making inert), vidveṣaṇa (generating enmity), uccāṭana (displacement) and māraṇa (causing death).

Śānti-rites are observed to cure disease, to remove bad luck due to an adverse astrological situation, and to thwart bad influences caused by the ritual practices of others. This types of pūjā is performed for either the Tantric's own safety, or on behalf of somebody else who seeks his occult help.

The other types are grouped collectively as *abhicāra* (or *krūra* karma) which may be translated as black magic.

Generally speaking kāmya-pūjā tends to be regarded as infamous, since its purpose is always worldly and has nothing to do with spiritual perfection. Yet the magical aspect of this form of pūjā and faith in its efficacy have a wide appeal for many who are not even Tantrics. As a matter of fact Tantrics, who are usually married men with families, often derive their income from performing the first type of *kāmya-pūjā* on behalf of other people.

The abhicāra-rites, on the other hand, are usually condemned. In fact Tantrics often suffer from public mistrust and fear stemming from the belief that they can cause harm. Tantra texts always advocate extreme caution in practising abhicāra. First of all, only Tantrics who have reached a very high spiritual level are allowed to practise these rites. This is to ensure that the public can rely on the discretion and disinterestedness of such men. It is also prohibited to practise abhicāra for personal gain of such men. It is also prohibited to practise against those who are innocent and harmless. The only permissible occasions for resorting to abhicāra are in cases of emergency, sudden attack, invasion, or to prevent a crime, etc. Even so, the TT (13,99-100) stipulates that a Tantric who performs māraṇa must follow this up with an expiatory rite that involves the penalty of giving away money or property and must, at the same time, undergo acts of penance and perform a vast number of japas. Nevertheless, these cautions do not prevent Tantrics from performing these rites to demonstrate their supernatural power (e.g. NT 20,53-55). Ordinary people both respect and shun them through fear lest, in anger, they cause harm.

The mode of performing these ritual pūjās does not significantly vary from that of daily worship. The main features are a) the yantra, b) the mantra, c) the deity. Each type of such a pūjā has its special yantra — a geometrical figure of a particular type drawn with special ingredients on a special surface. Inside this complex diagram, the special mantra earmarked for the act is written in a complicated pattern interspersed with various mystic syllables, amongst which the name of the beneficiary or of the victim is also written. Sometimes an effigy may be used (see ŚT. 19, 72-73 and 22, 123 ff.), or a part of the victim's body, e.g. a hair or nail. The mantra is always a very special and long one, expressing the purpose most effectively. The japa of this mantra is the most important factor of the ritual. In *abhicāra* rituals the deities are different from those in ordinary pūjās and often have dangerous characteristics (see ŚT 13, 126. Rati, Vāṇī, Ramā, Jyeṣṭhā, Durgā and Kālī are said to be the deities for śānti, vaśya, stambhana, vidveṣaṇa, uccāṭana and māraṇa respectively). At the beginning of each ritual the special deity is worshipped in the usual manner described under daily worship. Kārtavīrya, Nṛsiṃha, etc. are also important deities in this context. But any manifestation of the main deity can be substituted for an abhicāra-deity and, generally speaking, the fire-sacrifice with special offerings figures rather prominently in kāmya-pūjā.

The main feature is, of course, japa. Every ritual for a special purpose has its own stipulated number of repetitions of the mantra, which is usually not less than a hundred thousand times, or even more. The wearing of a talisman consisting of a mantra specially inscribed on a particular surface is not uncommon. For curing a disease or other ailment, or for purposes of subjugation, eating or drinking certain items that were offered in the ritual is often recommended.

In some forms of kāmya-pūjā it is customary to burn one or more lamps[61] continuously until the required number of japas has been completed. Should the lamp or lamps go out before then, the Tantric regards it as an indication of failure. Many other such obvious magical elements feature in kāmya-pūjā. If however the required ingredients are collected faithfully and correctly, the steps of the ritual followed without error, the mantras are correctly uttered and repeated the required number of times, and no sacrilege or impurity has crept into the performance — then the desired result should follow automatically.

But the result depends crucially on the capacity of the worshipper. Not just anybody can perform these rites. In the first place, only he who has undergone the final initiation is qualified to do so. Secondly, the performer should moreover have attained perfection (*siddhi*) in the worship of his own main mantra (*mūla-mantra*). That means that he must first successfully bring his *puraścaraṇa* ritual to an end, which makes it necessary to say a few words here about that ritual. The word *puraścarnṇa* means preliminary acts. After his final initiation, a Tantric is entitled to start practising the preliminary rites that will lead to his perfection in the mantra given to him as his main mantra.

There are five parts to puraścaraṇa: daily worship of the mantra and of the deity; daily performance of homa (fire-sacrifice); japa; offering the libation; and feeding brahmins (see KT 15.7-8). The Tantric takes a vow to perform a certain number of japas of mantra until he experiences perfect identity with his mantra and its deity. He regularly performs his spiritual duties of pūjā etc. and continues practising japa and yoga — the two main elements of Tantric yoga. He observes purity and austerity in his food and other basic daily needs. A strictly regulated and ethical mode of life is followed. Usually all this takes considerable time, depending on his personal capacity and spiritual acumen. Once this primary training comes to an end the Tantric has attained perfection in his mūla-mantra, he has completely mastered the technique of yoga.

In *kāmya-pūjā* the rites of homa, japa, etc. form part of the prescribed puraścaraṇa ritual for worship of the mantra and its deity. When this has been brought to a successful end, the worshipper becomes identified with the power of the divine and is empowered to use the mantra for the relevant act. He can then persuade that divine power to fulfil whatever he desires.

Use of a Corpse for Pūjā (Śava-sādhanā)

One of the extremely daring ways of performing *kāmya-pūjā* is to use a corpse as seat for the Tantric and, at the same time, as representing the deity. This rite is performed in a very lonely place, preferably near a cremation-ground. The corpse is chosen with great care and discretion. In certain cases, a child's corpse is preferable to any other. Only a *vīra*-type of Tantric is entitled to perform this difficult rite. He needs an assistant to help him in his sādhanā. This assistant is called *uttarasādhaka* and should be as spiritually advanced as the performer himself. This is a secret rite and the secrecy should be strictly observed. The corpse, which should be fresh, is bathed and consecrated in the usual manner with mantras, mudrās and nyāsa. The worshipper and his helper have also bathed in the same way. An important feature of this rite is that the participants must have had a good meal before starting pūjā. The usual steps of pūjā are observed with special emphasis on the protective rites. Śava-sādhanā is no rite for the timid to undertake, as the performers tend to have hallucinations of a most terrifying nature. By means of nyāsa, etc. the torso of the corpse is transmuted into the cosmic seat of the Goddess. As identified with Her, the worshipper sits upon it. Its face is conceived to be the deity's face and is worshipped as such. The Tantric pours alcoholic drinks into the corpse's mouth and feeds it with cooked meat. The uttarasādhaka sits a short distance away at the imaginary gate of the sacred enclosure. The hair of the corpse is tied into a topknot and sixteen upacāras are offered to the Goddess, who is envisaged as entering the corpse to enliven it. The Tantric then duly starts his japa (repetition of his mantra for the required number of times). The corpse is expected to start moving and then gradually to come to life, the divine life and ego having descended into it. The Tantric binds the deity, who speaks through the voice of the corpse, with a promise to grant him Her favour, and he then prays for fulfilment of his special desire. At the end of the pūjā he disposes of all the remaining ingredients of the pūjā and of the corpse itself, either in the water of a swiftly flowing river, or buries them in the ground. The Tantric must keep this act a secret for at least three to nine days, even though he must feed some brahmins after performing this pūjā (see KAN, Uttara 14). For achieving a particular end specified by the nature of the Kāmyakarma utilized, the worshipper prepares a yantra containing special signs and the mantra of the specific kāmyakarma is written down on that yantra in a highly technical manner (NT 18, 10-12).

NOTES

1 The term pūjā is briefly but thoroughly handled by Diehl, *Instrument and Purpose*, pp. 66-67 in a footnote.

2 See ṚV III, 62, 10.

3 E.g. the Tārā Gāyatrī: *aiṃ bhagavaty ekajaṭe vidmahe vikaṭadaṃṣṭre dhīmahi tannatāre pracodayāt.*

3a i.e. the normative one.

4 Although this is an experience, the word 'receive' is used because Tantrics regard this experience as a divine gift coming down (as it were from heaven): *śaktipāta.*

5 We have based our descriptions of pūjā mainly on this text with its offshoot the *Nityotsava,* where necessary supplemented by other texts.

6 Technically this is known as *Śaktipāta* (descent of divine power). It is said to come to the Tantric as a result of God's compassion

and ardour. This is envisaged as a projection of divine love manifest.

7 See ŚT p. 127 with Rāghavabhaṭṭa's comm. Amongst Tantrics there are somewhat divergent views about the form and number of these baths.

8 BrS, pp. 116-123.

9 Ibid.

10 Often in Tantric circle *yantra, mantra* and *devatā* are homologized, and the one is incomplete without the others; ŚT pp. 154f.

11 There are six limbs (aṅga), viz. hṛd (heart), śiras (head), śikhā (topknot),,netra (eyes), astra (weapon) and kavaca (armour or torso). Note that the last one differs from the last mentioned in the list given on p. 92.

12 See also KT, VI, 17.

13 *Saḍaṅganyāsa* starting with *karanyāsa, vyāpaka nyāsa, ṣoḍhānyāsa, aṇimā etc. siddhinyāsa* and *mūladevīyāsa.* These are most important (YHT III, 58-62).

14 The sixfold nyāsa (*ṣoḍhā-nyāsa*) of Gaṇeśa, *graha* (planets), *nakṣatra* (stars), Yoginī, *rāsi* (constellations) and *pīṭha,* and the great sixfold *nyāsa* of *prapañca* (world), *bhuvana* (universe), *mūrti, mantra, devatā,* and *mātṛkā* are considered important in the worship of Śrī. *Ṣoḍhā-nyāsa* is used for the worship of *śrī-yantra* (YHT III-8ff). The great ṣoḍhā-nyāsa is mainly used in the worship of Ardhanārīśvara.

15. It should be noted that there are diverse method of mantraśuddhi of which only one is mentioned here.

16 See YHT III, 170 and ŚT p. 132 with the commentary on the importance of *kuladīpa.*

17 This must be a rather late innovation and is not widely practised (MT. V. 82-88).

18 See plate 1.

19 Comm. on BhāvUp., p. 1ff.

20 See for instance: D.C. Sircar, *Text and Translation: Tantrasāradhṛta dhyānamālā.* JAIH, Vol. VI, parts 1-2, 1972-73, Calcutta, pp. 186-278.

21 The parts are the head, topknot, heart, eyes, weapon and armour, collectively envisaged as a separate deity called Ṣaḍaṅgayuvatī.

22 Āvaraṇa devatās surround the main deity in concentric circles.

23 Ritual concerning the consumption of food. Bodewitz, *Jaim Br*, pp. 254-256 and appendix.

24 Items 30, 31 and 34 are not parts of a general Tantric nitya pūjā.

25 Specially consecrated water with scents etc. Throughout the pūjā only this water is used.

26 Five products from a cow: milk, curd, clarified butter, urine and dung.

27 Saccharum Cylindrilum.

28 Certain other mantras are also uttered in which the worshipper peremptorily orders all evil spirits and obstructive elements to clear off at Śiva's command.

29 This praises the lines used in geometrical figures.

30 See plate 1.

31 Each deity's yantra is named after that particular deity.

32 Milk, curd, butter, honey and sugar.

33 The self of the goddess, *Śrī-cakra,* all mantras and the *siddḥa.*

34 See plate 4.

35 Gaṇeśa, the planets, stars, yoginī, constellations and holy places; these six go to make up a group that represents the main domain of the goddess.

36 Nyāsa of the nine geometrical figures of the Śrī-cakra.

37 These four ātmans are the various states of the self. Ātman is Brahman, antarātman is the enjoying jīva, the jīva in essence is paramātman, while jñānātman is Brahman as undifferentiated from jiva, Bhaskarāya's commentary Setubandha on YHT I, 12.

38 These are sarvasaṅkṣobhinī, sarvavidrāvinī, sarvākarṣaṇī, sarvavaśaṃkarī, sarvānandanī, sarvamahāṅkuśā, khecarī, bīja, yoni, trikhaṇḍā.

39 Note that only followers of Śrī-kula use the special arghya. Other sampradāyas do not always use it. Kālī-worshippers of certain vāmācāra (schools) add to the water a piece of cloth soaked in menstrual flow, and sometimes also a little semen.

40 Kaula Tantrics always follow the most orthodox form of esoteric rites involving the practice of drinking alcohol, eating meat and fish, and having sexual intercourse with a chosen partner during pūjā. The partner is sublimated to the position of the goddess and is called Śakti. She is initiated in the sect and, at the time of pūjā, is consecrated and worshipped. Her face, breasts and sex organ are specially revered. The tantric exerts himself to please her with food, drink and gifts. e.g. KT V, 85-7; ibid. ix, 49-58; ibid. x, 5; SL, Lakṣmīdhara's comm. pp. 182-3.

41 Opinions vary about this item. It seems that any tasty snack is generally acceptable as the fourth item.

42 See plates 5 and 6.

43 A mixture of curd, milk, clarified butter and honey.

44 These cups — starting with the main jug of wine — are arranged in a row from the left to the right of the sādhaka. See plates 7 and 8.

45 Nityotsava, p. 41.

46 These vary with each goddess. For Tripurā they are: Icchā Jñāna, Kriyā, Kāminī, Kāmadā, Rati, Ratipriyā and Nandā.

47 These are fixed steps in the ritual, common to all forms of worship. They are called *āvāhana, sthāpana, sannirodhana* and *sammukhīkarṇa.* See Rāghavabhaṭṭa's commentary on ŚT, p. 255.

48 Collectively these six parts and their respective śaktis are referred to as *ṣaḍaṅgayuvatī,* or *ṣāḍāṅgī* (Nityotsava p. 44).

49 One list of sixteen upācāras is given by the Mahānirvāṇa Tantra VI. 78 and 79. These are: water to wash feet, arghya, water to wash face and mouth, madhuparka, requisites for the bath, dress, ornaments, scents and unguent, flowers, incense, lamp, food, a second offering of water for washing face and mouth, amṛta and betel, tarpaṇa and salute.

50 See Bodewitz, JaminBr, pp. 243-245; 253-256; 310-314 and apendix.

51 Tāmbūla, a preparation of betel leaf (*pān*), areca nut, lime and other herbs, etc.

52 See KT XV, 15. 'when tired of performing japa one should perform dhyāna, when tired of dhyāna one should practice japa'.

53 See PrT pp. 221-225.

54 This is not a part of nityapūjā but a Kaula Tantric performs it often and so it is enumerated here for convenience.

55 In the case of cakra-pūjā, the sexual acts take place only after all rites have been completed and the food has been eaten.

56 It is very important for a Tantric to have good knowledge of astrology. In fact many Tantrics earn a living from fees obtained for preparing horoscopes and calculating auspicious occasions for performing sacraments for ordinary people.

57 This rite is performed in order to crush enemies in general and to avert misfortune caused by adverse constellations (*graha*).

58 Different varieties of thread can be used; for instance, gold or silver thread, silk, grass-fibre, cotton, etc. can all serve the purpose.

59 In the sense of lunar junctures.

60 Information received from Prof. V.N. Khiste.

61 See plate 2.

4. The Worship of Kālī According to the *Ṭoḍala Tantra*

To many Hindu Bengalis, Kālī is the most important divinity. Identified with the great Goddess, Devī Bhagavatī, she subsumes all other goddesses. She is held to be equal in status to Durgā and their annual festivals, which occur close to each other, are celebrated with the greatest grandeur: feasts are held, gifts are exchanged, and new clothes are worn in honour of the Goddess. Both Durgā and Kālī, facets of the same supreme Goddess, are fierce and aggressive. The Goddess is the embodiment of the divine power, potency, and dynamism. After the great dissolution of the worlds she regenerates the creation and sustains it until the time arrives when she must withdraw it into herself. She possesses both negative and positive elements in her divine personality. She is the nurturing mother of created beings as well as the sovereign cosmic ruler who maintains cosmic law and order through her invincible power and irresistible energy. She punishes the evil and rewards the righteous. Above all, she protects all her creatures and is especially kind and sweet to her loyal devotees, like an indulgent mother to her devoted children.

The cult of Kālī has a long history of development in which her character has undergone many changes. In an essay on "Śaivism and the Tantric Tradition", Alexis Sanderson explains that in the ninth and tenth centuries C.E., the Kashmiri Tantric exegetes classified and systematized Tantric texts according to the various cults, mainly of goddesses and fearsome gods. The main emphasis was on specific mantras and esoteric practices associated with those mantras, one of which is called the Seat of Awareness (*vidyā-pīṭha*). The texts dealing with the most esoteric Kālī cults are associated with the vidyā-pīṭha. The practices they prescribe include the so-called left-hand tradition (*vāma-mārga*), antinomian practices that involve alcohol, blood, and sex; these came to be called Kaula practices. The name *vidyā* here denotes esoteric mantras that are considered embodiments of the supreme knowledge or awareness that is indeed Kālī. Here she is called Kālī not because of her dark complexion but because she absorbs and transcends Time (*kāla*), and is thus the eternal transcendent reality (Kālasaṃkarṣiṇī). Kālī thus became the supreme godhead to this cult transcending even Śiva. This Kālī cult developed through various streams and survived in the cult of Guhyakālī, worshipped in Nepal as Guhyeśvarī and in Mithila (Bihar) even today (Sanderson 1990: 138-54). At the same period in Kashmir, there grew up a strong parallel Tantric cult known as the cult of the three goddesses, the Trika. They are Parā, transcendent; Parāparā; transcendent as well as material; and Aparā, material. The second and the third are related to the cosmic process of creation; the second is the state in which the transcendent unity of reality is disturbed and the goddess experiences the stir of polarized existence within herself, which heralds the next moment in the cosmic evolution of diverse creation.

As Sanderson points out, these two cults affected one another. "The cult of the three goddesses and that of Kālī were not sealed off from each other in the manner of rival sects. The *Jayadrathayāmala* shows that the devotees of Kālī had developed their own versions of the cult of the three goddesses. The Trika in its turn assimilated these and other new and more esoteric treatments from the left. Consequently we find a later Trika in which Kālasaṃkarṣiṇī has been introduced to be worshipped above the three goddesses of the trident" (Sanderson 1990: 146). This tendency continued throughout the history of the Kālī cult and is clearly noticeable in the *Śakti-saṃgama Tantra* (1.1.28-47), in which the three goddesses of the vidyās—Kālī, Tārā, and Chinnā, that is, Chinnamastā—form a kind of triad. Indeed, Sanderson has described how the adherents of the Kālī cult interpreted the name Kālī. "So, as Abhinavagupta tells us in his *Tantrāloka,* the autonomous consciousness which is the Absolute is called Kālī (i) because it throws, in the sense that it projects the universe, causing to appear as though beyond it ...; (ii) because through it the projection returns to ('goes to') its identity as cognition ...; (iii) because it knows the projected, in the sense that it represents it as identical with its own identity...; (iv) because it enumerates the projection, in the sense that it distinguishes each element from all the others within its own unity ...; and (v) because it sounds, in the sense that when it has dissolved the projection it continues as the resonance of internal self-awareness" (Sanderson 1990: 164).

In the Mahāvidyā cult, the primary goddess-emanations from Kālī the supreme and absolute consciousness form a horizontal triad at the cosmic differentiated level, that is Mahāmāyā, Sundarī and Bhairavī, to replace the Puranic triad of Brahmā, Viṣṇu, and Rudra/Śiva (Brown 1974; 118-80). Although Brahmā and so on were not totally removed from their cosmic functions, they moved to a subservient position.

The *Ṭoḍala Tantra,* translated below, was probably composed relatively late, in the fourteenth century C.E. It is a small Tantra that contains ten chapters (*paṭalas*) with 398 verses. It became very popular in Bengal, especially in the early modern period, and has been quoted as a scriptural authority in many Bengali priestly handbooks such as the *Purohita-darpaṇa,* on the ritual worship of Dakṣiṇā Kālī, also called Ādyā Kālī. Our text is mainly interested in the ritual worship of Kālī and other Mahāvidyās. It mentions all the Mahāvidyās, who are here more than ten in number, and also mentions their companions, who are different manifestations of Śiva. It succinctly gives all the ritual sequences needed for the worship of the first two Mahāvidyās, including the esoteric formulas (*mantras*) and the accompanying process of meditation (see Gupta 1977: 125-57). It also records a complete program of Śiva worship with mantras and so on, which seems to be the same for every manifestation. According to it, it is imperative to worship Śiva immediately after worshipping the relevant Mahāvidyā.

In the traditional way, the text is presented as a dialogue between Śiva and his divine spouse Pārvatī, who is the pupil and the interlocutor, whereas Śiva is the teacher of the sacred science (*śāstra*). Very little theological or ontological discussion is found in the text, though often it refers to the ultimacy of Kālī. The text gives important information about the esoteric meaning of the mantras of the first three Mahāvidyās and the practice of Tantric yoga; the esoteric kuṇḍalinī-yoga receives special treatment. Inheriting the Krama tradition of monistic power-theism (*śakti-advaya*), the *Toḍala Tantra* asserts that esoteric yoga is higher than esoteric rituals, as the latter involve differentiated awareness whereas yoga does not. This is elaborated by means of a description of kuṇḍalinī-yoga, giving a detailed parallel of the microcosm with the macrocosm. Kuṇḍalinī-yoga leads to release from saṃsāra as the yogin becomes one with the Goddess, having severed the veil of delusion, māyā, by means of vidyā. In connection with esoteric yoga practice, our text gives three important yogic postures: the yoni mudrā, svalpa yoni mudrā, and kākīcañcu mudrā. All are postures for practicing kuṇḍalinī yoga, where controlling the flow of air in the body by blocking all natural outlets of air is of the highest importance. Although it presents mantras and rituals concerning the Mahāvidyās, the treatment is so brief that the text needs to be supplemented by other handbooks, such as the *Tantrasāra* of Kṛṣṇānanda or *Kaulāvalīnirṇaya* of Jñānānandagiri (see Goudriaan and Gupta 1981: 139, 144).

In order to understand the theological background of our text, we have to turn to other scriptural sources from the medieval period (roughly 1200 to 1800 C.E.) They mainly belong to eastern India, and some may be from Bengal. By this time the Tārā-Ugratārā-Ekajaṭā cult of the Buddhist Tantric tradition merged into the Kālī and other Mahāvidyā cults presented in the *Toḍala Tantra.* To understand the history and nature of Kālī, the supreme Goddess, in eastern India in the medieval period (roughly 1200 C.E. to 1800 C.E.), three texts can be considered the most important. One is the *Śakti-saṃgama Tantra* (*ŚsT*), a large compendium of the rituals and mantras and other esoteric practices associated with Kālī and her other manifestations. This text, as well as the *Tantra-sāra* and the *Devīmāhātmya* (*DM*), which constitutes the final section of the *Mārkaṇḍeya Purāṇa,* have shaped the Tantric philosophy, theology, and practice of the Kālī cult in Bengal. There the *Devīmāhātmya* is simply called *Caṇḍī* (the fierce lady), and devout Tantrics recite it daily. In fact Kālī's iconography, as followed by the traditional image makers, shows traces of the description of the goddess Kālī in that text.

The *Devīmāhātmya* represents Kālī as a minor emanation of the Goddess, a demonic figure, fearsome and grotesque. Having emanated from the angry third eye of the supreme Goddess to help the Goddess in her battle against the demon host of Śumbha and Niśumbha, she was employed to lick up every drop of blood of Raktabījā, the demon general. Raktabīja's peculiarity was that even a drop of his blood shed on the earth produced countless clones. Kālī's lolling tongue symbolizes this blood-licking task. Her demonic nature is also symbolized by her fangs and by the countless severed heads and limbs dripping blood that cover her body. She is intoxicated by drinking blood, and in her frenzy she laughs loudly, baring her upper teeth.

The *Kālikā Purāṇa* (*KP*), on the other hand, describes Kālī as possessing a soothing dark complexion, as perfectly beautiful, riding a lion, four-armed, holding a sword and blue lotuses, her hair unrestrained, body firm and youthful

(*KP* 5. 52). A third view is found in such Tantric texts as the *Śakti-saṃgama Tantra,* where Kālī, naked, as seated on the supine body of *Śiva,* immersed in the pleasure of reverse sexual intercourse with him. These three separate views of the supreme goddess Kālī have influenced her modern iconography, although the third variety, the goddess seated on the inert body of Śiva, is rarely used outside esoteric worship. In the *Śakti-saṃgama Tantra,* though, we get two quite different descriptions of Kālī. In her supreme state, Kālī is, as Sanderson describes, just the light of pure consciousness, but in the creating state she is depicted in a form more awe-inspiring than charming.

The supreme Goddess is forever associated with the supreme god Śiva, the pair forming an indivisible unit. But in this late tradition, Kālī often supersedes Śiva and acts independently to initiate creation. Although creation is based on her aspect as Māyā, this often appears to be a biological activity. This point is emphasized in the iconography of Kālī and Tārā, both of whom appear to be having coitus with Śiva, who is lying like a corpse. Śiva's representation as a corpse makes it clear creation belongs to the Goddess. Therefore Śiva is not a corpse but is only depicted as one. The *Ṭoḍala Tantra* emphasizes this point. Kālī's association with Viṣṇu as Viṣṇu-māyā is also underscored in this tradition. In order to enhance the supremacy of the Goddess, the *Devīmāhātmya* took over the early Vaiṣṇava myth of the creation of the earth from the marrow and fat of two demons called Madhu and Kaiṭabha and replaced Viṣṇu with Devī as the slayer of the demons. The *Kālikā Purāṇa,* in fact, calls the cult of the supreme Goddess, Vaiṣṇavī Tantra, and the main mantra, which is a salutation to the supreme deity with some mystical syllables added, indeed addresses that deity: *Oṃ hrīṃ śrīṃ vaiṣṇavyai namaḥ.* This has been noted by Brown: "Thus does the Devī Bhagavatī, although eternal, manifest herself again and again for the protection of the world, O King"

(*Devīmāhātmya* 12.36), clearly echoing the famous description of Viṣṇu/Kṛṣṇa's avatāras in the fourth chapter of the *Bhagavad Gītā* (Brown 1990: 133-34). Both the *Ṭoḍala Tantra* and *Śakti-saṃgama Tantra* make some sort of equation between the ten avatāras of Viṣṇu and the ten great *vidyā* emanations of the Goddess. Her closeness to Viṣṇu/Kṛṣṇa is often mythicized when she is cast as Viṣṇu's sister or the embodiment of Viṣṇu's māyā. In late tradition the Goddess superseded all three cosmic gods—Brahmā, Viṣṇu, and Rudra.

The *Śakti-saṃgama Tantra* describes the creative activity of the goddess Kālī as follows: Dakṣiṇā (compassionate) Kālī, the primeval goddess, was dancing the dance of cosmic dissolution surrounded by howling jackals and other carrion-devouring beasts. The destroyed universe lay at her feet like a heap of corpses. Kālī is pure consciousness, totally transcendent, the unique Being. She subsumes both Śiva and the divine power, Śakti. At a certain primordial moment, Kālī suddenly saw inside herself her own mirror image or shadow, which is indeed delusion, Māyā. In that Māyā, Kālī created the imagined form of Śiva, who became the primeval god and Kālī's spouse. Kālī then created empty space, and the chaos of the destroyed universe disappeared as she engaged in sexual intercourse with Śiva, taking the reverse position and the active role. After a long coitus, Kālī produced one fetus, which developed into a perfectly beautiful girl whom Kālī called Sundarī, the beautiful lady. Her beauty completely deluded Śiva, who wanted to put into words his agitation and longing. Śiva's longing and desire for self-expression produced Speech, which from its central unity developed into the system of sounds, letters, and language, and became all-pervasive. Śiva, however, on creating Speech, first addressed the goddess Sundarī as his heart's desire, the loveliest in the three worlds, the exquisite sovereign deity and the ocean of nectarlike compassion. Next Śiva addressed Kālī as most terrifying, howling like a jackal, cruel-fanged and fearfully ugly, with lolling tongue and frightening roar. As Śiva uttered these two sentences addressing the two goddesses, Kālī, as if offended, suddenly disappeared, leaving Śiva with Sundarī, the product of delusion, to get on with the task of creation. Kālī, who is transcendent and the essence of the creation, transformed herself into the abstract cosmic dynamic power. But Śiva became utterly despondent and confused without Kālī; therefore the compassionate Kālī removed Śiva's confusion and infused him with unimpeded cognitive knowledge and desire to procreate. Moreover, in order to infuse him with power she taught Śiva the method of Tantric kuṇḍalinī yoga and gave him as his partner the beautiful goddess who is indeed the mother of the universe, Ambikā, the cosmic Creatrix (*ŚsT* 1. 1.22-45).

This myth neatly puts forward the idea that the transcendent supreme divinity is female; that she is the goddess Dakṣiṇā Kālī, who contains both the cosmic male and female polarity; that she is the sovereign cosmic ruler who regulates the system of creation and that the creation is based on cosmic delusion, which is her mirror image. This divine delusion, named Māyā or Mahāmāyā, is Kālī's divine capacity, which ensures that in spite of the perfect oneness of Kālī and Śiva, the latter is separated in an imaginary form by means of Kālī's delusory power. Śiva is then deluded into thinking himself to be a separate divinity from Kālī and so feels the attraction of the delusory image of Sundarī. Thus the main idea of monism, which emphasizes the unity of a single universal essence, and establishes the illusoriness of the dualistic worldview, is put forward through a creation myth. The polarized male and female cosmic divinities are results of delusion. In reality, the supreme goddess Kālī is unique and immutable, yet she is the source and foundation of all creation. Kālī, the eternally existent Reality, transcends both creation and dissolution of the creation. The appearance of her beautiful mirror image, Māyā, heralds creation as an evolutionary process, and at that point of primeval creation Kālī, the pure consciousness who exists beyond the reach of speech and phenomenal creation, disappears behind delusion and its influence—desire—and becomes the cosmic dynamic energy activating the ongoing process of creation. Śiva at the point of creation is the primordial conscious entity, Puruṣa. He possesses vidyā, omniscience, and icchā, sexual desire, to procreate; and he is called Sadāśiva who, together with Sundarī, becomes the primordial couple (*ŚsT* 1.1.103-6). In Tantric ontology, he is Śiva-tattva, the cosmic self. The evolving Śakti/Māyā, who is identical with the supreme Goddess, is known as Vidyā-tattva. Together with the individual self, Ātma-tattva, they constitute the cosmic realities who are ultimately one and same.

The nature of the supreme goddess, Mahādevī, and that of supreme delusion, Mahāmāyā, are expounded in the *Devīmāhātmya.* The Goddess is called Mahāmāyā, the great delusion when she is seen as responsible for the unsatisfactory and transient nature of this life. The real cause of this is human desire for possession and procreation, and Mahāmāyā deludes individuals by making desire their innate quality. But paradoxically the Goddess is also identified as supreme knowledge, Vidyā, which releases individuals from their bondage of desire and the consequent endless succession of lives and deaths. This is one of the many paradoxes that constitute the mystery of the Goddess's divine nature.

Another important statement in *Devīmāhātmya* identified Māyā with Prakṛti which, in the dualistic Sāṃkhya philosophy, is the primordial evolving matter. This identity was first recorded in the *Śvetāśvatara Upaniṣad* (4.9-10). Coburn (1996: 34) explains this as follows: "On the basis of such passages (*DM* 1.59 and 4.6) it seems safe to say that the *Devīmāhātmya* has shifted the focus of the Sāṃkhya school and the *Śvetāśvatara Upaniṣad* by understanding *prakṛti* not as the material shroud or possession of spirit but as itself supremely divine, as Devī herself." The *Śakti-saṃgama Tantra* (1.100) confirms this view by saying that the supreme Śakti, that is, the Goddess, is Prakṛti whereas her mirror image is the evolving power Mahāmāyā. Thus Prakṛti here refers to the supreme Goddess, who ultimately is the unique source and origin of all, there being nothing outside of her.

The *Ṭoḍala Tantra* endorses this theological tradition in its accounts of the nature of the goddess Dakṣiṇākālī and her other Vidyā emanations. Other important texts for the development of Kālī and her Mahāvidyā cult are the *Cīnācāra-krama Tantra, Mātṛkā-bheda Tantra, Gupta-sādhana Tantra, Kālikā Purāṇa, Brahma-vaivarta Purāṇa, Brahmāṇḍa Purāna* and other Tantric records of that period. The salient feature of this tradition is the total supremacy of the goddess Kālī. In the words of Brown (1990: 217-18):

> of the two genders, the feminine represents the dominant power and the authoritative will in the universe. Yet both genders must be included in the ultimate if it is truly ultimate. The masculine and feminine are aspects of the divine, transcendent reality, which goes beyond but still encompasses them. The Devī, in her supreme form as consciousness thus transcends gender, but her transcendence is not apart from her immanence. Indeed this affirmation of the oneness of transcendence and immanence constitutes the very essence of the divine mother, as presented in the Purāṇa (*Devī-bhāgavata*). And here we see what may be called "the ultimate triumph" of the goddess in our text. It is not finally, that she is infinitely superior to the male gods—though she is that, according to the myths in the *Devī-bhāgavata*—but rather that she transcends her own feminine nature as Prakṛti without denying it.

The speciality of the *Śakti-saṃgama Tantra* myth is that it neatly puts forward just this point. Prakṛti or the feminine source of the universe is Mahāmāyā, who is not Kālī but her mirror image. Kālī transcends her own evolving mirror image. In the universe of Mahāmāyā, both delusion and cognition function. In the case of Śiva, his delusion is restricted to his sexual desire for Sundarī, whereas his cognitive knowledge is otherwise untrammeled. In this sense, it is possible to find a parallel between the three goddesses Kālī, Mahāmāyā, and Sundarī and the three goddesses Parā, Parāparā and Aparā of the Trika tradition. Sundarī corresponds to the third deity of the Trika triad, that is, Aparā (ŚsT 1.1.102). The *Ṭoḍala Tantra* (1.7-8) confirms this with the statement that she is called the fivefold lady, Pañcami, because she is differentiated as the five cosmic elements.

Kālī and the Cult of the Ten Mahāvidyās

The *Ṭoḍala Tantra* describes the ritual worship of the ten sacred esoteric formulas, the Mahāvidyās. The word *vidyā* has various Tantric connotations. The great Goddess is Vidyā because she is perfect knowledge unimpeded by any differentiated or discursive cognition—cognition without any reference to anything cognized. This pure cognition brings about release. Vidyā also connotes an esoteric formula which, empowered by its Śakti deity, is capable of bestowing on its Tantric worshipper great power (*bhukti*) and eventually salvation (*mukti*). These ten Mahāvidyās or great mystic formulas are those of Kālī, Tārā, Ṣoḍaśī (also known as Sundarī or Tripurasundarī, meaning the Beautiful One in the Three Worlds), Bhuvaneśvarī (Sovereign of the Three Worlds), Bhairavī or Tripurabhairavī (the Fierce Lady), Chinnamastā (the Beheaded Lady), Dhūmāvatī (the Gray Lady, who is depicted in iconography as a widow with a crow as her symbol), Bagalā (the goddess of battle), Mātaṅgī (the goddess of the hunter tribes), and Kamalā (Lakṣmī). It is obvious that originally the number of formulas was not fixed at ten. Early texts, such as the *Ṭoḍala Tantra*, mention a few other formulas, including those of Durgā, Annapūrṇā, and Kullukā. The first two are universally popular goddesses, and the third became very important in the esoteric practices of the mantras and vidyās. The *Śakti-saṃgama Tantra*, being an encyclopedic text, mentions both a group of ten Mahāvidyās and also other lists of Mahāvidyās not confined to ten members.

The importance of this group of great formulas and their power goddesses grew enormously in late Tantric tradition and the goddess Kālī became foremost amongst them. She is considered the original power deity, designated Ādyā, the primeval lady. The *Ṭoḍala Tantra* deals only with the mantras and ritual worship of Kālī and Tārā, whereas Sundarī is treated in a rather fragmentary fashion. But the full treatment of their mantras, especially the monosyllabic seed (*bīja*) mantras, to some extent covers the other Mahīvidyās too, except for Dhūmāvatī. This last is a somewhat problematic figure: it is difficult to understand why she is included in this group of power goddesses. Like other ordinary deities, such as Gaṇeśa, her seed mantra simply consists of the first syllable of her name, *dhūṃ*. Thus, although the formulas of each of these goddesses are different, their identities are not always easy to determine and differentiate. It is also difficult to date the beginning of their popularity or the crystallization of the group of ten. The *Bṛhad-dharma Purāṇa* (*BdhP*) presents the myth of how the ten Mahāvidyās appeared in the following manner:

Śiva's wife Satī heard that her father Dakṣa was arranging the performance of a huge sacrifice to which all the gods and other celestials were invited except herself and Śiva. Incensed, she told her husband that she was going to her father's sacrifice to teach him a lesson in sensible behaviour. Śiva knew Dakṣa's animosity toward himself and Satī, and feared that Satī would be insulted, with catastrophic results, and so tried to dissuade her from going. Satī became irritated, and changed into her true

Kālī form, which she had suppressed when she had agreed to be born as the beautiful daughter of Dakṣa and Prasūti, in order to marry Śiva. Upon seeing her terrifying transformation, Śiva became completely confused and began to run away. Even her reassuring words failed to stop him. Then the Goddess appeared in one of her manifestations in each of the directions as Śiva tried to flee. Finally, at Śiva's request, the Goddess explained that she herself was the supreme reality Kālī, the source of all phenomena. At the request of Dakṣa and his wife, she had manifested herself as their exquisitely beautiful daughter Satī and then married Śiva. The ten manifestations who were blocking Śhiva's way in every direction were her own vidyā-manifestations. Before him, that is, to the east, appeared the Mahāvidyā Kālī; above him, Tārā; on his right (south), Chinnamastā; to his rear (west), Bagalā; on his left (north), Bhuvaneśvarī to his southeast, Dhūmāvatī; to his southwest, Sundarī; to his northwest, Mātaṅgī; to his northeast, Ṣoḍaśī; and immersed in his self was Bhairavī. At this revelation of the real identity and powers of the Goddess, Śiva apologized to her for assuming spousal authority and stopped resisting her departure to her father's home. As a result, Dakṣa was ruined, but escaped with his life; Satī, however, lost her life out of the anger and shame caused by her father's actions (*BdhP* 2.6.65-89, 128-52).

Let us now attempt to find out who these ten Mahāvidyās are. There seems to be nearly no difference between Kālī and Tārā in the eastern tradition. The *Mahācīnācāra-krama Ṭantra* 2.37 explains that in the Mahācīna tradition, antinomian practices are essential for Tārā worship. The *Ṭoḍala Tantra* agrees about these special features of Tārā. Although the *Toḍala Tantra* prescribes for Tārā's worship the use of the five esoteric ingredients (meat, fish, alcohol, woman, and sexual fluids) that signify vāmācāra practice, it appears to believe that these practices are not essential for Kālī worship. Perhaps this is why this text has been taken in Bengal to be the scriptural authority for the nonesoteric worship of Kālī, both in temples and in private homes. Other texts like *Bṛhat-nīla Tantra* and *Mahā-nirvāṇa Tantra* assert that these practices are essential for Kālī worship. However, the *Mahācīnācāra-krama Tantra*, having said that the four goddesses Dakṣiṇā Kālī, Tārā, Sundarī, and Bhairavī share the same style of worship, informs us in a later statement (2.38) that the latter two goddesses share another, presumably more orthodox, style of worship (that is, *dakṣiṇācāra*), but that the former two must be adored with antinomian practices (that is, *vāmācāra*). In the *Bṛhat-nīla Tantra*, Tārā is called Nīlasarasvatī and is described as resting on the corpse, that is, Śiva, in a fighting attitude with her left leg advanced and her right drawn back, young and smiling yet of awe-inspiring appearance, garlanded with severed heads, short, potbellied, powerful, and wearing a tiger skin. She has four arms and her tongue is lolling. She has flame-colored matted tresses held on the top of her head in a single mass on which the face of Akṣobhya is placed. She is also addressed as Ekajaṭā and Ugratārā. The popular iconography of Kālī, as already noted, is not very different from Tārā's, except for the hair: Kālī's hair is loose and dishevelled. All these peculiar features of Tārā show her close affinity with the Buddhist goddess Tārā (Saviouress), who is very popular among the Buddhists of Tibet and other Himalayan regions. The *Ṭoḍala Tantra* and *Śakti-saṃgama Tantra* also name Akṣobhya as Tārā's spouse, although a curious myth is offered in the *Ṭoḍala Tantra* to explain how Śiva came to be known by that name. The *Ṭoḍala Tantra* gives her seed mantra as *strīṃ*. Another source, namely, the Pāñcarātra *Lakṣmī Tantra*, equates Tārā with the supreme divine power that is identical with Vāc, the goddess Speech (Gupta 1972; 177-83; 286-96).

Ṣoḍaśī and Bhuvaneśvarī are, it seems, variations of Sundarī and Bālā and belong to the cult of Tripurasundarī or Lalitā; on this, see the *Paraśurāma-kalpa Sūtra* (*PkS*).

Bhairavī alias Tripurabhairavī also belongs to the same cult. Chinnamastā or the Beheaded Lady is depicted as a goddess standing in a fighting posture with her left leg forward and right leg drawn back. Her right hand holds a sword with which she has just severed her own head. Three streams of blood flow from her neck; that on her left is being drunk by a minor goddess called Ḍākinī, that on her right by Varṇinī, and the middle one spouts upwards and is being drunk by the goddess's own severed head. She stands on a prone woman who is in coitus with a supine man lying under her. This couple is considered to be Madana, the god of sexual desire, and his wife Rati, sexual pleasure. The goddess is the embodiment of the powerful mantra *hūṃ*, and is addressed as Vajravairocanī, which again points to a Buddhist goddess (Kinsley 1997: 144-66). A curious myth is recounted in *Śakti-saṃgama Tantra* (4.5.152-73) to explain this gory iconography. The goddess suddenly left her spouse Śiva in the midst of their amorous play. When she reappeared, Śiva asked her why she had disappeared so suddenly and why now she looked so pale. The goddess explained that she had to go to bathe together with her friends Ḍākinī and Varṇinī, who were hungry. After their bath, the goddess had provided meals for all three of them with her own blood as it gushed from her severed neck.

Bagalā or Bagalāmukhī is a golden-complexioned form of Tripurasundarī, the deity who presides over deadly weapons. It is difficult to identify Dhūmāvatī, who is tall, dark, rough, and sickly-complexioned. Her hair is thin and matted, and her disposition is restless and bellicose. She wears soiled clothes and rides a chariot with a banner displaying a crow. She is seen as an incarnation of all that is sordid, antisocial, and inauspicious in women, an antithesis of the goddess Śrī. She is depicted as a widow, who has allegedly gobbled up her husband Śiva in a fit of hunger. She was born from the smoking fire of the destruction of Dakṣa's sacrifice and the death of Satī. Frowning, she howls desolately and carries a winnowing fan. Lakṣmaṇa Deśika, the commentator on the *Śāradātilaka Tantra* (24.9-14), states that Dhūmāvatī is the same goddess as Jyeṣṭhyā.

The last two mahāvidyās are again familiar to the Lalitā cult. Mātaṅgī is the same as Śyāmalā in that cult. She is mainly considered to be the deity presiding over such fine arts as the power to compose poetry. She is exquisitely beautiful and is dark complexioned, but otherwise closely resembles Lalitā in appearance (*PkS* 6.1-39). The tenth Mahāvidyā is goddess Lakṣmī alias Śrī alias Kamalā, the spouse of Viṣṇu—although she too is closely related to the mantra of Tripurasundarī.

Tantric Esoteric Practice

The *Ṭoḍala Tantra* belongs to the corpus of Tantric scriptures that make up the Mantra mārga or Mantra path. The term *Mantra mārga* means the entire Tantric paradigm of ritual worship and meditation. Every mantra possesses a paradig-matical ritual system of its own, a pattern that has become more or less fixed, with variations to fit the relevant mantra and its deity, as well as the performer's intended application. Mantra-mārga is followed by Tantric practitioners for two broadly defined purposes: liberation from the bondage of endless transmigration (*saṃsāra*), or rewards such as supernatural power and achievements—mukti and bhukti respectively. The *Ṭoḍala Tantra* is more concerned with mukti and hence does not deal with the esoteric worship of any Mahāvidyās other than the first three: Kālī, Tārā, and Sundarī (or Bhuvaneśvarī). Seekers of mukti are more respected than seekers of power and achievement, although the latter are held in awe and are much sought after by lay devotees for personal gain, such as protection from disease and misfortune, and destroying enemies.

The four important constituents in such esoteric Tantric worship are the preliminaries, invocation, ritual service, and conclusion.

Preliminaries: First, the divine is represented by esoteric formulas, hand gestures (*mudrās*), symbols of the deity worshipped mainly on a diagram (*yantra*), and sometimes an image and a pitcher full of water. Second, the practitioner (*sādhaka*) must have been properly initiated by a competent sectarian guru. Third, the worshipper, the symbol of the deity, and the objects used for offering must be physically and mystically purified. Fourth is the ritual of security. Tantric esoteric practices are considered to be full of dangers. Often they are personified as harmful spirits that obstruct the worshipper's every movement. Therefore the worshipper must take measures to remove these spirits from the sacred area of the ritual worship, by making threatening sounds; by stamping one's foot, clapping, or snapping one's fingers; by frowning and looking angry, and scattering threatening objects such as white mustard seeds; by making threatening gestures imitating shooting arrows, and so forth. The fifth, and perhaps the most important preliminary rite is called nyāsa. This means the installation, limb by limb, of the sacred mantras, which are the sonic manifestation of the divine, onto the material body of the worshipper, thus replacing the mundane body of the worshipper with a sacred body. The same installation is performed onto the deity's symbol for the same purpose.

Invocation: The goddess is invoked, first into the center or heart of the worshipper, and thence onto the seat he has ritually prepared for her adoration.

Ritual Service: The deity is first adored in meditative imagination, in which all the objects of offering are of an abstract nature. Next, the Tantric practitioner worships the Goddess with various objects of material enjoyment. This is followed by the service of the Goddess's spouse, Śiva, and then her entourage, the minor gods and goddesses encircling her. This is followed by the offering (*bali*), which in the Mahāvidyā cult almost always implies an animal sacrifice, that is, beheading an animal in front of the image.

The animal offering is followed by a fire sacrifice. Then a short meditation is done by means of repeating the main mantra a certain number of times (*japa*). The ritual offerings culminate, for the followers of the vāmācāra, with the offerings of the five objects (meat, fish, etc.). Finally, the worshipper offers the deity all the merit he has accrued from performing the service. He also offers himself to the goddess. These last two ritual acts refer to two very important concepts: renunciation and loyal devotion. The first requires an utter annihilation of one's ego and greed. Even the greed for accumulating merit for the ego-person must be destroyed. The second is rooted in the concept of bhakti, which came to mean total surrender to one's adored deity. The devotee offers all that belongs to himself and then offers his individuality as well.

Conclusion: Having invoked a fierce manifestation of the Goddess and worshipped it with some parts of the already offered objects for his own success and that of his ritual service, the worshipper recites certain set formulas for his physical well-being, and then recites hymns to the Goddess. Having partaken of a little of the offered food as the Goddess's grace, the worshipper has fulfilled his daily obligatory ritual service of his Goddess and is free to follow his normal way of life.

Tantra Ritual Practice

The *Ṭoḍala Tantra* does not discuss Tantric initiation, and indeed, it does not discuss any theological concepts at all. It starts by describing the procedure for the ritual worship of Kālī. The first ritual act is to worship one's guru mentally. The guru is identified with the supreme deity Kālī when she is united with Śiva immediately prior to creation. This text is meant for experienced Tantric practitioners who are versed in the Tantric meditation on the kuṇḍalinī, the contracted and inert form of the creatrix goddess Kālī as she remains immanent in every creature (Eliade 1969: 200-

67). The aim of Tantric meditation is to arouse the kuṇḍalinī by means of breath control (*prāṇāyāma*) and one-pointed meditation (*dhyāna*) on the practitioner's deity, who when awakened longs to unite with Śiva and swiftly flies upward through the innermost passage of the practitioner's yogic body, which contains six spiritual centers. At the top of this passage, just above the practitioner's body, the creating Goddess is united with Śiva, and this divine area, transcending the creation at a point prior to creation, is imagined as a sphere or a lotus with countless petals (*sahasrāra cakra*). This united yet differentiated stance of the supreme Goddess and Śiva is what the Tantric practitioner endeavors to understand and identify with. This is liberation because it transcends creation. The practitioner's guru is already liberated and is thus one with this two-in-one divinity. Even before the practitioner actually leaves his bed, he performs the kuṇḍalinī meditation on his guru while repeating his name, declaring his total submission to him. Only then does he start his daily obligatory ritual acts.

Bhūtaśuddhi

The next important ritual is the purification of the practitioner's material body, which is composed of five cosmic elements (*bhūtaśuddhi*). This is again a form of meditation: the practitioner meditates on each of the five ontological elements, starting with the element of solidity/earth and ending with ether/undefined space. He eliminates each element by dissolving it into the element preceding it. Thus in his imagination he contracts the entire differentiated creation in its microcosmic form, arriving at the center of the countless-petaled lotus circle, where the energy of the Goddess burns away the impurities of his microcosm, eliminating any residual elements. Saturated and rejuvenated by the nectar produced by the coitus of the divine couple, the microcosm is recreated, pure and consubstantial with the divine. The import of such daily meditative rites as *bhūtaśuddhi* is to repeat the process of internalizing the theological explanation of salvation as a direct experience of one's true identity with vidyā, nondual pure awareness, which in turn is but the supreme goddess Kālī in her transcendental form.

Mantra and Nyāsa

After this renewed confirmation of his consubstantiality with Kālī, the practitioner can replace his purified mundane body with the divine personality, that is, vidyā, through the rite of *nyāsa.* In this rite the mantras and their sonic source (*mātṛkā*), the letters of the Sanskrit alphabet, are the most important concepts. Mantras are the sonic forms of their deities, just as the images are their visual forms. The mantras of Kālī and Tārā are therefore considered to be the mantra bodies of these two goddesses. The *Ṭoḍala Tantra* explains the concept of the Goddess's mantra physique in its sixth chapter. It is a Tantric custom to analyze the mantra of a deity into several components. The most important part is the seed or bījā mantra. Mahāvidyās like Kālī or Tārā have several such seeds, one of which is considered to be chief. The seed is the essence of a mantra. After the seed(s) comes the name of the deity. As the complete mantra is a sentence, the name is either inflected as a vocative, or is declined in the dative when it is followed by the term *namas,* which means "obeisance." Conventionally, formulas known as *vidyās* are considered to be of feminine gender, which requires them to end in *svāhā.* But in the case of the mantras found in the *Ṭoḍala Tantra,* several seed mantras are often inserted before the word *svāhā.* It is interesting to note that this word is used for offering Vedic oblations, and is mythologized as the name of the fire god Agni's spouse. However, a practitioner receives his personal esoteric mantra from his guru who, knowing the initiate's special disposition, chooses a specific variant of his chosen deity. This then becomes the initiated practitioner's main or mūla mantra. The main mantra, which is considered the full physical form of its deity, is divided into six main limbs (*aṅgas*). These are the heart, the head, the tuft of hair, the eyes, the weapon, and the armored torso. These six limbs symbolize the deity's entire body. In the rite of nyāsa the worshipper first invests his hands and fingers with sacred formulas and then invests his six limbs with the same parts of his main mantra. Because the supreme goddess is Vāc, Speech, the worshipper uses the mātṛkā mantra for some specific nyāsa, since that is Goddess's primordial manifestation. In the worship of Kālī, mātṛkā nyāsa is performed in six different ways.

Mudrā

Mudrā has more than one meaning. Its primary meaning is "seal", but in Tantric terminology, mudrā means a hand gesture or a posture of seated meditation (usually called āsana), and in the context of the five esoteric ingredients of offerings to the Goddess, it may either mean a female partner for ritual practice or just a snack. There are many uses of mudrās or hand gestures as the practitioner proceeds mentally to encounter divine and spiritual beings in his rituals. All actions at this state are accompanied by miming, and often they are so graphic that it is easy to understand their meaning. For instance, for the *dhyāna* or envisaging of the deity, the worshipper utters the deity's mantra of her iconography while acting out in gestures the deity's special attributes. Thus, while uttering Kālikā's dhyāna mantra— "*Oṃ*, you seated on a corpse, of fierce appearance with terrifying teeth, who bestows desired objects [on her devotees], who laughs [all the time], who has three eyes, holds in her hands a skull and a sword, whose hair is untied and tongue is lolling out incessantly drinking the blood [of the asuras]. One should envisage you, O Goddess, [as] having four arms whose other two hands gesture fulfilment of the devotee's wishes and who promises protection"— the adept gestures with his fingers, graphically symbolizing the attributes described in that

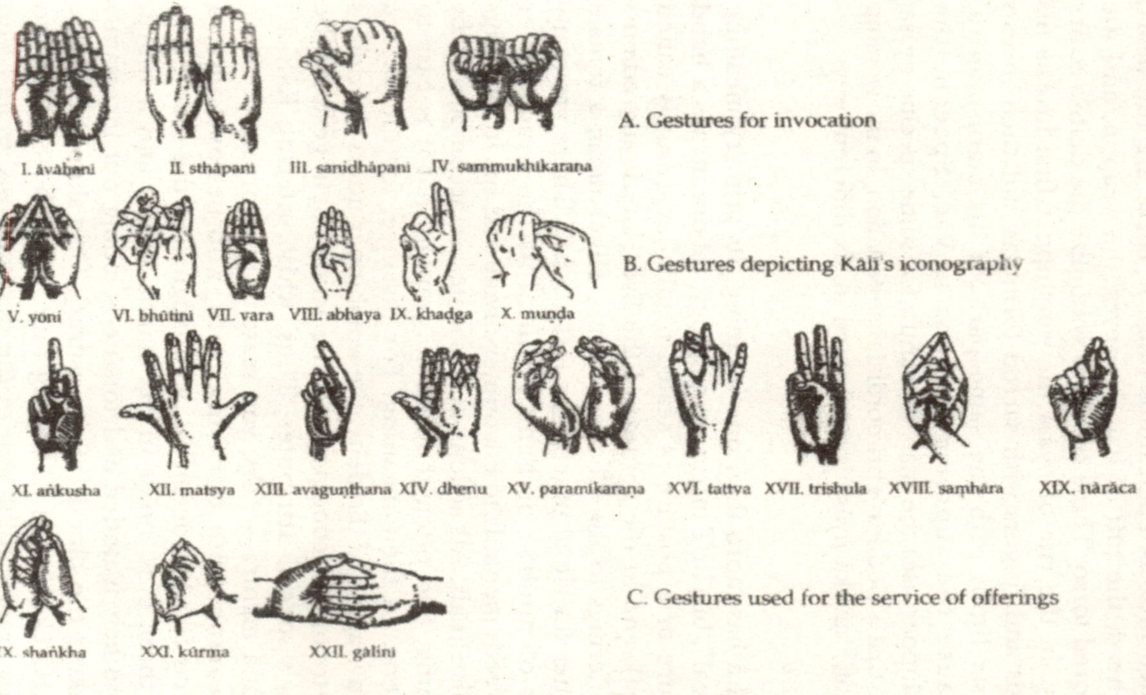
I. āvāhani
II. sthāpani
III. sanidhāpani
IV. sammukhīkaraṇa
A. Gestures for invocation
V. yoni
VI. bhūtini
VII. vara
VIII. abhaya
IX. khaḍga
X. muṇḍa
B. Gestures depicting Kālī's iconography
XI. aṅkusha
XII. matsya
XIII. avaguṇṭhana
XIV. dhenu
XV. paramīkaraṇa
XVI. tattva
XVII. trishula
XVIII. saṃhāra
XIX. nārāca
XX. shaṅkha
XXI. kūrma
XXII. gālini
C. Gestures used for the service of offerings

Fig. 1: Mudrās

mantra. These are called the yoni, bhutinī, vara, abhaya, khaḍga, and muṇḍa mudrās (see Figure 1).

The Devanagari edition of the *Ṭoḍala Tantra* was published in 1970, in *Tantra-saṃgraha* part 2, edited by Gopinath Kaviraj from the Yoga-Tantra department of Benares Sanskrit University, Varanasi. There are several Bengali published editions, as well. The edition I have used is *Ṭoḍala Tantra,* edited, translated, and commented on in Bengali by Pancanana Sastri (Calcutta: Navabharata Publications, 1976).

Further Reading

For further study, my essay on Tantric rituals in *Hindu Tāntrism,* by Sanjukta Gupta, Dirk J. Hoens, and Teun Goudraan (Leiden: E.J. Brill, 1979), pp. xxiii-xxxiv; Introduction to *Lakṣmī Tantra* by Sanjukta Gupta (Leiden: E.J. Bril, 1972); and *Hindu Tantric and Śākta Literature* by Teun Goudriaan and Sanjukta Gupta (Weisbaden: Otto Harrassowitc, 1981) are useful. Alexis Sanderson's essay "Śaivism and the Tantric Traditions" in *The World's Religions: Religions of Asia,* edited by Friedhelm Hardy (reprint London: Routledge & Kegan Paul, 1990), pp. 128-72, is a good source for the history of Tantric traditions. Thomas B. Coburn's essay "Devī: The Great Goddess," in *Devī: Goddesses of India,* edited by John Stratton Hawley and Donna Wulff (Berkeley: University of California Press, 1996), pp. 31-48; and Coburn, *Encountering the Goddess: A Translation of the Devī-Māhātmya and a Study of Its Interpretation* (Albany: State University of New York Press, 1991), are indispensable. The same is true of two books by C. Mackenzie Brown, *God as Mother: A Feminine Theology of India—An Historical and Theological Study of the Bṛahmavaivarta Purana* (Hartford, Vt., Claude Stark, 1974), and *The Triumph of the Goddess: The Canonical Models and Theological Visions of the Devī-Bhāgvata Purāṇa* (Albany: State University of New York Press, 1990). For an understanding of the concept of the ten Mahāvidyās one should read David Kinsley's two works, *Hindu Goddess: Visions of the Divine Feminine in the Hindu Religious Tradition* (Delhi: Motilal Banarasidas, 1987), and *Tantric Vision of the Divine Feminine: The Ten Mahāvidyās* (Berkeley and Los Angeles: University of California Press, 1997). On kuṇḍalinī yoga, I recommend Mircea Ediade, *Yoga: Immortality and Freedom,* 2nd edn., translated by Willard R. Trask (London: Routledge & Kegan Paul, 1969).

ṬOḌALA TANTRA

Chapter One

The Names of Different Forms of the Great God Śiva as Spouse of the Deities of Great Sacred Formulas

The goddess spoke:

1-2. O Lord of the universe, my master, who are the embodiment of all the sacred formulas (*vidyās*), [please] tell me when all the great formulas (*mahāvidyās*) are venerated in the three worlds, [and] what are the specific forms of the trumpet-holding Mahādeva who is seated on the right side of each of these [mahāvidyās]; O Lord! please enumerate [these forms] to me.

Śrī Śiva spoke:

3-4. Listen O beautiful and blessed one! Bhairava Mahākāla [a form of Mahādeva] should be worshipped by the right side of the benevolent (*dakṣiṇā*) Kālī, [because] Dakṣiṇā is always engaged in love-play with Mahākāla. One should worship Akṣobhya by the right side of Tārā.

5-7ab. O goddess, at the time of the churning of the [cosmic] ocean there arose [the poison called] Kālakūṭa. Then all the gods, together with their wives, became greatly disturbed. Since [Śiva, even when he] drank that deadly poison, remained unaffected by any kind of agitation, therefore, O great sovereign lady, he is famous as Akṣobhya ("Unagitated"). With him [the goddess] Tāriṇī, the great goddess of delusion, is ever engaged in love play.

7cd-9ab. O sovereign of the gods, one should worship the five-faced Śiva who has three eyes on each of his faces, on the right side of the great Tripurasundarī. Since the great Goddess is erotically excited [and is] ever [engaged in love play] with him [who has five faces], therefore, O great Goddess, she is known as the fifth.

9cd-11ab. One should worship Tryambaka [Śiva] by the right side of the blessed Bhuvanasundarī [Bhuvaneśvarī]. [Śiva] is called Tryambaka [associated with three mothers] because he makes love to the primaeval sovereign Goddess of the creation, in heaven, earth, and the nether region (*pātāla*). Accordingly he [Śiva] is renowned for being always united with Śakti and is venerated in all the Tantras.

11cd-12ab. One should with great care worship [Śiva] called Dakṣiṇāmūrti by the right side of Bhairavī. He is indeed the same as the five-faced [Sadāśiva].

12cd-13cd. One should worship Śiva as a headless trunk (*kabandha*) by the right side of Chinnamastā [the Beheaded Goddess]. He who does tāntric ritual worship of Kabandha [Śiva] certainly becomes the lord of all tantric perfection (*siddhi*). Dhūmāvatī, the great Vidyā, is manifest in the form of widow [hence there is no form of Śiva by her side].

14. The one-faced great Rudra (the Fierce One) is worshipped by the right hand side of Bagalā. He is famed as the annihilator [performing the contraction] of the creation.

15. By Mātaṅgī's right side one should worship Mātaṅga Śiva. He indeed is the Dakṣiṇāmūrtī who is in the form of universal bliss.

16. [A worshipper (*sādhaka*)] should worship Sadāśiva in the form of Viṣṇu by Kamalā's right side. O great sovereign Goddess, there is no doubt that he would achieve perfection (*siddhi*).

17. By the right side of Annapūrṇā [a sādhaka] should worship the great sovereign god [Śiva], the bestower of great liberation (*mokṣa*), who is the manifest *brahman* and who possesses ten faces.

18-19ab. [He] should carefully worship [Śiva as] Nārada by the right side of Durgā. The syllable *nā* stands for the creator, and the syllable *da* always represents the protector. Because the syllable *ra* symbolizes the destroyer Nārada, it is held [to represent the great god Śiva who creates, sustains, and destroys the universe].

19cd-19ef. For all other Vidyās, the seer (*ṛṣi*) [of the vidyā] mentioned in the formula is indeed her [the vidyā-śakti's] husband and should be worshipped by her right side.

Explanation of Śiva's Transformation into a Corpse Who Nonetheless Has Sexual Union with the Goddess

The blessed Goddess asked:

20. The [great Śakti] who is the first great Vidyā and also the second supreme Bhairavī who is the mother of the three worlds and is eternal—how can she be mounted on a corpse?

The blessed Śiva answered:

21-23. O great Goddess! she who is the primordial [divine being], herself Death/Time, exists [identified] as the heart [essence] of the glorious Śiva in the form of the destroyer. Therefore the supreme Death/Time [Mahākāla] is the destroyer of the universe. But when Kālī as the embodiment of destruction manifests herself in her true form, immediately at that very moment,

O Goddess, Sadāśiva appears in the form of a corpse and at that instant, O Lady with dancing eyes, she [Kālī] appears mounted on a corpse.

The blessed Goddess said:

24. The great god Sadāśiva as a corpse is a lifeless body. How could it then perform the sex act?

The blessed Śiva answered:

25. At the time that great Kālī [actively] manifests herself, Sadāśiva is devoid of active power. When, O Goddess, he is united with śakti, then he appears in the form of Śiva; [but though] when devoid of śakti he is virtually a corpse he still does not lose his manliness [his phallus].

End of the first chapter, called dialogue between Hara and Gaurī, of the most excellent of all Tantras, the *Toḍala-tantra*

Chapter Two

Brief Enumeration of Kuṇḍalinī Yoga

The blessed Śiva said:

1-4. Listen O Goddess! I shall briefly recount the essence of Yoga [meditation and Tantric mental adoration].

The [human] body is like a tree [in reverse form] whose roots are on top and branches hanging beneath. All the sacred places of the universe exist within this body. The very form of the macrocosm exists in the microcosm [of the human body]. There are thirty and a half million sacred places in the macrocosm, O You who are praised by the heroes [Tāntric practitioners]! Out of all of these, only a hundred and forty thousand sacred places are visible. Out of these, only fourteen [are noteworthy], and out of these fourteen], only three are auspicious. Amongst these [three again], O supreme sovereign Goddess, [the one called] Mahādhīrā bestows liberation (*mukti*).

5. Vāsukī [the divine serpent] is indeed Mahāmāyā [the cosmic goddess of delusion], who is manifest in the form of a serpent, coiled three and a half times, and resides in the region under the nether region (*pātāla*).

6-8. O supreme sovereign Goddess, listen carefully while I recount the seven heaven [upper regions] in their proper order. [These are] the region of the earth, of the atmosphere, of the celestials, then the region of maha [of the great saints], the region of jana [generation], the region of tapa [austerity] and, O Lady with an elegant face, the region of satya [truth]. Here ends the list of seven regions. O eminent lady! now listen carefully to the enumeration of the nether regions. [There are the regions of] atala, vitala, sutala, talātala, mahātala, pātāla, and after that rasātala.

9-17. The liberating [yogic duct, called nādī] Mahādhīrā ranges from rasātala to the end of satya, which exists inside the central [channel, that is, the spinal column, meru]. Mahāviṣṇu Śiva resides in the satya region and Vāsukī is full of intense longing to meet him. When Vāsukī, having pierced the six regions (*cakras*), rises up [to that region of satya], all the other flowing rivers [that is, the ducts] become upward flowing. In the body [the microcosm], O sovereign Goddess, the ducts remain in the following order. If [the sādhaka] presses down air through both the iḍā and piṅgalā ducts, which have the suṣumṇā between them, O sovereign Goddess, while repeating the prāṇa mantra [*so 'haṃ*], then the coiled one [Vāsukī] starts [moving upward through the suṣumṇā] following the order of the [six cakras], until she approaches the eternal and immutable lotus [the sahasrāra cakra]. With anxiety the coiled one enters that eternal abode. Simultaneously all other down-flowing [ducts] start flowing upstream. At that moment, O Goddess! [the sādhaka] should concentrate on the garland of letters. Then while repeating mentally 108 times his chief (*mūla*) mantra [received from his preceptor at the time of initiation] the intelligent [sādhaka] should bring the coiled one back to his mūlādhāra cakra [her original resting-place] in the same way, while refreshing the gods of the six *cakras* with the nectar [from the thousand-petaled lotus].

Yogic Mudrās, or Special Physical Positions for Kuṇḍalinī Yoga

17c-22ab. Now, my dear, I shall describe another yoga posture called the yonimudrā [the previous one was called śakti-cālanī].

The Mantra practitioner first sits down on his seat facing the east or the north. With his arms he firmly holds his two knees and then, O Queen of the gods, he brings his nose near the knees while sitting upright [that is, keeping his back straight]. O Queen of the gods [as before] he presses air down by inhaling (but, O Great Goddess! does not let the air escape by exhaling), and simultaneously continues repeating the prāṇa mantra. At the same time, as described before, he should repeat [his chief mantra] 108 times in his upright pose, [only this time] he repeats [the mantra] in reverse order. While thus [repeating his mantra], O You of glorious face, he brings [the kuṇḍalinī] back to the basic root cakra [*mūlādhāra*] through the same path while refreshing the gods of the six cakras with nectar.

22-cd-25. My dear, this yonimudrā removes all illness. O Goddess, without elaborating I can just say that it destroys great diseases and, O Goddess, without exaggerating I can say that this mudrā causes the realization of the mantra, brings about the direct perception of one's [true] self, and bestows on the practitioner the great liberation, mahāmokṣa. Had I possessed a hundred faces I would not have been able to exhaust all its details; but with only five faces how much can I enumerate? A Tantric practitioner practicing this mudrā becomes as beautiful as Cupid even if he began as a leper.

Here ends the second chapter of the Śiva-Pārvatī dialogue in the *Ṭoḍala Tantra* which is the best of all Tantras.

Chapter Three

The blessed goddess asked:

1. O God of gods, great God, the saver from the ocean of transient and recurring life [*saṃsāra*], O ocean of compassion, please tell me the great mudrā called baddhayoni.

Śiva answered:

2-4b. Listen, O Goddess, I shall briefly tell you the method of baddhayoni. O great Goddess, the mantra practitioner covers his anus with the tip of his penis. Then, O great Goddess, the intelligent practitioner gradually applies his fingers [to cover other apertures of his body] starting with the thumbs, to [cover] his ears, [and then in turn covering his] eyes, nose, and mouth [with rest of the pairs of fingers of his hands].

4cd-7. [Thus covering all his bodily apertures] he should then inhale through his nose and fill his mouth with air and as before press it downward [through the iḍā and piṅgalā ducts]. When [the coiled goddess unites with Śiva] the practitioner should envisage the primaeval Sound (*śabda-brahman*) and then envisage the garland of syllables (*varṇamālā*) while repeating his main mantra. Then, repeating the mantra *so 'ham,* he brings, O Goddess, [the kuṇḍalinī back to the mūlādhāra cakra] through the same central channel. On the way he refreshes all the cakra gods [with the nectar produced by the union of the goddess and Sadāśiva]. O Great sovereign Goddess! O Spotless One! I shall tell you [later] the achievements of one who performs this [kuṇḍalinī yoga seated in baddhayoni posture].

Kālī's Mantra or Vidyā

The blessed Pārvatī asked:

8. O Omniscient Īśāna! O Most excellent of the erudite, who possesses all wisdom! O Master of gods! please tell me the rare description of Kālikā's mantra system.

The Bīja [Seed] Mantra

The blessed Śiva answered:

9-13. O Ever-blissful Goddess, listen to my account of the excellent Kālikā mantra; even the mere discussion of its nature makes a man liberated in this life. For the first [seed mantra], cull the syllable *ka,* add to it *ī, r,* and the *bindunāda* [double nasalization, symbolized by a sickle shape topped by a point representing the normal nasalization]. O Auspicious One! this is the very rare perfect vidyā, the queen of all vidyās.

The Vidyā

Now listen to me explaining the next one. First utter this seed [mantra *krīṃ*] three times. Then cull the syllable *ha* connected with the nasal *bindu* and the vowel *u* [*huṃ*], [and utter] it twice [after the first three]; and now I tell you the next one [that is the third seed mantra]. Then, O Sovereign Goddess [utter the syllable *ha* joined with *r, ī,* and the nasa l] and repeat it again [*hrīṃ hrīṃ*]; then add [Kālikā's] vocative, then again three of the first seed mantra, then twice the kūrca mantra [*hūṃ*] and twice the māyā mantra [*hrīṃ*] and finally *svāhā*. This mantra of twenty-five syllables is the queen of all vidyās and is very rare.

14. When this great vidyā is preceded by the vāgbhava mantra [*aiṃ*, the seed mantra of the supreme speech, Vāc], its inherent deity is Śrīkālī; when preceded by the praṇava mantra [*Oṃ*], its deity is known as Siddhikālikā.

15-16. When the mantra consists of two of the goddess's own mantras [*krīṃ*] followed by one kūrca mantra [*hūṃ*], O great Goddess, this trisyllabic supreme vidyā is known as Cāmuṇḍākālikā. There is no vidyā like this one for bringing about success. The six-syllabled vidyā [*om krīṃ krīṃ krīṃ phaṭ svāhā*] and the three-syllabled vidyā [*krīṃ krīṃ hūṃ*] are of equal power.

17-18ab. O Auspicious one! three of [Kālikā's] own seed mantra [*krīṃ krīṃ huṃ*] followed by the [vocative] *śmaśānakālike*, then again the three seed mantras and finally *svāhā*, [together] constitute the fourteen-syllabled mantra that is worshipped in all the three worlds.

Eight Forms of the Kālī Vidyā

18cd-21ab. Dakṣiṇākālikā, Siddhikālikā, Guhyakālikā, Śrīkālikā, Bhadrakālī, Cāmuṇḍākālikā, and the supreme Śmaśānakālikā and Mahākalī, O Goddess! these are the eight [forms of goddess Kālī]. O Sovereign Goddess! First utter Kālī's own seed mantra, then her name in the vocative followed by another Kālikā seed mantra, and finally and *svāhā* [*krīṃ kālike krīṃ svāhā*]. These eight forms of Kālikā's mantra are secretly expressed in all Tantras.

The blessed Goddess said:

21cd-23ab. I have [now] heard the very secret mantras of the great Kālikā. Now I wish to hear Tārā's royal mantra. O Īśāna! if you love me do tell me her mantra, whose mere mention prevents one from drowning in the ocean of [transitory] existence.

Tārā Bījas

Śrī Śiva answered:

Having uttered the moon seed [*saṃ*] add the syllable of fire [*r*] and *t* to it, together with the left eye [*ī*]. My beloved, this royal mantra, this single-syllabled vidyā [*strīṃ*] is venerated in three worlds. *Īśāna* [*h*] united with the nasal and the left ear [*ū*] [forms] the monosyllabic vidyā [*hūṃ*], which is [Tārā's] second royal mantra.

The Tārā Vidyā

23cd-32ab. Śiva [*h*] with the fire [*r*] and the left eye [*ī*] and the nasal added to it [*hrīṃ*] [should first be uttered]. Then the first seed [*strīṃ*] and then the second [*hūṃ*], then utter the weapon, astra mantra [*hrīṃ strīṃ hūṃ phaṭ*].

Different Forms and Efficacies of the Tārā Vidyā

When this vidyā is preceded by praṇava [*Oṃ*], then [the Goddess] is called Ugratārā. When without the Praṇava this vidyā is called Ekajaṭā, the bestower of supreme liberation (*mokṣa*). With neither praṇava nor astra mantra [that is, *hrīṃ strīṃ hūm*], this trisyllabic vidyā is called Mahānīlasarasvatī. When the [trisyllabic] vidyā is preceded by the vāgbhava [seed mantra], it bestows [on the practitioner] the status of the god of speech. This supreme vidyā when preceded by the seed mantra *śrīṃ* bestows wealth and prosperity. When this great vidyā is preceded by the seed mantra māyā [*hrīṃ*], it bestows sure success and perfection (*siddhi*). When it is preceded by the kūrca [*hūṃ*], it reveals the entire system of speech. When this supreme vidyā is preceded by the seed of the sky [*haṃ*], it bestows the liberation of total resorption. When this geat vidyā starts with the prāsāda [seed mantra, *hauṃ*] it brings about the union of the practitioner with Śiva. When this mantra starts with the seed [mantra] of prāṇa [*prūṃ*] it bestows on the practitioner the fulfilment of whatever he wishes. When this supreme vidyā opens with the seed of Kālī [*krīṃ*] it bestows both liberation and prosperity.

Ritual Worship of the Deity

32cd-50abc. Now I shall describe the method of worshipping Kālī and Tārā. Arising in the morning, the practitioner who knows his mantra [and its method of meditation] first mentally worships his guru in the topmost cakra consisting of a thousand petals. Then, having pierced the six cakras, he should repeat his main mantra 108 times. Thereafter, having bowed down [to his preferred deity] he should perform his ritual bathing. He should start this bathing ritual with the following declaration of his intention (*saṃkalpa*): "Today [here he mentions the day and date and then] the solar month, [I bathe myself] for the pleasure of the deity." Then he bathes in the pure water.

Then he should utter *Oṃ* and then *gaṅge ca,* followed by *yamune,* then having uttered *godāvarī, sarasvatī, narmade* and *sindhu kāverī* he utters the words *asmin jale sannidhiṃ kuru* [Oṃ the rivers Ganges, Yamunā, Godāvarī, Sarasvatī, Narmadā, Sindhu, and Kāverī please abide in this water]. [While uttering this mantra the practitioner] with the hand gesture called the goad (*aṅkuśa*) should [in imagination] pull these sacred rivers from the orb of the sun and settle them [in the water in which he is bathing] by carefully showing four relevant hand gestures. Then having protected the water with the hand gesture called the fish [and scooping a palmful of water and covering it with the other palm], the worshipper repeats his [deity's seed] mantra [*krīṃ*] eleven times. Then, throwing this water toward the sun, he should repeat his main mantra twelve times while [in imagination] washing [Kālikā's] feet three times. Then [in imagination] he should three times bathe himself with that rinse water flowing from [Kālī's] feet while repeating the mantra. This is done by showing the gesture of the water pot (*kumbha*) while repeating his main mantra three times.

Then, O Queen of gods! he should decorate his forehead according to the custom of his sect. Then he performs ācamana [ritual cleansing of his mouth and hands] with water while uttering the mantras of the three tattvas—*ātmatattva, vidyātattva,* and *śivatattva.* The mantras consists of each tattva preceded by praṇava and ending with *svāhā* [this is the name of the wife of the god Agni, Fire].

[At this point he has left his bathing place, cleanly and decorously attired, and reached the actual place of worship, carrying a pitcher full of water brought from the water source. In this water pitcher] he invokes the sacred rivers with the same *gaṅge ca,* etc. mantra [following the aforesaid procedure]. Then he dips a bunch of kuśa grass into the sanctified water and with it sprinkles water on the ground [where he will hold his ritual worship]. Then in the same way he should sprinkle himself seven times. Then he performs his aṅganyāsa. Then, O Goddess of the celestials, he with his left hand [scoops up water] and repeats three times the [pañcabhūta] bīja mantras: *haṃ, vaṃ, yaṃ, laṃ* and *raṃ.* Having thus encapsulated that water with that pañcabhūta mantra, the practitioner should sprinkle himself seven times with his finger in the gesture of tattva [reality] while uttering his main mantra. This act at once removes all his sins.

Then, O Great sovereign Queen, the adept transfers the rest of the water from his left hand to his right and in imagination inhales it through his iḍā duct [inside his left nostril], which water then cleanses his inner body. Thereafter, he should exhale that water through his piṅgalā duct [inside his right nostril]. Here he imagines that water to be black and the embodiment of sins; he immediately throws the water onto a slab of rock with the mantra *phaṭ*. Then he should wash his hands, perform *ācamana* and, having performed breath control, offer libation to his lineage god and then offer *arghya* [an offering of a few rice grains, tips of dūrvā grass and sanctified water] to the Sun god and *arghya* to his chosen deity.

50d-53. Thereafter he should repeat the great words of the [Kālikā] *gāyatrī* [the famous Vedic mantra with which brahmans worship the Sun every day, as follows]; first one should take the praṇava [*Oṃ*], then utter *kālikāyai*, then *vidmahe;* then *śmaśānavāsinyai dhīmahi*, then *tan no ghore pracodayāt.* While uttering this mantra, the worshipper should three times scatter the consecrated water upward.

54ab. Then, O great Goddess, having performed aṅganyāsa the worshipper again performs *ācamana.*

Tārā Gāyatrī *is Described with a Brief Mention of the Deity's Dhyāna as the Sun Deity*

54cd-56ab. O Great Goddess! Having envisaged in meditation one's chosen deity [here Tārā] in the orb of the sun, one should utter *Oṃ tārāyai vidmahe mahogrāyai dhīmahi jan no devī pracodayāt.* Then, having performed breath control, he should repeat this mantra 108 times.

Now, O Queen of gods, I offer in the form of aphorisms (*sūtrākāra*) an account of the system of worship.

Preliminaries

56cd-58. First proclaim universal well-being (*svasti-vacana*), then the announcement of one's intention to worship (*saṃkalpa*). Next, one should carefully place the pitcher [full of consecrated water], followed by the act of *ācamana* with mantras; next comes setting the pitcher of water for *arghya* for general purposes; then sprinkling the entrance [with consecrated water for purification], finishing that ritual by worshipping the entrance. Then, having removed the three categories of hindrances [concretized as evil spirits, belonging to the ground, atmosphere, and close to the body of the worshipper and the material objects around him gathered for the ritual] he removes [other evil] spirits [with mantras, sprinkling of water and threatening gestures].

Starting the Actual Worship

59-60ab. Having adored the seat, the intelligent worshipper first of all bows down to his guru. Then he purified his hands, claps them three times, and then performs the rite of consolidating and safeguarding the area surrounding his person (*digbandhana*). Then he encompasses himself with fire. Then he performs bhūtaśuddhi.

Nyāsa

60cd-64ab. He should then first perform the *nyāsa* of the six limbs of the *mātṛkā* [the full Sanskrit alphabet], then the *nyāsa* of the *mātṛkā* on his inner body. Then he utters the *dhyāna* mantra [the mantra that gives the deity's iconography] of the *mātṛkā*. He should perform the same nyāsa of the sage, and so on [the sage poet, the meter, and the deity of his mantra]. Then he performs *nyāsa* of his hands and his limbs [identifying them with] the letters of the Sanskrit alphabet. Then he performs the six types of *nyāsa* [of his main mantra]. Then he performs *vyāpaka* [extended] *nyāsa*. With concentration he performs the *nyāsa* of the *tattvas*; then, O Goddess!] he performs the *nyāsa* of the seed mantra. He performs the *vyāpaka nyāsa* in seven different ways using his main mantra. Then in deep concentration he visualizes his deity, whereafter he worships that deity mentally [with imagined ingredients].

Adoration of the Deity

64cd-68ab. [The adept] prepares the consecrated special liquid for special *argyha*. Then he worships [the deity's] seat. Next he again performs the visualization of the deity in deep meditation (*dhyāna*) and this time he sees her with her eyes open. [All the time he utters specific mantras and appropriate gestures to accompany his ritual acts.] Then he in similar manner welcomes the deity. Then while purifying all objects of offering he shows the gestures of the cow's udder, and so on. [These are called the *dhenu mudrā*, the symbol for the celestial cow whose milk is nectar; the *avaguṇṭhana mudrā*, which symbolizes safety and cover; the *gālinī mudrā* which symbolizes the fusing of the sacred and the mundane water; and the *nārāca mudrā*, which symbolizes iron arrowheads to ward off any polluting evil spirits]. Then he performs the *nyāsa* of the deity's six limbs. Then he performs the rite of establishing life [in the image or other representation of the deity]. Then he worships [with offerings] his principal mantra and its deity, the Goddess. Then he requests the Goddess to authorize him [to exercise the power of the mantra]. Then he worships the deity's attendant deities like Kālī, and so on. [They are Kālī, Kapālinī, Kullā, Kurukullā, Virodhinī, Vipracittā, Ugrā, Ugraprabhā, and Dīptā. The second circle of her assistants consists of Nīlā, Ghanā, and Valakā, and the third circle consists of Mātrā, Mudrā, and Mitā]. Then he worships her attendant mother-goddesses Brāhmī, and so on, and their Bhairavas, Asitāṅga, and so on. [They are Brāhmī, Vaiṣṇavī, Māheśvarī, Cāmuṇḍā,

Kaumārī, Aparājitā, Varāhī, and Nārasiṃhī; and Asitāṅga, Ruru, Caṇḍa, Krodha, Unmatta, Kapāli, Bhīṣaṇa and Saṃhāra]. Then he worships [the deity's consort] Mahākāla. Then he worships the Goddess's [weapons, that is,] her sword, and so on. Next he worships the lineage of his guru. Then the ritualist repeats the worship of Kālī. This is followed by the offering of bali [a sacrificial animal, or in some cases nonvegetarian food for the spirits]. This is followed by the fire sacrifice. Then, having performed *prāṇāyāma* [as a preparation for *japa*], he performs mantra repetition (*japa*) of his main mantra [which is a form of one-pointed meditation]. Finally, the intelligent worshipper dedicates the merit of his *japa* to the deity and then performs *prāṇāyāma* for a second time.

Esoteric Worship of Goddess with Alcohol and Other Ingredients

68cd. At this moment the worshipper may, O Goddess, collect [esoteric ingredients such as] alcohol [meat, fish, fried food/a partner for intercourse, and the sexual fluids].

Concluding Section of the Worship

69-71. Afterward, the worshipper offer the deity *arghya* and also dedicates himself to the Goddess. Then he recites the Goddess's eulogy and then recites her protective *kavaca* ["armor," a special hymn used as a mantra, which guards every part of the worshipper's body]. Finally he prostrates himself. Afterward he mentally utters the formula, "I am Śiva," while making the gesture of bidding her farewell. He then draws a diagram on the southwestern corner and offers *arghya* and other offerings to the goddess Ucchiṣṭacanḍālī. He then himself puts a mark on his forehead with the sandal paste offered to the Goddess and partakes of some of the offered food. Thereafter he can do whatever he wishes.

Alternative Brief Ritual

Alternatively, the initiated Tantric ritualist who has composed and fixed his mind in devotion and meditation may perform a shortened version of the worship.

First he performs the *nyāsa* of the poet-sage, and so on, of his main mantra; then he purifies his hands [with *nyāsa*] followed by *nyāsa* of his fingers and the extensive nyāsa of his body. Then he performs the nyāsa of his six limbs. Then he claps his hands three times [to remove obstructing spirits], then encircles his surroundings with [a fiery barrier]. Then he performs breath control followed by *dhyāna* on his mantra deity and then mentally performs her worship. Then he prepares and places the pitcher of *arghya* water, and worships the seat [of the Goddess]. On that he invokes the Goddess after having meditated on her image. Then he performs her ritual welcome, and so forth, followed by establishing life in her symbol, *jīvanyāsa* or *prāṇapratiṣṭhā*, and finally worships the supreme Goddess. Then he worships the attendant deities Kālī, and so on, as well as the eight śaktis, Brāhmī, and so on, along with their bhairavas. Then having worshipped Mahākāla he worships his guru's lineage as well as the Goddess's attributes and weapons such as the sword. This is followed by a repeat of the worship of the Goddess. Then the foremost of all worshippers practices breath control before performing his *japa*. He dedicates the [merit of his] *japa* to the Goddess's hand. He performs the concluding breath control, prostrates himself, recites the Goddess's panegyric and *kavaca* and causes the special *arghya* to be offered. He then dedicates himself [to the Goddess] and bids her farewell with the gesture of resorption. He draws a diagram on his southwestern side and worships Ucchiṣṭacaṇḍālī. In conclusion, he partakes of some of the offered food and then he may do as he pleases.

5. Maṇḍala as an Image of Man*

The surviving texts of *Tantra* go back to about 1500 years, but the ideas they contain may well be centuries older. Thus the Tāntric tradition, coexisted with the Vedic tradition, which is the other, more important Indian religious tradition. Indeed, one reason for the later date of Tāntric texts is that they were written or redacted by high-caste Hindus coming from the Vedic tradition, who were naturally slow to accept Tantra. In the early stage of the development of Brahmanical religious practices, the discipline of yoga, the hallmark of Tāntric religious practice, was followed mainly by social dropouts. The adherents of the Vedic or Brahmanical religion did *not* at first encourage such yogic practices. So it took a very long period for the two traditions to accept and influence each other openly. But classical Hinduism both non-sectarian and sectarian shows the result of assimilation of the two traditions.

The Tāntric form of religion is found in all indigenous Indian religions: Hinduism, Buddhism and Jainism. But in this paper I shall discuss the influence of Vedic tradition on certain central concepts and ritual practices of the Hindu Tantra. There are Vaiṣṇava, Śaiva and Śākta Tāntrics who respectively regard Viṣṇu, Śiva or the Mother Goddess as the Supreme Deity. Varieties within these main groups are many and complex. However there are features common to all the three groups and I will therefore dwell on the

* This paper was originally drafted for the symposium, "The Destiny of Man" organized by Dr T.S. Maxwell as part of the Festival of India in London, April 1982, as an extension of the exhibition *In the Image of Man.* I wish to thank Dr Maxwell for suggesting further revision.

similarities and ignore the differences. Tāntrics, practitioners of Tantra, are religious sectarians. This term has a precise meaning in Hindu context. Sectarians are monotheists. They regard a particular deity as supreme.

In Hindu soteriology, the creation is cyclical and God the Supreme Deity creates and sustains His creation and creatures; destroys the universe; and rewards and punishes as well. Punishment takes the form of concealing Himself from the person punished; and conversely, to favour is to reveal Himself to a devotee. The goal of a religious practitioner is to escape the non-ending involvement with the cycle of creation and destruction and the last divine function grants him just that. The person who practices Tantra, the *sādhaka*, must be formally initiated into the cult of his sect, that is, the worship of his chosen deity (*iṣṭadevatā*), by a *guru*. The *guru* has supreme importance in Tāntric religion. Only he can guide one to one's goal. One must trust him implicitly and obey him in everything.

Tantra is, as the term suggests, very much a matter of practice, rather than mere faith or understanding. In particular, Tantra is a matter of ritual and of meditation; the two always take place together. A distinctive feature of Tantra is that it can be undertaken for either of the two goals: religious salvation or worldly power. All Indian religious techniques are thought to bring the practitioner power, but most systems discourage the exploitation of the power. Tantra does not. It is frankly both a religious and a magical technique. Moreover, the magic can be for good (white magic) or for evil ends (black magic). Many Tāntric sects, especially the Vaiṣṇava sects, deplore the use of black magic, but they all believe that a successful *sādhaka* acquires powers which he can use as he sees fit. It is for this reason that the aspect of the Supreme Deity with which the *sādhaka* wishes to relate is called Śakti, or Power.

An account of some basic ideas of Tāntric philosophy or, perhaps more accurately, Tāntric theology is in order, because it is closely linked to the practice of Tantra. We must begin by stepping back for a moment to take a broader view. Two ideas have run through Hindu religious thought from the very beginning. The earliest form of Hinduism, which is commonly known as the Vedic religion or Brahmanism, was centered on the phenomenon of sacrifice. However different Hinduism came to be later, it never lost sight of this idea of sacrifice, even when the term came to be used in a metaphorical way. Certain leading ideas which had been put forward in Vedic literature as a theory of sacrifice never lost their influence and importance.

According to the *Ṛgveda* (10.90), the Creator God created the universe, the cosmos, by performing a sacrifice; and what he offered in that sacrifice was Himself for, indeed, nothing else existed. Thus the universe was made out of the body of God. The cosmos is consubstantial with God. Hinduism never quite lost sight of this idea, and this paper is chiefly concerned with that idea proposing that the cosmogramic *maṇḍala* symbolizes this identification. A second idea can be traced back to the very same myth. The Creator God was the first, the prototypical sacrificer, and the sacrificer in Hindu thought stands for man, or at least for a religious man. We should therefore follow the example of the Creator and offer sacrifice; and in doing so, we are to realize that parts of us as individuals correspond to the parts of the universe, in the same way as in the Divine Sacrifice. This idea may not be as unfamiliar as the first, because it is found in many mystical traditions. It is generally known as the equivalence between the microcosms, the human individuals; and the macrocosm, the world.

But early Indian religious thinkers took a further very important step. They put these two ideas together. If God is the universe, and man also corresponds to the universe, it follows logically that man corresponds to God. This idea is crucial to all Hindu paths to salvation.

In the Indian tradition, the correspondence between man and God is not worked out in physical detail: it did not lead to the kind of idea familiar in the Christian tradition, that man is formed in the image of God. Attention was concentrated rather on what could be the essence of man and, indeed, of God. One result was the concept that man has some eternal animating principle: the familiar concept of the soul. By the equation I have described, one can immediately deduce that man's essence, his soul, is made of the same stuff as God, who is the soul of the world. A popular metaphor was that our souls relate to God as sparks to a fire. They are the same thing provided one is able to realize this.

Now, if God and the world are the same thing, two problems arise immediately. The first is: why is this fact not obvious? There must in fact be, or *appear* to be, some kind of difference between God and the world. So what kind of difference is that?

The second problem is the following. Obviously there are two very different kinds of things in the world. In the Western tradition, one would probably say that there are things which are alive, and things which are not. The Indians saw it a little differently: they said that there are things which are conscious, and things which are not. And obviously God is more like what is conscious than He is like what is unconscious.

Following this line of thought, Indian theologians arrived at the conclusion that the crucial thing about God is His consciousness—it is, indeed, His defining characteristic, His very essence. And the same is thus true of the individual soul: it is pure consciousness. The Tāntric theologians completely endorsed that Brahmanical idea. Consciousness here is very narrowly understood. It is absolutely not thought. Thought is discursive and complicated. Consciousness is simple, indeed unitary. It is the pure light source, which makes the world visible, knowable. This comparison of consciousness to light is very important. Consciousness is thus conceived as being itself totally inactive; yet it is the condition which makes all activity possible.

Tāntric philosophy says that ultimately the unconscious bits of the universe, like stones, are also God and hence consciousness, but a consciousness that has decided to conceal itself (*ātmasaṇkoca*) Here we come to the double concealment which God decides on; firstly, He conceals the fact that His true form is identical with the individual soul; and secondly, he conceals His true nature as consciousness to manifest Himself as unconscious phenomena. The world of the Tāntric, then, is ultimately all God, but it contains a vast range of things, from things as gross as stones to things as subtle as God. Mind, for example, comes somewhere between these two extremes. We thus have three ranges, scales, or gamuts, all of which coincide. Looking from God downwards, we have the range from conscious to unconscious, the range from simple to complex, and the range from subtle to gross. These three ranges are co-ordinate; in fact, they are different aspects of the same thing. Moreover, movement down the scale is precisely what happens when God creates the universe.

A *maṇḍala* contains circles enclosing one central point. It is an image of the cosmic happening or cosmic act. The circles, considered to appear centrifugally, depict these ranges. Another metaphor used by Tāntric to explain this image is that of throwing a stone into an expanse of still water. The disturbance thus created produces a pattern of ring-like waves moving outwards from the centre of disturbance, while remaining centred on it. The *maṇḍala* arrests this metaphor in lines.

Tāntrics hold to the ultimacy of the personal God. As we shall see in a moment, His personal attributes play a fundamental role in their system. Nevertheless, their monotheism cannot be clearly understood unless one remembers the pervasive Hindu tradition of God as an impersonal essence, devoid of all duality, best described as 'not this, not that.[1] This tradition helps to explain why, in Tāntric theology as we are about to see, so little can be predicated of the masculine God—whether he is conceived and worshipped as Śiva or Viṣṇu. This apparent paradox, that God is everything and yet nothing can be predicated of Him, is solved by the Tāntric by introducing the concept of Śakti, the feminine principle.

It is important to understand that we are dealing here with a hypostatization, indeed, a personification. Basically, *śakti* is simply an abstract noun, derived from the verbal root *śak*, 'to be able to'. Like most abstract nouns in Sanskrit, it is grammatically feminine.

Śakti cannot be adequately translated by a single word. The concepts of power, potency and potentiality are all subsumed under it. God has the potentiality to be everything in the world, the power to do everything in the world—had He not, He would not be God. Ultimately, this power, this potentiality, is nothing different from God. The enlightened mystic can perfectly realize that unity. But he also realizes that God's active aspect, everything which is other than pure consciousness, is his Śakti.

The theory of Śakti is the key point of Tāntric theology, and the symbolism of Śakti moulds Tāntric ritual. Like God Himself, but one step down, so to speak, Śakti can be seen as one or many. It is a single principle, the aspect of God which can become manifest. Śakti is conceived as a feminine principle and is mythologized as the wife of God, inextricably entwined with Him in loving embrace, which fact is symbolically represented by the central point of the *maṇḍala.* On the other hand, everything in the world is an aspect of Śakti; and just as Śakti has been hypostatized from the divine essence, an adjective made noun, an attribute regarded as a principle, so everything else can be referred to as if it were a separate thing, though it is really only an aspect of Śakti, of God's creative self-manifestation.

It will be remembered that consciousness is compared to a light. In Tāntric theology, God has two complementary aspects called *prakāśa* and *vimarśa*—'illumination' and 'consideration' or 'thought'. The first is God's essence, but by itself it achieves nothing. God's thinking (*vimarśa*) is the first stage in His creative activity of making Himself manifest. *Vimarśa* is also the Supreme Śakti. God's thought, which is at the same time the deployment of His creative power, creates the universe at every moment; His withdrawal of His thought, His reversion to a state of pure consciousness, destroys it, reabsorbing it into the primal unity. God chooses by His discursive thought to conceal His true nature as pure consciousness to all individuals. But a *sādhaka* may by his rigorous tāntric practices and devotion move God to favour this devotee to escape the bondage of worldly existence by revealing His true divine Self to him/her. This is His grace. We thus see that in Tāntric theology the active aspects of Godhead, viz. His omnipotence and omniscience belong really to Śakti, His Power. Śakti's knowledge is a form of discursive thought (*vimarśa*). The concept of Śakti, the active aspect of the Godhead clearly shows us that Śakti's processing the acts of creation through her divine attributes like omnipotence, omniscience and so forth disturb the bliss of God's pure subjective consciousness, His transcendence.

We come now to the individual or, more precisely, to the individual Tāntric practitioner, the *sādhaka*. He is ultimately identical with God. He believes that in his essence he is both omnipotent and omniscient as well as the transcendent consciousness. His goal is to realize this fact, in the full sense of the word 'realize'. By completely believing and understanding it he will make it a reality. This realization is to be achieved through ritual (in which mimesis plays an important part), and through meditation, much of which is based on visualization.

We need now to take a closer look at how the *sādhaka* identifies with God. His aim is to identify with God in three forms, which are all present in the ritual. The first of those forms is his *guru.* The second is the form of God as sound, as revealed in the *mantra.* The third is the form in which God can be visualized. And this is where the *maṇḍala* is used.

In a recent paper[2] Sir Ernst Gombrich writes of three, competing theories of how art relates to human emotion. The oldest he calls the magico-medical theory that art creates moods and evokes emotions. The second theory, current in the European Renaissance, is that art depicts reality, like a play. The artist is seen "to hold, as it were, the mirror up to nature". The third theory, introduced by Romanticism, sees art as a symptom, an expression of the artist's inner state. While all these theories are relevant to this discussion, it is to the fourth theory, Sir Ernst's own, that I wish to draw attention. It is that the artist gets feedback from his creation, and interacts with the tradition within which he works.

"The... theory... of the ancient world which concentrates on the effects of art on the emotions, almost as if the means of the artist were comparable to incantations or even to drugs, seems to me the most important of them all. But, I would urge that the first to feel this effect, and indeed to seek it out, is the artist himself who discovers and selects the kind of emotion he wishes to cultivate and express".[3]

The description perfectly suits the purpose and effect of the *maṇḍala,* used by the *sādhaka.* That familiar, symmetrical linear diagram is a cosmogram, representing God/Śakti, in the form of the created universe, deployed in multiplicity. Of course it is moot whether the *maṇḍala*—diagram—can be called an art-form or an art-expression. Looking at a well-made *maṇḍala* I think that, like an anthropomorphic image of a deity, it could be so regarded. The *sādhaka* employs this visual aid in order to create the appropriate emotion and to focus his concentration. As a result, he can easily identify himself with this artistic expression of God, a linear image. The *sādhaka* uses symbols, the meanings of which have become fixed and easy to recognize in the orthodox Hindu tradition.

The basic form of a Hindu Tāntric *maṇḍala* consists of a square, which encloses a circle, which in turn encloses a triangle, in the centre of which is point. The word *maṇḍala* means 'circle', and it is the circle with its central point which is common to all Tāntric traditions, Hindu, Buddhist and Jaina. The circle represents the cosmos emanating from God at its centre. The central point is known as *bīja*, 'seed', or *bindu*, 'drop'. The circle is called *cakra*, literally wheel, of which *bindu* is the hub. The connection between hub and rim of a wheel is, of course, a spoke (*ara*). In Tāntric iconography, the spokes are shown not as lines but as lotus petals placed symmetrically. That is why, for example, the thousand-spoked wheel (*sahasrāra-cakra*) is depicted as a thousand-petalled lotus. The spokes are also rays of light. They symbolize both the facts that God is connected to everything, being immanent in the cosmos; and that he is the unmoved mover, as the centre-point of the hub is still while the wheel revolves. By contrast with the circle and the point, the square and the triangle do not appear in every *maṇḍala*. The triangle is essential to the Śaiva/Śākta *maṇḍala*. There it represents the female principle in the form of the 'womb' (*yoni*), which encloses the seed. Macrocosmically, it thus shows God's first self-differentiation, His initial manifestation through His Śakti. Microcosmically, it represents man's fall from the primal unity. Ignorant man, who is subject to constant rebirth in *saṃsāra*, is even further from the centre, on the rim of the wheel. The square which forms the outer boundary of the *maṇḍala* has a gap in the middle of each side called *dvāra*, 'gate'. The sides are aligned to the cardinal directions. The square is usually called *bhū-pura*, 'earth citadel' or *bhū-prākāra*, 'earth rampart'. In the Tāntric cosmogony, *bhū*, 'earth', is the grossest of the thirty-six levels of cosmic creation, the farthest from God. It may refer both to the element earth, and to the earth on which we stand.

The *sādhaka* physically goes into the *maṇḍala* at his initiation. What concerns us here, however, is that he does so in imagination every time he does his daily ritual, his yoga.[4] He thinks of himself as entering the outermost square,[5] the grossest form of creation, by the gate facing him as he begins his meditation, and gradually progressing through the divine realm of the goddess towards the centre, the *bindu*. The progress is from gross to subtle, from unconscious to conscious, from complexity to unity, from lower to higher levels of reality. He imagines the destruction of each stage, once he passes through it, thus recapitulating the destruction of the cosmos, and its reabsorption into primal unity. When he reaches the centre, he has realized his identity with God. At that point, he realizes that creation emanates from him.[6] He then identifies himself with the universe, which is represented in the *maṇḍala*. His body is now the universe. In ritual, this identification is both visualized and acted out in the performance of *bhūtaśuddhi* (purification of one's gross body) and *nyāsa* (replacement of this body with the divine one).

I have already remarked on the power of an art object over the emotion of its beholder, and that the first beholder on whom this power is tested is the artist himself, who draws on symbols and motifs from his own tradition. The *maṇḍala* is one of the few art forms of which the sole beholder is often the artist himself. The tradition on which the *sādhaka* draws is deeply influenced by the prestigious Vedic tradition. I offer as a hypothesis that the square enclosure of the *maṇḍala* has Vedic antecedents. Vedic models turn up throughout Tāntric ritual. The Tāntric texts take pseudo-Vedic titles, calling themselves *saṃhitā* and *āgama*, both originally terms for the Veda. The daily Vedic ritual of fire sacrifice is always performed just after the daily Tāntric ritual. This latter ritual, indeed, is referred to as *bahiryāga*, 'external sacrifice', and its accompanying meditation as *antaryāga*, 'inner sacrifice'. Moreover, the symbolism of Vedic sacrifice is incorporated in the meditation on the six *cakras* in the body. The *maṇḍala* with its enclosing square is the Tāntric analogue to the sacred area in which the Vedic sacrifice takes place, the fire altar. The square symbolically represents the fire alter, for in Vedic domestic ritual the platform on which the sacred fire is kindled is usually square. Thus the *sādhaka* enters his sacred enclosure, sacred ground (*bhū*) just as the Vedic sacrificer enters his.

In a brilliant article[7] Malamoud describes the symbolism of the Vedic fire altar for the *agnicayana*. Though this particular altar, which is for a *śrauta* not a domestic ritual, is not square (it is in the shape of a bird), it represents the body of the creator god Prajāpati, who has dismembered himself to create universe, and with whom the sacrificer (*yajamāna*) is identified. One can draw parallels between Malamoud's description and the Tāntric *maṇḍala*:

"The fire altar is made of five layers of bricks separated by four layers of lose earth. There is a fifth layer of loose earth on top; on it are put gold vessels in which ultimately the fire is lighted.... For some [texts] the layers of loose earth are the mortal parts of Prajāpati, namely hair, skin, flesh, bones and marrow, whereas the layers of brick represent his immortal parts, namely spirit, hearing, sight, voice and breaths. In building the altar of bricks, one grips the mortal parts in the immortal, which act to protect them; one thus makes the whole immortal".

Similarly, the *maṇḍala* serves to divinize or immortalize the *sādhaka*. Again:

"For other texts... Prajāpati is the year. The five parts of his body dispersed during the creative process are the seasons. The five layers of brick reconstruct the five seasons. But Prajāpati is also space, the five layers are the five points of the compass: east, south, west, north and the zenith".

This explanation stresses the equivalence between God and the macrocosm—both represented in the altar and *maṇḍala*, with its square diagram oriented to the cardinal directions and its central point showing the zenith. God has deployed Himself in time and space.

"In the centre of the first layer is placed a golden human statuette, an image of Puruṣa ('Man')... [which] at the same time is an image of the human sacrificer for whose benefit the sacrifice is performed. (Besides, the statuette is an image of Agni, since it rests on a lotus, which is the birthplace of Agni.) *The altar and the sacrificer are thus consubstantial.* [My italics]. The entire edifice, bricks and statue, is an offering, and the rite must be so conducted and interpreted as to display the identity of the sacrificer and the offering."[8]

Tāntric ritual is conducted *without* the Vedic fire, so there seems to be no analogue in the case of the *maṇḍala* with the role of the fire in the ritual of the *agnicayana.* That apart, the parallel is so clear as to require few words. The *sādhaka* enters the square of his *maṇḍala* to become identified with the cosmic sacrificer and sacrifice, the Puruṣa of *ṚV* 10.90, when he enters the sacrificial area. The *maṇḍala* as a representation of the cosmos repeats the identification which the *Brāhmaṇa* texts establish between the cosmos and the fire altar. Moreover, the cosmos and the fire altar both represent God, whether He be called Prajāpati or Śiva. Finally in both cases the religious practitioner, the *yajamāna,* in the Vedic case and, the *sādhaka* in the Tantric case, becomes identified with the deity represented by the alter or the *Maṇḍala.*

NOTES

1 Kṣemarāja, *Pratyabhijñā-hṛdayam,* ed. Jaydev Singh, Varanasi, 1961, passim.

2 E.H. Gombrich, "Four Theories of Artistic Expression", *Architectural Association Quartely,* XII, 4, 1980, pp. 14-19.

3 Ibid., p. 19.

4 *Yoginihṛdaya-tantra,* ed. G. Kaviraj, Varanasi, 1963, Chs. 1, 3.

5 Śivacandra Vidyārṇava, *Tantratattva,* new edn., Calcutta, 1973, p. 526.

6 *Pratyabbijña-hṛdayam,* 16-20.

7 Ch. Malamoud, *La Brique Percée: sur le jeu du vide et du plein dans l'Inde brahmanique,* in *Figure du vide, Nouvelle Revue de Psycbanalyse,* XI, prin-temps 1975, pp. 205-22.

8 Ibid., p. 211, translated from the French by Richard Gombrich.

6. The Religious and Literary Background of the Navāvaraṇa-Kīrtana of Muttusvāmī Dīkṣitār: Dīkṣitār's Cycle of Nine Hymns to Goddess Tripurasundarī/Śrī-cakra

1. Introduction

Muttusvāmī Dīkṣitār was born in 1775 and died in 1835. He is one of the three great poet-composers who gave the classical music of South India its present distinctive shape. The youngest of those three giants, Dīkṣitār, was the most versatile and innovative of them all.

The language of his songs, which is almost entirely Sanskrit, shows his mastery of classical erudition. It is musical, colourful and used with great economy. His knowledge of Sanskrit grammar, poetics and literary norms and of the classical tradition of rich imagery and subtlety of expression gave his songs a rare depth of meaning and yet a deceptive simplicity. In their expression the songs are fine examples of a classical heritage. Moreover, as V. Raghavan[1] said, Sanskrit was the most suitable medium to convey the complex religious idea borne by the songs. Following an ancient tradition, Dīkṣitar composed his songs as object of offering in his worship of the relevant deity.

Also the themes of these songs, invariably addressed to a deity, often belonging to a particular temple, come from an ancient religious heritage. That heritage has been formed by a constant exchange of ideas between two most important medieval religious traditions. The first of these is self-surrendering and ecstatic devotionalism (*prāpatti-bhakti*), and the second is the esoteric, ritualistic gnosticism known as *tantra.* The complex synthesis resulting from this exchange was already more than a thousand years old at Dīkṣitār's time. During that long period, many sects and cults were created; and these further developed and changed their original forms. Even the old orthodox brahmanical Hinduism, the non-sectarian "standard" (*smārta*) Hindu religion, underwent many metamorphoses.

Dīkṣitār was born in a *smārta brāhmaṇa* family which maintained traditions of Vedic ritual and Sanskrit learning. Moreover it was a family of musical tradition. His father, Rāmasvāmī Dīkṣitār, was a famous musician, poet and composer, a scholar, and a very religious man. For the sake of a peaceful and creative life he moved to the city called Tiruvārur, an important pilgrim centre of many temples, among which the temple of Tyāgarāja was the chief.

The fame of Rāmasvāmī Dīkṣitār travelled far and wide and even the Mahratta king of Tanjavur became his patron. Later he moved to Manali as the chief musician and the music master at the court of the rich local landlord Veṅkaṭakṛṣṇa Mudaliar. Rāmasvāmī was a pious man and often went on pilgrimages to visit famous temples, to whatever deity they were dedicated. It is said that Muttusvāmī was born as a gift of grace granted by Skandasvāmin, the six-faced god, Kumāra, of the temple of Vaidyeśvara. It is also said that Rāmasvāmī was very much influenced by the tradition of singing hymns (*bhajana*) at the religious centre of Govindapuram and twice monthly himself sang the entire suite of songs of the *Gītagovindam,* composed in the twelfth century A.D. at Puri (Orissa) by the poet-composer Jayadeva. *Gītagovindam* is a cycle of eighteen songs describing Kṛṣṇa, the pastoral incarnation of Viṣṇu, and his amatory exploits in company with the milkmaids. Ever since its composition the *Gītagovindam* has been sung every day at the temple of Viṣṇu at Puri as part of the daily ritual worship.

This short sketch of Rāmasvāmī Dīkṣitār's life[2] makes it clear that Muttusvāmī grew up in a typical South Indian cultured *brāhmaṇa* family of notable composers musicians. Moreover his father imbued the family with the spirit of the contemporary devotionalism typically expressed in hymn or prayer singing at important temples. In the history of South Indian devotionalism, temples and their main deities influence the everyday life of the devotees. They constantly feel the presence of these great gods who are partially incarnated in the temple images. Being a *smārta brāhmaṇa* also meant being free of sectarian bigotry; *smārta* tended to eclecticism and generally adhered to a pan-Indian Sanskrit-based culture. Like his father, Muttusvāmī frequently made pilgrimages to famous temples and composed and sang hymns to the local manifestations of god.[3]

While still young, Muttusvāmī left Manali in the company of a famous *yogin* of the Saṃkara-school of monks, a friend of his father, called Cidambaranātha, and went to Varanasi. There he was initiated into the Tantric cult of *śrī-vidyā* (the personification of occult knowledge), in a tradition which had its centre in Kāñcīpuram of Tamil Nadu. For five years he stayed in Varanasi, and in that great centre of Indian tradition learned among other things a great deal more about Indian classical music. It is said that on his return to Manali he went straight to the great temple of Skandasvāmin at Tiruttani, and there received his first experience of occult perfection in the form of grace of the god of the temple.

From then on he adopted the personal signature, Guruguha, which means, "he whose spiritual guide is god Guha or Skandasvāmin". His chosen personal deity was Śrī or Kamalāmbā, the presiding Goddess of Śrī-vidyā, also commonly known as Tripurasundarī, Lalitā, Sundarī, Ṣoḍaśī or Bālā.

2. The Kīrtana

The work analysed in this monograph is called the *Navāvaraṇa kīrtana*, which can be translated "Hymn to the Nine Enclosures". The nine enclosures will be explained in section 3 (vi) below. Here we explain the religious background of the term *kīrtana*.

From the second half of the first millennium A.D. till today Hinduism has been dominated by the monotheistic religion of *bhakti*, "devotion". The devotee (*bhakta*) surrenders to God's grace. This self-surrender is called *prapatti*. It is made with faith in God's boundless love and sympathy for all His creatures and in particular for his dedicated, self-effacing devotee.

This form of Hinduism, *prapatti-bhakti*, began in South India.[4] From the beginning of Tamil religious literature, in the early centuries A.D., poets mention God as present in temples and shrines in His full glory, even while at the same time they believe in His transcendence. This divine presence is localized in images. The *bhakti* religion denigrated complicated ritual in favour of simple service to God and the spontaneous display of pious emotion. Overwhelmed by his love for God, the devotee craved for His nearness and felt it to be available in the temples, where God had taken up residence to favour His devotees and enjoy their love. Tamil poet saints, both Śaiva and Vaiṣṇava, moved from one holy place to another to pour out their religious feelings in beautiful hymns to the forms of God manifest in the temples. Often such a saint remained associated with a particular temple.

Whatever the form of the particular temple image, to the ecstatic devotee it was his own chosen deity who appeared in it. Dīkṣitar stood in this tradition. His *Navāvaraṇa Kīrtana* was composed to praise and adore the deity of the Kamalāmbā temple at Tiruvārur. Dīkṣitar also composed many other song cycles dedicated either to one deity in a temple or to various deities in the famous temples of one place of pilgrimage; the latter cycles are called *sthalākṛti*.[5]

In all theistic religion the worshipper communicates to his god or gods through some form of prayer. The most compact form of Hindu prayer is *mantra*. *Mantra*, Hindu sacred speech, will be discussed in section 3 (v) below; it has various levels of significance, but concerns us here because prayer is one of them. Thus a believer will often repeat his *mantra* not only in the course of ritual devotions but also when he is emotionally disturbed.

However, a *mantra* is a formula, and allows little scope for expressing emotion. It was hymns of praise (*stuti, stava, stotra,* the terms are synonymous), through which devotees came to express their understanding of God and their feeling for Him. Like the Vedic poets, the later Hindus composed poetry to communicate their religious experience through the available literary medium. The mystic songs of Buddhist Tantric poets like Saraha and Kāṇha speak of their practice of *yoga* and their esoteric experience of the divine. In his hymns, Kramastotram, etc. Abhinavagupta describes the nature of his revered deity in so far as he is describable, and reveals his own serene devotion.[6] The best example of such poetic expression in connection with the cult of *Śrī-vidyā* and goddess Tripurasundarī is the *Saundaryalaharī,* which has profoundly influenced all members of the sect, including Muttusvāmī (see section 3 (iii) below).

South Indian devotionalism produced the vernacular hymns of the Tamil poet saints, the Ālvār and Nāyanmār. As this *prapatti-bhakti* spread through India, it gave rise to new forms of prayer-hymns variously known as *kīrtana, bhajana* and *dohā.* The characteristic feature of these lyrical hymns is a declaration of total surrender to one's chosen deity, who is envisaged as both infinitely loving and exquisitely beautiful. In these lyrics the poet's religious experience has become identical with aesthetic experience as defined by the classical Indian literary tradition. (To a limited extent this phenomenon can also be compared to Christian bridal mysticism).

This type of lyrical hymn developed most among Vaiṣṇava, whose religion valued and encouraged ecstatic experience. The two most important North Indian Vaiṣṇava sects, those founded by Vallabha and by Caitanya, have produced marvellous poets in this genre. But the earliest example of such lyrical poetry in Sanskrit is the *Gītagovindam*, which can be said to have been the main single source of inspiration for all later religious poet-singers, irrespective of cult or sect.

Kīrtana like *stava* or *stotra*, literally means "laudatory hymn". *Kīrtana* are of two types. In the *nāma-kīrtana* the deity is extolled by singing his or her names. The *līlā-kīrtana* recalls the deity's exploits described in the mythological texts (*purāṇa*).[7] Our text is in the first category. Such texts are particularly adapted to the outpouring by poet and singer (who may be the same person) of intense religious feelings. According to the Sanskrit literary tradition, these lyrics can express any of the whole gamut of human emotions.[8] But each song or cycle of songs should evoke a particular mood in all its phases of development till it reaches its ecstatic climax in the minds of both performer and audience. The *kīrtana* evokes the aesthetic experience of love for the divine (*bhakti rasa*). Among the various moods which may be experienced by religious devotees, the *smārta* and the Tantrics mainly accept three, namely the mood of repose (*śānta rasa*), of total self-surrender like a bond-slave (*dāsya rasa*), and tender love like that of a mother for her child or vice versa (*vātsalya rasa*). The *Navāvaraṇa Kīrtana* presents a combination of all these three moods. Schematizing somewhat, we may say that Dīkṣitār derived the *śānta rasa* from his *smārta* religiosity, the *dāsya rasa* from his *prapatti-bhakti*, the *vātsalya rasa* from the tender filial love which a Tāntric devotee feels for his Goddess.

The *bhakti rasa* of the devotee derives from his realization that his deity is of a perfect beauty transcending worldly experience. In Indian aesthetic theory the perfection of a beautiful object evokes in the beholder emotions so acute that they transport him from his mudane existence to the transcendent state of pure bliss. In the religious context this aesthetic object is the deity. The exquisite beauty and charm of the divine person evoke in the devotee feelings of wonderment and love which transport him to the realm of transcendent bliss. To the devotee his adored deity is beautiful and to love a marvellously beautiful god is no more than natural. That is why in later Vaiṣṇavism so much emphasis is laid on the beauty of Kṛṣṇa and his favourite companion Rādhā. Because of the different character of their mythology, Śaivism and its close relative Śāktism may initially have found this ideology of beauty inappropriate. But if the problem existed, it was overcome: though Śiva and the Goddess are often depicted in terrible forms (see 3 (ii) below), to the devotee they still appear as the manifestation of perfect beauty.

A creative artist can express his experience of aesthetic bliss in his own idiom, be it painting, sculpture, poetry, music or dance. Dīkṣitār, who was poet, composer and musician, used all these skills to give expression to his sensations of love and wonder at the beauty of his Goddess.

Abhinavagupta, the great theorist of Sanskrit literary aesthetics, propounded his *rasa* ideology on the basis of his own Śaiva Tantric views. He stood in the tradition of such theorists as Bhaṭṭanāyaka and Ānandavardhana and both of them approached the subject of literary aesthetic experience from the idealistic point of view. It is a retrospective experience of the same category as that of *Brahman*. According to Abhinavagupta, *rasa* is another name of Śiva, the supreme principle. His eternal inherent character is bliss. Śiva is ecstatic in his own bliss (*ānandaikarasāhlādī*) and the exuberance of that feeling results in His will to create. This ecstacy and His desire to create have resulted in this our world of phenomena, full of inherent vitality and beauty. *Rasa*, aesthetic delight, is an independent entity inherent in all monumental entities. But *rasa* finds its self-expression in the creative act symbolized in the *yāmala* (see below) concept of Śiva and his divine energy. This ideology of desire meant in the literary context that the erotic *rasa* (*Śṛṅgāra*) was considered the most felicitious of all *rasa*.[9]

Dīkṣitār too equates his deity, Tripurā, with the *śṛṅgāra rasa.* He drew on the one hand on the classical Sanskrit tradition of aesthetics and on the other on the tradition of *bhakti* lyrics and music composition.[10]

3. Dīkṣitār's Śāktism

(i) General character of Tantrism

Tantrism is a form of Indian religion in which ritual (known as "external worship") and meditative practice (also known as "internal worship") are indissolubly linked.[11] All Hindu Tantrics are monotheists, whether they consider the ultimate Godhead to be Viṣṇu or Śiva. They also consider the world to be real, not an illusion, and to be created by God.

Tantrism does not advocate renunciation of the world and its pleasures. On the contrary, the Tantric practises his religion for both worldly and supramundane ends. One who practises *tantra* is called a *sādhaka* ("achiever") and his practice is called *sādhanā* ("achieving"). He aims to achieve various powers (*siddhi*) or "achievements" in this world, powers both over others and over the normal constraints of nature. He also aims to achieve release (*mukti,* mokṣa) from rebirth, salvation. In the last resort he must choose between these two goals, but until he has achieved a vary high level they are congruent; spiritual and worldly advance go hand in hand.

Salvation consists in the realization that ultimately one is identical with the supreme Godhead, the object of one's adoration. The "internal worship" thus consists in achieving this identification with the deity, a process which takes place in elaborately prescribed stages. To each of these stages of mental progress correspond ritual actions which are carried out as one meditates. These ritual actions conspicuously involve stereotyped gesture (*mudrā*), formulaic utterance (*mantra*) and diagram (*cakra, maṇḍala, yantra*).[12]

Tantric practice is esoteric. One can only become a *sādhaka* through initiation (*dīkṣā*) by a teacher (*guru*). The *guru* himself embodies God and his initiation is a manifestation of God's grace.

Śrī-Vidyā, the cult into which Dīkṣitār was initiated, is a form of Tantrism known as Śākta, a word which derives from *śakti.* In Sanskrit generally *śakti* means "power", "potency", "potentiality"; in religion, it refers to God's creative energy, which is said by theologians to be both the efficient and the material cause of the world. In a general sense all Hindu Tantrics may be said to be *śakti-upāsaka,* worshippers of Śakti. The distinction between Śaiva Tantrics and Śākta Tantrics is a subtle one which need not here concern us.

What however must concern us is that Tantric theory and practice combine a great many symbolic systems and conflate different levels of understanding, so that they need lengthy explanation to be intelligible to the outsider. The different systems derive from different levels of sophistication, so that what may be merely metaphorical to the advanced initiate, may be understood literally by the simple outsider or beginner. From the point of view of the enlightened man who has attained ultimate truth, Tantric thought and action deal mainly with metaphors; from this point of view *śakti* is an abstraction, the aspect of Godhead accessible to human thought. As one moves down the scale of sophistication, such abstractions become successively hypostatized, deified and personified. This *śakti* becomes something one can talk about as an entity in its own right; an object of visual or phonic form; a mythological character, a goddess. All these levels are simultaneously present in *sādhanā.*

At the least sophisticated level, Śakti is the Goddess, Devī. Just as there are innumerable Goddesses (commonly called Mothers) in the villages of India, there are innumerable forms of Śakti; and just as the wise man understands all the village goddesses to be but one Goddess (much as Our Lady of Lourdes is the same as Our Lady of Paris), the wise Tantric will understand all *śakti* to be but aspects and emanations of the one Śakti.

(ii) Śākta mythology and the personality of the Goddess

As the Goddess has many forms and many aspects, she has many mythologies and many names. As the wife of Śiva she can be called by the feminine form of Śiva's names or epithets. One of Śiva's epithets is Tripurāntaka, "Destroyer of the Triple Citadel", a reference to a myth in which he destroys demons. The Goddess's name Tripurā must have derived from this, though its original meaning has been lost and the "three citadels" are given esoteric meanings.[13]

The Goddess can also be identified with any goddess in exoteric Hindu mythology; with Sarasvatī, the goddess of learning; with Kālī, the dark goddess of destruction; with Lakṣmī or Śrī, the goddess of fortune, prosperity and beauty — even though exoterically the latter are considered to be primarily names of the consort of Viṣṇu. Since Lakṣmī/Śrī is depicted as seated on a lotus, she is also called Kamalā ("Lotus Lady").

Śiva has both benign and terrible aspects. His very name, Śiva, meaning "benign", "auspicious", seems originally to have been an apotropaic euphemism, for his name in the Ṛgveda is Rudra, "Terrible". The same ambivalence inheres in the character of the Goddess. Indeed, the older Śaiva/Śākta cults, those dating from the first millennium A.D., seem for the most part to have concentrated on her dreadful aspect. This aspect is strikingly personified in the figure of Kālī or Mahākālī, whose name originally meant "the (Great) Black Lady"; but since Sanskrit *kāla*, "black", has a homonym which means "time", her name is also taken to refer to the Time which brings death to the individual and periodic destruction to the universe.

The cult of *Śrī-Vidyā* on the other hand is devoted to the benign form of the Goddess. Whether she had any historical connection with the Buddhist goddess Tārā we cannot be sure, but in some Vaiṣṇava texts, e.g. the *Lakṣmī Tantra*, she is also referred to as Tārā. Most of the names under which the Goddess is known in this tradition refer to her qualities as the personification of the Indian ideal of lovely womanhood. The perfect woman is sixteen years old (Ṣoḍasī), beautiful (Sundarī), prosperous (Śrī, Kamalā), sweetly youthful (Bālā), tender (Lalitā). She also personifies wisdom or knowledge (Vidyā) and so represents the logos (*śabda, nāda* — see section (v) below). This logos, as will be further explained below, is God's intuitive knowledge of the cosmos, the source of all creation; so the Goddess is the Matrix (Mātṛkā, Ambikā).

The goddess's opposite characteristics as benign and terrible are given coherence in myth by stories of how her terrible aspect is used to confront and conquer demons, the forces of evil. The single most famous mythological text about the Goddess is the *Devī-māhātmya*; it tells how she became the crusher (*mardinī*) of the buffalo demon (*mahiṣāsura*). Scarcely less important is the story found in the appendix to the *Brahmāṇḍa Purāṇa*. That appendix is called the *Lalitopākhyāna*, "The Lalitā Story". As we have seen Lalitā is identified by the devotees of *Śrī-vidyā* with Tripurasundarī, their central personification of the Goddess. The *Lalitopākhyāna* gives a coherent account of the Goddess's first appearance, her conflict with the demon Bhaṇḍa ("Treacherous"), who was menacing the world, and her final triumph over him. It also accounts for the subsidiary deities of the cult; Śyāmalā ("Dark Lady") is the chief minister (*mantranātha*) and companion of Tripurā as well as the divine source of music (*saṅgītamātṛ*); Vārāhī alias Vārtāḷī is the Goddess's military commander-in-chief and hence is called the "Punisher" (Daṇḍanātha, Daṇḍinī). All these deities are included in the temple worship of Tripurā. Of course, since all goddesses are manifestations of the one Goddess, Śyāmalā, etc. can also be identified with Lalitā/ Tripurā; we shall see that in his compositions Dīkṣitār uses all these names for her. The *Purāṇa* further tells the story of Lalitā's marriage to Śiva in his Kāmeśvara (Cupid) manifestation (see section (iv) below), and gives a concise explanation of how to worship Lalitā in the Tantric way. The narration ends with a long hymn enumerating the Goddess's thousand names, the *Lalitāsahasranāma Stava.* Pious worshippers of the Goddess still recite this hymn before her image daily. The multiplicity of her names is thus familiar to her worshippers; what may seem confusing to us is thus transparent to them.

(iii) The Śrī-vidyā cult: History

We do not know exactly when the cult of Śrī/Tripurā spread in Northern, Western and Southern India, but it cannot have begun very much before the previous millennium. The followers of the cult call themselves the *Śrī-kula* or *Śrī-saṃpradāya* ("Family" or "tradition" of Śrī). They have had a remarkable tradition of meticulous scholarship. Their two earliest scriptures, the *Nityaṣoḍaśikārṇava Tantra* and the *Yoginīhṛdaya Tantra,* are conspicuous among the early texts of the genre for their scholarly language, their expert handling of the subject matter, and accounts of *tantra-yoga* (ritual and meditation in Tantric *sādhanā*), more detailed and methodical than others found outside the self-conscious works of the Kashmir Śaiva philosophers.

The three basic texts of the cult are the two just mentioned and a later one, the *Tantrarāja Tantra.* These Tantra have exhaustively and systematically described the religious discipline of worship and meditation, practised by the followers of the Śrī-cult for occult power and worldly prosperity as well as for salvation. A very late compendium of the subject is the *paraśurāmakalpasūtra.* There are also several late Upaniṣads forming the sacred scripture of this sect.

Among the commentators on these texts the names of Jayaratha (twelfth century A.D.), Śivānanda (thirteenth century A.D.) and Maheśvarānanda (thirteenth to fourteenth century A.D.) are important. The first hailed from Kashmir but the latter two were respectively from Kerala and the Cola country. Maheśvarānanda also wrote the Prākṛt text *Mahārthamñjarī* on the philosophy of the Tāntric Śrī cult. The *Tripurārahasya-jñānakāṇḍa* is the other important treatise on its philosophy. Lastly one should mention Bhāskara Rāya, the last great Tantric and commentator of the same sect. He was a prolific writer with many commentaries and independent Tantric works to his credit. A *brahmin* from Mahārāṣṭra, he was a contemporary of Dīkṣitār. He travelled widely in India and won many disputes against the rival Hindu sects. The cult is also associated with Śaṃkara, the well known philosopher and religious reformer from Kerala (ca. 700 A.D.) propagating the view of idealistic monism. Gauḍapāda, often regarded as the great grand teacher of Śaṃkara, is considered to be the author of a famous treatise called the *Saubhāgyavardhanī*. Śaṃkara himself is credited with the fine poetical composition of a long hymn, the *Saundaryalaharī*. This is a late work and is a very important one for the followers of the Śrī-cult.[14] One cannot exaggerate its influence on Dīkṣitar himself who in his own hymns closely followed the exposition of the Goddess Tripurasundarī as revealed in the Saundaryalaharī. The followers of the Śrī-sect take each verse of this text for a *vidyā* revealing one aspect of the Goddess. Each of these aspects is worshipped as a *śakti* with a specific mystical diagram for receiving special occult powers. This is an example of how a simple hymn can be elevated to the status of a *mantra* or *vidyā*. In fact the *Navāvaraṇa Kīrtana* too is sometimes treated as such.

4. Śākta Theology

Since the theology of the Srī-cult permeates Dīkṣitār's songs, we must now try to explain it, as briefly as so complex a matter allows. The basic philosophical tenets of this school are the same as those of the Kashmir Śaiva sect. This is a monotheism which accepts no reality independent of the Supreme God. It is known as the system of non-duality (*advaya*). Inheriting the older view that absolute reality is the monistic principle, unqualified Brahman, the Tāntrics, who are monotheists, equate that monistic principle with *parama* (supreme) Śiva, i.e. Śiva in His highest and most abstract form. *Parama* Śiva is manifest in the empirical universe as His Power, Śakti. Thus the universe is Śakti, the Goddess. All phenomena — the unconscious matter and material objects and the conscious souls — are manifestations of Śakti and are essentially Śakti. Only Śakti here conceals her real identity behind a limited aspect of hers. These are, as it were, rays from the central Power, Śakti and in this way Śakti creates the diversity from the simple central unity which is herself. Śakti is this single integral unity which is both empirical and transcendental.

God, as the creator, has five cosmic functions. He is the creator, the sustainer and destroyer of the universe — functions which are exoteric and in the Hindu mythology commonly assigned to Brahmā, Viṣṇu and Śiva. Besides these three He also is the dispenser of cosmic and moral laws which concern the individual souls. This requires God's self-concealment from individuals, because essentially individuals are not different from God and thus they are not bound by any such law. But God's divine power to delude the souls make them forget their true nature. This power is called *māyā.* This is God's fourth cosmic function, the concealment by means of His *māyā*, and this creates the individuals. Finally, God also is the bestower of grace which saves his true devotees.[15] He executes these functions through a series of assignments of His sovereign power (*ājñā*) to the Goddess in Her various manifestations. The Goddess, God's divine personality *ahaṃtā* (literally "I-ness") is a hypostatization of abstract ideas such as the divine consciousness (*prakāśa*), will (*icchā*) and discursive knowledge (*vimarśa*). Indeed, the whole of Tāntric theology can be understood as a series of hypostatizations, which in the context of religious practice — the peculiarly Tantric combination of ritual and meditation — takes the further step of becoming personifications. The language of Tantric theology is no more paradoxical than that of Christian theology, for example; but to readers from an alien culture it can at first sight seem opaque. Tantric theology, like the Christian theology, has to deal with two related paradoxes; that of unity in multiplicity; and that of time and eternity — God (and souls) are both in and outside time. For the Tantric these two paradoxes are intimately related. Whereas for most Christians the first paradox is confined to the nature of God (the world being only multiple), the Tantric, whose monotheism arose from an earlier monism, sees the world as real and yet as identical with God. God is ever active in creation and yet still - the unmoved mover, as the Christians say. All this requires the use of highly figurative language. Prominent in that language is the use of sexual symbolism. And we must remember that in Hindu thought the feminine is the principle of activity, the male of passivity and at the same time of authority.

Those who are aware of the doctrine of the Trinity will not find it difficult to understand the concept of God and His Power (Śakti) as two in one, or to take the further step of seeing Śakti personified as a Goddess, much as the holy Ghost appears as a Dove. But then one must be prepared to see this process many times repeated, as the unity of Śakti is in turn dissolved into several aspects, which are hypostatized and personified, some of them again to undergo the same kind of dissolution. For example, Tripurasundarī is God's Power and at the same time she is God's thought, *vimarśa.* As the active source of the creation she is called the Mother (*Ambikā*). From Her emerge Her three primary creative aspects, God's Will (*icchāśkti*), God's omniscience (*jñānaśakti*) and God's omnipotent creative dynamism (*kriyāśakti*). All these *śaktis* are envisaged as different goddesses. Moreover the primal duality (like some of the other steps in this differentiation of God's unity) is expressed by Tantric theologicans in several different ways, to establish different metaphysical verities. Seen in Himself, God is an undivided whole, without parts. Śakti however can be seen as plural, and thus as having parts. These parts are called *kalā*, a metaphor taken from astronomy: a *kalā* is that theoretical segment of the moon which is added each lunar day of the waxing fortnight and disappears each lunar day in the waning fortnight. In Indian theory there are sixteen such *kalā*: fifteen segments plus one standing for the whole. These *kalā* are also personified as goddesses called Nityā. Thus the Goddess, Śakti, can be dissolved, as it were, into fifteen Nityā; and yet even amongst them She is identified primarily with Kāmeśvarī, the one who stands for the whole group. (Her name Ṣoḍaśī, which we mentioned above as referring to a sixteen-year-old girl, also means "the sixteenth" in this context. Such a "group" of divinities can be called a *cakra* or *maṇḍala*, the very term used for the cosmogram essential to Tantric ritual (see section 6 below).

God creates because his undifferentiated unity is affected by desire (*kāma*). *Kāma* is often personified, in common myth, as the Indian Cupid. In this context, Śakti is personified as Kāmakalā, "the differentiated desire". Śiva and Śakti are also personified as Kāmeśvara and Kāmeśvarī, "Lord and Lady of desire". This duality is referred to as a twin (*yāmala*) concept; by this is meant that the two are ultimately one, just like the Christian doctrine of God's three persons.

Śakti accounts for everything in the world including individual souls. The world is God in the sense that it is God's voluntary self-limitation. The material world, lacking consciousness, is extremely limited. Also limited, though less so, are individual souls; they possess consciousness, but not that perfect consciousness which is God's and which enables an individual to realize his true identity with God. Thus each soul (*jīva*) is also a śakti and one name for Śakti is Haṃsinī,

"She with the swan", because the swan is an ancient symbol for the soul.

The next duality we must consider is that of *prakāśa* (illumination) and *vimarśa* (reflection). Supreme Brahman, Parama Śiva, is consciousness, light, the sole illuminating principle: He alone reveals all. As Śiva's personality, the Śakti too is the light, *prakāśa,* without which no experience takes place as nothing becomes revealed. But as *prakāśa* she is completely fused and identical with Śiva: the Supreme Deity (*para*) and the supreme divine personality, are in no way distinct, since in the supreme state Śiva is unqualified, undiscernible and immutable. For creation to take place, the idea of creation (both as act and as product) dawns in the Supreme Deity. That is the primal manifestation of His divine personality, its contemplative aspect, *vimarśa. Vimarśa* is God's thought.[16]

The cosmos is created through divine agency (*kartṛtva*), agency which is irresistible, adamant and dependent on itself alone (*svātantrya*). God's potent contemplation has three aspects pertaining to the act of creation: three kinds of *śakti*: (1) divine Will, the desire to create and the sovereignty (because a sovereign's will is his command), *icchāśakti,* (2) divine Knowledge, omniscience, to which all created phenomena are distinctly revealed even before their creation, *jñānaśakti*; (3) divine Activity, which translates all creative desires into deeds, *kriyāśakti.* The divine personality, Śakti develops into Will (*icchā*), Knowledge (*jñāna*) and Action (*kriyā*) in that order. God's desire to create the universe pulsates and in a flash reveals the universe imprinted as it were on Śakti, God's thought.

Śakti's creating is nothing but Her expanding or unfolding Herself in waves of minor manifestations of Herself, secondary *śakti* which are like rays proceeding from the central Energy. These minor manifestations account for all phenomena in a scale of decreasing abstraction and subtlety, down to the gross, empirical world.[17]

The supreme Śakti is Śiva's personality and personality never exists without the person, in this case God. Thought does not exist outside the conscious thinker, just as will presupposes the willer. Thus the supreme Śakti combines both God, Śiva and His thought, *vimarśa,* His impulse to create. She combines his intuitive vision of the creation and His creative thrust.

Desire is the first pulsating (*spanda*) of the creative potency. This pulsating Energy (*Śakti*) energizes the whole of active creation and is to be experienced in living beings as their vital breath (*prāṇa*).[18] But God, the supreme consciousness, the locus of *prakāśa* and *vimarśa,* abides ever with the supreme Śakti and with every single manifestation of Śakti. This ever-abiding presence is called Sadāśiva — the ever-abiding Spirit. The whole gamut of creation — from Śakti down to inanimate objects like the stump of a tree — possesses this Spirit. Due to the variable nature of Śakti, this Spirit is explicit in some and hidden in others. The distance of the minor manifestations of Śakti from the central Energy not only determines their comparative subtlety and grossness but also their comparative transparency and opacity to reveal the inner Spirit.

In order to facilitate understanding the process of creation and the nature of each cosmic principle the Tantric religion utilizes the system of mythology and personifies each abstract principle as a deity. In Tantric ontology the pair of Śiva and Śakti head the list and are equated with God's will, *icchāśakti.* God Sadāśiva comes next and is *jñānaśakti,* the locus of divine intuition. The third is Īśvara, the *kriyāśakti.* He controls and wields sovereign power over the universe. The next position is given to the occult knowledge inherent in the *mantra* which are also gods.[19] For the gods, as will be explained in the next section, are identical with the *mantra* which the *sādhanā* (practice) can use to control them. From the theological point of view, these gods/*mantra* represent various aspects of God's power; so they too are Śakti. They are the mediating means to salvation. The *sādhaka* (Tantric practitioner), following his personal liking and disposition selects one of the gods belonging to the above-mentioned Tantric ontology. This choice is made at the time of his initiation and his *guru* may help his selection. Then the *sādhaka* follows the Tantric path to achieve his soteriological goal of realizing total union first with his adored deity and hence with God and as a natural consequence with the world. He has to realize that the world is no more or less than the contents of his consciousness. The light of that consciousness is refracted among a vast multiplicity of objects, but really those appearances are nothing but the light, the light which shines within him and is at the same time God. The distinction between subject and object which appears in one's experiences is pragmatic only; once he has grasped the omnipotence of his subjectivity he can deploy it to any purpose. He, the eternal subject, is beyond any external constraint; he has shaken off the fetters (*pāśa*) which made him but a beast of burden (*paśu*) to the Lord (*pati*). These fetters were but clouded consciousness, unawareness that he is himself the Lord. The world of the Tantric is all God and yet unlike God it contains a vast range of things, from things as gross as stones to things as subtle as God. In this world there are three ranges, scales or gamuts, all of which coincide. Looking from God downwards we have the range from conscious to unconscious, the range from simple to complex, and the range from subtle to gross. These three ranges are coordinate; in fact they are different aspects of the same thing; God's Śakti.

5. Sādhanā: The Means and the Mantra

We need now to take a closer look at how the *sādhaka* identifies himself with God. In his *sādhanā*, the Tantric, as he learns from his *guru*, aims to identify with God in three forms, which are all present in the ritual and meditation of the Tantra-yoga system. The first of these forms is his *guru*. The second is the form in which God can be visualized, which is present in an image. One such image is the symbolic diagram called a *cakra* or *maṇḍala* (circle). The *cakra* in our present context is the Goddess's image as the cosmos. Thus the *śrī-cakra* or the *navāvaraṇa maṇḍala* (the circle of nine enclosures) is the cosmic image of Tripurasundarī. The third form of God is the sound. His form as what is called a *mantra* or a *vidyā*. Thus it is that *śrī-vidyā*,[20] the complete and esoteric *mantra* of the Goddess Tripurasundarī is identical with *śrī-cakra*, the cosmic image of the same Goddess and both are objects of adoration for the followers of the cult of Śrī. One merely conceives the Goddess visually, the other sonically. In fact the role of the sacred formula (*mantra*) in Tantra cannot be exaggerated.

In order to understand the position of *mantra* in Hindu religion, we must return for a moment to the earliest Indian religious speculations. These aimed to explain not only the efficacy of the sacrifice but also why the words accompanying the sacrifice were necessary. As early as the Ṛgveda, the *mantra* is praised as (the form of) Agni (the fire-god) hidden in the sacrificer's heart; it is also said to guard important deities like Agni. In the hymn to Speech (*vāc*), Speech is said to be all-pervasive; it supports such exalted deities as Mitra, Varuṇa, Indra and Agni (Ṛgveda X.71.1 and 181.2). In the Upaniṣad a close link is established between consciousness, which on the empirical level is homogeneous with the life-breath (*prāṇa*), the mind, which is the faculty for discursive thought and speech (Cf. ChU. VII.3.1; I.5.3; I.4 and IX.23.2; BĀU. I.5.3.7).

The grammarians of Sanskrit and the Mīmāṃsakas, the theorists of the Vedic ritualism, developed closely related theories of the nature of speech and language. Patañjali, in the introduction to his great commentary on Pāṇini, the ancient Indian grammarian of ca. fifth century B.C., developed the theory that there exists an eternal sound which is the basis of any mental assessment of the meaning of significant sound. This essence of significant sound is called *śabda-sphoṭa,* "the bursting/illuminating sound"; it contains the meaning of all meaningful sounds of human language.[21]

Basing himself on Patañjali, Bhartṛhari (sixth century A.D.) built up his philosophy of grammar, in his Vākyapadīya. One can at once notice the close affinity of this grammarian and philosopher to the Tantric tradition; his ideas were further developed by the Śaiva Tantrics of Kashmir.[22] He and his followers put forward the fundamental thesis that the source of knowledge and of all created phenomena is the eternal sound-principle *śabdabrahman.* This is by nature a simple unity and self-illuminating consciousness. *Śabdabrahman* is further equated with the Vedic all-pervasive speech (*vāc*).

In the Tantric ideology of the Tripurā cult, the supreme deity is Śiva, but He is only apprehended in the goddess Tripurā, His Śakti. Śakti's essential nature is pure intelligence or pure thought (*vimarśa*). In fact Śakti is not only the Divine thought and Will manifest, but also the supreme principle of significant sound (*vāc/śabdabrahman*). Just before creation actually takes place, the whole of it in every detail is instantaneously imprinted on God's thought, *vimarśa,* like a blueprint. This flash of total cognition of the creation is called *pratibhā* (illumination, inspiration); it is the vision of what He wills to create which is considered the prior knowledge indispensable to the creator (Cf. *Tripurārahasya, Jñānakāṇḍa,* XX, 31-37). Thus it is that *vāc,* the principle of sound, is taken to be the immediate source of creation. In various Tantric texts it is described thus: "as the reflection of a mountain may be caught in a mirror, so also the creation is caught in pure divine thought, i.e. in the Goddess".[23] One should remember, though, what the Tantric thinker really meant is not a mirror but a canvas on which the creation is painted. Thus the Goddess is not only the evolving matter of which the universe is made, but also its substratum. At the same time as the divine thought, she is the intelligent creator or the artist. This last idea helps us to understand how Dīkṣitār's religious ideology was intricately related to his artistic creativity. It is believed that the individual creative power (*pratibhā*) is just a limited manifestation of the cosmic Śakti.

The initial content of Śakti as the divine thought is thus precisely language, the theoretical body of all possible sentences designating all possible states of reality. This then gives rise to the phonic matrix of language, the range of sounds used to form human speech.[24] And this matrix in turn, gives rise to language as we know it. As the *Lakṣmī Tantra* puts it: "I (Śakti) am the state of *pratibhā* inherent in all created object and adhering to each of them through all their different phases [of existence].... I am essentially consciousness and bliss, the source of all *mantra*; the absolute; the mother of all sounds; *śakti*, not subjected to appearance and disappearance".[25]

Thus *mantra* are the purest and the most potent manifestation of the Goddess, the essential principle of sound, the concrete form of the divine omniscience. The *Tripurarahasya, jñānakāṇḍa* writes that *śrī-vidyā*, the *mantra* which is symbolized in the diagram of nine figures (*navāvaraṇa cakra*), is indeed the Goddess Tripurasundarī, the cosmic creatrix, Śakti.[26]

The Sanskrit sounds or letters, fifty in number are taken to be the primary concrete manifestation of the goddess Speech (*vāc*). They constitute the final stage of the creative process of *vimarśa's* evolution. This final stage, Sanskrit speech, is called *vaikharī*. The highest manifestation of *vāc* is the transcendent form called *parā* or *nāda*; the next stage is the same as *prātibhā* but is designated *paśyantī* or *bindu*, ideal speech. Before appearing as concrete speech, *vāc* has another intermediary stage, subtle speech, which is called *madhyamā*. It is the form of speech just before it is uttered.

The fifty letters are considered to be the source of all *mantra*. The vowels, sixteen in number and preceding the consonants, are called the moon-sounds (*soma-varṇa*). Among the consonants, the mutes, twenty-five in number, are called the sun-sounds (*sūrya-varṇa*) and the remaining letters, sonants "pervasives" (*vyāpaka*), are called the fire-sounds (*agni-varṇa*). *Soma, sūrya* and *agni* are taken to be the goddess's luminous body. Each of these three has its circle of *śakti* called *kalā. Soma*, naturally has sixteen, *sūrya*, twelve (cf. the twelve *āditya*) and *agni*, ten.[27]

In Tantra a secret spell is called *vidyā*, a term which really means knowledge or scholarship. It is a form of *mantra*, which is the general term for occult formulas. A *vidyā* contains syllables and words. The syllables which stand independent, without being a part of a word, possess secret meanings known only to the initiated. Each *mantra* has a seed (*bīja*) or essential part. The *śrī-vidyā* consists of sixteen independent syllables arranged in three groups: *hrīṃaeīlahrīṃ; hasakahalahrīṃ; sakalahrīṃ*; and the seed or essential part of this *vidyā* is *aiṃhrīṃsauḥ*.[28]

It should be clear by now that the sound and language aspect of the Goddess who is identified with the *mantra* is very important to the Tantric who meditates mainly concentrating on this aspect of his adored deity. The religious practitioner seeking knowledge — the intuitive knowledge which is the essence of all knowledge and hence all creative power — worships the *vidyā*. *Śrī-vidyā* which is as much a spell as wisdom, is worshipped not only by the aspirants of salvation but also by the creative artists, the poet, the musician, the composer, etc. The practitioner realizing the true meaning of this *vidyā* acquires *pratibhā*, which is the essential nature of the Goddess *Tripurasundarī*, whose sonic form *śrī-vidyā* is and who during the meditation of the Tantric is manifest in the cosmogram, *Śrī-cakra*.

Tripurasundarī, thus being the essence of intuitive knowledge, *pratibhā*, is especially worshipped by the creative artists and poets. In Sanskrit poetics, only those who possess *pratibhā*, "poetic vision" which is in the last analysis the same as God's creative vision, are real poets. It is the supreme wisdom which can create novel phenomena, and the poet possesses the intuition which once in a while flashes forth the unique *pratibhā* resulting in the creation of true poetry.[29] A poet is one who possesses inspiration and even in the Atharvaveda he is said to possess *medhā*, which is a faculty akin to *pratibhā*.[30] Thus the notion of a poet's possessing occult power is an old Indian tradition. The lucky ones are born with it or one can acquire it by propitiating the Goddess and by practising Tantric *yoga*. In the Tantric *yoga* tradition practising music is a variant yogic discipline.

6. Sādhanā, The Religious Practice

The Śrī-cakra and its nine enclosures (āvaraṇa)

Tripurasundarī, the divine creative inspiration and vision as well as the cosmic matrix, is conceived as the starting point of the creation. As has been said already, the creative act is indeed a double concealment of God's and hence of Śakti's real nature. The cosmic creative act with all the three coordinating ranges is, in its entirety, captured in the diagram of *Śrī-cakra*. It is the image of cosmic happenings, depicted in geometrical figures intertwined to create nine circles or rather enclosures made of squares, circles and triangles, centripetally arranged around the central point representing Tripurasundarī. The flash of creative *pratibhā* in the pulsating *vimarśa* (divine thought) is like throwing a stone in the still water. The disturbance created produces a pattern of ring-like waves moving outwards from the centre of disturbance, while remaining centred on it. *Śrī-cakra* arrests this metaphor.

The number nine is very important in this *cakra*.[31] The basis diagram is made of nine triangles, four having their apex turned upwards and five turned downwards respectively representing Śiva, Śrīkaṇṭha and his Śakti, Śrī, Tripurasundarī. These are interesecting each other to form smaller triangles arranged as enclosures telescoping one into another. This diagram is often worshipped in three-dimensional form where the enclosures are arranged in tiers with its central point, the axis, placed on the top. These enclosures, five in total, encircle the central point, *bindu*. These five enclosures are then encircled first by a circular form containing eight lotus-petals and representing an eight-petalled lotus flower and then by another circular form containing sixteen lotus-petals. This entire diagram is finally enclosed in three squares, drawn in white, red and yellow, the sides being exactly on the cardinal directions. In the middle of each side is an opening to indicate a gateway. This last enclosure is called the citadel of the earth (*bhūpura*).

It is perhaps now time to say a few words about the term "enclosure" (*āvaraṇa*). The *cakra*-diagram is used in Tantric practice to fix one's concentration on one's deity. Tripurasundarī's cosmic creative act with all the three coordinating ranges subtle to gross, simple to complex and light to opacity, is seen as self concealment covering herself behind a series of self-manifestations. These manifestations are essentially *śakti*, but they reveal only a partial aspect of the cosmic Śakti. At each stage of creation a particular series of such *śakti* emerge from the central Śakti and provide a cover for this Śakti. The term *āvaraṇa* means "cover". Thus each emerging circle of *śakti* becomes an enclosure hiding the Goddess Tripurasundarī inside it. The square figure in the *Śrī-cakra* represents the grossest state of creation, i.e. the pragmatic world of the man. The *śakti* present in this state represent the gross and limited forms of the cosmic Śakti. These are minor goddesses and they possess powers to grant a Tantric minor occult powers. By showing this unimportant form of *śakti*, power, these minor *śakti* effectively conceal the real nature of the divine Śakti and mislead many Tantric practitioners. In this sense too the word *āvaraṇa*, cover, is used.

The Tantric receives the knowledge of the secret meaning of these figures of the *cakra* at his initiation rites. Thereafter, he must every day in his meditation identify himself with each one of these circles of *śakti* in the reverse order of creation, until he penetrates into the central mystery of the *bindu* and its essence the cosmic Śakti. According to the Tripurā-school, there are nine centres arranged vertically in every person. The *śrī-cakra*, the miniature macrocosm, is thus an aid to the ritual and meditative practices of a Tantric worshipper of Tripurasundarī to realize the essential nature of the Goddess. This realization brings salvation to him.

The lowest or first enclosure, the square one, is called the *trailokya-mohanacakra* (the circle that deludes the universe). The second enclosure consists of the larger lotus figure and is called the *sarvāśāparipūraka* (the circle that fulfills all desires). The third enclosure is called the *sarvasaṃkṣobhinīcakra* (the circle that agitates all). The lotus has special symbolic meanings in Hindu theology. It symbolizes, amongst other things, the act of God's self-concealment, *māyā,* inflicting on the individual soul's pseudo-limitations of time and space. These two enclosures thus represent the first stages of the creation of the universe. The *śakti* manifest on these levels are respectively designated as the secret deities and the very secret deities. They, when propitiated, can fulfill the aspirant's desired goal, which still is worldly. At these levels the Tantric is still a victim of desire — a desire not for minor object but for power and dominance over people. That is how he regards his deity — a sovereign and despotic cosmic power, ruling the cosmos. These first three enclosures thus completely hide the unity and simplicity of the supreme Being.

With the fourth enclosure, the Tantric starts his real encounter with the real nature of Śakti. The deities here are called the sectarian *śakti.* This *cakra,* called the *sarvasaubhāgyadāyaka* (that which grants all good-luck), consists of fourteen tiny triangles. A triangle symbolizes a womb and signifies *śakti* as the source of all phenomena, the cosmic mother. Thus the Tantric begins to realize the true nature of his deity as the cosmic source but still he sees her diversified.

The fifth cakra or *āvaraṇa*, consisting of ten little triangles is called the *sarvārthasādhaka* (the fulfiller of all aspiration). The deities present on this level are designated as those who are beyond the *kula*, i.e. a specific sect. The sixth *cakra* too consists of ten little triangles and is called *sarvarakṣākara* (the universal protector). The deities of this *cakra* are regarded as the seminal *śakti* who help the Tantric's spiritual regeneration. The Tantric rises above the bonds of the mundane life and becomes aware of his own cosmic nature.

The seventh enclosure is called the *sarvarogahara* (remover of all ill) *cakra*. It is made of eight small triangles and the deities here are called the esoteric *śakti* who are close to Tripurasundarī. The Tantric who comes in contact with them is in close range to his understanding the esoteric knowledge revealing the true nature of the supreme Goddess and thus is very close to his salvation.

The eighth *āvaraṇa* is just one triangle which is called the *sarvasiddhi-prada* (that which grants all perfection) *cakra*. Here the deities are three in number and represent the fundamental creative aspects of Goddess Tripurasundarī, Her sovereign Will, Omniscience and Omnipotence. As the primary aspect of the creating Śakti these *śakti's* are called the very esoteric goddesses who can reveal to the Tantric the mystery of creation and the true nature of its creatrix.

These three *śakti's* are worshipped as the goddesses Bhagamālinī, Kāmeśvarī and Vajreśvarī and are also designated respectively as Vāmā, Jyeṣṭhā and Raudrī. These last three names indicate their cosmic functions as the goddess of creation, the goddess of sustenance and the goddess of destruction respectively. Understanding these deities, their cosmic functions and their real nature, the *sādhaka* realizes the divine act of creation as the diversification of the central cosmic unity, symbolized in the ninth or the last *āvaraṇa*.

The last *āvaraṇa* is called the *sarvānandamaya* (that which is permeated by all-bliss) *cakra*. It is the central point (*bindu*) of the entire diagram. The Goddess, worshipped here, is called Mahā Tripurasundarī. As the source of the creation she is also called Ambikā, the mother. She is the cosmic flux (*spanda*), the ever-vibrating Śakti. As the *sādhaka* realizes Her to be the quintessence of all *śakti*, She is called the supreme as well as the subsidiary esoteric Goddess. But the Mahā Tripurasundarī is not a simple form. She combines both the primal polarity in the principle of God's Śakti and the eternal transcendental unity of the same principle. The first polarized divine principle *vimarśa*, here personified as Kāmakalā, and the supreme unity of *prakāśa* underlying it are combined in Ambikā. The *sādhaka* understands that, on the one hand, Ambikā is the starting point of the creation but at the same time, for the individual in quest of true gnosis of reality, She is also the final resting point. In view of this latter sense Ambikā is also called Śāntā (the restful one). The *sādhaka* achieving identity with Her also achieves total quiescence. This is the end of both sonic creation and the phenomenal creation (*śabda* and *artha*).[32]

Śrī-cakra is a graphic record of Śakti's creation by means of gradual unfolding and multiplying of Herself. The creation is divided into nine categories; four types of consciousness (*ātman, antarātman, paramātman* and *jñānātman*), the good and the evil (*dharma* and *adharma*), cognition, objects of cognition and the cognizer. Seeing from above, from God's point of view, the first enclosure, *bindu*, is the primary polarization of the transcendental unity. It is still undifferentiated. The second triangular enclosure shows the first step of differentiation. The third enclosure contains the nine categories. The fourth and the subsequent enclosures reveal the further differentiation of Śakti and the gradual emergence of the empirical categories which more or less follow the scheme of the orthodox Sāṃkhya system. The practitioner's *sādhanā* requires him to step by step identify himself with these enclosures; first from the outside in a concentric way and then in the reverse order. He does this by means of vivid imagination and concentration as well as Tantric ritual acts accompanying these imaginations. The more clearly he can envisage these principles the better is his understanding of the mystery of creation and closer he comes to the realization of the supreme reality, God. At the beginning of his *sādhanā,* he needs the concrete and personified forms to apprehend the total pattern, then he grasps the process of the recurring hypostatizations until at a very sophisticated spiritual and intellectual level, he realizes the abstract concept of Śakti and Her acts and finally grasps the underlying stillness, the perfect quiescence of God who is Brahman and Unique. Similarly, the *mantra* — the sonic symbol of the deity — are used, first just as means of concrete and understandable formulas. Then as the *sādhaka* rises spiritually, he gradually penetrates into the underlying essence of Speech, *vāc.* He uses a *mantra* as a concentrated and esoteric sonic symbol of the divine — but at the same time he may try to convey his deepest understanding of this deity and his closest feelings for her through the medium of poetry. He most naturally wants to have a personal dialogue with his most adored deity — an interior dialogue. This finds expression in the form of a hymn.

NOTES

1 V. Raghavan, *Muttuswami Dikshitar (1775-1835)*, in: *Journal of the National Centre for the Performing Arts,* Bombay, September 1975, p. 22.

2 See ibid., for a detailed description of Dīkṣitār's biography.

3 K.R. Rajagopalan, *Group Kirtanas of Dikshitar,* in: *Kalakshetra Quarterly,* vol. VI, no. 1, Madras (no date), pp. 13-18.

4 S. Gupta, *From Bhakti to Prapati – The Theory of Grace in the Pāñcarātra System,* Sanskrit and World Culture, SCHR. OR. Berlin, 1986, pp. 537-542. Friedhelm Hardy, *Viraha-bhakti: The Early History of Kṛṣṇa Devotion in South India,* Delhi, Oxford University Press, 1983.

5 V. Raghavan, op. cit., p. 21.

6 K.C. Pandey, *Abhinavagupta, A Historical and Philosophical Study,* Chowkhamba Sanskrit Series, vol. I, Benares, 1935, pp. 409ff.; Lilian Silburn, *Hymnes de Abhinavagupta,* Tradutis et Commentés, Paris, 1970.

7 V. Raghavan, op. cit., p. 20; S.B. Dasgupta, 1946.

8 Sanjukta Gupta, *Studies in the Philosophy of Madhusūdana Sarasvatī,* Calcutta, 1966, pp. 194-230.

9 Cf. Āndavardhana, Dhvanyāloka on II, 8 and III, 43 and Abhinavagupta's Commentary on these places.

10 See Rachel Fell McDermott, 2001.

11 Sanjukta Gupta, Dirk Jan Hoens, Teun Goudriaan, *Hindu Tantrism,* Handbuch der Orientalistik, Zweite Abteilung, 4. Band. 2. Abschnitt, Leiden, 1979, pp. 121ff.

12 Ibid., pp. 90ff.

13 Nityaṣoḍaśikārṇava Tantra, IV, 4, tells us that the goddess has three forms, supreme (*para*), subtle (*sūkṣma*) and gross (*sthūla*); Yoginīhṛdaya Tantra too says the same thing. But Prapañcasāra Tantra says that being the embodiment of the three Vedas (*trayī*) she is called Tripurā; also because she is supreme and beyond the three cosmic gods Brahmā, etc., she is called Tripurā; moreover, she pervades the three worlds and so she is called Tripurā. Another explanation is that she is indeed the three Tantric principles, Śiva, Śakti and Jīva. There are many more such explanations forwarded by different Tantric traditions.

14 Teun Goudriaan and Sanjukta Gupta, *Hindu Tantric and Sākta Literature, A History of Indian Literature,* vol. II, fasc. 2, Wiesbaden 1981, pp. 58-74.

15 Cf. *Pratyabhijñāhṛdayam,* 4; Sanjukta Gupta, *Lakṣmī Tantra: A Pañcarātra Text, Translation and Notes,* p. XXVI.

16 Tripurārahasya, jñānakaṇḍa 16, 66; *Pratyabhijñāhṛdayam* 12.

17 Cf. Ibid. 7.

18 Cf. Ibid. 7.

19 These are called the *vidyeśvara.*

20 *Srī-vidyā* contains three clusters of sounds which are respectively called the *vāgbhava bīja/kūṭa, kāmarāja bīja/kūṭa* and *Śakti bīja/ kūṭa.* It has altogether fifteen letters, *ha, sa, ka, la, hrīṃ; ha, sa, ka, ha, la, hrīṃ; sa, ka, la, hrīṃ*; the special deity of the *vāgbhava kūṭa* is *jñānśakti* and is the main *citśakti* which reveals the supreme gnosis. *Kāmarāja kūṭa's* main deity is *kriyāśakti* and it brings yogic ecstacy. *Śakti kūṭa* deity is *icchāśakti* and is able to reveal the identity of the soul with the supreme principle, Śiva. Different esoteric traditions of this school use these *kūṭa* with slight change of the initial letter. These variations have produced different schools called *kādi, hādi, sādi* or *kahādi* schools. Cf. Tripurārahasya, jñānakaṇḍa 20, 18ff.

21 K. Kunjanni Raja, *Indian Theories of Meaning,* Adyar Library Series 91, Madras, 1963, pp. 98-148.

22 Bhartṛhari, *Vākyapadiya,* cantos I and II, edited and translated by K. Raghavan Pillai, Delhi 1971, pp. 27-32 and 157.

23 Tripurārahasya, *jñānakaṇḍa* 20, 31. Technically this idea is called the theory of reflection (*ābhāsavāda*). K.C. Pandey, op. cit., p. 195f.

24 *The Introduction to the Nityāṣoḍaśikārṇava Tantra,* edited with introduction by Vrajavallabha Dviveda, Varanasi, 1968, pp. 62-69.

25 *Lakṣmī Tantra* XVIII, 16f.

26 Tripurārahasya, jñānakaṇḍa 20, 16-38; Yoginīhṛdaya Tantra I, 8-24.

27 *Prapañcasāra Tantra* 3, 11-12.

28 Goudriaan and Gupta, op. cit., p. 59.

29 Krishnamoorthy, 325-329.

30 Shende, 15; Abhinavagupta's Commentary on *Dhvanyāloka* 34.

31 There are nine enclosures in the *Śrī-cakra,* nine triangles. The Sanskrit letters are also divided into nine groups; corresponding to the nine enclosures there are nine yogic centres in the human body; and there are nine important hand postures (*mudrā*). *Nityāṣoḍaśikārṇava Tantra,* Introd.

32 Cf. *Saundaryalaharī* v. 2. and Bhāskararāya's comm. on v. 1; *Paraśurāmakalpasūtra* V. 12; *Nityāṣoḍaśikārṇava Tantra* IV and *Yoginīhṛdaya Tantra* I.

MUTTUSVĀMĪ DĪKṢITĀR'S KAMALĀMBIKĀ NAVĀVARAṆA KĪRTANA

Sanskrit text, English translation and Notes

Navāvaraṇa-dhyānakīrtana

Toḍī-rāga

Pallavī

Kamalāmbike āśritakalpalatike caṇḍike

Kamanīyāruṇāṃśuke karavidhṛtaśuke mām ava (Ka......)

Anupallavī

Kamalāsanādipūjitakamalapade bahuvarade

Kamalālaya tīrtha vaibhav Śive Karuṇārṇave (Ka.......)

Caraṇa

Sakalalokanāyike saṃgītarasike

Sukavitvapradāyike Sundarīgatamāyike

Vikalebaramuktidānanipuṇe aghaharaṇe

Viyadādibhūtakiraṇe vinodacaraṇe aruṇe
Sakale Guruguhakaraṇe Sadāśivāntaḥkaraṇe
Akacaṭatapādivarṇe akhaṇḍaikarasapūrṇe (Ka.......)

Invocation to the Goddess manifest in the nine enclosures

This first hymn precedes the group of nine. It is called "concentration" (*dhyāna*) and its function is to create a mental image of the Goddess for Her worshipper to concentrate on. Singing these songs is a form of worship (*pūjā*), and every form of *pūjā* starts with such an invocation, in order to realize the divine presence. The parrot in Her hand shows that the Goddess is here visualized as Śyāmalā (the Tantric version of the poetic muse), also called Sarasvatī; she is Tripurā's specific aspect as music. The use of names of the Goddess in other aspects merely recalls the essential identity of all her aspects.

TRANSLATION

Pallavī

O Lotus Mother, creeper fulfilling the wishes of those who shelter under you! O Fierce One, you wear soft red silk. You hold a parrot in your hand. Save me![1]

Anupallavī

Your feet, Lotus-tender, Lotus-throned Brahmā and the rest[2] worship. You grant many wishes. You are the wealth of the holy home of Kamalā.[3] O Lady Śivā, ocean of compassion save me ......

Caraṇa

O heroine of all worlds, you delight in music; you bestow poetic genius, beautiful lady. You transcend cosmic delusion. You are apt to grant salvation at death;[4] you remove all sins. Your rays are the five elements headed by space. Your feet are enchanting, [your complexion is] red. You are differentiated [into aspects]. You created [me] the disciple of Guha. You are the mind of Sadāśiva. You are the sounds of Sanskrit [divided under] *a, ka, ca, ṭa, ta, pa,* etc. [groups].[5] You are the fullness of bliss undifferentiated and unique. Save me .....

NOTES

1 The lotus flower (*kamala*) symbolizes beauty, water, the time, etc. It also represents bounty, fertility. Śrī/Kamalā is iconically conceived as seated on or residing inside a lotus; she holds lotuses in Her hands and is surrounded by lotuses.

2 "the rest" here means Viṣṇu and Rudra/Śiva. Brahmā, Viṣṇu and Rudra are the traditional three cosmic gods and their worshipping the Goddess indicates Her cosmic sovereignty. Cf. *Saundaryalaharī* verse I. But in the Tāntric theology of the Tripurā school two more cosmic gods are added to these three, Sadāśiva and Īśvara. Iconographically the Goddess is envisaged as seated on the couch made of Sadāśiva in a supine position. This couch is held up by Īśvara, Brahmā, Viṣṇu, Rudra. See also note 2 on hymn 4.

3 *Śrīpura* is the *Śrī-cakra*; it also indicates the temple of Kamalāmbā at Tiruvārur, where these nine songs were composed to worship the deity in this temple.

4 Although in Tāntric religion salvation in this life is admitted, the poet seems to believe that salvation is attained only after death. As on several other points, he accepts Śaṃkara, the Advaita Vedānta philosopher's view.

5 There are fifty letters in Sanskrit language: sixteen vowels starting with *a,* and forming the first group; and thirty-four consonants. Of these latter the first twenty-five are arranged in five groups according to their places of utterance. Then comes the group of four semi-vowels and the last group of five sibilants. Each of these eight group is called after the first letter of the group, i.e. *a, ka, ca, ṭa, pa, ya, śa.* For the Tripurā-cult a ninth group is added, viz. *kṣa.*

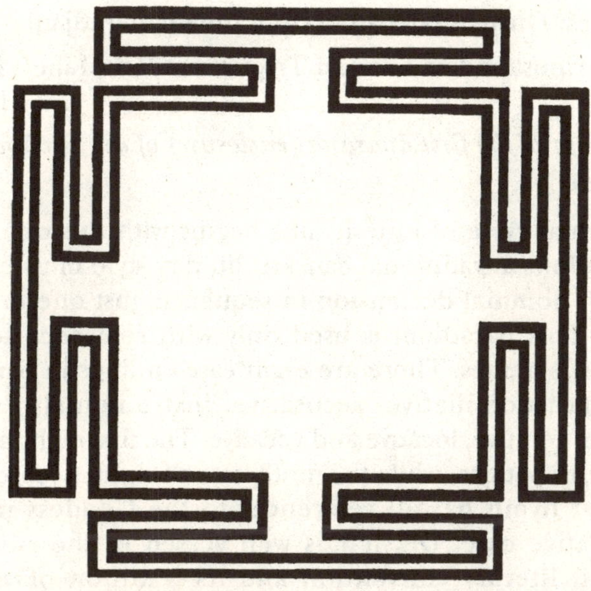

Prathamāvaraṇakīrtana

Ānandabhairavī-rāga

Pallavī

Kamalāmbā saṃrakṣatu māṃ hṛtkamalanagaranivāsinī
(Ka....)

Anupallavī

Sumanasārādhitādbjamukhī Sundaramanaḥpriyakarasakhī
Kamalajānandabodhasukhī kāntātārapañjaraśukī (Ka....)

Caraṇa

Tripurādicakreśvarī aṇimādisiddhīśvarī
Nityākāmeśvarī kṣitipuratrailokyamohanacakravartinī
Prakaṭayoginī suraripumahiṣāsurādimardinī
Nigamapurāṇādisaṃvedinī

Tripureśī Guruguhajananī Tripurabhañjanarañjanī
Madhuripusahodarī talodarī Tripurāsundarī Maheśvarī
(Ka....)

The hymn of the first āvaraṇa (enclosure) of the navāvaraṇa maṇḍala

The actual cycle of nine hymns begins with this one. The poet follows a traditional Sanskrit literary style in using the cases of nominal declension in sequence, just one to each hymn. This paradigm is used only with reference to the Goddess's names. There are eight case-endings in Sanskrit grammar: nominative, accusative, instrumental, dative, ablative, genitive, locative and vocative. The first eight hymns follow this pattern, while the ninth uses all eight. Accordingly the first hymn has all references to the Goddess in the nominative case. Dīkṣitar is well versed in the rules of Sanskrit literary convention and its tradition of verbal ingenuity. One of the important features of Sanskrit poetry is its use of many figures of speech. The Sanskrit poets considered them to be useful tools for the achievement of aesthetic perfection and made free use of them. Being deeply rooted in this tradition, Dīkṣitar too uses many such ornamentations such as simile, metaphor, punning, alliteration of various kinds and so on. Another important point of his style is that these laudatory hymns are modelled on the *nāma stuti*, a genre of laudatory hymns listing the deity's many names revealing his various characteristics. In these hymns, Dīkṣitar closely follows the content of the *Lalitā-sahasra-nāmam*, a laudatory hymn to Lalitā. It is appended to the *Brahmāṇḍa Purāṇa.*

TRANSLATION

Pallavī

May lady mother Kamalā protect me, she who resides in the lotus-city of the [human] heart, may Kamalāmbā protect me.
(Refrain.....)

Anupallavī

She who is worshipped by the gods; who possesses a lotus face; who is the beloved friend of Sundara (Śiva), delighting His mind with her deeds;[1] the lotus-born one who is happy with her [inherent] bliss and knowledge;[2] the charming one who is the parrot in the cage of *tāra.*[3] (Refrain......)

Caraṇa

May the one who is the goddesses Tripurā, etc. of the cosmos/cosmogram (*cakra*); one who is [emanated as] the deities of the occult powers, *aṇimā,* etc.;[4] who is the *nityā,* Kāmeśvari,[5] who is inherent in the [*āvaraṇa*] called the circle which beguiles the three worlds, which [represents] Her citadel, the earth; who appears [in that citadel] as the *yoginī* (the tangible forms of the spirits inherent in the *mantra,* the divine powers which are experienced by the Tāntric practisers); she who (as Durgā, etc.) destroys the enemies of the gods like the buffalo-demon;[6] she who reveals the Tāntric and mythological scriptures;[7] the Goddess of the three *pura;*[8] the mother of the preceptor Guha;[9] the beloved of [Śiva] who destroyed the three [demonic] forts; who is the sister of [Viṣṇu], the enemy of the demon Madhu; who is slender-waisted, Tripurasundarī, the great Goddess.

(Refrain .....)

NOTES

1 There are two readings *priyasakhī* and *priyakarasakhī.* The first simply means that she is Śiva's beloved. But that seems unlikely as it is repeated in the *caraṇa.* The second reading is better, since it refers to the Goddess as the God's power of action (*kriyāśakti*).

2 i.e. *vimarśaśakti.*

3 *Tāra* is another name of the well known *mantra* "*oṃ*", which is the quintessence of the Vedas and the primary manifestation of *Śabdabrahman.* The Goddess as *Śabdabrahman* is inherent in this quintessential manifestation of speech, which is the source of creation.

4 Traditionally a successful Tantric practiser acquires eight occult powers. *Aṇimā* (power to become almost etherial), *laghimā* (power to become weightless), *mahima* (power to become very great), *īśitva* (power to reign over all), *vaśitva* (power to subjugate all), *garimā* (power to become inordinately heavy), *prāpti* (power to obtain whatever one wishes) and *prākāmya* (power to fulfill all wishes).

5 *Nityā* are primary goddesses or emanations of the divine Energy. They are sixteen in number with Kāmeśvarī at the centre and fifteen others around her, symbolizing the central creative Energy and the initial decentralization of this power. Their names are: Kāmeśvarī, Bhagamālinī, Nityaklinnā, Bheruṇḍā, Vahnivāsinī, Mahāvajreśvarī, Śivadūtī, Tvaritā, Kulasundarī, Nityā, Nīlapatākā, Vijayā, Sarvamaṅgalā, Jvālāmālinī, Citrā, Mahānityā.

6 The goddess becomes incarnate to destroy the evil which appears in the form of various demons. The *Devī-māhātmya*, the last part of the Mārkaṇḍeya Purāṇa, enumerates most of them.

7 The sacred Tantra literature is called *nigama* to distinguish it from the *āgama*, the Vedas. Purāṇas are the mythological literature.

8 There are various explanations put forward by different texts, regarding the term *tripura* (the three dwellings). One of these is that the Goddess is the essence of the three realities, Śiva, the souls (*jīva*) and the divine knowledge (*vidyā*).

9 Guha or Skandasvāmī, Pārvatī's son, learned the secret lore of the Tripurā cult from his parents, when he was a baby and rested on his mother's arm.

Dvitīyāvaraṇakīrtana

Kalyāṇī-rāga

Pallavī

Kamalām Ambāṃ bhajare re mānasa kalpitamāyākāyaṃ tyaja re (Ka........)

Anupallavī

Kamalāvāṇīsevitapārśvāṃ kambujayagrīvāṃ naṭadevāṃ
Kamalāpurasadanāṃ mṛdugadanāṃ kamanīyaradanāṃ kamalavadanāṃ (Ka......)

Caraṇa

Sarvāśāparipūrakacakrasvāminīm Paramaśivakāminīṃ
Durvāsārcitaguptayoginīṃ duḥkhadhvaṃsinīṃ haṃsinīṃ
Nirvāṇanijasukhapradāyinīṃ nityakalyāṇīṃ Kātyāyanīṃ
Sarvāṇīṃ madhupavijayaveṇīṃ sadguruguhajananīṃ
Nirañjanīṃ garvitabhaṇḍāsurabhañjanīṃ
Kāmākarṣinyādirañjaniṃ
Nirviśeṣacaitanyarūpiṇīṃ ūrvitattvādisvarūpiṇīṃ (Ka....)

The hymn of the second āvaraṇa

All references to the Goddess are here in the accusative case.

TRANSLATION

Pallavī

O my mind, do worship Kamalāmbā. Do give up [attachment for worldly subjects, which are] illusory, the creation of *māyā* (cosmic delusion). (Refrain....)

Anupallavī

She who is flanked by Lakṣmī and Sarasvatī;[1] whose [exquisite] throat has defeated [the beauty] of the conch shell, before whom all gods bow down; who resides in the city of Kamalā; who talks softly; who has charming teeth and a lotus face. (Refrain.....)

Caraṇa

[Worship] Her who is the mistress of the circle [called] Fulfiller of All Wishes; who is desired by Parama Śiva; who is the secret *yoginī* worshipped by Durvāsas;[2] who destroys all sufferings; who is the goose;[3] who bestows the salvation which is but the bliss of one's own self;[4] who is ever auspicious; who is Kātyāyanī; Sarvāṇī; whose plaited hair triumphs [in beauty] over the honey-bees; who is the mother of the perfect preceptor Guha; who is unblemished; who destroyed the vain demon Bhaṇḍa;[6] who delights [the minor śakti] Kāmākaṣiṇī, etc.;[7] who is the embodiment of unqualified consciousness,[8] and who is manifest as [the five material elements] such as earth.[9] (Refrain ....)

NOTES

1 Like the three Hindu cosmic gods Brahmā, Viṣṇu and Rudra, the Goddess too, in Her three cosmic functions, is manifest

in three forms, each corresponding to one of the three gods. The Goddess Herself is manifest as Mahāmāyā or Mahākālī and is related to Rudra, the cosmic deluder and destroyer; Lakṣmī is related to Viṣṇu, the sustainer; and Sarasvatī or Mahāvidyā, the cosmic omniscience, is related to Brahmā, the creator.

2 The yogic esoteric form of the Goddess is indeed Her secret *mantra* form. The Tāntric *yogin* worships and meditates on this *mantra* to attain occult power and salvation. Durvāsā was one of the savants who founded a subsect of the esoteric Tripurā sect. The subsect established by Durvāsā includes such early savants as Dattātreya and Paraśurāma; the latter is traditionally held to be the author of an aphoristic work, called the *Kalpasūtra*.

3 *Haṃsa* (goose) symbolizes the cosmic Śakti inherent in the human soul; the *yogin* envisages that it soars to its original transcendental existence free from the bondage of experiences of the empirical life and the bondage of death and rebirth.

4 Release, *mukti* is not a new achievement but regaining one's pristine existence as identical with the divine reality, which is just bliss.

5 This is the name of the Goddess who is considered to be the sister of Viṣṇu. According to Bhāskara Rāya, she is the daughter of the sage Kata. Cf. Bhāskara's commentary on the Lalitā-sahasra-nāmam 113, p. 235.

6 The Goddess in Her incarnation as Lalitā marched against this evil demon and destroyed him. The story is told in the last chapter of the *Brahmāṇḍa Purāṇa*.

7 There are fifteen presiding *śakti* in the second *āvaraṇa*. Their names all ending in *ākarṣiṇī*, meaning "she who pulls", indicate that the esoteric purpose of this diagram is that the practiser gains supernatural spiritual power over other people and objects. The names are Kāmākarṣiṇī, Buddhyākarṣiṇī, Ahaṃkārākarṣiṇī, Cittākarṣiṇī, Smṛtyākarṣiṇī, Śarīrākarṣiṇī, Śabdākarṣiṇī, Sparśākarṣiṇī. Rūpākarṣiṇī, Rasākarṣiṇī, Gandhākarṣiṇī, Nāmākarṣiṇī, Bījākarṣiṇī, Ātmākarṣiṇī and Amṛtākarṣiṇī.

8 This is the transcendent and undifferentiated form of the Goddess – a hypostatization of the divine consciousness (*saṃvit*) termed *prakāśa*, 'revelation'.

9 The five elements are earth, water, fire, air and the void/space.

Tṛtīyāvaraṇakīrtana

Śaṃkarābharaṇa-rāga

Pallavī

Śrīkamalāmbikayā kaṭākṣito 'haṃ
Saccidānandaparipūrṇabrahmāsmi (Śrī .....)

Anupallavī

Pākaśāsanādisakaladevatāsevitayā
Paṃkajāsanādi pañcakṛdbhāvitayā
Śokaharacaturapadayā mūkamukhyavākpradayā
Kokanadavijayapadayā Guruguhatattraipadayā (Śrī ...)

Caraṇa

Anaṃgakusumādyaṣṭaśaktyārayā
Aruṇavarṇasaṃkṣobhaṇacakrakārayā

Anantakoṭyaṇḍanāyakaśaṃkaranāyikayā
Aṣṭavargātmakaguptatarayā varayā
Anaṃgādyupāsitayā aṣṭadalābjasthitayā
Dhanurbāṇadharakarayā dayāsudhāsāgarayā (Śrī ...)

The hymn of the third āvaraṇa

The case ending attached here to the Goddess is the instrumental and is thus theologically highly significant. All the cosmic acts of God are carried out by His Śakti, which is His creative thrust. Both aspects of God, as the creator and as the saviour, are concretized in the Goddess, His Śakti. In the refrain of this hymn that second aspect of the Divine, which is the most important one for the religious practiser, is emphasized: the poet declares that he has attained salvation, a gnostic salvation, through the instrumentality of the Goddess, the embodiment of divine grace.

TRANSLATION

Pallavī

I have been glanced at (i.e. received the kind attention, which is grace) by Mother Kamalā [and now] I am [identified with] Brahman, the fullness of existence, consciousness and bliss.[1] (Refrain....)

Anupallavī

By the one who is served by all gods led by Indra; who is [constantly] contemplated by the lotus-seated (Brahmā) and other [cosmic gods], who perform the five cosmic acts;[2] whose feet are adroit in removing grief; who restores the primary sentence even to the dumb;[3] whose feet beat red lotuses [in beauty]; who is indeed that three-worded [sentence] which is Guruguha himself.[4]

(Refrain ...)

Caraṇa

By one who is embodied as Anaṃgakusuma and the rest of the *śakti*[5] who preside over the third [*āvaraṇa*]; who is the red *saṃkṣobhaṇa cakra,*[6] who is the beloved of Śiva, the master of countless millions of universe;[7] who is even more secret [than the *mantra* of the previous *cakra*], being in the form [of the alphabet] grouped in eight sections;[8] who is excellent; who is worshipped by [such savants as] Manmatha and others;[9] who resides in the eight-petalled lotus;[10] who carries a bow and arrows in her hands; who is the ocean of the nectar of compassion. (Refrain......)

NOTES

1 In Tāntric theology God's grace is termed "*śakti-pāta*" (descent of Śakti). Without this no salvation is possible. Thus tough believers in gnostic soteriology, the Tāntric still belong to the *bhakti* tradition of grace. The poet communicates this combination of divine grace and gnosis (of the soul's being identical with the transcendental Reality, the unique, immutable, conscious and blissful Brahman) in their right sequence – "I am glanced at by the Goddess and I am saved from the bondage of *saṃsāra* and its suffering".

2 The five acts are creation, sustenance, destruction, delusion and granting grace. Cf. Sanjukta Gupta, *Lakṣmī Tantra: A Pañcarātra Text,* In the Tripurā system these acts are associated with Brahmā, Viṣṇu, Rudra, Sadāśiva and Īśvara.

3 The primary sentence refers to the Upaniṣadic statement "thou art that". (*tat tvam asi*), Chāndogya Upaniṣad, 6; it declares the identity between Brahman and the human soul.

4 This enigmatic compound is an example of the figure of speech known as *anuprāsa,* a form of alliteration, playing on the word *pada. Pada* means both a foot and a part of speech. Besides, the poet again takes up the theme of the *pallavī* – the juxtaposition of the Goddess's grace symbolized as her kind

glance or her feet, the worshipper's final resort and the gnostic idea of salvation. He thus underscores the importance of grace in Tantra as the prerequisite for salvation. The three-worded sentence is the above-mentioned "thou art that".

5 Anaṅgakusuma, Anaṅgamekhalā, Anaṅgamadanā, Anaṅgamadanāturā, Anaṅgarekhā, Anaṅgaveginī, Anaṅgāṃkuśā and Anaṅgamālinī; these are subsidiary *śakti* presiding over the third *āvaraṇa*; they represent mental faculties lying behind the acts of speech, taking or grasping something, movement, defection, sexual act, loss, gain and indifference.

6 The third *āvaraṇa* represents the psychological level of the individual's world-consciousness and involvement, which is called attachment, *rāga*. This word also means tinge, hue, etc. and is often related to red tint, the colour of *rajas*, cosmic dynamism.

7 In Tāntric cosmology worlds, *brahmāṇḍa* (cosmic egg), are many.

8 The reference is to the *mātṛkā mantra*, which is the fifty Sanskrit letters. These are divided into eight groups, *varga;* the vowels, twenty-five mutes divided into five groups, viz. guttural, palatal, cerebral, dental and labial, the four semi-vowels (ya, ra, la, va), and finally the aspirants. The *mātṛkā mantra* is considered to be the source of all *mantra* and also the source of the creation.

9 There are twelve traditional savants of the Tripurā sect, each one establishing a subsect worshipping the Tripurā *mantra* in slightly different forms. The names of these savants are Manu, Candra, Kubera, Lopāmudrā, Manmatha, Agastya, Agni, (or Nandikeśvara), Sūrya, Indra, (or Ādiśeṣa), Skanda, Śiva and Durvāsā. Of these Lopāmudrā, Agastya, Manmatha and Durvāsā are the most imprtant names.

10 The lotus situated at the individual's heart is known as the eight-petalled lotus and is the seat of God, the inner controller *antaryāmin*. Since the Goddess is indeed the divine personality, it is her seat too. This lotus is also known as the *cakra* of the heart. But this *cakra* is not to be counted on the nine *cakra* or centres of the spiritual body of the *yogin* accepted in the Tripurā sect of the *yogin*. These nine centres are covered by the nine *āvaraṇa* of the *śrī cakra* in a different form of equation.

Caturthāvaraṇakīrtana

Kāmbhoji-rāga

Pallavī

Kamalāmbikāyai kanakāṃśukāyai

Karpūravīṭikāyai namas te namas te (Ka....)

Anupallavī

Kamalākāntānujāyai Kāmeśvaryai Ajāyai

Himagiritanujāyai hrīṃkārapūjyāyai

Kamalānagaravihāriṇyai khalasamūhasaṃhāriṇyai

Kamanīyaratnahāriṇyai kalpitakalmaṣaparihāriṇyai (Ka...)

Caraṇa

Sakalasaubhāgyadāyakāmbhojacaraṇāyai

Saṃkṣobhiṇyādiśaktiyutacaturthāvaraṇāyai

Prakaṭacaturdaśabhuvanabharaṇāyai

Prabalaguruguhasampradāyāntaḥkaraṇāyai
Akalaṃkarūpavarṇāyai Aparṇāyai suparṇāyai
Sukaradhṛtacāpabāṇāyai śobhanakaramanukoṇāyai
Sakuṃkumādilepanāyai carācarādikalpanāyai
Cikuravijitanīlaghanāyai cidānandapūrṇaghanāyai (Ka...)

The hymn of the fourth āvaraṇa

The grammatical point here is the use of the dative case-ending for all nouns referring to the Goddess. In theology this indicates the total surrender of the devotee's own self to the mercy of the divine. Just as the previous hymn presents the ancient theistic view of salvation, a combination of gnosticism and the theology of grace, in this hymn the special medieval development of emotional devotionalism (*prapatti-bhakti*) – originated in South India – is being illustrated. This juxtaposition of both the older and the medieval brand of theism is characteristic of the late medieval/early modern Śaivism in Southern and Eastern India. This special form of self-surrendering mysticism found expression in the songs of such famous poet-composers as Dīkṣitar of South India, and Rāmprasāda of Bengal. (See Goudariaan and Gupta, *Tantric Literature*, p. 196 f.)

TRANSLATION

Pallavī

I salute you, I salute you O lady mother Kamalā, who wears golden clothes and [chews] betel flavoured with camphor.[1]

(Refrain....)

Anupallavī

[I surrender myself) to you who are the younger sister of the husband of Lakṣmī;[2] who are Kāmeśvarī;[3] who are the unborn one; who are the daughter of Mount Himālaya; who are worshipped with the [mystic] sound *hrīṃ*;[4] who live at leisure in the city of Kamalā; who destroy the dishonest; who wear a string of lovely jewels; who remove the sins we have committed. (Refrain....)

Caraṇa

To you, who possess lotus-like feet which bestow all good fortune; [who embody] the fourth *āvaraṇa* containing the *śakti*, Saṃkṣobhinī, etc.,[5] who sustain the fourteen manifest worlds;[6] who are the heart of the strong tradition [to which] Guruguha [belongs]; who are of flawless beauty and complexion; who are [called] Aparṇā;[7] who are the beautiful bird;[8] who hold in your lovely hands a bow and arrows;[9] who [as the diagram] contain fourteen triangles;[10] who are besmeared with red paint; who are the fashioner of static as well as movable phenomena; whose [black] hair triumphs over the blue clouds; and who are the concentrated plenitude[11] of consciousness and bliss. (Refrain.....)

NOTES

1 The *Saundaryalaharī* (24) describes the Goddess distributing bits of a camphor-flavoured betel, which she is in the habit of chewing, to the assembled gods as a sign of Her favour. Dīkṣitar in this hymn of self-surrender recalls that image of a benign Goddess. See Rāmeśvara's commentary on the *Kalpasūtra* p. 141.

2 Cf. Gupta, *Lakṣmī Tantra*, Introduction, p. XXIX.

3 This is the image of the Goddess in coitus with Śiva, also called Kāmeśvara (the lord of sexual desire); it symbolizes Her role as the creatrix.

4 This is the highest *mantra* of the Goddess and stands for Her essential manifestation as Sound/Speech. This is the counterpart of *Oṃ*. As *Oṃ* is the manifestation of *śabdabrahman*, so *hrīṃ* is the manifestation of the Goddess Vāc.

5 This *āvaraṇa* represents the most benign manifestation of the Goddess, the embodiment of the grace that fulfills all

aspirations of Her devotees. It is called the circle, *cakra* "which grants all prosperity" (*sarvasaubhāgyadāyaka*). This *cakra* indicates a stage of a Tāntric's spiritual achievement in which he obtains all sorts of occult powers (*siddhi*). These powers are expressed in Tāntric religion in concrete terms as female deities (*śakti*). As the design of the *cakra* contains fourteen triangles – the symbol of *śakti* or the female procreative energy – there are fourteen *śakti* in this *cakra*. These are Sarvasaṃkṣobhiṇī (she who disturbs all), Sarvavidrāviṇī (she who breaks/frightens all), Sarvākarṣiṇī (she who attracts all), Sarvastambhinī (she who makes everybody immobile), Sarvajṛmbhinī (she who makes everybody sleepy), Sarvavaśaṃkarī (she who subjugates all), Sarvāhlādinī (she who delights all), Sarvasammohinī (she who enchants all), Sarvarañjanī (she who pleases all), Sarvonmādinī (she who maddens all), Sarvārthasādhakā (she who fulfills all aspirations), Sarvasampattipūraṇī (she who increases all property), Sarvamantramayī (she who embodies all *mantra*), Sarvadvandvakṣayaṃkarī (she who destroys all dualities). These name are suggestive of specific Tāntric magic spells and rituals called in Tantra the six types of rituals (*ṣaṭkarman*). These are esoteric rites and spells (*vidyā*) and are kept close to the tradition of different sects (*sampradāya*). The powers which are acquired by the Tāntric practisers are called *bhukti* and the possessors of such powers enjoy them by divine sanction (*ājñā*). But this too is sanctioned in the form of divine grace and so the *cakra* is here compared with the Goddess's feet. Cf. *Lalitāsahasranāmastotram* 2, 67 and 69.

6 These are arranged vertically – seven above ground and seven underground.

7 The goddess as a maiden practised severe penance in order to please Śiva and to move him into marrying her. At the final stage of this ascetic practice, she refused all food including even fallen leaves of the tree under which she was seated, lost in deep meditation. Hence she is called "she who refused the fallen leaf (*parṇa*)".

8 The dynamic *śakti* is manifest on the cosmic level as the cosmic vibration or flux, and on the microcosmic level as the life breath (*prāṇa*). *Prāṇa* is envisaged as a wild goose. Cf. *Lalitāsahasranāmastotram* 2, 95.

9 The image of the Goddess Tripurā depicts her as holding a bow of sugar-cane and five arrows made of flowers (*Saundaryalaharī* 6).

10 This is the outermost *āvaraṇa* made of triangles. It represents the grossest manifestations of *śakti* belonging to the manifest worlds.

11 The poet in this last address refers to the transcendent Goddess, to convey his own realization of the One-ness of Śakti.

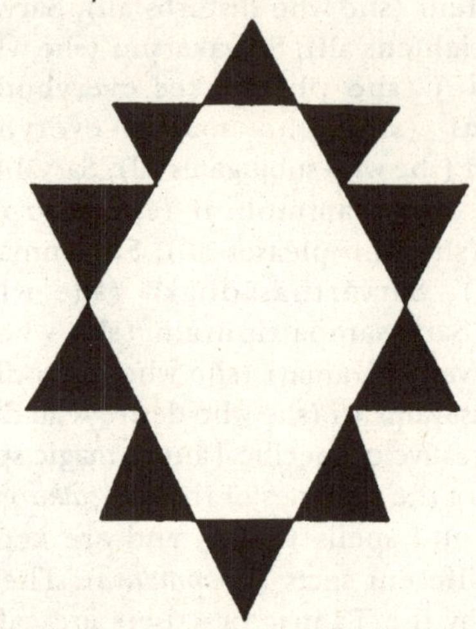

Pañcamāvaraṇakīrtana

Bhairavī-rāga

Pallavī

Śrīkamalāmbāyāḥ paraṃ na hi re citta

Kṣityādiśivāntatattvasvarūpiṇyāḥ (Śrī....)

Anupallavī

Śrīkaṇṭhaviṣṇuviriñcādijanayītryāḥ

Śivātmakaviśvakartryāḥ kārayitryāḥ

Śrīkarabahirdaśāracakrasthityāḥ

SevitaBhairavīBhārgavīBhāratyāḥ (Śrī ....)

Caraṇa

Nādamayasūkṣmarūpasarvasiddhipradādi-
Daśaśaktyārādhitamūrteḥ śrotrādidaśakaraṇātmaka-
Kulakaulikādibahuvidhopāsitakīrteḥ
Abhedanityaśuddhabuddhamuktasaccidānanda-
paramādvaitasphūrteḥ
Ādimadhyāntarahitāprameya-
Guruguhamoditasarvārthasādhakasphūrteḥ
Mūlādinavādhāravyāvṛttadaśadhvanibheda-
jñayogibṛndasaṃrakṣaṇyāḥ
Anādimāyāvidyākāryakāraṇavinodakaraṇa-
paṭutarakaṭākṣavīkṣaṇyāḥ (Śrī......)

The hymn of the fifth āvaraṇa

This hymn uses the ablative of the nouns referring to the Goddess. That case presupposes a difference between phenomena. Thus the poet here uses the ablative in a negative way to negate all differentiation of the empirical world. In this hymn the poet reveals the essential nature of Tripurā. She is the cosmic sound/speech (*vāc*) and the cosmic dynamism (*spanda*), Śiva's active Energy, representing the unity of all phenomena.

TRANSLATION

Pallavī

O [my] mind, there is nothing else but the glorious lady mother Kamalā; than the one who is the essence of [the categories] from the earth up to Śiva.[1] (Refrain......)

Anupallavī

[There is nothing else but her] who is the mother of Śrīkaṇṭha,[2] Viṣṇu and Brahmā; who created the universe which is in essence [nothing but] Śiva;[3] who is the agent of all actions; who resides in the sacred outer *cakra* possessing ten triangles; who is served by Bhairavī (Kālī), Bhārgavī (Lakṣmī and Bhāratī (Sarasvatī). (Refrain.....)

Caraṇa

[There is nothing else but] her who is of the subtle form *nāda*[4] and is propitiated by the ten *śakti* Sarvasiddhipradā, etc.;[5] who is famous for being worshipped in various religious modes, such as *kula* and *kaula,* as the power identical with the ten sense and motor organs;[6] who is the manifestation of the supreme non-dual, non-differentiated, ever pure, enlightened and free [Self]; the reality which is consciousness and bliss as well; who is [an integral whole without any parts such as] the first, the middle and the last;[7] who is unknowable; who is entertained by Guruguha; who is manifest as the Achieving all-purposes [*cakra*]; who inheres in the nine centres (*cakra* of the mystial yogic body), viz. *mūlādhāra,* etc.[8] and who, surpassing these, knows how to pierce through the sounds;[9] who protects the group of *yogin*; whose mere glance is capable of dispelling beginningless delusion and ignorance[10] and the laws of cause and effect.[11]

(Refrain ......)

NOTES

1 Tāntric ontology recognizes thirty-six categories (*tattva*) divided into three levels of creation. First is the pure creation headed by Śiva with Śakti, followed by Sadāśiva, Īśvara and pure knowledge, *vidyā.* Next comes the intermediary creation, which contains both pure and impure elements. This consists of ontological categories, *māyā, kalā, vidyā, rāga, kāla* and *niyati. Māyā* is Śakti in her active character, while the following five are her five functional aspects with which she delimits the individual souls by deluding them into believing themselves

to be differentiated, of limited knowledge, consequently full of desire for things to possess, impermanent and limited by their own *karman*. This is the period or process, which transforms the pure conscious entity into many limited transient souls (*jīva*). The third stage of the creative process is stamped as impure. It is headed by matter (*prakṛti*), then *buddhi, ahaṃkāra, manas,* the five sense organs, five motor organs, the five essences of the five cosmic elements, and the five cosmic elements, viz. space, air, fire, water and earth. This third list is that of Sāṃkhya ontology.

2 This is a name of Rudra.

3 This is called the outer *cakra* possessing ten triangles, because the next *cakra*, which is placed inside it, also possesses ten triangles. This *cakra* is called "achieving all-purposes", *sarvārthasādhaka.*

4 *Nāda* is *śabdabrahman*, the primary sound, and Śakti is its essence.

5 These ten *śakti* are: Sarvasiddhipradā (giver of all magical powers), Sarvasampatpradā (giver of all riches), Sarvapriyaṃkarī (performer of all pleasant deeds), Sarvamaṅgalakarī (she who grants all good luck), Sarvakāmapradā (giver of all desires), Sarvaduḥkha vimocinī (remover of all miseries), Sarvatyu praśaminī (diminisher of all sorts of fear of death), Sarvavighna-nivāriṇī (remover of all obstacles), Sarvāṅgasundarī (perfect beauty) and Sarvasaubhāgyadāyinī (she who grants all favours).

6 The Goddess is here represented by the ten *śakti* who are considered to be transcendental (*kulottīrṇā*) goddesses (*yoginī*). The supreme Goddess who inheres in every individual as the life-breath, *prāṇa*, becomes in the empirical stage further differentiated as the ten sense and motor organs which are instrumental in performing all individual acts and the cognition inspiring the acts. In this way the dynamic aspects of Śakti, known as *kriyā-śakti*, is further differentiated at the individual level.

7 The transcendental reality is one and integral and is not made of any parts.

8 These are nine centres conceived vertically and representing the individual microcosm. Kuṇḍalinī, the dynamic Śakti on this microcosmic level, lies in the lowest of these centres, called "the lotus of the root", *mūlādhāra*. The other centres are *svādhiṣṭhāna, maṇipura, anāhata, madhyamā, vajrakaṇṭhā, lambikā, viśuddhikā* and *ājñā*. (NS 245-246, and the Introduction 113-116). At each of these centres the Goddess remains manifesting Her primordial form as speech, which the *yogin* can, through his power of concentration, experience. Once the lowest one is experienced the *yogin* spiritually rises above it and attempts to experience the next. At the end of all nine centres, he arrives at the tenth, which is just the threshold to the Goddess's transcendental state. This centre is known as *dvādaśānta*.

9 These ten sounds are: at *mūlādhara* – the faint sound of resonance "cini"; at *svādhiṣṭhāna* – more pronounced resonance "cini cini"; then at maṇipura – the sound of a bell; in *anāhata* – the sound of a conch shell. The sound of the *vīṇā* (a string instrument) is how *śabda* is experienced in *madhyamā*. Then successively, the sounds of cymbal, bamboo flute, horn (or bassoon) and drum are experienced in *vajrakaṇṭha, lambikā, viśuddhikā* and *ājñā*. Finally at the tenth centre, which is situated just above the human head, the sound is experienced as a clap of thunder. Cf. Bhāṣkararāya, *Varivasyārahasya*, pp. 47-75.

10 *Māyā* is God's Śakti in her function as the deluder of individuals. *Avidyā*, on the other hand, is the limited or partial knowledge belonging to individuals.

11 As ultimately there is just one integral reality, in the last analysis there is no creator, no creation and no knowledge or experience of differentiated phenomena. There is neither cause nor effect. It is the effect of *māyā* to bring *avidyā* into the individual's mind and make individuals believe in the law of cause and effect, which is the root of all *karman*. Once an individual *yogin* realizes his mistake – the mistake of thinking that the world is differentiated and full of phenomena – and recognizes his identity with non-dual transcendence, he is free from *karman* and is released (*mukta*).

Ṣaṣṭhāvaraṇakīrtana

Punnāgavarāli-rāga

Pallavī

Kamalāmbikāyās tava bhakto'haṃ Saṃkaryāḥ
Śrīkaryāḥ saṃgītarasikāyāḥ Śrī (Ka.....)

Anupallavī

Śubhaśarekṣukodaṇḍapāśāṃkuśapāṇyāḥ
Atimadhuratara vāṇyāḥ Sarvāṇyāḥ Kalyāṇyāḥ
Ramaṇīyapunnāgavarālivijitaveṇyāḥ Śrī (Ka.....)

Caraṇa

Daśakalātmakavahnisvarūpaprakāśāntar-
Daśārasarvarakṣākaracakreśvaryāḥ
Tridaśādinuta-ka-ca-vargadvayamayasarvajñādi
Daśaśaktisametamālinīcakreśvaryāḥ

Tridaśaviṃśativarṇagarbhiṇīkuṇḍalinyāḥ
Daśamudrāsamārādhitakaulinyāḥ
Daśarathādinutaguruguhajanakaśivabodhinyāḥ
Daśakaraṇavṛttimarīcinigarbhayoginyāḥ Śrī (Ka....)

The hymn of the sixth āvaraṇa

Here the poet expresses his devotion to the Goddess in Her form as Mālinī[1] and as the presiding deity of music, viz. Śyāmalā. Here the genitive case is continuously used to illustrate the *dāsya bhakti*.

TRANSLATION

Pallavi

I am your devotee, mother Kamalā; of the bestower of well-being; of her who brings prosperity; who is a *rasikā* of music.[2]
(Refrain....)

Anupallavi

[I am the devotee of her] who holds in her [four] hands the auspicious arrows, the sugar-cane bow, the noose and the goad; whose speech is exquisitely sweet; of Sarvāṇī, of the auspicious one; of her whose braided hair conquers [the beauty of] lovely black bees [swarming round] the *punnāga* tree.[3] (Refrain....)

Caraṇa

[I am a devotee] of the Goddess of the circle, "Protecting All", whose essential nature is the fire and who is identical with the ten *kalā*;[4] manifest in the [inner] circle possessing ten triangles; of the Goddess of the circle of Mālinī,[5] which has ten *śakti*, Sarvajñā, etc.[6] who are [the ten letters] of the *ka* and *ca* groups – she is worshipped by gods and others; of her who is Kuṇḍalinī encompassing the fifty letters [of the Sanskrit alphabet]; She is Goddess Kaulinī propitiated by ten *mudrā*;[7] She is worshipped by Daśaratha and others and bestows the *śiva* knowledge on him whose *guru* is Guha;[8] She is the inner power of her Radiations, which are the functions of the ten sense and motor organs.[9] (Refrain.....)

NOTES

1 The Goddess as the *mātṛkā* is the source of all experience and knowledge. As explained above, the first concrete manifestation of *śabda* is the *mātṛkā* (letters of the Sanskrit language). But the esoteric form of this *mātṛkā* representing Tripurā is called *mālinī* and the letters are arranged in a special order, not the one generally in use.

2 Pun: both "the essence of music" and "a connoisseur of music". The Goddess is the Muse who favours poets and musicians with their inspiration. Cf. *Saundaryalaharī* 15-17.

3 The poet makes a play on words and coins a rather stiff compound in order to underscore his choice of the musical mode (*rāga*) *punnāgavarāli*.

4 The Sanskrit letters are divided into three groups depending on their mystic nature. The vowels are called "the moon letters" and they possess sixteen *kalā* or parts. Each part is a *śakti*. The twenty-five mutes are called "the sun letters" and they possess twelve *kalā*. The rest of the letters are called "the fire letters" and they possess ten *kalā*. Cf. *Prapañcasāra* Tantra III.11-12.

5 *Mālinī cakra* is a particular diagram where the Sanskrit letters are arranged in a concentric pattern in this order: *na, ṛ, ṝ, ḷ, ḹ, tha, ca, dha, ī, ṇa, u, ū, ba, ka, kha, ga, gha, ṅ, i, a, va, bha, ma, ḍa, ḍha, ṭha, jha, ñ, ja, ra, ṭa, pa, cha, la, ā, sa, aḥ, ha, ṣa, kṣa, ma, śa, aṃ, ta, e, ai, o, ou, da, pha*. Cf. J.A. Schoterman, Appendix.

6 *Sarvajñā, Sarvaśakti, Sarvaiśvaryapradāyinī, Sarvajñānamayī, Sarvavyādhivināśinī, Sarvādhārasvarūpā, Sarvapāpaharā, Sarvānandamayī, Sarvarakṣāsvarūpinī* and *Sarvepsitaphalapradā*. See *Nityāṣoḍaśikārṇava Tantra* I.173-175.

7 These are *Sarvasaṃkṣobhinī, Sarvavidrāviṇī, Sarvākarṣiṇī, Sarvāveśakarī, Sarvonmādanī, Mahāṃkuśā, Khecarī, Bījā, Yoni* and *Trikhaṇḍā*. A *mudrā* is a hand-gesture. It also means a seal. The worshipper in Tāntric religious practices must constantly use these gestures to sanctify his acts with the divine seal of sanction. See *Yoginihṛdaya Tantra* I.57-71 with Amṛtānanda's commentary.

8 Śivajñāna is the saving gnosis of Śiva, which gnosis itself *is* Śiva.

9 See *Pratyabhijñāhṛdayam* 12 and its commentary. Under the delusion of *māyā*, the *jīva* becomes limited in his knowledge and starts experiencing differentiated phenomena. He, as the experient, is influenced by minor *śakti* manipulating him as the individual agent. *Khecarī śakti* makes him believe himself to be the empirical subject of his experiences, *gocarī śakti* controls his mind, *dikcarī śakti* controls his senses and organs and *bhūcarī śakti* becomes manifest as the content of his experience.

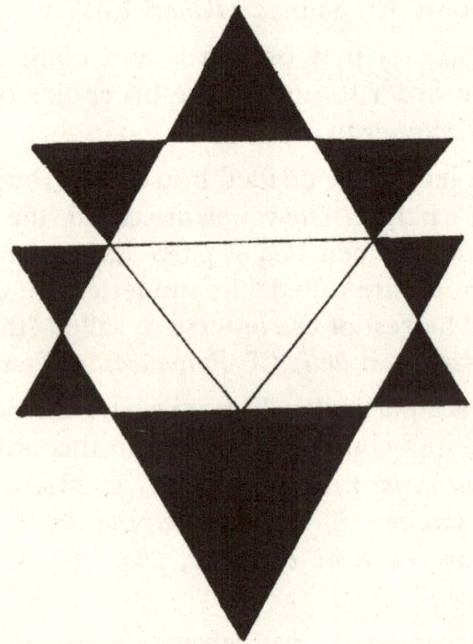

Saptamāvaraṇakīrtana

Sahānā-rāga (Śrī.....)

Pallavī

Śrīkạmalāmibikāyāṃ bhaktiṃ karomi
Śritakalpavāṭikāyāṃ Caṇḍikāyāṃ jagadambikāyāṃ (Śrī.....)

Anupallavī

Rākācandravadanāyaṃ rājīvanayanāyāṃ
Pākārinutacaraṇāyāṃ ākāśādikiraṇāyāṃ
Hrīṃkāravipinahariṇyāṃ hrīṃkārasuśarīriṇyāṃ
Hrīṃkāratarumañjaryāṃ hrīṃkāreśvaryāṃ Gauryāṃ
(Śrī.....)

Caraṇa

Śarīratrayavilakṣaṇasukhatarasvātmānubhoginyāṃ
Viriñciharīśānaharihayaveditarahasyayoginyāṃ
Parādivāgdevatārūpavaśinyādivibhāginyāṃ
Carātmakasarvarogaharanirāmayarājayoginyāṃ
Karadhṛtavīṇāvādinyāṃ Kamalānagaravinodinyāṃ
Suranaramunijanamodinyāṃ Guruguhavaraprasādinyāṃ
(Śrī.....)

The hymn of the seventh āvaraṇa

The grammatical point here is the use of the locative case with reference to the Goddess, the locus and the essence of creation. As explained above, Śakti as the primal *Śabda* represents God's creative intellect (*saṃkalpa*), in which the creation is reflected before the actual act of creation. Thus as *śabda* or *vāc* the Goddess is the locus of the universe – a locus or blueprint which God uses when He creates the universe through the dynamism of His Śakti. The use of the locative also indicates Her being the last resort on whose mercy the suffering devotee throws himself in anguish and fear, to be protected from all the evils of *saṃsāra.* In Her fearful image (Caṇḍikā) She destroys the evils and protects Her devotees. Finally Her essential characteristic is the sublime reality which is bliss and is thus the goal of all *yogin* worshipping Her in Her *mantra* form, the most essential form of which is the seminal *mantra, hrīṃ*.

TRANSLATION

Pallavi

I give my devotion to lady mother Kamalā; to her who resides in the garden palace of the wishfulfilling gem (heaven); to Caṇḍikā to the mother of the universe. (Refrain....)

Anupallavi

To Her who has a face [beautiful as] the full moon; whose eyes are like the lotus [bud]; whose feet are praised by Indra; whose rays are [the five elements], the space, etc.;[1] who is the gazelle in the forest of *hrīṃ*; who is the embodiment of *hrīṃ*; who is the blossom of the tree which is *hrīṃ*; who is the goddess of *hrīṃ*; who is Gaurī.[2] (Refrain.....)

Caraṇa

To her who rejoices in her own self of superior bliss – the self which transcends her other three forms;[3] who is the secret *yoginī* known [only] to Brahmā, Viṣṇu, Rudra and Hayagrīva;[4] who is differentiated as the *śakti* Vaśinī, etc. and as [the four states of development of] the deity of speech;[5] who is the healing *rāja yoga* that removes all illness, which is essentially transient;[6] who plays on the *vīṇā* she holds in her hands; who delights the city of Kamalā;[7] who charms the gods, men and sages; who grants Guruguha the boon of her grace. (Refrain.....)

NOTES

1 The material or phenomenal world is a projection of Śakti, who is of course its locus as well. The primary form of the

material world consists of five elements, viz. space (*ākāśa*), air (*vāyu*), fire (*tejas*), water (*ap*) and earth (*pṛthivī*).

2 The Ṛgvedic hymn to the goddess Śrī (ṚV Khila, 2, 6) is one of the earliest hymns on the goddess and is held in high esteem by the worshippers of the goddess Lakṣmī/Śrī. In that hymn the goddess is addressed as the swift-moving gazelle (*hariṇī*). Here the imagery is that of the swift-moving *śabda* which is identical with knowledge and consciousness. Every *mantra* is divided into two parts, the soul and the body. The soul part is called the seminal *mantra* (*bīja mantra*) and is the essential part of the *mantra*. The poet here has drawn on all poetic embellishments to reproduce the experience of the *yogin* who, at an advanced stage of his yogic practice, concentrates on the *bīja mantra, hrīṃ* as the essence of the Goddess's sonic, i.e. primordial form. Using figures of speech like alliteration, word-repetition (*yamaka*) and metaphor, the poet reveals the sensation of the *yogin* as being immersed in the sound and the personality of the *mantra hrīṃ*, the personality which is that of the cosmic awareness (*bodhaśakti*) inherent in human beings as the *Kuṇḍalinī*. Usually *Kuṇḍalinī* remains dormant, but the *yogin*, through his meditation and other yogic techniques, arouses it and raises it to its transcendent state, his awareness accompanying it. This process is envisaged as the swift flight of a gazelle or a lightning flash, hence the simile of the gazelle and the address Gaurī (the fair one), i.e. light.

3 The Goddess as the creatrix of the universe has three states in which one can comprehend Her: the supreme, the subtle and the gross. But Her transcendent state is beyond creation and is incomprehensible.

4 Hayagrīva, "the horse faced", is the form of Viṣṇu in which he represents the phenomenon of sacrifice and symbolizes the essence of Vedic and hence fundamental knowledge.

5 *Śabda* is transformed from its pristine state to the empirical state in four stages – *parā* (supreme), *paśyantī* (omniscient), *madhyamā* (intermediary) and *vaikharī* (manifest). The concept was primarily developed among the philosopher-grammarians.

6 This *āvaraṇa* is called "remover of all ill", *sarvarogahara* circle. *Roga* here does not mean illness, its usual sense, but evil, the basic cause of worldly sufferings, which is the transience of

all worldly phenomena. *Rāja-yoga* is an advanced form of *yoga*. In this *yoga*, the *yogin* in meditation completely merges his individuality in the unqualified *Brahman*. In this meditation the *yogin* loses all consciousness of the differentiated creation. Some scriptures say that there are four types of *yoga* practices – *mantrayoga*, *haṭhayoga*, *layayoga* and *rājayoga*. Cf. *Yogaśikhopaniṣad* 1.129; *Śiva Saṃhitā* 5.17. These texts also seem to maintain that the *rājayoga* is the most advanced form of yogic practice, in which all sense of differentiation disappears from its practiser's consciousness. The *Yogaśikhopaniṣad* 1.137 further adds that *rājayoga* means the union of the female principle with the male principle, the union between Śakti and Śiva.

7 The *śrī-cakra* is called *śrīpura*, the city of Śrī Kamalā.

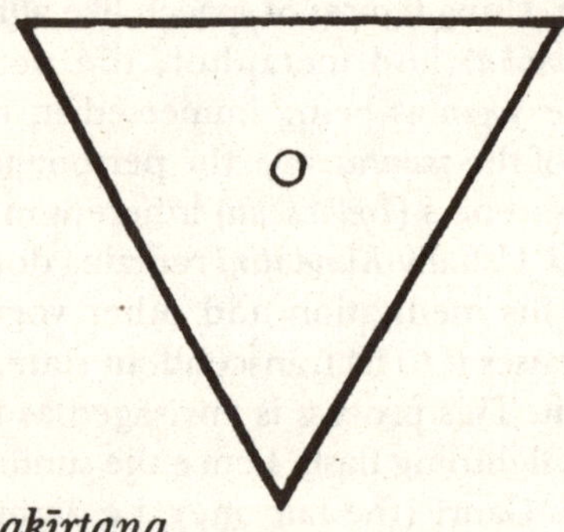

Aṣṭamāvaraṇakīrtana

Ghaṇṭā-rāga

Pallavī

Śrīkamalāmbik'evāva Śive karadhṛtaśukasārike (Śrī...)

Anupallavī

Lokapālinī Kapālinī Śūlinī lokajananī Bhagamālinī

Sakṛd ālokaya māṃ sarvasiddhipradāyike Tripurāmbike Bālāmbike (Śrī ....)

Caraṇa

Santāptahemasannibhadehe sadā'khaṇḍaikarasapravāhe
Santāpahare, trikoṇagehe Sakāmeśvarīśaktisamūhe
Santataṃ muktighaṇṭāmaṇighoṣāyamānakavāṭadvāre
Anantaguruguhavidite karāṃgulinakhodaye
Viṣṇudaśāvatāre antaḥkaraṇekṣukārmuka-
Śabdādipañcatanmātraviśikhātyantarāgapāśa-
Dveṣāṃkuśadharakareti rahasyayoginīpare (Śrī ....)

The hymn of the eighth āvaraṇa

In this hymn the poet prays for his salvation. All the nominal case endings are in the vocative.

TRANSLATION

Pallavī

O you auspicious lady mother Kamalā, protect me, do protect me; O you kindly one, who carry a parrot and a myna in your hands;[1] (Refrain.....)

Anupallavī

O sustainer of the worlds; you carry a skull; bearer of the trident; O mother of the worlds; O Bhagamālinī;[2] please cast your glance at me just for once;[3] O giver of all perfections (occult powers); O mother Tripurā; O mother Bālā.

(Refrain.....)

Caraṇa

O you whose body is like burnished gold; O you who are the eternal stream of undifferentiated, unique bliss; O remover of sufferings; O you who reside in the triangle accompanied by the *śakti* Kāmeśvarī, etc. O you wide doorway where the jewelled bell constantly announces salvation;[4] you who are known [only] to [god] Ananta

(Ādiśeṣa) and Guruguha;[5] you from whose [ten] finger-nails appeared the ten incarnations of Viṣṇu;[6] O you the supremely secret *yoginī* who holds in her four hands, it is said, the sugarcane bow [symbolizing] mind, five arrows [symbolizing] the five essences, sound, etc. of the five elements,[7] the noose [symbolizing] attachment and the goad [symbolizing] hatred. (Refrain......)

NOTES

1 The manifestation of Tripurā in which she is conceived as holding a parrot is called Śyāmalā, the goddess of poetic genius. The parrot and the myna – both talking birds – are often mentioned in a compound to indicate the same bird and not really two separate birds, yet by convention the myna is the female counterpart of the male parrot. Here the poet plays on the word *sāra* meaning "essence", signifying thereby that the goddess is the inherent Śakti of *śabda,* manifest as the seminal *mantra Oṃ/hrīṃ* symbolized in the parrot.

2 The word literally means one who is wearing a garland of female organs and here the goddess is *kriyāśakti.* As the creatrix of the universe she is connected with Brahmā. The first address here is directed to Vajreśvarī, who as the goddess of sustenance is connected with Viṣṇu. The second deity addressed here as the bearer of the skull and trident is Kāmeśvarī, the goddess of destruction, and is connected with Rudra. See Śivānanda, *Subhagodaya* 41-42.

3 To cast Her benign eyes on Her devotee signifies the final *śaktipāta,* i.e. the *yogin* receives the Goddess's full grace. That is why this *āvaraṇa* is called "giver of all perfection" circle. The *yogin* here attains all powers (*bhukti*) and is close to his liberation (*mukti*) as he is about to be merged in the Goddess.

4 *Mukti,* which is not any new achievement of the *yogin* but recognition of his own fundamental and real self, is only an experience. This is achieved through the understanding of the *mantra* of Tripurā and especially Her *bīja mantra, hrīṃ.* This sonic form of Śakti, when experienced with perfect realization

of its true sense, is the last state of differentiated experience of an individual, hindering his experience of the identity of his self with the undifferentiated ineffable Brahman. Thus it is imagined as the threshold of that supreme experience which is salvation, and *hrīṃ* as the gong of the doorbell. The *yogin* who attains the spiritual level of a complete understanding of the true nature of *hrīṃ* automatically passes into the state of liberation without any further hindrance.

5 Ādiśeṣa, i.e. Mahāviṣṇu, and the sixfaced god Guha are two important gods who are counted amongst the twelve original founders of the Tripurā sect.

6 Cf. *Lalitāsahasranāma* 82. Viṣṇu's ten incarnations are: Mīna, Kūrma, Varāha, Nṛsiṃha, Balarāma, Paraśurāma, Rāma, Kṛṣṇa, Buddha and Kalkī. Compare *Gītagovindam.*

7 Corresponding to each of the five elements there exist five essences, *tanmātra* ("just that"). The essence of earth is smell, of water is taste, of fire is visibility, of air is tactileness and of space is audibility.

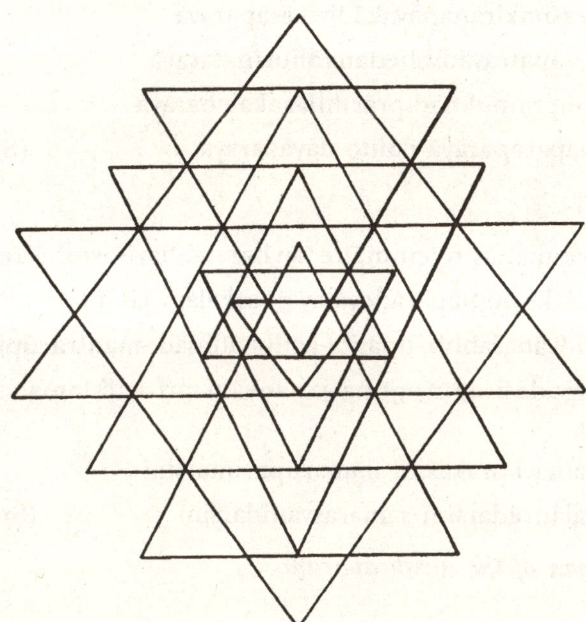

Navamāvaraṇakīrtana

Āhirī-rāga

Pallavī

Śrīkamalāmbā jayatī Ambā Śrīkamalāmbā jayatī
Jagadambā Śrīkamalāmbā jayatī śṛṅgārarasakadambā
Madambā Śrīkamalāmbā jayatī
Cidbimbapratibimbendubimbā Śrīkamalāmbā jayatī
Śrīpurabindumadhyasthacintāmaṇimandirastha-
Śivākāramañcasthitaśivakāmeśāṃkasthā (Śrī.....)

Anupallavi

Sūkarānanādyarcitamahātripurasundarīṃ
Rājarājeśvarīṃ Suvāsinīṃ
Śrīkarasarvānandamayacakravāsinīṃ cintaye'haṃ
Divākaraśītakiraṇapāvakādivikāsaparayā
Bhīkaratāpatrayādibhedanadhurīṇatarayā
Pākaripupramukhādiprārthitasukalebarayā
Prākaṭyaparāparayā pālito dayākarayā (Śrī.....)

Caraṇa

Śrīmātre namas te cinmātre sevitaramāharīsavidhātre
Vāmādiśaktipūjitaparadevatāyāḥ sakalaṃ jātaṃ
Kāmādidvādaśabhir upāsita-kādi-hādi-sādi-mantrarūpiṇyāḥ
Premāspadaśivaguruguha jananyāṃ prītiyuktamaccittaṃ vilayatu
Brahmamayaprakāśinī nāmarūpavimarśinī
Kāmakalāpradarśinī sāmarasyanidarśinī (Śrī......)

The hymn of the ninth āvaraṇa

The poet here uses all the cases for the nouns referring to the Goddess. The *pallavī* is completely in the nominative case. The first three lines of the *anupallavī* contain the accusative case. The rest of the *annupallavī* demonstrates the instrumental case. The first line of the *caraṇa* contains the dative case, the next line the ablative case. The genitive case is applied in the next line and the locative case in the line thereafter. The last two lines are in the vocative case.

TRANSLATION

Pallavī

Hail mother Kamalā, hail my mother Kamalā. Hail mother Kamalā, mother of the world. Hail my mother, mother Kamalā, a flower of the *kadamba* plant[1] in her sexual pleasure. Hail mother Kamalā, who as the orb of moon shows the reflection of the original orb (i.e. void) of consciousness.[2] She who resides inside the *bindu cakra* which is the city of Śrī and inside the temple there, which is made of the wish-fulfilling stone; who is in the embrace of Śiva, the lord of sexual desire, on the throne which is [Sadā] Śiva.[3]

(Refrain.....)

Anupallavī

I contemplate Mahātripurasundarī, who is propitiated by the goddess with a boar's face and others; on the suzerain empress,[4] the auspicious lady,[5] who dwells in the circle "Replete with All Bliss", which increases good luck. I am protected by her who makes the sun, the moon and the fire manifest themselves;[6] who is skilful in removing the three terrible sufferings;[7] who possesses the beautiful form assumed to grant the prayers of Indra and the other [gods];[8] who is manifest both as the supreme and as empirical objects; the compassionate. (Refrain....)

Caraṇa

I salute you, auspicious mother; pure consciousness; worshipped by Lakṣmī, Viṣṇu and Brahmā. Everything is born of the supreme deity who is worshipped by the *śakti, Vāmā,* etc.,[9] who has the form of the *mantra* which begins with the letter *ka,* or *ha,* or *sa* – the *mantra* which is worshipped and meditated on by the twelve [savants], Kāma, etc.[10] Let my loving mind be dissolved in her whose beloved is Śiva and who is Guruguha's mother. O you who embody the light which is Brahman; who are the [divine] omniscience which contains all phenomena and their names; who are [the gnosis] that reveals *Kāmakalā* and who are the insight [revealing the] perfect identity.[11] (Refrain ......)

NOTES

1 In the *bindu cakra,* the centre of the *Śrī cakra,* Tripurā remains in sexual embrace with Śiva. This biological symbol is used to underscore Her being the mother of the universe from whose womb all is born. The world is created by God in His bliss and ecstasy of love. Creation is the effect of His sport (*līlā*), which is love-making. Śakti in mythological and iconographical symbolism is conceived as His partner in the love-making. Hence She is called *Kāmakalā,* God's love-partner. The acute sensual pleasure experienced by the Goddess produce horripilation in her. The yellow flowers of the *kadamba* tree is round with stamens standing out all over it like a frightened hedgehog.

2 Here the play on the word *bindu* is intended to indicate the mystical theory of the two *bindu,* which often makes Tāntric cosmogony rather obscure. The primal *bindu* symbolizes the void which is the undifferentiated transcendental consciousness of Brahman, the ineffable reality which *is* consciousness but is conscious *of* nothing, there being nothing else in existence. This is also called *cidgagana* (the sky of

consciousness). The second *bindu*, which is compared to the orb of moon because it is luminous but not transparent, is the second stage of creation. God's desire to create is *śabda* and its first concrete though still transcendent form is *nāda*. God's creative thought is further concretized into a comprehensive idea of all phenomena to be created, ideal speech, present in God's mind as His omniscience. This is the reflection of the future creation stamped on the divine thought (*vimarśa*). This *bindu* is also called *paśyantī*. Cf. Lakṣmaṇa Deśika, *Sāradātilakam*, the introductory verses.

3 Kāmakalā and Śiva recline on a throne which is the supine figure of Sadāśiva. He is supported on the heads of Brahmā, Viṣṇu, Rudra and Īśvara. This image depicts the cosmic gods together wth Śiva and Śakti in the creative act. Tripurāmbikā represents this divine couple, who are but a single principle.

4 Tripurā is the divine sovereign, Śyāmalā is Her minister and the boarfaced Vārāhī is Her army general.

5 A *suvāsinī* is a married woman, who is always considered to be auspicious because of her potential as mother.

6 These represent the *mātṛkā*.

7 These are those belonging to the human soul (*ādhyātmika*), those caused by supernatural sources (*ādhidaivika*) and those of this earth (*ādhibhautika*).

8 The reference is to the Goddess's manifestation as Kauśikī, who defeated the demons Sumbha, etc. See Devīmāhātmya Ch. V ff.

9 Reference to the three deities of the eighth *āvaraṇa*. *Vāmā*, literary "pouring out", means the Goddess's act of self-projection.

10 See p. 240 on the hymn of the third *āvaraṇa*.

11 *Sāmarasya* is the central Tāntric concept of monistic theism. All diversities are merged in the final unity of non-dual reality, which is bliss.

Śrī-rāga

Pallavī

Śrīkamalāmbike Śive pāhi māṃ, Lalite

Śrīpativinute sitāsite Śivasahite (Śrī....)

Samaṣṭicaraṇa

Rākācandramukhi rakṣitakolamukhī
Ramāvāṇīsakhī rājayogasukhī
Śākambharī śātodarī candrakalādharī
Śaṃkarī Śaṃkaraguruguhabhaktavaśaṃkarī
Ekākṣarī Bhuvaneśvarī Īśapriyakarī
Sukhakarī Śrīmahātripurasundarī (Śrī......)

TRANSLATION

Pallavī

O lady mother Kamalā, O Lalitā, protect me. O you who are worshipped by Viṣṇu, who are [as Lalitā and as Śyāmalā], both fair and dark; who are united with Śiva. (Refrain....)

Samaṣṭicaraṇa

O you whose face is the full moon; [you] who protect Kolāmukhī (Vārāhī); who are a friend of Lakṣmī and Sarasvatī; who are happy by the royal union;[1] O Śākambharī,[2] O slim one, O wearer of the crescent moon, O beneficial one, O controller of the devotees of Guruguha, the beneficial [god]; O you who are the single syllable (*hrīṃ*), O mistress of the universe, beloved of God, bringer of happiness, the supreme lady Tripurasundarī; (Refrain....)

NOTES

1 *Rājayoga* is the union of Śiva and Śakti. See note 6 on the hymn of the seventh *āvaraṇa*.

2 Mother nature; Devīmāhātmya XI.45 says that when the earth was suffering from a drought lasting for one hundred years, Śakti sustained the creatures with vegetation grown from Her own self.

7. The Domestication of a Goddess: Caraṇa-Tīrtha Kālīghāṭ, the Mahāpīṭha of Kālī

From her [Ambikā's] broad forehead, clouded by frowning eyebrows, there sprang out at great speed Kālī of ferocious face, brandishing her sword and noose and the strange skull-staff. A garland of severed heads ornamented her body. She wore a tiger hide, and her emaciated form looked terrifying. From her wide-open mouth protruded an awful, lolling tongue. Her eyes red and sunken, she emitted screams that filled up all directions.

"Devī-Māhātmya" 7:5-7

Kalīghāṭ, the landing stage sacred to Kālī on the old course of the river Ganga at Calcutta, is regarded as an important seat of the Goddess (*mahāpīṭha* or *śaktipīṭha*) and is visited by thousands of pilgrims every day. As a major Indian pilgrim center, it is limited neither by the Bengali language nor by the cultural specialization of the local priests, for the temple authorities hire many non-Bengali priests to accommodate pilgrims hailing from other parts of India.[1] In this breadth of appeal, Kālīghāṭ clearly reflects the changing character of Calcutta itself, which was established in 1690 by Job Charnock of the East India Company. From the early nineteenth century, when it was the capital of the Indian empire as envisaged by Lord Wellesley, Calcutta gradually became the most important city of the Raj. Even when the capital was moved to Delhi in 1911, Calcutta, with its large, busy port, remained the trading and economic center of northern and eastern India. This naturally brought great number of people from other regions of the country, who in turn became woven into the rich fabric of Calcutta's socio-economic life.

In spite of this rich mixture, however, Calcutta retained its highly specific, Bengali social and cultural identity, and the visitors who pursued their own business interests there also tended to adopt local traditions. This cultural interplay has been and continues to be noticeable in several arenas, including religion.

One particular feature of Bengali religiosity is a deep-seated devotion to mother goddesses. The most important public religious festivals in Bengal are connected with two goddesses, Durgā and Kālī, the goddess of war and victory and the goddess of death and regeneration, respectively. Even today West Bengal is dotted with traditional temples of the Goddess, such as the Yogādyā Mā Temple in the Burdwan district.[2] Many of these temples were at one time patronized by local zamindars or sanctified by the presence of some famous holy man, as was the case with the Tārāpīṭha Temple and its great Tāntrika, Vāmākhyāpā. The most recent such center is the temple of Kālī at Dakṣiṇeśvar in north Calcutta, where Sri Ramakrishna taught his own interpretation of the traditional religion of India and nurtured the religious personality of his greatest disciple, Swami Vivekananda.

The concept of the Goddess, mainly identified with Kālī, is full of contradiction and ambiguity. On the one hand, she is seen all over India as the epitome of demonic ferocity and cannibalism, as is clearly depicted in her iconography: corpse-earrings; the long necklace of freshly severed heads and the belt made of amputated forearms; her nakedness or tiger's skin loincloth; her dress and ornaments dripping blood; and her grotesque habit of tearing apart the live bodies of her victims, lapping up their gushing blood with her lolling tongue and getting drunk on it. In other words, she is death and destruction. On the other hand, she is also the life-giving and life-protecting cosmic mother whose breast milk sustains the world and regenerates her creatures, weakened by the process of life and death and wearied by suffering.[3]

Partly in support of this second, life-affirming aspect of the Goddess, her wild and demonic iconography is toned down in favor of a dark but beautiful form for the benefit of Bengali religious sensitivities. Her red, round, bulging, unfocused eyes are made large, elongated, and serene; her disheveled, matted hair is changed into abundant, long, black, wavy tresses; and her greedy, lolling tongue and blood-smeared mouth are hidden behind cosmetic unguents, flower, decorations, and ear and nose ornaments. Her nakedness is often covered, as at the Kālīghāṭ Temple, with an expensive sārī. She is the perfection of youthful, charming, and feminine beauty.[4] At the same time she is the active, sovereign, divine power controlling the universe. As both Kālī the Reaper and Kālī the Supreme Savior,[5] she is a cosmic mother, who may punish wrongdoers but in her infinite kindness is ever ready to forgive them and to save them from misery and transience.[6] According to her devotees, all other goddesses, worshipped at different places under different names and on various festive occasions (for instance, Tārā, Durgā, Sarasvatī, Lakṣmī, Pārvatī, and even village goddesses) are but facets of this unique mother goddess Kālī.

The thousands of pilgrims who flock daily to the Kālīghāṭ Temple treat Kālī very much like a human mother, bringing her their domestic problems and prayers for prosperity, and returning when their prayers are fulfilled to express their gratitude. Their attitude to the Goddess is guided by their religious traditions and training, their spiritual and intellectual capacities, and the guidance of their temple priests. I myself have witnessed such a priest guiding a group of pilgrims and worshipping the Goddess on their behalf with mantras meant for the worship of Sarasvatī, the goddess of learning and arts. The day in question was Sarasvatī Pūjā, and no one had any problem worshipping a non-vegetarian Tāntric goddess with mantras intended for a vegetarian goddess, who, notwithstanding her identification with Kālī at the highest philosophical level and in other parts of India,[7] is treated in Bengal as one of her minor aspects

Calcutta and the House of Kālī by the River

Over the past hundred years, railroads and the publicity provided by newspapers and other periodicals have greatly enhanced the importance of the Kālīghāṭ, *mahāpīṭha.*[8] The small Kālī Temple used to be served by one priest, allegedly a Tantric practitioner as well, who personally managed every aspect of the temple's activities. Because of the increased prestige of the temple, largely owing to modern communications, the numerous descendants of the early priestly line have gained enormous power and prosperity. This raises the interesting question of the relationship between the religious sensitivity of the members of this priestly lineage and that of their pilgrim-clients. Do their religious attitude clash, or have they been peacefully integrated? As we shall see, the variety of religious attitudes towards Kālī seems not to be a problem, either for the priests, hereditary or temporary, or for the pilgrims, with their various cultural backgrounds.

In West Bengal, the great sacred centers dedicated to the Goddess as the divine active power (*Śākta pīṭhas*) have a different character from the religious temple centers of pan-Indian reputation. Unlike the temple of Jagannātha at Puri or of Mīṇākṣī at Madurai, for instance, Kālīghāṭ allows of pilgrims to worship in a relaxed, informal way. Yet it is easy to detect the ever-present managerial influence of the temple's priestly clan. Here we encounter two streams of Hinduism: the domestic religious sphere of the temple priests, who consider the deity in the temple to belong to their family tradition; and the Hindu tradition of the Purāṇas and Tantras, however that may be understood by Hindu pilgrims from far and wide

Figure 1: The Kālīghāṭ Temple. Photo by Jayanta Roy, February 2001.

In the course of several visits to the Kālīghāṭ Temple (Fig. 1) during a stay in Calcutta in 1995, I was able to witness the "domestication" of Kālī by the family and kinsmen of the Hāldārs, the priestly clan who enjoy ownership of this famous temple and manage its affairs with complete authority. In the process of such domestication, which follows the household religious ethos of the original forefathers who started the lineage some two hundred and fifty years ago, several important innovations have been made. Two points strike me as essential for understanding the religious attitudes of the temple priests and pilgrims. The first is the fusion at this religious center between two religious streams: the non-vegetarian Śākta (Tantric) tradition and the vegetarian Vaiṣṇava (Kṛṣṇaite) tradition. Since the seventeenth century, both have been strong in Bengal, and they have spawned a syncrestistic religious attitude that ignores sectarian boundaries. The second point is the fact that the religion of a family that owns or manages a revered Kālī temple may differ from that of most of her devotees, and may consequently influence the cult. Here at Kālīghāṭ, the family religious tradition of the Hāldār *sevāyets* is Vaiṣṇava, and this impinges on the temple's own ancient tradition, the Tantric cult of Dakṣiṇākālī.

Mother Kālī (Mā Kālī) and the Impact of Vaiṣṇava Religiosity

Let me now elaborate the first point. By the eighteenth century, largely under the influence of the Vaiṣṇava tradition, the religious attitude of Bengalis toward the supreme Goddess had completely changed. One can see this by comparing Kālī as she appears in the early sixth-century "Devī-Māhātmya" section of the *Mārkaṇḍeya Purāṇa* with Kālī as she is transformed in texts postdating the famous tenth-century *Bhāgavata Purāṇa*, which celebrates the youthful Kṛṣṇa. The "Devī-Māhātmya" describes the goddess Ambikā as the supreme *māyā* (delusive power) who appears in various manifestations to deliver gods and others from threatening demons. Kālī here assumes a subordinate form, as she emanates from the Goddess only to help her in fighting demons. The eleventh-to twelfth-century *Devībhāgavata*

Purāṇa, however, clearly modeled after the popular Vaiṣṇava *Bhāgavata Purāṇa,* records a different legend (5.23.1 ff.). In this case, the supreme Goddess is Pārvatī. In order to slay the demon kings Śumbha and Niśumbha and their demonic hosts, she emanates an exquisitely beautiful goddess, the Mother (Ambikā), also called Kauśīkī. As if exhausted of all positive feminine beauty, Pārvatī then turns completely black and becomes terrifyingly menacing, like the night of world destruction (*kālarātri*). In this dark form, she is called Kālī. Ambikā and Kālī go where the demons reign and start singing delightfully, attracting their enemies' attention. A great battle ensues. Eventually, the goddesses slay all the terrible demons, freeing the universe from evil. In this Purāṇa, therefore, Kālī as Pārvatī, Śiva's spouse, is Kauśīkī's equal; this allows her to have a leading role in the battles fought and makes a clear theological point: the two goddesses are but one single divine power, subsuming all other forces and gods (5.23-29). Indeed, most of the late Purāṇas popular in Bengal show the blurring of sectarian boundaries; other popular deities are presented in their legends in such a way as to be taken as aspects of the supreme Goddess. For instance, the goddesses Ṣaṣṭhī (the protectress of children); Śītalā (the goddess of smallpox and other epidemics), and Manasā (the snake goddess) are all incorporated in the fifteenth-century Śākta *Brahmavaivarta Purāṇa.* Even Rādhikā, the cowherd woman beloved of Kṛṣṇa, is elevated to the status of the divine power, the cosmic mother, in Śākta Purāṇas such as the *Devībhāgavata* and *Brahmavaivarta Purāṇas.*[9] Seen from this perspective, then, there is nothing incongruous in being a devotee of Kṛṣṇa/Viṣṇu and Kālī at the same time, or in finding Ṣaṣṭhī, Śītalā, and Manasā integrated into the temple worship of Kālī. We shall presently see both phenomena in our temple at Kālīghāṭ

The Vaiṣṇava tradition of the medieval Purāṇas was not the only influence upon Śākta sensibilities. Starting from the fifteenth century, Śrī Kṛṣṇa Caitanya's ecstatic Kṛṣṇa *bhakti* also had a tremendous impact upon conceptions of Śākta deities. As a result of both such vaiṣṇava influences, by the eighteenth century in Bengal Kālī was transformed from a wild, ferocious deity of death to a benign youthful mother, albeit capricious and crazy,[10] who charmed her devotees. One famous example is Rāmprasād Sen, who poured out his ecstatic adoration in excellent lyrics that, sung by popular singers, conveyed this regeneration of Kālī to every corner of Bengal.

The new attitude was charged with emotion, an ecstasy of tenderness such as exists between friends, lovers, husband and wife, parents and children, and even master and servant. Such loving bonds of closeness made devotees overlook the Goddess's divine sternness and suppressed all awareness of her fearful aspects. While continuing to maintain that Kālī was the supreme deity, the cosmic controller of creation, omnipotent to save and to nurture, her traditional violence was converted into playfulness, and her blood-curdling, roaring laughter into the sweet, amused laughter of a teenage girl. Similar to the image of the teenage Kṛṣṇa in the *Bhāgavata Purāṇa,* Kālī was viewed as a beautiful, tender youthful mother, like that idealized in the mind of a very young child. From the eighteenth century on, her cult attracted vast numbers of goddess worshippers, and both the "*Devi-Mahatmya*" and the *Devībhāgavata Purāṇa* became very popular.

Vaiṣṇava Innovations at a Śākta Temple

The close association of the Vaiṣṇava and Śākta traditions in Bengal is illustrated by six innovations instituted in the ritual regime by the Hāldār *sevāyets* at the Kālīghāṭ Temple, presumably since the time of Bhavānīdās, the founder of their lineage. (1) An icon of Vāsudeva (Kṛṣṇa/Viṣṇu) has been placed in a niche in the inner sanctum where the Kālī image stands. All of my informants told me that Vāsudeva is the *gṛhadevatā* or *kuladevatā* (family or lineage deity) of the Hāldārs, and that it was their ancestor Bhavānīdās who installed the icon in the temple. Its role in the temple ritual is very important even today. (2) Kālī is daily decorated with a clear Vaiṣṇava mark on the ridge of her nose. (3) During the most famous and important Bengali festival of Kālī, Kālī Pūjā, the Goddess in the temple is worshipped as Lakṣmī, and no animal sacrifice is offered to her on that day. (4) The temple bursary does not pay for the daily animal sacrifice at the temple. (5) Animals are taken inside the temple to be sacrificed only twice a year. After their beheading, the heads are allowed to stay inside the inner sanctum overnight and are then immersed in the Ganga the next morning. (6) No animal is allowed to be sacrificed during the daily *bhoga-pūjā* when Kālī is offered food. I shall elaborate on each of these innovations in describing the layout of the temple and the ritual schedule. All of them indicate that a gradual synthesis of Vaiṣṇava and Śākta traditions must have changed the original (Tantric?) character of this *mahāpīṭha.*

Kālīghāṭ is situated on the bank of the Ganga in southern Calcutta and is a busy trading center. It is one of the famous fifty-one *pīṭhas* (seats, or sacred centers) dedicated to the Goddess, and has been mentioned in various Bengali religious texts from the sixteenth century on.[11] Each of these fifty-one *pīṭhas* is sacred because a part of the lifeless body of Satī, an ancient manifestation of the Goddess, fell on that spot. The well-known Satī myth of Indian antiquity appears in different forms in various texts. One recent version recounts the story as follows. In ancient times the Goddess was born as a daughter of Dakṣa Prajāpati and married Śiva. Dakṣa considered Śiva to be unacceptable to the celestial community, and so when he organized a great sacrifice, he pointedly refrained from inviting Śiva and Satī. On hearing the news of this sacrifice, Satī went to her father and demanded to know why Śiva was the only god not invited.

Dakṣa launched into a diatribe against Śiva in front of all the assembled gods. At this insult, Satī fell dead on the spot. In terrible anger and grief, Śiva destroyed Dakṣa's sacrifice and beheaded Dakṣa. Then, in desperate sorrow, he carried Satī's corpse on his shoulder and roamed the universe, desolate and disconsolate, oblivious of all his duties. On the decision of the council of the gods, Viṣṇu finally relieved Śiva of his gruesome burden by cutting Satī's body into fifty-one pieces, which fell to earth bit by bit and were scattered over a wide area. Wherever a piece of this sacred body landed, a Satī center grew up to commemorate her great power and fidelity.[12]

Figure 2: The Kālī Image of Kālīghāṭ Temple. Photo by Jayanta Roy, February 2001.

As legend would have it, four toes from Satī's right foot fell at Kālīghāṭ.[13] The image of Kālī in the temple does indeed consist of what the devotees call the face and the feet; hence the name *caraṇa-tīrtha* (pilgrimage place of the feet) became popular. The image is decorated with splendid jewelry and a costly sari that completely conceals the image, showing just the face and hands with their attributes and part of the feet firmly set on a pedestal (Fig. 2). Even the head is encircled by a sari in the Bengali style. The face is mounted with three large golden eyes and a large, lolling golden tongue, on top of which the Goddess's upper lip and upper set of teeth are engraved. No other facial features are visible. No blood-dripping corners of her mouth or fangs are shown. Four silver arms are also mounted on the sides of the image; one holds a sword, one a severed head, and two make the usual gesture of granting safety and fulfilling the devotees' wishes. One of the main desires of every pilgrim is to touch the Goddess's feet and occasionally to offer a votive object like miniature sword or, if the pilgrim has come in gratitude for the cure of some disease, a small replica of the healed part of his or her body. More generous gifts include money, jewellery, in expensive sari, or even a royal canopy made of gold or silver, in recognition of Kālī's supreme sovereignty and compassion.

The main temple is a simple rectangular building, consisting of one large room, the inner sanctum, surrounded by an elevated, circumambulatory, open balcony (Fig. 3). Two doors open from this balcony, one in front of the image for a full view of the Goddess as one is circumambulating her, and one at the side, opening onto a flight of steps leading down to the inner sanctum. The pedestal rock on which the Goddess stands is situated almost in the middle of this room, facilitating a second circumambulatory passage. Devotees touch the Goddess's feet after presenting her with their ritual offerings (*pūjā*). On the wall of the inner sanctum, in a niche, an image of Vāsudeva is kept. Recently, this image has been covered with metal latticework doors, so I could not see it.

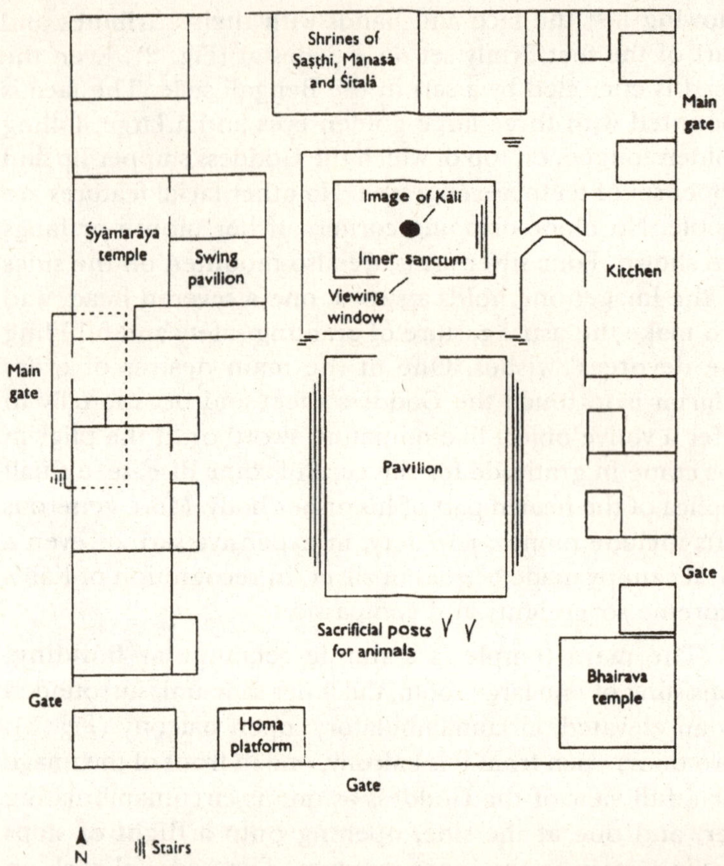

Figure 3: The floor plan of the Kālīghāṭ Temple, created by Sanjukta Gupta. Figure not drawn to scale

On one side of the main temple, there is a smaller temple to Śyāmarāya (the Dark King), containing images of Rādhā and Kṛṣṇa. This is flanked by two storerooms and a small kitchen. Adjacent to the Rādhā-Kṛṣṇa Temple is the swing pavilion (*dolmañca*) kept for their annual festival. On another side of the main Kālī Temple, there are shrines of the goddesses Ṣaṣṭhī, Manasā, and Śītalā. The cults of all these minor temples and shrines are integrated within the

Kālī Temple's special annual ritual events and are managed by the *sevāyet* Hāldārs and their appointed priests. The *pīṭha's* actual Bhairava, or ferocious form of Śiva, is Nakuleśvara.[14] But his temple, built long after the temple of Kālī Mā and even Śyāmarāya, stands a little way outside the present-day main temple complex and its encircling wall, and is much more easily accessible to the public. Although the management of the Nakuleśvara Temple is also in the hands of the Hāldārs, its priests are from Orissa and follow their own program, independent of the main temple routine. It is not clear to me why the Hāldārs have not appointed a Bengali priest for this temple.

The sacrificial post (Bengali, *hāḍikāṭh*, Sanskrit, *yūpa*) for the main temple stands at present on one side of the temple pavilion (*nāṭyayamañca*) near a side door at the far end of the precinct, neatly enclosed by a low wall. The temple in front of this area is that of a Bhairava who is not Nakuleśvara Śiva, and whose identity I failed to determine. He is related to the actual ritual of animal sacrifice, and the severed heads of the animals are offered to him. Opposite this Bhairava Temple is the pavilion for the ritual fire sacrifice (*homavedī*). This area, containing the enclosure of the fire sacrifice, the animal sacrifice, and the Bhairava Temple, is accessible through three doors set in the temple enclosure walls, and it appears to be slightly distinct from the main temple area that is the center of the pilgrimage, which is served by two main gates. One of these gates leads to the small water tank called the Kālī-kuṇḍa, into which the fossilized part of Satī's body is alleged to have originally fallen. The other leads to the temple of Nakuleśvara Śiva. A huge rectangular pavilion (*nāṭyamandira*) stands between the main temple and the sacrificial area, with flights of marble stairs on each of its long sides, and its short sides facing the main temple and the sacrificial area, respectively. Its marble floor is level with the balcony of the main temple, and a devotee siting there can see the image through the temple door facing it. This pavilion is not structurally connected with the temple and was erected thirty years latter. The temple kitchen, with a wide verandah in front of it, sits across a small yard from the side of the main temple. The cooked food is transported across this yard to the inner sanctum by means of a bridged corridor.

From the layout of the additional temples and other utility structures, it seems to me that there has been a conscious effort both to incorporate local deities like Ṣaṣṭhī, Śītalā, and Manasā, as well as Kṛṣṇa and Rādhā from Bengali Vaiṣṇavism, and to downplay Kālī's connection with blood sacrifice and even with ferocious Bhairavas. This is an ongoing process and is still continuing. As far as I can remember, the only part of the temple to have been "tidied up" in the past thirty years is the sacrificial area; this is so as to shield it slightly from the prying eyes of pilgrims and visitors. In other Kālī temples, the beheading of the animal is performed right in front of the temple's main door, or near to it, symbolizing that the sacrifice is being made in the Goddess's full sight.[15]

The daily cycle of Mā Kālī's ritual worship begins at 4 A.M., when the Hāldār priest responsible for the day's worship enters the inner sanctum with an assistant priest, who cleans up and removes all previous offerings, garlands, and so on.[16] Special care is taken to clean the feet of the image, which is then decorated with fresh garlands before the temple door in front of it is opened to the public, although people are not allowed inside the inner sanctum. A simple ceremony of worship is followed by *ārati* (waving of various objects, including, at the end, lamps). This is always performed by the same member of the Hāldār family and is done grandly, with great devotional emotion.[17] At 6 A.M., the main ritual worship commences inside the sanctum to the right of the image. This is known as Mā Kālī's daily morning worship (*nitya-pūjā*). So far as I could check, the worship follows a handbook, which could very well be the famous *Purohit-Darpaṇ (Mirror for Priests)*, compiled and edited by the late Surendramohan Bhaṭṭācārya. This handbook describes various rituals and mantras in Bengali, quoting Tantric sources as authorities, and it has run into more than thirty-five editions since it first appeared in 1891.[18] At this early morning worship no *homa* (fire sacrifice) is performed. Nor is a *yantra* (a mystic diagram representing the deity) drawn, but a *yantra* flower is placed on the body of the image – a substitution recommended by the *Purohit-Darpaṇ.*[19] Mr. Śānti Bhaṭṭācārya told me that the ritual program is based on the *Toḍala Tantra,* a fairly late text that describes the rituals of the ten Mahāvidyās. Interestingly enough, this text equates the ten Mahāvidyās with the ten *avatāras* of Viṣṇu.[20]

This worship of Kālī takes about two and a half hours. Vāsudeva is also worshipped, and his icon is brought down and placed inside the sacred ritual area. As far as I could see, it was more a Purāṇic than a Tantric rite, as there is no sequence involving a fire ritual. After the priests have finished the formal ceremony, the public is allowed to come down into the inner sanctum and touch the Goddess's feet; in this, they are aided by ordinary ritualist Brahmans who are not temple priests but who are allowed into the temple to officiate for pilgrims. The latter give their offerings to such priests, who then offer them to Kālī. The officiating priests get a small fee for their services from their pilgrim clients, while the Hāldārs receive whatever is offered to Kālī. These officiating priests hail from various parts of India and are appointed by the Hāldārs to serve the pilgrims, who also come from all over India.

At 2 P.M., the inner sanctum is closed to the public, and the early afternoon worship starts. As I have not witnessed this, I can only state that my informants told me that it is much the same as the morning worship, except that in the afternoon, cooked food is offered, whereas in the morning, the Goddess only eats fruits and sweets. I did see the cooked meal offerings as they were being conveyed from the kitchen to the temple and to the sanctum. The meal appeared to be simple, resembling the normal midday meal any affluent traditional Bengali would eat: a couple of rice dishes, a few vegetable curries, fish and goat-meat curries, some fried items, and rice pudding. After the food is offered, the priest shuts both doors of the main sanctum for about forty-five minutes. I must add an interesting detail here. I was told by the priest that the temple cook first prepares all the vegetarian and sweet dishes and offers these to Vāsudeva in the kitchen. Only then are the meat dishes cooked and transferred, with the vegetarian and sweet ones, to the inner sanctum for the ritual offering to Kālī. After the Goddess's meal is complete, the priest goes in and finishes the rituals that follow the food offering.[21] The temple servants then convey the food back to a room next to the kitchen, where the chief *sevāyet* of the day stands. He not only receives all the day's gifts offered to the Goddess by the pilgrims but also bears the cost of the daily food ritual and other offerings furnished by the regular temple suppliers. In addition, he supervises the process of cooking and offering the food, and thereafter distributes it–now known as *prasāda* (deity's grace)–amongst the other *sevāyets*, priests, servants, cooks, caretakers, and some special pilgrims; like myself. Finally, he oversees the feeding of a large number of beggars who are already gathered in the enclosed quadrangle. This is ritually called *daridra-nārāyaṇa-sevā* (serving Nārāyaṇa manifest as the poor) and has an obvious Vaiṣṇava overtone; the beggars are given only vegetarian food.

From 4 P.M. on, the public is allowed in again, and their offerings are administered by the *sevāyets* or their agents. The temple priest can now go home and take the *prasāda* as his midday meal and breakfast rolled into one. He then rests or attends to his private affairs, returning to the temple later for the Goddess's evening rituals. These commence with another *ārati*, which is much more elaborate than that performed in the early morning. Then a cold supper (*śītal*) consisting of fruits and sweets is offered to the Goddess, and the public can once again approach her. After about 11 P.M., the public is excluded. Finally, Kālī's bed is made ready, and she is freshly clothed and decorated with flower garlands, preparatory for sleep. One feature of these nighttime rituals is the restoration of her Vaiṣṇava mark (*rasakali* or *tilaka*), which is made of special sandalwood paste and consists of a dot between her eyes above a vertical line where the ridge of the nose would be. It is an interesting ritual point that in the afternoon when Kālī is about to be offered food that includes cooked fish and meat, the priest wipes out her Vaiṣṇava mark; it remains absent until she retires at night. When the Goddess is ready for bed, the priest and temple attendants close the temple doors, lock up all the other rooms of the temple enclosure, and finally lock the gates.

Not only has the Vaiṣṇavism of the Hāldārs impinged on the Goddess's Tantric tradition–making her, at least in their eyes, a Vaiṣṇaite Kālī–but popular cults have been merged into hers, and special *pūjās (naimittika pūjā* or *utsava*) are performed at the temple for other deities who are somehow related to the ritual program of the main temple, whose shrines are accommodated in the temple complex.

For example, on every new moon day, Kālī is worshipped in the dead of night according to a special Tantric system, and one hundred offerings of clarified butter (*āhūti*) are poured onto the sacred fire that follows the Tantric *pūjā*.[22] Yet it is not clear to me whether any animal is sacrificed from the temple side. Many devotees visit the temple on that day and offer animals to the Goddess, but this always occurs in the morning, and their offerings are treated as something not belonging to the inner Kālī worship. There are other interesting *naimittika pūjās* performed in the temple. For instance, I am informed that on the annual Kālī Pūjā day, which coincides with the pan-Indian Hindu festival of lamps and fireworks (Dīpāvalī) on the autumnal new moon day, the image at the Kālī Temple receives special worship, but as Lakṣmī, not Kālī. No special Kālī *pūjā* is offered to her that day, although countless pilgrims make it a point to visit her, preferably in the evening, since it is a specially auspicious day for Kālī. In addition, many animals are sacrificed by the pilgrims. It is well known that this Bengali Kālī Pūjā was inaugurated in the eighteenth century by the famous Rāja Kṛṣṇacandra of Navadvipa; thus it is not an ancient tradition.[23] It is also true that in the rest of India, Hindus worship Lakṣmī, not Kālī, on this day. But Bengalis have their own special annual festival for Lakṣmī, on the full moon day preceding Kālī Pūjā. The tradition at Kālīghāṭ of substituting Lakṣmī for Kālī worship on this occasion was probably introduced by Bhavānīdās. Is this evidence for Kālī's Vaiṣṇavī form as she is envisaged by the Hāldārs?[24] Even more strange, the most important festival of the temple community is observed on Rāmanavamī, the birthday of Rāma, when all the employees of the temple serving Mā Kālī get gifts of new clothes and money. The evening before, the swing festival of Kṛṣṇa, Dol-Yātrā or Cāṅcar is held with great pomp and grandeur at the swing pavilion. The next day, the images of Rādha and Kṛṣṇa are taken out of their temple and are placed on a vehicle, which is conveyed in procession, to the accompaniment of a band, along a special route within the temple complex. The Hāldārs celebrate the festive day by playing the color-throwing game. The very oddity of not performing these rites on the usual vernal full moon day also indicates that this is an old family tradition.[25] The temple also celebrates the birthday of Kṛṣṇa, Janmāṣṭamī, and, on the previous day, the festival of Nanda, Kṛṣṇa's father.

It should be noted, too, that the temple bursary does not pay for any daily sacrifice of goats. These are brought by private devotees and pilgrims to offer, but neither blood nor raw meat enters the temple. After the beheading, the *sevayet* of the day receives the head, and the body is given back to the donor. There is only one exception: the first goat offered as a sacrifice to Kālī is retained by the *sevāyet* for Kālī's food offering. I have been vaguely told that the *sevāyet* pays the donor money as the price of the goat meat. If no one agrees to give up his or her claim to the carcass, the *sevāyet* of the day has to buy a live goat and offer it himself.

Only twice annually does the temple fund pay for a goat sacrifice: once on the annual festival day for the goddess Manasā, who shares a shrine behind the main temple with the goddess Ṣaṣṭī; and once on the ninth or Navamī day of the annual Durgā Pūjā festival, when three goats are offered to the Goddess. The lineage norm of the Hāldārs allows animal sacrifices only on these two occasions. On Durgā Navamī, three goats are taken into the temple, where the preliminary rites are performed. One is offered in the name of the lineage guru (*kulaguru*) of the Hāldārs, who initiated them into Kālī worship, and the other two are offered in the name of the main Hāldār lineage. After the goats have been ritually beheaded, the heads are carried inside the main sanctum, where they are kept overnight; they are immersed in the Ganga the next day.[26] Another point brought to my attention by Mr. Vidyut Hāldār is that no animal sacrifice is allowed to take place while food is being offered to Kālī. This attitude toward animal sacrifice is very unusual for a Kālī worshipper and shows a certain uneasiness on the part of the Hāldārs about animal sacrifice. Sometimes, this feeling can be very intense. For example, I encountered total hostility to my taking a photograph of the temple precinct, lest I try to capture with my camera the cruel custom of decapitating a poor goat.

Pilgrims' Perspectives on Kālī

The importance accorded to Vāsudeva, the application of a Vaiṣṇava *tilaka* on the Goddess's forehead, and the special observances of the temple ritual calendar all show the influence of the Hāldārs' Vaiṣṇava tradition. In contrast, the general public view of Kālī at Kālīghāṭ is reflected in the legends about the temple and its image. Since the image is the great goddess Kālī, and since the temple encompasses one of her famed seats, Kālīghāṭ is considered a great Tantric power centre.[27] The earliest legends about the temple concern two Brahman Tāntricas named Brahmānanda Svāmī and Ātmārāma Brahmacārī. The former was not a Bengali. Once, while he was deep in meditation, the rock on which he was sitting floated down the river Ganga, eventually arriving at Kālīghāṭ, where it came to rest on the riverbank. Meanwhile, Ātmārāma Brahmacārī–sometimes presented as Brahmānanda's disciple in Tantric practices (*sādhanā*) and sometimes treated independently – learned in a meditative vision that part of Satī's body was lying at the bottom of a nearby pond. When it was brought up, it looked like a piece of black rock. For various complex reasons, the sculptor who was using it to carve Kālī's image could not finish the job. Hence the image consists of the Goddess's face and feet, while other parts remain unfashioned.[28] This incomplete image was then placed on the rock that Brahmānanda had used at his meditation seat.

Ātmārāma is involved in many other legends as well. One of these claims that he was highly honored by Rājā Vastana Rāy, uncle of Rājā Pratāpāditya Rāy of Jessore and a courtier of the Mughal emperor, in the seventeenth century.[29] Mr. Śānti Bhaṭṭācārya, the chief temple priest and author of a popular article on the history of the Kālīghaṭ Temple, maintains that Brahmānanda came from the Nilgiri mountain range in Tamilnadu and that he and his pupil Ātmārāma established a Tantric pupillary lineage at Kālīghāṭ. The last of this lineage was a certain Bhuvaneśvar Brahmacārī, a Tantric Kaula practitioner.[30] He had one daughter, named Umā, born of his union with his partner in Tantric practice, a woman whom he later married.

The final phase of the history of the Kālī Temple concerns Bhavānīdās Cakravartī, founder of the Hāldār lineage. I mention one version of how he became temple priest and beneficiary. For some reason, young Bhavānīdās, already married and the father of a son, made a pilgrimage to Kālīghāṭ. Bhuvaneśvar liked him and tried to persuade him to marry his daughter Umā as a second wife and to settle down at Kālīghāṭ as the *sevāyet* of the temple. By this time, the temple possessed a sizeable landed property and, being situated on the route to the East India Company's prosperous trading port of Calcutta, was a flourishing pilgrim center. Bhavānīdās found the proposal attractive and agreed. He married Umā and then, having brought his first wife and her son to Kālīghāṭ, took the position of *sevāyet.* This started the last phase of the priestly lineage at the Kālī Temple.

During the early period of the prosperity of Calcutta under the East India Company, the Kālī Temple became famous and flourished so much that the Hāldār family members felt that they could not handle all the affairs of the temple. About two hundred years ago, the Hāldārs employed a certain Śrīpada Bhaṭṭācārya from Somra, a village in the Hoogly District, to perform the actual daily worship of the image in the temple as the temple priest. The present chief priest, Mr. Śānti Bhaṭṭācārya, is the eighth generation descending from this Brahman. He explained that as the duties are very onerous, involving fasting every day until about 4 P.M. and working almost non-stop from 3:30 A.M., none of his children, brothers, cousins, or other male members of his clan want to do the job. He has therefore hired additional priests and is training them to help him execute the many long and complex ritual acts carried out daily in the temple. The day I witnessed the early 6 A.M. ritual worship of the Goddess, the officiating priest was Mr. Kārtik Mukherjee. He had been recruited just a few years ago. It was interesting to notice in this quiet young man (in his mid twenties) a sober and humble kind of devotion for the Goddess and to his duties.

For years, the Hāldārs enjoyed full authority over the temple management and evolved a self-regulating, kin-based association to run the temple affairs and to make an equal distribution of its assets and income. Recently, however, they came into legal conflict with the Sābarṇa Caudhurīs, who suddenly claimed ownership of the temple lands.[31] This led to government interference and to the establishment of a legal executive committee, formed democratically from members of the Hāldār lineage but also including nominees from Calcutta University and Calcutta Corporation, with the supreme authority held by a high government administrator. Yet the Hāldārs still retain their full authority over the day-to-day running of the temple's businesses and its considerable daily income, so they face no problem in introducing subtle changes and innovations into the temple's ritual services.

The aforementioned peculiar ritual practices at the Kālī Temple complex, as introduced by the Hāldārs, derive from Bhavānīdās's Vaiṣṇava background. There is nothing to suggest that he had any Tantric learnings (he was certainly neither a Kāpālika[32] nor a Kaula), or even that he showed any propensity to ecstatic adoration of Kālī. He was a traditional orthodox Brahman householder with strong Vaiṣṇava inclinations, and it is evident that his and his descendants' loyalty to Vāsudeva as their lineage deity has remained unchanged. It is even conceivable that the Vāsudeva icon in the niche of the inner sanctum is the very image that once belonged to Bhavānīdās. Although he applied himself to his duties as the caretaker, manager, and priest of the temple, in all probability being initiated into the Kālī mantra by his father-in-law when the latter handed over the proprietorship of the temple to him, he took measures to play down the Tantric aspects of the Goddess's worship, notably the blood sacrifice. The same is true for the rest of the Hāldār family, even though they acquired a hereditary Śākta lineage guru not long after Bhavānīdās's time.[33]

Mr. Vidyut Hāldār and other informants told me that they worship the Goddess in her Vaiṣṇavī form. One can see this both in the six ritual innovations described above and in the lack of attention paid to be obvious Śākta monuments associated with the main temple. The Hāldārs appear to have very little to do with the day-to-day functions at the shrine of Nakuleśvara Śiva, the main Bhairava of Kālīghāṭ, and the Kālī-kuṇḍa, or temple pond sacred to Kālī, has only recently been renovated after a long period of neglect. The obvious lack of interest on the part of earlier generations of Hāldārs in these older goddess-centered parts of the Kālī Temple complex is thus noteworthy.

What emerges from these small but very specific traditional variations in the ritual patterns of this Kālī Temple is that the Vaiṣṇava learning of Bhavānīdās and his descendants have influenced their method of Kālī worship. Although the thousands of pilgrims daily visiting the temple definitely do not think her so, to the Hāldārs she is one and the same as Lakṣmī or Śrī or Ambikā–or indeed Kālī as recorded in the *Devībhāgavata Purāṇa.*

The ancient, strict, Kāpālika associations of the temple, revealed in the legends concerning Brahmānanda Svāmī, Ātmārāma Brahmacārī, and Bhuvaneśvara Brahmacārī, and in other legends about highway robbers performing human sacrifice at the temple, appear to have been completely wiped out both from the present-day temple rituals and from the arrangements of the various shrines within the Kālīghāṭ complex. However, for pilgrims visiting the temple, Mother Kālī is both compassionate and fierce. Contradiction is inherent in her, and she is easily prone to take offense. Declaring their total dependence on her mercy, pilgrims entering the temple loudly call on her, "Mother! O Mother!" The majority of these devotees believe that she is satisfied by receiving blood sacrifice, and a great number of goats are sacrificed every day by devotees seeking her favors. Some devotees even offer their own blood to show their loyalty and devotion. To them, she is neither vegetarian nor connected with Viṣṇu, but is the great Goddess extolled in the Tantric and Purāṇic tradition.

NOTES

For providing me with much of the information on the Kālī Temple at Kālīghāṭ, I am indebted to several members of the Hāldār family, the hereditary owner-managers (*sevāyets*) of the temple. *Sevāyet* literally means "servicing man," but technically it refers to a temple priest who has the right to enjoy the temple's income. Such a person therefore has the responsibility for the management of the temple property, as well as its day-to-day running, including all associated rituals. The title *hāldār* or *hāolādār* (land custodian) was awarded to a descendant of the first *sevāyet* at the temple by Nawāb Alīvardī Khān of Murshidabad (1740-56). At present the Hāldārs are divided into five lines according to the ages of the five grandsons of Bhavānīdās Cakravartī (Hāldār), the first of the family to become associated with the temple. I am especially grateful to Mr. Vidyut Hāldār, who hails from the primary line, is the most important *sevāyet* of the Goddess at Kālīghāṭ, and is one of the few *sevāyets* to work full-time, and to his uncle Mr. Aruṇkumār Mukherjee, now the secretary of the Kālī Temple Trust Committee. In addition, I thank Mr. Śānti Bhaṭṭācārya and Mr. Kārtik Mukherjee, the chief priest and his assistant at the temple, who gave me a lot of their time and allowed me to sit inside the temple during the main morning ritual worship of the Goddess.

Epigraph: For the Sanskrit original, see *Devī-Māhātmyam: The Glorification of the Great Goddess*, ed. and trans. Vasudeva S. Agrawala (Ramnagar: All India Kashiraj Trust, 1963), p. 96. The more familiar form of Kālī is described in a late hymn called the *Karpūrādistava*, attributed to Mahākāla, or Lord Śiva. In this text, Dakṣiṇākālī, which is also the name of the Goddess in the temple at Kālīghāṭ, is naked and wears a girdle of severed arms; babies' corpses serve as her two earrings; and blood flows from the corners of her mouth. She resides in a terrible cremation ground and is seated on a corpse (Śiva). See *Karpurādistava*, as translated in Sir

John Woodroffe's *Hymns to the Goddess and Hymn to Kali* (1913; Wilmot, Wis.: Lotus Light Publications, 1981), pp. 288-335.

1 See Indrani Basu Roy, *Kālīghāṭ: Its Impact on Socio-Cultural Life of Hindus* (New Delhi: Gyan Publishing House, 1993); and Surajit Sinha, "Kali Temple at Kalighat and the City of Calcutta," in *Cultural Profile of Calcutta* (Calcutta: Indian Anthropological Society, 1972), pp. 61-72.

2 This is another ancient Kālī-*pīṭha*. See *Paścimbaṅger Pūjā-pārvan o Melā*, ed. Aśok Mitra (Indian Census, 1961), vol. 16, pt. 7-B, no. 5, pp. 258-67.

3 See E. Alan Morinis, *Pilgrimage in the Hindu Tradition: A Case Study of West Bengal* (Delhi: Oxford University Press, 1984), pp. 174-75. It is said that the secret images of Tārā inside the outer wooden image at the Tārāpiṭh Temple shows the Goddess suckling Śiva her husband to restore his life and to annul the effect of the cosmic poison he drank to save creation.

4 Sanjukta Gupta, "Tantric Śākta Literature in Modern Indian Languages," in Teun Goudriaan and Sanjukta Gupta, *Hindu Tantric and Śākta Literature*, vol. 2, fasc. 2 of *A History of Indian Literature*, ed. Jan Gonda (Wiesbaden: Otto Harrassowitz, 1981), pp. 178-80.

5 *Lakṣmī Tantra: A Pāñcrātra Text*, trans. with notes by Sanjukta Gupta (Leiden: E.J. Brill, 1972), Introduction, p. xxvi.

6 Kālī is said to exercise the fivefold cosmic functions of creating (*sṛṣṭi*), sustaining (*sthiti*), and destroying (*laya*) the world, deluding or punishing (*tirodhānā* or *nigraha*), and granting the reward of her grace (*anugraha*). See ibid., pp. 69-72.

7 For example, the Lalitā cult of Kanci and the Śāradā cult of Sringeri in Tamilnadu.

8 See Sinha, *Kali Temple at Kalighat*, and D.C. Sirkar, *The Śākta Pīṭhas*, 2nd ed. (Delhi: Motilal Banarsidass, 1973), pp. 24 and 87, for the development of Kālīghāṭ's reputation as a great seat of the Goddess.

9 For further discussion of the parallel treatment of the Goddess in medieval Śākta texts and of Kṛṣṇa in the *Bhāgavata Purāṇa*, see studies by Cheever Mackenzie Brown: *God as Mother: A Feminine Theology in India* (Hartford, Vt.: Claud Stark, 1974); and *The Triumph of the Goddess: The Canonical Models and*

Theological Visions of the Devībhāgavata Purāṇa (Albany: State University of New York Press, 1990).

10 "In the marketplace of this world, the dark mother sits flying her kites. One or two in a hundred thousand snap the string and fly away bondless, and how she laughs, clapping her hands!" Rāmprasād Sen, in Śivaprasād Bhaṭṭācārya, *Bhāratcandra o Rāmprasād*, 2nd ed. (Calcutta: Modern Book Agency, 1967), p. 297. See also C. Mackenzie Brown, "Kālī, the Mad Mother," in *The Book of the Goddess Past and Present: An Introduction to Her Religion*, ed. Carl Olson (New York: Crossroad, 1987), pp. 110-23.

11 See the *Manasāmaṅgala* by Bipradās (1495), the *Caṇḍīmaṅgala* by Mukundarām Cakravartī (1590), and the *Pīṭhanirṇaya/ Mahāpīṭhanirūpaṇa* and *Gaṅgābhaktitaraṅginī* (both eighteenth century). These are discussed by Sinha, "Kali Temple at Kalighat," p. 62, and Sirkar, *Śākta Pīṭhas*, pp. 4, 32-41.

12 See Sirkar, *Śākta Pīṭhas*, pp. 5-7. In earlier texts like the *Tantrasāra* of Kṛṣṇananda Āgamavāgīśa, the number of *pīṭhas* is said to be fifty. Ibid., pp. 17-24.

13 There are different views on this point. According to some informants, these limbs are still kept in a silver box hidden in the body of the image in the inner sanctum. Once a year, on Kālī's sacred bathing day, known as her *snāna-yātrā*, a direct descendent of Bhavānīdās's eldest family line changes the dress and decoration of this body part, the nature of which is a family secret. See Apūrba Caṭṭopādhyāy, "Kālīghāṭer Kālīpujo," *Sāptāhik Bartamān*, November 9, 1996, pp. 8-11.

14 Every goddess-*pīṭha* has a special Bhairava as a guardian (*kṣetrapāla*) of the sacred area. See Sirkar, *Śākta Pīṭhas*, pp. 39-41.

15 Morinis's description of goat sacrifice as performed at the Tārāpīṭh Temple is interesting. The priests wave the animal toward the temple of Tārā to emphasize that it is being sacrificed to the Goddess. See *Pilgrimage in the Hindu Tradition*, pp. 184-85.

16 I mainly obtained this information from Mr. Vidyut Hāldār and Mr. Śānti Bhaṭṭācārya.

17 This gentleman, known as Kānāi Hāldār, is not compelled to perform the *ārati*, but does so willingly and meticulously. Probably, Kālī is his chosen personal deity (*iṣṭadevatā*). In "Kālīghāṭer Kālīpūjo," p. 9, Apūrba Caṭṭopādhyāy states that this *ārati* practice had been introduced only about twenty-five years earlier.

18 The first edition appeared in parts; it took eleven years, until Bengali era 1311 [1904], before the manual was completed. A good edition which, however, includes only a portion of the *Purohit-Darpaṇ*, is the *Sarva-deva-devī-pūjā-paddhati* (*Method of Worshipping All Gods and Goddess*), ed. Vāmadeva Bhaṭṭācārya and corrected by Prabhākar Kāvyasmṛtimāmāṃsātīrtha, 4th ed. (Calcutta: Calcutta Town Library, 1355 [1948]). Bengali Era publication dates, which are 593 years fewer than those of the Gregorian calendar, are used in most Bengali books, and the Gregorian year is given in square brackets following the Bengali date in the notes that follows.

19 See the 38th edition of the *Purohit-Darpaṇ* (Calcutta: Satyanārāyaṇ Library, 1393 [1986]), p 384.

20 For a detailed discussion of Tantras from eastern and northeastern India that contain Vaiṣṇava themes, see Teun Goudriaan, "Hindu Tantric Literature in Sanskrit," in Goudriaan and Gupta, *Hindu Tantric and Śākta Literature*, pp. 82-84.

21 See Sanjukta Gupta, Dirk Jan Hoens, and Teun Goudriaan, *Hindu Tantrism* (Leiden: E.J. Brill, 1979), p. 156. Mr. Kārtik Mukherjee told me that Ucchiṣṭacaṇḍālī, the goddess who is always invoked at the end of a Tantric Kālī *pūjā* as the first to accept the offered food (*prasāda*), so as to safeguard it from harmful spirits, is never called upon in the daily *pūjā* of Kālī.

22 See ibid., pp. 162-53.

23 Chintaharan Chakravarti, *Tantras: Studies on their Religion and Literature* (Calcutta: Punthi Pustak, 1963), pp. 89-93.

24 See Caṭṭopādhyāy, "Kālīghāṭer Kālīpūjo," p. 10.

25 Ibid., pp. 8-11. In addition to their devotion to Vāsudeva, the Hāldārs have probably long been worshippers of Rāma. Holi, or the festival of colors that accompanies Rādhā and Kṛṣṇa's swing festival, is normally held on the full moon day previous

to the ninth day of the bright fortnight in Caitra (March-April), when Rāma was born.

26 Goat sacrifice on the occasion of Durgā Pūjā is a very common custom among Bengali upper-caste landowners, and the Hāldārs as the *sevāyets* of Kālī did at one time own much land. This holding has somehow dwindled to just the land on which the temple complex stands, plus a few hundred square metres outside it.

27 See Dīptimay Rāy, *Paścimbaṅger Kālī o Kālīkṣetra* (Calcutta: Maṇḍal Book House, 1391 [1984]), pp. 38-54.

28 I must quote a popular local Bengali verse reporting the unusualness of the image: "Kālīghāṭer kathā; āge beḍoy hāt pā, pare beḍoy māthā" ("The strange thing about Kālīghāṭ is that first emerge her hands and feet, and then emerges her head").

29 In some legends, Vasanta Rāy is replaced by Mansingh, the great general of the Mughals.

30 Kaula refers to a particular mode of esoteric Tantric ritual practices wherein certain objects held to be impure by orthodox Hindus are offered to the deity. These include impure foods like meat and alcohol. In addition, ritual sexual intercourse with a woman outside one's own caste is practiced in order to collect and offer to the deity the resulting sexual fluids. Such Kaula practitioners are mainly worshippers of the Goddess as the supreme divine Power, Śakti.

31 Job Charnock of the East India Company bought three villages from the Sabarṇa Caudhurīs that together formed the nucleus of modern Calcutta.

32 Kāpālikas belong to an ancient Śaiva ascetic sect. A Kāpālika must always carry his begging bowl made of human skulls, or *kapālas;* hence the name. From the inception of this sect, its followers have practiced antinomian religious rites.

33 It is said that Bhavānīdās's grandsons appointed three hereditary types of Brahman ritualist: a *kulaguru* (lineage preceptor), a *bhaṭṭācārya ṭhākur* (temple priest), and two *miśra* assistants (Brahmans acting as aides to the temple priests). See Basu Roy, *Kālighāt,* p. 21.

8. Kings, Power and the Goddess[1]

Until quite recently, any Indian king was considered the locus of all temporal power in the area he ruled. Indeed, in Nepal this is still so. All Indian princes, and even the big zamindars in British India, used to believe that their will and command should reign untrammeled within their territories. This sovereignty of the royal will was of course based on political and economic strength; but it also had to be sanctioned by the local temple of the Goddess, who symbolized Power. To his subjects, the king's supremacy is consolidated when they are convinced that he holds the divine authority (*ājñā*), the mandate of heaven, concretized as *śakti.* The king is regarded as married to Lakṣmī or Śrī, the personification of regal power and prosperity.[2] He is annually blessed by Durgā, the goddess of victory and prowess in battle. Royal rituals confer and express the king's *śakti,* which is embodied in his regalia as well as his person.

In his famous essay on ancient Indian kingship,[3] as well as in other writings, Louis Dumont has described the interdependence of the king and his royal chaplain (*purohita*). The chaplain guarantees the king's legitimacy and performs ritual on his behalf. More recent work on kingship has discovered the king's intimate association with various feminine principles and/or goddesses and criticized Dumont's account as faulty or incomplete.[4] In our view, this is hardly fair to Dumont. He is describing the state of affairs before the rise to dominance of Hindu monotheism in the early centuries of the Christian era. The *purohita* is the representation of Vedic religion, the officient of Vedic (*śrauta* and *gṛhya*) ritual.[5] This stratum of ritual has never become wholly obsolete, but throughout Hinduism it has long been overlaid by the ritual of the monotheistic sects, ritual which is accurately known as *tāntrika.* Tantra is also a major current of Hindu theology which centres on the concept of God's Power (*Śakti*). It is the aim of this paper to show that for at least the last thousand years, perhaps longer the concept of power in its political and social application has been intimately connected with tantric theology – so intimately, one might suggest, that the one cannot be adequately understood apart from the other. To give a full exposition of either would lie outside the scope of a single paper; but we hope that a brief summary of the tantric concept of *śakti* on the one hand and a few historical examples on the other may serve to establish the connection.

This connection has been made by Geertz in his evocative interpretation of the nineteenth-century Balinese state/royal city. (*Negara* is derived from Sanskrit *nagara,* "city".) Geertz writes of the court:

> The message the *negara* was designed to convey, and in its ritual life did convey, is ill-described by the mere statement, correct enough in itself, that the king was a kind of corporeal god. To the degree that it can be abstracted at all from the vehicle of its expression, the message was that the king, the court around him, and around the court the country as a whole, were supposed to make themselves into facsimiles of the order their imagery defined.[6]

First a very few words are necessary to remind readers of the pre-tāntric position. We need not go back to Vedic times (c. 500 BC) but only to the turn of the Christian era, when Hindu monotheism was superseding the Vedic pantheon. The great classical texts on kingship, Manu's *dharmaśāstra* and Kauṭilya's *Arthaśāstra,* probably date from the first two centuries AD. In Manu, the king is primarily the protector of the law of the universe, *dharma.*[7] Originally *dharma* was a cosmic principle of law and order which transcended even the gods; but for monotheists that is impossible: *dharma,* like everything else, must be created and guaranteed by God. The king is God's chosen occupant of the divine viceregal office in his territory: God made him out of parts of other major, regal gods. It is his duty to maintain *dharma* by punishing those who offend against it and rewarding its defenders: the latter means principally that he must care for learned and virtuous *brāhmaṇas,* who are the custodians and interpreters of *dharma.* Manu emphasizes the king's duty to punish the wicked. The emblem of royal power is the mace or scepture, literally the 'stick' (*daṇḍa*) – a word which is also used to mean 'punishment'. Chastisement of malefactors among his subjects and external enemies is not wholly differentiated: *daṇḍa* is the sword of both justice and war.[8]

The god most closely identified with royalty at this period is Viṣṇu. His iconography represents him as the cosmic sovereign, the *cakravartin* – literally 'being in the wheel', i.e., at the centre of the circle. He wears a crown and holds a mace and wheel. The mace symbolizes punishment and the wheel his sphere of control, in this case the entire universe. His standard bears the royal eagle Garuḍa. In purānic theology, likewise, Viṣṇu is the divine Person (Puruṣa – the Christian theological overtone of this translation is intentional) whose function it is to maintain the world (*sthiti-kartṛ*), just as it is the function of the ideal *kṣatriya* to do likewise.

The fact that Viṣṇu is a king – which Śiva is clearly not – does not however mean that every king is Viṣṇu. The general principle is rather – and we shall see the significance – that the king is identified with the highest male god of the locality. Thus the King of Varanasi (Kāśī Nareśa), though he lives in Ramnagar and has other links with Rāma, is greeted as Śiva incarnate, since Śiva reigns supreme in Benares. In this way, as in others, the king comes close to personifying his kingdom.[9]

On the other hand we must not forget that like other high caste Hindus the king will inherit a family deity (*kula-*

devatā) in his partrilineage. This can be a source of confusion. Thus the family or dynastic deity of the kings of Vijayanagara was Narasiṃha, the Man Lion form of Viṣṇu, so they were Vaiṣṇavas; but the local god was Virūpākṣa with shrine within the palace itself. The local river is the Pampā, and Indian rivers are always feminine, so Virūpāksa, as the local god, was of course the "Lord/Husband of Pampā", Pampeśvara; and by the same token the monarch was Pampeśvara too.

In more recent times, the same motivation made the ruler of Mysore adopt the local powerful Goddess Cāmuṇḍā and her (so-called) sister, Uttanahalli Ammā as the royal divinity. About this process, Surajit Chandra Sinha writes, "The report indicates how the cult of Chamundesvari complex has been supported by its association with various castes and by the over-riding patronage of the former ruling family of Mysore".[10] To explore this pervasive metaphor of marriage and mastery we must now turn to tantric theology.

TANTRA

Tantra is a form of religion in which worldly, temporal goods and theology are perfectly integrated. It advocates the worship of power for the attainment of power. During the latter half of the first millennium AD, when other Hindu theologies were increasingly influenced on the one hand by the passive, other-worldly ideology of renunciation and on the other by the self-surrendering, unresisting emotionalism of *bhakti,* tantra supported neither meekness nor passivity. Tantra is undertaken for both salvation, *mukti,* and personal gain and power, *bhukti. Bhukti,* literally 'enjoyment', is realized through power.

The person who practises tantra is known as a *sādhaka,* literally, an 'achiever', and one who has attained the goal of his practice is a *siddha,* 'he who has achieved'. The *sādhaka* worships the supreme divinity as the vital power of the cosmos, the essence of all will, action and knowledge, and aims to possess the power by becoming that divinity. This requires considerable explanation.

God, Man and Power

Two ideas which have run through Indian religious thought from its very beginnings in the Vedic sacrificial cult are basic to tantric theology. Both occur in *Ṛg Veda X.*90, a hymn known as the *Puruṣa-sūkta.* According to the hymn the creator god created the universe by performing a sacrifice. What he offered in that sacrifice, since nothing else existed, was inevitably himself. Thus the world is made of the body of god and is consubstantial with god. The second idea is that the creator god was the first sacrificer, the prototype of all later sacrificers, and that he was by same token the prototype of man, for in Vedic thought it is the essence of man to sacrifice. Thus man too, when he sacrifices, somehow performs a cosmogonic act with the materials of his own person – though for the latter the human sacrificer finds something which is explicitly a substitute. From this line of mystical speculation about the sacrifice arose a widely pervasive theory of a correspondence between the microcosm of the individual and the macrocosm, the world.

Combining these two ideas of equivalence, the early Indian thinkers took the further step to arrive at the logical conclusion that man corresponds to god. This correspondence was not pursued into physical detail and did not lead to the view familiar in the Christian tradition, that man is formed in the image of God. Attention was concentrated rather on what could be the essence of man – and indeed of God.

For Hindu theologians the crucial thing about God was his consciousness. It was his defining characteristic, his very essence. The same is true of the individual soul: it is pure consciousness. Consciousness is here narrowly understood. It is absolutely not thought, for thought is discursive and complicated. Consciousness is simple, indeed unitary. It is the pure light source which makes the world visible, knowable. This comparison of consciousness to light is very important. Consciousness is thus conceived as totally inactive, as light is; yet it is the condition which makes any activity – mental or physical – possible.

In late Vedic religion the highest divinity was an impersonal principle, *brahman* – a neuter term. Hindu theology then developed the concept of a supreme personal god, usually a form of Viṣṇu or Śiva and therefore masculine. But the theistic theologians never abandoned the concept of brahman. Equating it with the highest personal deity, the only ultimate reality, they built ambiguity into their system. God's personal attributes play a fundamental role in tantric thought; yet that thought cannot be clearly understood unless one remembers the tradition, never rejected, that god is an impersonal essence devoid of all duality, best described by negation: 'Not this, not that'. This heritage helps to explain why in tāntric monotheism, whether the supreme god is Śiva or Viṣṇu, nothing can be predicated of him.

It is the theory of *śakti* which is the hallmark of tāntric theology and the symbolism of *śakti* which moulds tāntric ritual. Like god himself, *śakti* can pragmatically (including for religious purposes) be seen as one or many. (This will not seem strange if one remembers that to have power is inevitably to have powers.) Everything in the world, from souls down to stones, is an aspect of *śakti*, because it is a manifestation and effect of god's power; and just as *śakti* has been hypostatised from the divine essence, an adjective made noun, an attribute regarded as a principle, so everything else can be referred to as if it were separate entity. There are thus many *śaktis*, designated according to context, in a complex hierarchy of being. But if properly understood they are but aspects of the one *śakti*, one name for which is *svātantrya-śakti*, (god's) 'autonomous power'. God is the only true agent, for no one can tell him what to do.

While *śakti* is precisely Power, one must remember the distinction between power and authority. We here move on to the level of personification. Śakti is dependent for her authority on god; she has none of her own. It may not be fanciful to suggest that in this she recalls the Hindu wife, who however active is theoretically acting always only on the authority of her husband, the inert centre of her world. More relevant to our present purpose is that while she *has* no authority, she *is* authority, concretized or personified as god's *ājñā*. This word literally means 'command'; in our context we can also translate it as 'authority' or 'mandate'. The sign of royal authority is the *mudrā* or seal which the king gives to his officers. Śakti is called *mudrā*. To have god's *mudrā* is thus to have his authority, to be empowered to act on his behalf. A person thus empowered is called *ājñādhara*, 'bearer of authority', 'wielder of the mandate'; the term is common to (tantric) religion and politics.

To move to the still more concrete level of myth, Śakti is god's wife. Since she is related to him as personality to person, their inextricable connection is symbolized by her being united with him in sexual embrace. She is the Goddess, Devī. As on the theological, so on the mythological level, Devī can be one or many: her innumerable aspects have as many names – and as many myths attached to them. But almost all Hindus are aware that all goddesses are embodiments of god's power, which however fragmented into aspects is unique. Thus the local name or form of the divine feminine principle makes no difference to its function as the repository of power.

Tantra may appear to us to be a form of idealism, since the world is precisely the content of god's thought. (To explain the process of creation, the deployment of *śakti* as thought, would take us too far afield.) However, tantra holds the world to be real. What is ultimately unreal is multiplicity. It is the failure to realize that we are identical with god and have the same power which causes us the sufferings and dissatisfactions of normal life. The *siddha,* who has understood the truth, reposes in the bliss of pure consciousness.

Geertz has well summarized this theology as it has appeared in the social setting of a court. In Bali the Supreme God was Śiva; so Śakti (= sekti) was His wife. Geertz writes:

> Finally, *sekti* is the Balinese word for the sort of transordinary phenomenon that elsewhere is called *mana, baraka, orenda, kramat* or, of course, in its original sense, charisma: "A divinely inspired gift or power, such as the ability to perform miracles".
>
> At bottom, however, sekti rests on a distinctive view of how the divine gets into the world; and most particularly on an elusive and paradoxical conception (and not only to external observers) of the relation between, on the one hand, the subsistent "forms" or "shapes" the divine takes (the Balinese word is *murti,* "[a] body", "physical" from the Sanskrit *murta,* "settled into any fixed shape") and , on the other hand, the dynamic "manifestations" (the Sanskrit is *śakti,* the energy or active part of a deity) that, in those forms and through those shapes it variously has. Brahma and Visnu are said to be sektis – that is, roughly, "activations" – of Siva. So is Siva's wife. So, indeed, are all the gods and goddesses. The king, the lord, the priest, and the ascetic are all said to be *sekti* (*not,* as often has been said, "to possess" it) to the extent that they are, in turn, instances of what they adore. Royal regalia, priestly ritual objects, sacred heirlooms, and holy places are all sekti in the same sense: they display the power the divine takes on when it falls into particular shapes. Sekti is "supernatural" power well enough – but supernatural power which grows out of imaging the truth, not out of believing, obeying, possessing, organising, utilising, or even understanding it.

THE INDIVIDUAL

The *sādhaka* believes that he is ultimately identical with god and hence in essence omniscient and omnipotent. His goal is to realize that fact, in the full sense of the word 'realize': by completely believing and understanding it he will make it a reality. This realization is to be achieved through a combination of ritual, in which mimesis plays an important part, and meditation, much of it based on visualization. One aspect of the mimesis is that the *sādhaka* during worship – worship of the deity with whom he is attempting to identify – makes various hand gestures called *mudrā*; we remember that these 'seals' indicate his being the bearer of divine authority. Acting them out is thus a part of his personating god. Another aspect of this personation is that he tries to unite with the feminine principle, the goddess. If a woman can be found to act the part of Śakti, he first adores her, to propitiate her and win her over, and then replicates the condition of the cosmic god by having intercourse with her – thus incidentally finding a short cut to divine bliss.

Another logical conclusion to be drawn from this theology is that if every soul is really god, the apparent distinction resting on a mistake, then every soul must be identical with every other. This conclusion is indeed drawn, and applied in certain contexts. To become a *sādhaka* one must be initiated by a guru. The guru is an advanced *sādhaka:* in fact, theoretically he should be a *siddha*, who has realized his identity with god and thus has god's mandate (*ājñādhara* again) to deploy god's *śakti* and perform transactions between souls. In particular, the guru can take the pupil's soul out of the pupil's body and put it in his own and then replace it, and he can similarly transfer his soul to the pupil's body. Though such transactions are not discussed in philosophical tantric texts, they are a part of the practice. The temporary exchange of souls is a feature of a *sādhaka's* final initiation.[12]

The *sādhaka* is to realize that the world is neither more nor less than the contents of his consciousness. The light of that consciousness is refracted among a vast multitude of objects, but these appearances are really nothing but light. The distinction between subject and object is pragmatic only: once he has grasped the omnipotence of his subjectivity he can deploy it to any purpose. He, the eternal subject, is beyond any constraint; he has shaken off the bonds (*pāśa*) which made him but a beast of burden and victim (*paśu*) to the Lord (*pati*). He is the Lord now.

In Tāntric theology, god's power is manifested in five acts. There are the creation, sustenance and reabsorption of the world. The other two are the power to conceal himself (which is at the same time punishment, for this concealment envelops the individual soul in delusion and hence leads to suffering) and, conversely, the power to reveal himself and so grant his grace (*prasāda*) to the *sādhaka*. When the *sādhaka* is so favoured and becomes *siddha*, does his power manifest itself in exactly the same five acts? They have the same names, but not – or so it must appear to unelightened onlookers – exactly the same application. The world he creates, sustains and destroys is his own, the contents of his consciousness; he is constantly making and unmaking his own world in his ritual and meditation. More relevant to the topic of this paper is his deployment of the power to punish and the favour.[13] This deployment is instantiated in what we would call white and black magic. An important tāntric text says that if the adept does not wish to derive any profit for himself by his *śakti*, he should offer his services to the king in times of national distress. There are some miracles which should be performed only by a king.[14]

Both the ritual practice of tāntric magic and the theory underlying it are extremely complex and cannot be described here. But to complete this extraordinarily compressed account of those features of tantra which are most relevant to Indian kingship, we must briefly mention *mantra* and *maṇḍala*.

In tantra, god is said to take three forms. One is the guru. The first sign of god's favour to an individual is his sending a guru. God's favour is called *śakti-pāta,* 'descent of power'; this is manifest in the guru, who incarnates *śakti.* The second form of god is the iconic form, that form which can be visualized. (This of course applies to the gods of the entire pantheon, who are all aspects of the supreme god.) The third form, and by no means the least important, is the sonic form, *mantra.*[15] Like god and like *śakti, mantra* can be conceived as single or multiple, but is multiple for pragmatic purposes; and like everything else, a *mantra* is *śakti* – crucial feature of a tantric initiation is that the guru reveals to the disciple the *mantra* of the deity, the power, he is to worship by ritual and meditation. The *mantra* is a syllable or string of syllables. It is secret; only the initiated know which *śakti* it stands for and is. While the supreme god has his own *mantra,* each individual *mantra* can be the stepping-stone to acquiring god's all-pervasive and comprehensive *śakti.* But until one becomes a *siddha,* one's power is partial: the potential of one's *mantra* is still limited to one's particular purposes, e.g., predicting Derby winners.[16]

The *maṇḍala* or *cakra* is cosmogram, essential to tāntric worship. When it is in use the same object is also known as a *yantra.* The primary meaning of *maṇḍala* is 'circle, round object'. and we have seen above that *cakra* literally means 'wheel' and hence 'round object' likewise. The cosmogram is indeed often (albeit then enclosed in a square frame) in accordance with general classical cosmography. But this is not the meaning of the terms which is uppermost in the minds of worshippers. Both *maṇḍala* and *cakra* are commonplace political terms meaning 'domain' sphere of influence.[17] We have met the concept of Viṣṇu as *cakravartin,* cosmic sovereign. The Goddess is invariably conceived as seated at the centre of the cosmogram, *cakra-vartinī*; thus she is literally 'in the centre of the circle', but the predominant meaning is 'cosmic sovereign', *cakreśvarī.* She is thus conceived at the controlling centre of the world whether she is literally depicted there or not, and this applies to exoteric as well as esoteric worship. Initiates of course know, by the double equation explained above, that the goddess is equally the *whole* cosmogram, a fact they seek to realize in their daily worship; but the exoteric, pluralistic interpretation has the direct links with state ritual and political theory.

The most famous of the cosmograms, the *Śrī-cakra*, is a concentric diagram of squares which enclose circles which enclose nine intersecting triangles which centre on a dot. The outermost lines are three squares oriented to the cardinal directions. In the middle of each side is an opening which represents a gateway. These squares are collectively called *bhūpura*, 'the citadel of the earth'. The term *Śrī-cakra* is polysemic. The important point for us is that it means 'the domain of Śrī'. Śrī means Fortune and it is a commonplace that all kings are married to her – in mythology she is also the wife or sister of Viṣṇu. But the main point here is that she is the Goddess, who is seated in that dot in the centre, and is thus the Supreme Power, Parā Śakti. She is 'the mistress of the *cakra*', *cakreśvarī*, and the aim of the *sādhaka* is to win her and so become 'lord of the circle', *maṇḍala*. It is no coincidence that is a term for the successful despot in the *Arthaśāstra*,[18] to which we now turn.

KINGS AND ŚAKTI

The *Arthaśāstra* discusses in what one can characterize as rational and pragmatic terms how to maintain and use royal power. The kingdom, it says,[19] has seven essential components: the king (here called *svāmin*), minister, territory, treasury, fortifications, army and ally. While the *Arthaśāstra* does not talk of the king's role as chastiser of the wicked with the fervour of Manu, as it is little concerned with *dharma*, the repressive aspect of rule is – perhaps naturally – equally to the fore. This stress on the king as *nigraha-kṣama-puruṣa*, "the man with power to repress", is an important ideological link between the political theory of Manu and Kauṭilya on the one hand, and Tantra on the other. The tāntric adept has a standard black magic repertory of six things he can do to his enemies, and as we have seen, he is encouraged to put this repertory at the king's disposal.

By about the twelfth century we find clear tantric influence in treatises on statecraft. In the *Mānasollāsa*, composed in that period by King Someśvara, we find the same list of seven years earlier. But Someśvara says that this king's *śakti*, in the form of his authority (*ājñā*), controls all the other components – a clear use of tantric terminology.[20] He also stresses that the king should take great care in selecting his *purohita*. While this preserves the ancient tradition that the *purohita* is a counsellor,[21] we suspect that here an old term is camouflaging a change, as by that time one would expect the performer of Vedic rites to have a purely ceremonial function. The term *purohita* may here refer to the *rājaguru*, the king's spiritual guide. We cannot prove this; but there is ample literary evidence that kings early in the present millennium sometimes had close relationship with tantric adepts. No doubt, in so far as it was thought to enable the king to defend his people, it was also considered quite suitable – even though *brāhmaṇa* authors express disapproval. Kalhaṇa, the chronicler of medieval Kashmir, records that King Kalaśa (eleventh century) openly became a pupil of the tāntric guru Pramādakaṇṭha.[22] Another Kashmiri *brāhmaṇa, Kṣemendra (twelfth century)*, portrays a king as being bamboozled by a female tantric.[23] He elsewhere refers to *kāyasthas*, civil servants, joining a *rati-cakra-mahotsava*, a tāntric rite involving group sex.[24] Though these authors stigmatize Tantra as degenerate hedonism, it was widespread in Kashmiri ruling circles and among the high officials, many of whom were *brāhmaṇas*.

In the fourteenth century, Iban Battuta, visiting the Chandella kingdom at Khajuraho, saw yellow-skinned ascetics preparing aphrodisiacs for the king.[25] Ascetics who prepare aphrodisiacs are almost sure to be tāntric.

However, it is not our case that the Indian king has necessarily had close links with tantrics and their esoteric practices. What we are arguing is the pervasiveness of the tāntric doctrine of power and its symbolization in goddesses. The concept of *śakti* as the supreme cosmic despotic power became almost universally current in the Hindu community. A king was considered successful only when granted the divine favour of the transference of sovereignty to his own person – though clearly in his case it will not be eternal. Within his territory he is viewed as the supreme *ājñādhara*; were he not, he could not be victorious against his foes. The exoteric form of this *śakti* most conspicuous in Hindu states has been Durgā.

Images of this goddess start to show many royal insignia from about 500 AD on. Her association with Viṣṇu became very close. In South Indian iconography Durgā usually carried the wheel (*cakra*) of Viṣṇu and his battle trumpet (*śaṅkha*).[26] The form in which she slays the buffalo demon, Mahiṣamardinī, was particularly associated with royalty and victory in battle, and from early times Durgā in this form is often shown with a lion, emblem of royalty. A king's throne is a 'lion throne' (*siṃhāsana*), its feet being carved with lion motif; when the king ascends it (first at his consecration) he is joining the goddess there and making her 'his' *śakti*. This can be expressed by saying that the goddess is manifest in the throne. Even the Maharaja of Kolhapur recently interviewed by Adrian Mayer, though clearly not very interested in these religious traditions, ascended the *siṃhāsana* for his consecration, though he dismissed it as 'just sanctifying the whole thing', and 'just a show to impress the people and to declare that I am here'.[27] His own attribution of *śakti* was to the *gaddī*, a form of throne probably introduced under Muslim influence, but evidently his Hindu subjects expected him (and his wife – the goddess by no means excludes a human counterpart) to sit on the lion throne. Moreover, *gaddī* too means 'throne', only it is not a *siṃhāsana,* the lion throne, and is not associated specifically with Durgā.

The Pallava temples at Mamallapuram bear ample witness to the importance Durgā had for that warring dynasty. Many centuries later, the kings of Vijayanagara observed the Durgā, *navarātri*, every year with great splendour. The festival was a major political occasion, an annual ceremony of reintegration much like the *rājasūya* sacrifice in ancient times. The local name of the Goddess who incorporated the royal power was Pampā, originally – as we have seen – the name of the local river; but the festival, as at other courts, was Durgā's. All the tributary chiefs and provincial governors, revenue collectors, foreign ambassadors, eminent merchants and bankers of the capital – in brief, everyone of any importance – were to attend the durbars on that occasion. They paid tribute to the king, even if only in token form, and the king rewarded them.[28]

This custom of celebrating the Durgā *navarātri pūjā* with great pomp continued until very recently at royal and even zamindari courts, even when there were no provincial governors or tributary chiefs to swear allegiance. In Mysore the British political agent and other British officers attended the durbars. There a procession of the court and army, headed by the king mounted on an elephant, marked the end of the king's *pūjā* of the goddess for the nine auspicious days. During that *pūjā* it was customary to reconsecrate the throne and to consecrate at the Goddess' altar the weapons of the king and his warriors. In Mysore these consecrated arms were displayed in the final procession on the morning of the tenth day.[29]

While Durgā is predominantly associated with battle, other forms of the Goddess are more the benevolent despot.

An important cult which developed in mediaeval India, mainly after AD 1000, was that of Lalitā, the cosmic regent. She was adored as the incarnation or personification of autonomous power (*svātantrya*). She has her own court, with a goddess as her chief minister and a theriomorphic goddess as the general of her imperial army. Her territory is the cosmos. Whatever her esoteric theology, for the general public she was the sole ruler of the cosmos and all the other gods were her courtiers. She was worshipped in the *Śrī-cakra* cosmogram.[30]

In exoteric myth and theology as understood by the general Hindu public, one divine form of *śakti* is easily equated with another, since all are but instances of the same general principle. This is evident in temples even nowadays. Royal power has been worshipped under the names of Rājeśvarī, Kālī, and many others, and temples to the Goddess as Power are still being built. The goddess of the famous Ambāji temple near Mount Abu is Renukā, whose original mount was a tiger. But on a recent visit we found that her temple now is surrounded by all the goddesses of Lalitā's court, while she has a different royal mount for each day of the weak: lion, tiger, elephant, sedan chair, etc.

In the area of modern Rajasthan, the tāntric Nātha sector flourished greatly in the medieval and early modern period. The family goddess of the Rānās of Mewar has always been Kālī. When King Mansingh of Amber, the Moghul general, attacked and defeated King Pratāpāditya of Jasohara in Bengal, he carried off in his loot Pratāpāditya's family image of Kālī, called Jasoreśvarī, 'mistress of Jasohara'. He also carried off her hereditary priests and their families. This image is still worshipped in Amber fort and the priests there are descendants of the original priests and still talk Bengali. Pratāpāditya was a famous king and daring warrior; by defeating and imprisoning him Mansingh took over his *śakti*. Mansingh took his royal captive to the Moghul emperor but kept the Kālī image for himself.

The influence of the Nātha sect on the Rajput kings of Jaisalmer, Udaipur and other states reached its peak around 1800. At that time the Nātha yogin Ayas Dev Nāth became famous for his piety and spirituality. The king of Jodhpur, also called Mansingh, on his accession to the throne of Marwar made Ayas Dev Nāth his *rājaguru* and always followed his political advice. This is a clear case of a tantric *siddha* taking over the classical role of a *purohita.* King Mansingh built a huge temple complex, Mahāmandir, for his guru, close to the palace. Ayas Dev Nāth, who had a reputation for clairvoyance, acquired immense political power. After his death the Nātha gurus were so powerful and despotic that the British political agents of Jodhpur struggled against them and subdued them with great difficulty.[31]

The same attitudes and customs survived in zamindari courts under the British. When in 1863 the widow of a deceased landowner of Sivagangai (Malabar) won a suit against another claimant to the land, she chose to be consecrated and accede to power on the final day of the *navarātri* festival. The zamindars of Shivagangai and Ramnad (also in Malabar) used to go out on the final day of *navarātri* and shoot sacred arrows at a tree representing the buffalo demon, *mahiṣāsura.* They thus identified with Durgā in the destruction of *adharma.*[32]

Symbolism as Emulation and Compensation

After about AD 1000 there were no great Hindu empires. Kingdoms were small and generally unable to cope with the Muslim invaders. Perhaps under the influence of the theory expounded in the *Arthaśāstra* and its successors, they regarded their immediate neighbours as their natural foes and thus generally failed to band together to repel foreign invaders. The general pattern throughout the present millennium (with the notable exception of Vijayanagara) has been the increasing fragmentation and decreasing importance of Hindu kingdoms. The native rulers and zamindars under British rule had little autonomy. We suggest that possibly the increasing popularity of tantra and resort to magical means to maintain power was a substitution of fantasy for reality.

In Bali too, the courts Geertz describes had more pomp than power.

> All the enormous gorgeousness was an attempt to set up, in terms of drama and decoration, an authoritative pattern of political analogy. As Siva was to the gods, the gods were to the kings, the kings were to the nobles, the nobles were to the perbekels, and the perbekels were to the people; "inside" and "outside", "little world" and "big world", or *murti* to *sekti*; all were versions of the same reality.
>
> Whether it centred on burning a corpse, or filling down a row of teeth, or consecrating a palace temple, a state ceremony transformed the lord whose corpse, teeth, or temple were being laboured over into an icon, a figuration of the sacred in itself sacred. He became one more of the "activations" of the "divine shapes" at the same time that he himself became such a shape, from which further activations automatically arose. The meaningful structure of the rituals was constant, however varied the symbolic detail. The "little world" of the experienced and the "big world" of the experienceable were matched in two directions; on the inward side toward the lingga [= *lingam*] in the lotus; on the outward, toward the state in the society. And in being so matched, they represented the lord as at once an image of power – that is as, *murti* and (or, rather, therefore) as an instance of it as *sekti*. The basic idiom is again emulative. Seeing Siva as the exemplary shape and the king as its activation, the people see the king as exemplary shape and the state as its activation, the state as exemplary shape and society as its activation, society as exemplary shape and the self as its activation.[33]

I myself (SG) grew up in Dumraon, a very large zamindari in Bihar. As the official deity of this state was Kṛṣṇa, the *navarātri pūjā* was less conspicuous and the king took no part in it till the ninth evening, when after the final *pūjā* the priest of the Rājrājeśvarījī temple brought the king the Goddess' blessings and *prasāda.* Even so, the royal procession on the tenth day with the king on the royal elephant was the greatest event in the calendar. It was followed by a grand durbar in which officials and eminent subjects paid the king tribute in the form of money, and the king distributed presents and feasted his assembled subjects.

In 1941 I witnessed a great tāntric black magic ritual. The prince wished to eliminate his chief enemy and rival. He brought in a large group of tāntrics from Mithilā, the district of northern Bihar which has long been a famous centre of tantra. The rites lasted for many weeks. Soon after they ended the enemy did die in an accident. Ever afterwards the chief of those tantrics, a *siddha,* lived in a state house with a big garden and performed tantric sacrifices every night for the king's benefit. It is noteworthy that the zamindar was a non-believer in any form of Hinduism and never showed any interest in religion. Nevertheless, he did not hesitate to accept the advice of his councillors to resort to tantra for political purposes. Questions of power belong to the area of politics, not of personal faith or soteriology.

Political use of tantra is no less widespread today. The names of Ānandamayī Mā and Yogī Dhīrendra Brahmacārī were connected with that of Mrs. Gandhi. On the local level, a frustrated tāntric of repute and influence in Varanasi has told us that he performed tantric rituals on behalf of several politicians who sought his help before the elections. But alas, they have proved an ungrateful lot. Now that they are in power they are failing to repay their tantric priest by finding his sons good jobs.

Now that India is a democracy, power no longer lies with kings, princes or zamindars; it rests with the politicians and their backers, the big businessmen. But the symbolism of *śakti* has lost none of its persuasiveness with the Indian public Since power is now enjoyed by common people, such common people are now acquiring control of *śakti* worship. A recent study of a popular temple of the goddess in Cuttack has shown how the power to regulate the temple's affairs has changed in recent years. The zamindar who used to be its patron has now virtually no hand in its management; control has passed to a group of local dignitaries, new men. Thus he who no longer has any of the substance of power also loses it on the symbolic level.

NOTES

1 This paper is a slightly revised version of one I gave to the meeting of British Anthropologists of South Asia held at SOAS in April 1984.

2 This personification generally subsumes the King's marriage to *Bhū*, 'Earth', i.e., the king's territory. The view that the king has two wives, Lakṣmī/Śrī and Bhū, is probably confined to Southern India.

3 Louis Dumont, "The Conception of Kingship in Ancient India", in *Religion, Politics and History in India* (Paris and The Hague, 1970), pp. 62-88.

4 Notably Frederique Apffel Marglin, "Kings and Wives: The Separation of Status and Royal Power", and Adrian C. Mayer, "Perceptions of Princely Ṛule: Perspectives from a Biography", in T.N Madan (ed.), *Way of Life: King, Householder, Renouncer; Essays in Honour of Louis Dumont* (New Delhi, 2nd impression, 1982), pp. 156-7, and p. 127, respectively.

5 *Manusmṛiti* VII, 78.

6 Clifford Geertz, *Negara: The Theatre State in Nineteenth-century Bali* (Princeton, 1980).

7 *Manusmṛiti* VII, 3-15.

8 Even in recent times this symbolism of *daṇḍa* was kept up; it was the symbol of royal power and prerogative. We quote from the memories of Maharani Gayatri Devi of Jaipur. "The funeral procession of her husband the late Maharaja of Jaipur started at nine o'clock the next morning... At the forefront of the procession were richly caparisoned elephants with the chief mahout carrying the gold rod bestowed by the Moghul Emperors on the rulers of Amber", Gayatri Devi and Shanta Rama Rau, *A Princess Remembers: The Memories of the Maharani of Jaipur* (New Delhi, 5th edition, first published in London 1976).

9 Cf. Somadeva, *Nītisūtra*, 29, 15 – c. ninth century – where the king is said to be the living form of the three high gods: Brahmā, Viṣṇu and Śiva. See also J.J. Preston, *Cult of the Goddess: Social and Religious Change in a Hindu Temple* (New Delhi, 1980), p. 25.

10 B.B. Goswami, S.G. Morab, *Chamundersvari, Temple in Mysore*, Anthropological Survey of India (Calcutta, 1975), pp. 22-3, and Foreword by Surajit Chandra Sinha.

11 Geertz, *op. cit.*, p. 106.

12 Bhaskararāya, *setubandha* (a commentary on the *Nityaṣoḍaśikārṇava Tantra*), 4.56. *Ājñā* is here explained as the essential consciousness of the guru, who at the time of initiation projects it via his own eyes and through those of the initiated into the essential consciousness of the latter. In this way he momentarily infuses the disciple's consciousness with the supreme *śakti* in her pristine form. *Nityaṣoḍaśikārṇava Tantra*, with *Setubandha* of Bhāskararāya; Anandasrama Sanskrit Series, Vol. 56 (Bombay, 1976).

13 *Kulārṇava Tantra* 10, 130-35; II, 71 (Calcutta, 1977).

14 *Lakṣmī Tantra: A Pāñcarātra Text*, translated with notes by Sanjukta Gupta (Leiden, 1972), pp. 312-3, 315-6, 318-20, 323-4.

15 A synonym for *mantra* in *tantra* is *vidyā*, 'knowledge'. Knowledge is power.

16 Field notes, Varanasi 1981-2.

17 The title of the sixth chapter of the *Arthaśātra Maṇḍalayoni*, "The Source of a Realm". A *maṇḍala* is the smaller-scale domain (like a zamindari) which accepts the king as overloard.

18 *Arthaśāstra* VI, 2; Somadeva 29, 19.

19 *Arthaśāstra* Vi, 1, 1.

20 *Mānasollāsa* II, 8. 696.

21 *Arthaśāstra* I, 7, 4 and I, 9, 5ff.; Somadeva XI, 2 and 24. The latter author tends to equate the *purohita* with the king's *guru*.

22 Kalhana, *Rājatraṅginī* VII, 278.

23 *Samayamātṛkā* II, 95-6.

24 Mentioned in Devangana Desai, *Erotic Sculpture of India: A Socio-Cultural Study* (New Delhi, 1975), p. 176.

25 *The Rehla of Ibn Baṭṭuta*, p. 186, quoted by Deṣai, *op. cit.*

26 R. Nagaswamy, *Tantric Cult of South India* (Delhi, 1982), p. 177; see also plates 42, 43, 52, 76.

27 Mayer, *op. cit.*, p. 143.

28 T.V. Mahalingam, *Administration and Social Life under Vijayanagara*, Madras University Historical Series No. 15, 1940, pp. 238-340.

29 C. Hayavadana Rao, *The Dasara in Mysore: Its Origin and Significance* (Bangalore City, 1936), pp. 21-8.

30 *Brahmāṇḍa Purāṇa* part 3, appendix: the episode of Lalitā.

31 Padamaja Sharma, *Maharaja Mansingh of Jodhpur and His Times, 1803-1843* (Agara, 1972), pp. 153-9, 176-82.

32 Information taken from Pamela G. Price, "Resources and Rule in Zamindari South India, 1802-1903: Sivagangai and Ramnad as Kingdoms under the Raj", unpublished PhD thesis, University of Wisconsin at Madison, 1979, Ch. VIII.

33 Geertz, *op. cit.*, pp. 107-8.

34 Preston, *op. cit.*, pp. 25 and 38.

9. Hindu Tantric and Śākta Literature in Modern Indian Languages

I. Introduction

From the earliest period Tantric mystics have used lyrical poetry to praise the deity and to express their ecstatic experiences of the divine. Naturally they have been inspired to pour out their emotions in songs and ballads in their own vernacular language. As a result the best pieces of Tantric vernacular literature often bring out the living emotions of the poet much better than do their comparable Sanskrit counterparts. Though the vernacular poets adhere to the Sanskrit literary traditions, released from the formal structure of the Sanskrit language they express subtler nuances of emotion and religious experience. Thus they have produced a livelier and more sensuous literature in vernacular than they could in Sanskrit. This spontaneous literature brings to light a very important aspect of Tantric religion and is therefore of great interest to a student of the history of religion. Tantric literature of this inspiration differs radically from that written in Sanskrit. The Sanskrit Tantras are treatises which attempt to systematize the ritual worship and meditation used by the Tantrics for winning the deity's favour, favour which culminates in the adept's experience of the divine in deep meditation, a type of experience which Eliade has called enstasis.[1] The Sanskrit Tantras, though meant for instruction, rarely elaborate on this ultimate experience. Even when they broach it–usually in frustratingly technical and symbolic language intelligible only to initiates–they only discuss stages on the way to it; but of its quality they rarely attempt to speak. That is not surprising, since the experience is beyond ordinary comprehension and transcends the realm of language, which describes the world shared by men. The type of Sanskrit Tantric literature which comes nearest to his vernacular Tantric literature is the great body of *stavas, stotras* and *māhātmyas*–prayers, hymns and ballads.

However, the Tantric poets did not entirely repress all impulses to communicate their beatific experience, and did try to express the inexpressible. To this purpose they used two patterns. On the first, the more indirect, the poets described the deity in mythological terms, detailing the specific god's or goddesse's exploits. They dwelt on the deity's beauty and power, and their own all-consuming love for and total dependence on their God. They eulogized the deity's grandeur and prayed in abject submission.

Secondly, more daring, the mystic would try directly to communicate his experience. To do this he had to resort to traditional poetic imagery and to poetic paradox–a much practised form of communication amongst the exponents of mystic religions. For instance, often used is the image of a fragile boat manoeuvred upstream by a single boatman in bad weather, keeping its helm fixed in the direction of the goal. This expresses the difficult task a yogin has to steer his mind, steadfast through all distractions, keeping his attention fixed on the goal. Common also is the moralistic image of an innocent and harmless deer perpetually in danger of destruction because it is made of delectable flesh and so is its own worst enemy. This symbolizes the human being whose soul is prey to desires. Even commoner is erotic imagery–a device which claims both antiquity and universality. The mystic and the goal he aspires to–cosmic as well as transcendental union with the Absolute Reality–are conveyed by a series of relationships between lover and beloved. Sometimes erotic imagery is made more striking by being mixed with paradox. The mystic likens himself to a high-born individual who has gone mad and become corrupt and uncouth, who united with a partner equally grotesque enjoys an erotic dance in wild and hideous yet blissful abandon. Beauty and the grotesque are juxtaposed on equal terms to convey the transcendent.

Images from daily life naturally proliferate in a literature of which the hall-mark is spontaneity. The complex play of emotion in a young wife living in her husband's joint family– her mute struggle with his relatives, her total lack of freedom, her desperation as the cook of an impoverished family which often unexpectedly swells at mealtimes– is a favourite theme for the mystic poet endeavouring to depict his own poignant helplessness on his spiritual journey. Other tensions in the daily transactions between kinsmen have also been extensively explored. The indignities and humiliations suffered by a poor relative at the hands of rich kinsmen; the revulsion felt by a mother at the sight of her son-in-law– poor, dependent, yet insufferably complacent and demanding–such images are used to express a yogin's indifferent attitude towards the existing social system and the exquisite repose achieved through disciplined meditation. To show the different dimensions of the Tantrics' personal world from the normal social life of attachment and self-consciousness in society, the image of an utterly indifferent person lay to hand. The unnatural and much distrusted *kāpālika* and his natural habitat, the cremation ground, figure often in the Tantric poets' songs.

The extensive use of paradox and riddle to produce an effect of mystery was common to all mystic poets. Munidatta, the commentator on the Buddhist songs composed in early Bengali or Hindi, the *Caryāpadas,* explained this special style as *sandhyā bhāṣā,*[2] an allusive language, twilight language or code language. The Sanskrit counterpart of this style of writing has been briefly discussed in the Hevajra Tantra.[3] None of the Hindu Tantric texts contains a comparable treatment, though the style they use is the same as the Buddhist.

Before a detailed discussion of this literary genre, it seems to me important to mention the place these songs and ballads found in Tantric ritual. As in the public and private worship of Śaivas and Vaiṣṇavas in South India vernacular lyric poetry (Tamil: *prabandham*)[4] has an integral position, so too the Tantrics use their vernacular literature as an integral part of the ritual worship of their goddess in both its private and public forms. In Bengal and other parts of Northern India, ballads to the Goddess used to be ceremonially sung during her annual festival.[5] In Kerala, songs to Kālī (*paṭṭu* and *toṭṭa*) are used as *mantras* during the ritual worship and till recently these songs were treated as a secret tradition.[6] Nepalese Vajrayāna Buddhists still use their *caryā* and *dohā* songs in rituals and continue to regard them as esoteric like their *mantras* and other sacred literature.[7] The last part of the worship of a deity consists of the worshipper singing hymns on the deity.[8] Thus in the ritual context these songs replaced the Sanskrit *mantras, stavas, purāṇas* and *māhātmyas*, which used to occupy that final position.

But not all Tantric poetry is confined to a ritual context. All over India poet devotees, whether Tantric or not, have left behind a rich body of devotional songs on Tantric themes, the emotional appeal of which is still alive. These compositions stand on their own feet as poetry and music even if one disregards their religious relevance. To give but two examples: in South India, Muttusvāmī Dīkṣitar composed a vast number of songs in praise of the Goddesses Kālī, Durgā, Tripurā; in Bengal, Rāmprasād Sen likewise composed songs to Kālī. Both these collections of songs enriched the general tradition of classical Indian music, and are as popular with non-Tantrics as with Tantrics.

In some religious sects ritual worship became minimal and yogic meditation and the singing of devotional hymns took its place. The various sub-sects of Bāuls and Sahajiyās, the Nātha yogins and Siddhas (to name but a few of these sects), greatly minimized the ritual part of *upāsanā* and correspondingly increased the *stuti.* The poets of these sects have produced an enormous number of lyric songs which are mystic in nature and devotional in tone. Many of these poems contain Tantric postulates even though the Goddess does not occur in them. The deity is often the undefined ineffable Reality abiding in all beings as the innate self. Although many of these sects follow the system of Tantra-yoga in their pattern of meditation, their lack of interest in the complicated Tantric form of ritual worship prompts their members to consider themselves non-Tantric. Of course one must hasten to add at this point that it is extremely difficult to decide what is Tantric and what is not. The general technique of Tantra Yoga became so diffused amongst the mystics of India that even Muslim mystics borrowed it and used its terminology in their mystic lyric songs. For instance Lālan Fakir of Bengal (18th century A.D.), a disciple of Sirāj Sāi, extensively used terms from Tantra Yoga in his songs, betraying his close acquaintance with it (e.g. "What beauty radiates from the two-petalled [lotus]; seeing this beauty my eyes become dazzled. This beautiful form surpasses the dazzling brightness of the jewel of the snake or of moonlight" etc.).[9] But it can be safely said that most of these poets adhere to the faith in a cosmic Energy (Śakti) as an intrinsic aspect of the Supreme Divine–a conceptual concretization of this Divine's absolute dominance, knowledge and bliss.

For the specifically Śākta Tantric, on the other hand, Śakti is the Supreme Power, and though in theory the Supreme God is the locus of this power, Śakti representing His sovereignty (*svātantrya*), the worshipper regards Her as the active independent Power while the male supreme God recedes somewhat into the background. Independent Power really means the Goddess's indomitable power to achieve any goal. She executes the five divine acts, viz., creation, sustenance, destruction, punishing (*nigraha*) the ignorant and favouring (*anugraha*) her devotees. She is the cosmic dynamism, actuating creation, and she is the ultimate source of creation and creatures. She by her own free will evolves herself into phenomenal creation. She also has the indomitable power to destroy, if necessary, her own creation. In her creative aspect she is a benign, beautiful goddess, the cosmic mother; in her destructive aspect she is the dark and awesome goddess Kālī. Thus the same Goddess has come to represent supreme power in both its aspects, divine and demoniac, at its most benign and at its most terrible. In her benign aspect the Goddess is always the same: the daughter of Himālaya (the mountain range) and the wife of Śiva. In this form she is exquisitely beautiful and charming and her nature has no trace of the terrifying form. This aspect of the Goddess has generated many myths showing the sentiment of love in various forms–conjugal, maternal, filial. These stories have been handled imaginatively by numerous poets and mystics all over the subcontinent and throughout the medieval and modern periods. The cosmic parents are often depicted, both in literature and in the visual arts, as a divine family with one or two sons, Skanda and Gaṇeśa. Traditionally an Indian lady is referred to in discourse as the mother of her children (i.e. by a teknonym); accordingly the Goddess is often called 'mother of Skanda' or 'mother of Gaṇeśa'. This lovely image of domesticity serves the purpose of bringing the deity to the emotional level of reassuring intimacy with the adoring poet. Her awesomeness as indomitable power remains concealed from the poet's active imagination; only Her protective benevolence is glorified.

In Her terrifying form the Goddess has quite a different image from that of Umā, the daughter of Himālaya. The most familiar ferocious images of the Goddess are Durgā, Mahiṣamardinī (vanquisher of the Buffalo demon) and Kālī (the dark Goddess). Various mythological accounts of the birth of the terrible Goddess–be it Durgā or Kālī–represent

Her as the essence of the divine power of destruction and death. Durgā in fact represents heroic power—the power to fight, conquer and punish the demons and the anti-gods. Kālī on the other hand personifies the unqualified power of destruction, supremely gruesome and grotesque. If Durgā or Caṇḍī (the Fierce), as She is often called, represents virtuous fury, Kālī represents simply fury unrestrained. Theoretically she is not accompanied by Śiva; only Her hosts accompany Her and She is surrounded by desolation. But theologically She is identified with Śiva's spouse, the cosmic Goddess. The fierceness of Her image did not hinder Her devotees from beginning in the 18th century to assimilate to Her all the benevolence of the Cosmic Goddess: "The happy One is in my heart; ever is she playing there. I meditate on thoughts that come to me, but never do I forget her name. Though both my eyes are closed, yet in my heart I see her, garlanded with heads of men."[10]

In the poet's imagination Her demoniac expression changes to an expression of fathomless compassion and tenderness. The gruesome and dishevelled figure of Kālī turns into a lovely woman with loose tresses framing Her figure. The poet declares that he adores the "dark form, because Śyāmā (the dark Goddess) is the loose-haired charmer of the mind". In this manner the devotee's mind effects a complete identity between the horrific, fierce, yet protective Goddess and the benign and bewitchingly lovely Cosmic Mother, the wife of Śiva, the Great God (*maheśvara*). To the devotee there is but one sovereign Goddess (*Īśvarī*). She possesses a bewildering variety of contradictory characteristics, but these very oppositions in Her help the devotee to realize Her transcendental supremacy and bliss.

As is to be expected, vernacular Tantric literature often reflects local cultural phenomena. The widespread Vaiṣṇava *bhakti* movement had its impact on this literature too, especially in areas like Bengal, Bihar and Orissa where during the fourteenth and fifteenth centuries Vaiṣṇava preoccupation with the youthful Kṛṣṇa and His divine sports at Vṛndāvana strongly influenced the Tantric poet's imagination. The common Tantric image of the Goddess as Kumārī, the virgin Umā, the young daughter of Himālaya, inspired devotees to experience a love for the Goddess akin to that of a doting father for his daughter. Poets like Rāmprasād Sen have often described the deity as a loving little daughter, understanding, sympathetic and even almost docile to Her adoring devotee, as a daughter to her father, her power expressed in a manner more persuasive than coercive. As in the Vaiṣṇava literature, the Tantric poet's personal feelings towards his deity are expressed through the medium of mythological personalities of the divine family. The grief and anxiety of Menakā, Umā's mother, form the subject of many Bengali and Maithilī hymns to the Goddess. The emotional turmoil of Menakā, the sorrows, worries and frustrations suffered by a helpless mother who longs for her sweet and beloved married daughter and yet is completely powerless to take any action suited to the emotional state of the poet-devotee to perfection. The literary motif of separation of mother and child proved to be very fertile.

It is impossible to do justice to vernacular Tantric literature, even when only the theme of Śakti is selected, in a few pages. Firstly because it is vast, for it has been composed over the last thousand years in every language of India and in many different genres. Secondly, because scholarship on this subject is still in its infancy, and in the literature of some languages Tantric material has not yet been collected, let alone analysed. Finally, because my own linguistic limitations force me to confine myself to a few language, mostly North Indian, and to attempt only a preliminary survey of this type of literature. Since I am thus forced to make what must in any case appear an arbitrary selection and since I wanted to avoid just presenting a list of unavailable works most of which I myself could not examine, I concentrate on Bengali and handle it more exhaustively; while for other languages I give a few examples and try to convey their distinctive flavour, hoping that the part may give not too misleading an impression of the whole.

The main genres we shall find are these. First, the lyric poetry of mystical experience with which this introduction has been primarily concerned. Secondly, hymns of praise (*stuti, stava,* etc.) to the Goddess. Thirdly, lengthy ballads relating myths of the Goddess. Fourthly, drama, in the Sanskrit tradition. Finally yogic manuals. I have excluded scholarly works in vernacular, which began to be produced about a century ago and are still coming out, as falling outside the creative period of Tantric literature.

I deal most fully with Bengali for three reasons. Firstly, from the late medieval period Bengal became an important centre of Tantric activities and produced a vast corpus of literature. Secondly, this literature is available almost in full due to the excellent efforts of several scholars in the field. Finally, late seventeenth and early eighteenth century Bengal witnessed a revitalization of creative Hindu Tantrism which produced a sizable body of mystic hymns notable for its expression of emotional devotion (*bhakti*) towards the Goddess. This deserves special notice.

Mithilā (Tirhut), the land adjacent to Bengal, presents a similar situation. An ancient and influential Śākta Tantric tradition has existed in that country and continues even today. The royal court of Tirhut has been the greatest patron of Śākta Tantrism and Tantric literature. When the Muslim invasion forced the court to shift to within the territory of Nepal, the Śākta poets accompanied the court there and continued ballads and songs about the Goddess and the Maithilī Tantric literature has certainly influenced Bengali Tantric literature. It seems that in both lands the local Hindu princes were of Śaiva and Śākta faith, and the poets of repute in both Mithilā and Bengal often enjoyed princely patronage. That is why in both lands this genre formed an important part of the official vernacular literature.

The same is to some extent true in other parts of India. But the Tantric literature written in Hindi, Rājasthānī and Panjābī has not yet been fully explored. All I can do in these languages is to show a few representative pieces in order to introduce the reader to these areas, which urgently need investigation.

In the South too there exists a rich body of Tantric Śākta literature. The Siddhas, the Kannakī/Pattinī cult, some Śaiva literature–all these genres have produced literature falling broadly within the Śākta Tantric category.[11] In Kerala the cult of Kālī has always been quite strong and also distinctive. One example of this distinctiveness is the existence of a group of hymns in Malayalam used just like *mantras* in the ritual worship of Kālī. These are called *toṭṭas* and *paṭṭus.*[12]

Several famous composers of the seventeenth and eighteenth centuries from Tamil Nadu, Karnaṭaka and the Deccan plateau composed songs in Śākta Tantric themes. For example, the Navāvaraṇa Songs describe the mystic diagram (*cakra*) of the Goddess consisting of nine geometrical figure (*Śrīcakra*).[13] But I have decided to leave the entire area of Western and Southern Indian literature on Śākta Tantric material to await future study.

The prototype of mystical Tantric literature is the group of songs known as the Caryā songs and Dohās. Although these are definitely non-Hindu Tantric songs, I must here give a very brief account of them. The reason is this. These early songs are claimed to be the oldest literary record of Hindi, Bengali and other Indo-Aryan languages of N.E. India. Not only have the literary forms and even metres of these songs influenced the latter religious poems in Hindi, Bengali, Assamese and Oriya, but also the themes and motifs drawn from daily life are adopted by these vernaeular literatures. Although predominantly Buddhist, some of the poets like Luipa[14] possibly had close connection with Hindu Tantrism as well. These poems were primarily meant to be sung, and although containing a mystical message, they became very popular because of their simple diction and charming lyricism as well as their deep religiosity. The tradition was kept up in Hindi literature through the *dohās* of North Indian saints like Dādū, and Kabīr, and the Nātha sect.[15]

The religious and philosophical content of these early Tantric songs is very homogeneous and knows no sectarian boundaries. The essential feature, common to all Tantric denominations, is a disciplined path of spiritual endeavour which aims at personal perfection. The model Person is the Absolute, transcendent and immutable. This Person is innate (*sahaja*) in all beings, though all but forgotten by these beings and anyway beyond their awareness. The Tantric aspires directly to experience total identity with this Absolute Person; and yet this identification is not an absorption of the Tantric's self into the Absolute, in that most of the time he is conscious of the fact that the Absolute remains ineffable whereas the individual is subject to change and limitation. Moreover the awareness of this polarity in fact opens up an infinite number of possibilities in mystical experience. The polarity is symbolized by the relationship between man and woman and the love they share. Even after the experience of union, the Tantric in a mystical way retains a sense of separateness which allows him to experience *bhakti* or loving adoration for the Absolute. This realization of both identity and separateness combined produces in the individual an experience which is reposeful bliss and at the same time ecstatically joyous (*sahajānanda* or *mahāsukha* in Buddhist parlance, *ullāsa* in the Hindu). The Siddhas, i.e. the Tantric poets of the Caryā songs and the Buddhist Dohās, were yogins of the Buddhist Vajrayāna system. But they composed songs for an audience of ordinary people, using popular language and endeavouring to be clear and instructive.

Legend claims that Saraha, a Siddha, composed a vast number of Dohās to make both ordinary people and royalty understand his religious ways and experiences. Concerning the deluded ways of ordinary people Saraha sings:[16]

1. Bees know that in flowers
   Honey can be found.
   That *saṃsāra* and *nirvāṇa* are not two.
   How will the deluded ever understand?

2. Mind, immaculate in its very being, can never be
   Polluted by *saṃsāra's* or *nirvāṇa's* impurities.
   A precious jewel deep in mud
   Will not shine, though it has lustre.

3. Once in the realm that is full of joy
   The seeing mind becomes enriched,
   And thereby for this and that most useful;
   even when it runs
   After objects it is not alienated from itself.

These prototypes of the later vernacular mystical songs and poems possessed meanings on different levels. Drawing similies from the ordinary objects of the everyday world, the poets often achieved aesthetic success. At the same time the real meaning underlying the pictorial description conveyed in symbolic language presents a different dimension of experience which appeals directly to those who have shared the poet's intimate religious experiences. Here is a poem addressed to an outcaste girl, who symbolizes Buddhist wisdom (*prajñā*), which is to realize that everything is without a changeless essence.

O Ḍombi, your hut is outside the town.
The shaven Brāhmaṇas passing by keep on touching it.
O Ḍombi, I shall cohabit with you.
I am the shameless Kāpālika Kānha, the naked yogin.
There is a lotus with sixty-four petals;
The wonderful Dombi dances on that lotus.
O Ḍombi, I ask you in confidence,
On whose boat do you come and go?
Ḍombi, you sell string and baskets.

> For your sake I have given up my actor's paraphernalia.
> O you are a Ḍombi, breaking the (dam of the) lake I shall feed you lotus stalks.
> O Ḍombi, I shall kill and take life.

The unclean Ḍombi, whose caste functions connect her with corpses and carrion, naturally lives outside the town, away from the pure castes. The poor Ḍombi lives in a hut, yet her charm attracts Brāhmaṇas members of the purest caste, who defy the pollution caused by contact with her hut. Kānha Yogin is himself born in a high caste, but has turned into a Kāpālika, a naked member of a weired sect, indifferent to all social conventions, and he has no compunction in proposing to live with the impure Ḍombi. The utter impossibility of such a connection suggests a symbolism and makes it clear that the underlying meaning refers to some unconventional religious practices. The bliss of the two, viz. Kānha and Ḍombi, in union is described in just two lines. The bewitching slender girl lightly dances on the lotus of sixty-four petals. The lover is mystified at her incomprehensible movements. The lotus is the highest level of Tantric yogic experience where the transcendental Ḍombi is occasionally intuited by fortunate yogins. The Ḍombi plies her caste trade in selling wicker baskets, etc. But Kānha has given up his job and has abandoned his basket containing the paraphernalia of professional actor. Instead he now indulges in such crazy acts as breaking down a dam to collect lotus stalks for the Ḍombi, and is not averse even to killing. These last two enigmatic lines really refer to esoteric Tantric notions and technical terms. But outwardly they appear to refer to the fact that association with Ḍombi has destroyed all brahmanic convention in Kānha, and he now behaves as thoughtlessly and aggressively as one expects from the male members of Ḍombi's caste. Even his taste has changed, and he feels no aversion to wearing unclean ornaments like a bone-necklace. This last object too has a different technical meaning in the Buddhist Tantric tradition.[17]

Thus these songs present a series of pictures from a pretty Ḍombi girl's life in juxtaposition with her high caste, uninhibited and repulsive yogin-lover to convey a mystical message fully understood only by adepts. Only a fellow Tantric can understand the quintessential description of Kānha Yogin's own yogic efforts and religious experience.

These songs are mostly sung to set melodies. But we are not sure who composed the music; possibly the poets themselves did. Parallels can be drawn from comparatively recent composers–poets like Tyāgarāja, Śamaśāstri, Dīkṣitar and Rāmprasād Sen. The other possibility is that professional composers set their poems to music; the Maithilī musicologist Locana records that a famous composer set the text of the great poet Vidyāpati Mithilā to music.[18]

II. Tantric Literature in Bengali

For historical reasons Bengali Śākta literary genres can best be arranged in this order: (1) ballads; (2) hymns and mystic poems; (3) technical treatises.

It is strange that the Caryā songs had no immediate successor in Bengali religious literature. Their genre somehow fell out of fashion, while the model of epic narrative poetry (*purāṇa*) induced the vernacular poets to write long narrative poems in ballad style. The popularity of narrative poetry is reflected in the fact that around the fourteenth century the Mahābhārata, the Rāmāyaṇa and several Purāṇas were translated or rather rendered into Bengali. This made the vast mythological material of the Epics and Purāṇas available to vernacular poets, and their audience too was now familiar with this type of literature. This *purāṇa* style combined with the popular ballad form of poetry to produce the new genre of mythological literature in the vernacular known as *maṅgala* (auspicious ballads).

By ancient tradition, dramatic performances accompanied the celebration of a god's annual festival.[1] Sections of certain Sanskrit *purāṇas*, such as the Devī Purāṇa and the Brahmavaivarta Purāṇa, were similarly recited in such annual rituals: for instance, the Devīmāhātmya section of the Mārkaṇḍeya Purāṇa is always recited at the end of the *pūjā* on each of the three days of the annual festival of Durgā. A related custom was that in the ritual worship of local deities old ballads were sung, especially at the end. These two customs, the Sanskritic and the non-Sanskritic, fused in the composition and ritual use of *maṅgalas.*

Maṅgalas were part recited and part sung by professional in the ritual worship of the deities about whom they were composed. Locana (op. cit) tells us that a certain Bhavabhūti obtained perfection in poetic skill through divine grace and composed a poem on the model of a purāṇa (*kāvyaṃ purāṇapratimaṃ cakāra*). Another example of Sanskritic influence is that each *maṅgala* begins with an account of the cosmogony in which the deity it is composed to honour plays a major role. This pattern was applied, for example, in the Manasāmaṅgala.[2] The snake goddess Manasā, a non-purāṇic deity, became the centre of an important cult which at one time flourished over much of Northern and Eastern India. In the fifteenth century some redactor or redactors with Sanskrit education assembled the ballads, hymns and legends which had grown up around her into the Manasāmaṅgala. This text is ceremonially sung for the four days of that goddess's annual festival, and the Dharmamaṅgala is sung during the twelve days of the annual festival of Dharma.[3] The recitation of a *maṅgala* is preceded by a special preliminary rite. Naturally this ritual application influenced the structure of these texts. Every *maṇgala* is usually divided into more or less equal parts, matching in number the days of the *pūjā* of the relevant deity. Each of these parts is called a section in sequence (*pālā*). Every *maṇgala* contains near the end a summary recapitulation of its story. The major narratives are in simple metres which are easy to chant; this is then frequently enlivened by the addition of short poems which are sung to melodies as hymns. The later versions of *maṅgalas* often indicate the melodies of the songs, and the text becomes virtually a collection of hymns.[4]

Although there are several *maṅgalas* on important cult deities, only the *maṅgala* texts on the goddesses Caṇḍī/Durgā and Kālī/Annadā are of interest to us. It is interesting to note that although the redactors of these *maṅgalas* theologically maintained that all these goddesses are different names of the same Goddess (cf. the *cautiśa* hymn sung by Kālaketu in the Caṇḍīmaṅgala of Mukundarāma to propitiate the goddess Caṇḍī), yet the contents of these two sets of *maṅgalas*, viz. the Caṇḍīmaṅgala and Annadāmaṅgala, are quite different. Moreover the Caṇḍīmaṅgala texts are older than those of the Annadā or Kālikāmaṅgala. On the other hand, there is no problem about the identity of the goddess Annadā/Kālikā, whereas Caṇḍī's identity is rather complex. The two narratives recounted in the *maṅgalas* to Caṇḍī to establish her greatness (*māhātmya*) in bringing unprecedented luck (*maṅgala*) and giving protection (*abhaya*) to her devotees present her as the goddess of the wild beasts in forests and domestic animals in pastures, i.e. a goddess who protects animals of the forest and pasture. Sukumar Sen traces her origin to the Ṛigvedic goddess Araṇyānī.[5] However, the deity of the Caṇḍīmaṅgala is certainly identical with Durgā, who destroyed the Buffalo demon and who also is Umā, Śiva's spouse. The two narratives, curiously enough, describe the Goddess in a disadvantageous position. In the first narrative the deity is determined to show her capacity to bring prosperity and power not only to likely candidates such as the king of Kaliṅga but also to a most unlikely candidate, Kālaketu, a wretchedly poor person of humble origin whose only livelihood is to hunt wild animals and sell the meat in the market. Why such a prestigious goddess as Durgā should need to make a show of her great power is not very clear. In the second narrative she seems to be more logical in her actions, if one believes that among the rich and socially influential trading community of Bengal the worship of Śakti, the Divine Sovereign Power, was not very popular and needed more recognition. In the Tantric Śākta tradition Śakti, who is mainly conceived as the Divine partner of Śiva, is completely identified with Śrī, the goddess of prosperity. This is evident in the Śaiva Śākta Śrī cult, in which Śakti is worshipped in a diagram called the diagram of Śrī (Śrīyantra or Śrīcakra). In the *maṅgala* texts Durgā is indeed called Maṅgalā, or the one who brings prosperity and is benign (*abhayā*).

However, the assimilation of Caṇḍī of the Caṇḍīmaṅgalas to the Purāṇic goddess Durgā was complete by the end of the middle ages and is accepted by the Sanskrit tradition. The Sanskrit *Bṛhaddharma Purāṇa* (15th or 16th century) attaches the stories of the Caṇḍīmaṅgala to the goddess Durgā or Devī (the Goddess).

> You who are the fake salamander who gave Kālaketu the boons,
> You are the embodiment of good luck and are called Maṅgalacaṇḍī.
> From the hands of king Śālivāhana you saved the father and son,
> O lotus-born, while you presented yourself as swallowing and regurgitating elephants.[6]

In some Caṇḍī images the salamander is present. The salamander plays an important role in the first story of the Caṇḍīmaṅgala, in which the goddess comes to the hero Kālaketu's house in the guise of a salamander. She is usually envisaged as seated on a red lotus and possessing four arms and hands. Her complexion is red. A sketch of an ancient image of the goddess (from the period of the Bengali king Lakṣmaṇa Sen) shows two elephants pouring water on the image (S. Sen, appendix). This again reminds one of the goddess's connection with Lakṣmī (i.e. Gajalakṣmī).[7] The twin elephants are connected with the goddess Caṇḍī in the second story of the *maṅgalas.* Halāyudha (twelfth century) in his *Brāhmaṇa-sarvasva* describes the *dhyāna* and ritual worship of Maṅgalacaṇḍī.

The extant *maṅgalas* of Caṇḍī are not very old. The oldest goes back to the sixteenth century of the Christian era. But the tradition goes back much further, though it is difficult to know just how far.

The biographer of Caitanya, Vṛndāvana Dāsa (the *Caitanya Bhāgavata*), makes it clear that in his time (c. middle of the sixteenth century) the singing of the ballads of Maṅgalacaṇḍī was very popular.[8] Indeed Mānik Datta, the earliest known author of the Caṇḍīmaṅgala, must have flourished before then. It seems possible that the worship of the goddess Caṇḍī became so popular at that period (cf. Vṛndāvana Dāsa 1/8), that talented and educated poets of Śākta faith began composing long ballads on the basis of older ballads and legends on Maṅgalacaṇḍī. Each work, though essentially telling the same stories, possesses distinctive marks of the poet's personality. The oldest extant Caṇḍīmaṅgala is that of Dvija Mādhava (1579)[9] and is called the Sāradāmaṅgala.

The most popular and beautiful work of the CM is that of Kavikaṇkan Mukundarām Cakravartī, a learned *brāhmaṇa* from the neighbourhood of Burdwan. He had to leave his home under adverse circumstances and move to Midnapore. There he obtained royal patronage and composed a Caṇḍīmaṅgala (A.D. 1590) which he called the Abhayāmaṅgala. He was a talented poet with refined taste and made many improvements on the original legends. He displayed real ingenuity in coordinating the two rather discordant legends of the Caṇḍīmaṅgala. The charm of the poem is much enhanced by short devotional songs added at appropriate places.

Amongst the other Caṇḍīmaṅgala authors mention should be made of Dvija Rāmadev, Kṛṣṇarām Dās, Muktārām Sen and Rāmānanda Yati.

Like all *maṅgala* texts, a Caṇḍīmaṅgala starts with short laudatory hymns to different gods. After that a short account of creation is given. This account agrees with that given in two other major kinds of *maṅgala*, Dharmamaṅgala and Manasāmaṅgala. The ineffable and immutable Creator Dharma first creates the primal goddess Ādyāśakti and then the three cosmic gods Brahmā, Viṣṇu and Śiva. After that the rest of creation comes into existence.

After this cosmogony, the main body of the *maṅgala* text begins. This is divided into three parts, viz. Devī khaṇda or the section on the Goddess; Ākṣeṭi khaṇḍa or the section on the Ākṣeṭi[10] hero; and Baṇik khaṇḍa or the section on the tradesman. The first section is usually short and describes the origin of the Goddess Durgā, her birth as Pārvatī and marriage to Śiva and their ensuing divine conjugal life. This section serves to link the two separate legends about the spread of the Goddess's worship among different sections of the population. For ritual purposes, as explained above, the text is divided into eight uneven parts called *pālā*, which do not correspond to the narrative boundaries. The recitation of the text used to be an intrinsic part of the annual worship of the goddess Maṅgalacaṇḍī. This took place for four days, starting on a Tuesday, and each section is meant for one half of a day's performance.

The story of Durgā mainly follows the Sanskrit Purāṇic tradition, although sometimes a certain demon Maṅgala replaces the Buffalo demon. Stories of Śiva's wife Satī, daughter of Dakṣa, and of her regenerated form Pārvatī, the daughter of Himālaya, appear more or less in the usual Purāṇic form till the birth of her two sons Gaṇeśa and Kārttikeya. But when the poets picture the conjugal life of the divine couple their imagination leads them to produce a vivid account of contemporary Bengali middle-class society at its poorest.

At this point both Śiva and Pārvatī lose their divine grandeur and serenity. Pārvatī is depicted as a typical spoilt, inconsiderate, indolent and rather sharp-tongued daughter of rich and influential parents. Śiva too is presented as a type character, a penniless *brāhmaṇa* sponging on his rich parents-in-law, indifferent to others' comforts, demanding and self-indulgent. The poets entertained their audience by giving a brilliant picture of the chaotic condition of Śiva's homestead, with his impetuous sons and an incongruous collection of animals chosen as mounts for each member of the divine family. As soon as Pārvatī starts her independent household away from her parents, dire poverty and Śiva's lack of consideration lead to marital quarrels and matters grow serious. A harassed and vexed Pārvatī wails to her companion Padmā about her misfortune:

> Father's snake and son's peacock perform antics.
> Gaṇeśa's rat gnaws holes in the begging sack and I get the blame.
> How can I prevent the natural enmity between the lion and the ox?
> O poor me, how luckless I am!
> The perpetual fight between the peacock and the snakes
> Makes me a victim of abuse.

Since Śiva's income is both inadequate and irregular, Padmā advises the Goddess to replenish the family income by popularizing her own worship among mankind. Accordingly the goddess persuades her husband to put a curse on the younger son of the god Indra to be born as a man on earth in order to propagate her worship there.

Here starts the first legend. The goddess sets a trap for Indra's pious son to incur Śiva's displeasure. He falls for it and is cursed. Meanwhile, the Goddess rewards the king of Kaliṇga with prosperity and in gratitude he starts worshipping her.

Indra's son takes birth in the house of a poor hunter as his son and is named Kālaketu. He grows up to be a skilled and powerful hunter, marries Phullarā and starts hunting for a living. He kills wild animals indiscriminately. The distressed animals approach the Goddess for redress. Pārvatī comes to Kālaketu in the guise of a salamander which he catches. Soon she changes into a beautiful young girl to beguile the hunter. Kālaketu and his wife are first puzzled and then grow angry and apprehensive. Finally the Goddess reveals her identity and with her favour Kālaketu becomes the king of a newly established kingdom called Gujarāt. Kālketu and Phullarā become great devotees of Pārvatī. But Kālaketu comes into conflict with the king of Kaliṅga and is imprisoned. The latter intends to execute Kālaketu, who starts praying to the Goddess with a hymn. This hymn of praise to the deity[11] has the traditional Tantric pattern:[12] the initial letters of the lines are the consonants arranged in alphabetical order; but the first three nasal, *ṅ*, *ñ* and *ṇ*, which do not begin aṅy Bengali words, are replaced respectively by the three vowels *u*, *i* and *a*, because when reciting the alphabet they are named *uṅa*, *iña* and *aṇa*. Since there are reckoned to be 34 Bengali consonants (including *kṣa*) this type of hymn is called *cautiśā*('of thirty-four'). The authors of these hymns had in mind the cosmic form of the Goddess as unmanifested Sound (Śabdabrahman), the first manifestation of which is the alphabet (*varṇamālā*), the source of all *mantras* and also of the physical universe. Some poets like Dvija Rāmdev[13] were more erudite in Tantric Śākta theology and knew the *mātṛkā* concept of the Goddess, so they used only the vowels instead of the consonants. This indicates that Kālketu prayed to the Goddess Śakti with the most essential of all *mantras* and obtained immediate fulfillment (*siddhi*). Indeed soon after this Kālaketu obtains once again Pārvatī's active favour: not only does he become free and regain all his possessions, but also all his dead army is restored to life. Thus having established the greatness of

Śakti's power and influence, Kālaketu dies at a ripe age and Indra gets back his younger son. This is the end of the first legend about the Goddess, the Ākṣeṭi khaṇḍa.

The next story is about two rich merchants, Dhanapati and his son Śrīmanta. Merchants were at the time more devoted to Śiva than to Śakti. Therefore probably her devotees wanted to make this community accept the Goddess as this supreme deity who would confer safety and prosperity. A celestial dancer is cursed to be born on the earth. She takes birth as Khullanā, the daughter of a rich merchant called Lakṣapati and his wife Rambhā. When she comes of age, a famous merchant, Dhanapati, marries her as his second wife. Lahanā, her co-wife and cousin, is the mistress of Dhanapati's household and naturally she becomes angry and jealous at the second marriage. She harasses Khullanā and when Dhanapati is away on a business trip forces her to become the family goatherd, the most menial job. While grazing the herd in the forest Khullanā loses one goat and, frightened of her co-wife's wrath, roams in the wilderness in search of it. There she encounters a small band of women, worshippers of Caṇḍī, who on listening to her story advise her to perform rites for the Goddess. Under their guidance Khullanā does so and obtains the Goddess's grace. Her goat comes back and Lahanā too becomes less hostile and relieves her of her goatherd's job. Dhanapati comes back home after a successful business trip and Khullanā is united with him. Soon Khullanā becomes pregnant and in the fifth month of her pregnancy her husband once again gets ready to go away to trade, this time abroad, to Ceylon. He gives Khullanā a written order that if a girl is born she is to be called Mahāmāyā. If a son is born, he is to be called Śrīmanta, and in case Dhanapati is delayed in Ceylon, he should at a suitable age go in search of his father. On the eve of his journey Dhanapati acts sacrilegiously to Caṇḍī's symbol (a jug full of water) while Khullanā is engaged in her worship, since, misled by Lahanā, he thinks Khullanā is engaged in witchcraft. This antagonizes the Goddess and as a result he meets with misfortune. While sailing to Ceylon he sees a miracle: a girl of sixteen seated on a lotus on water, swallowing and immediately disgorging an elephant. The merchant tells this story at the court of the king of Ceylon. The king disbelieves it and wants to see for himself by going to that spot together with the merchant. But the girl is no longer there. The king throws the merchant into prison as a fraud and he languishes there. Time passes. Khullanā gives birth to a son, Śrīmanta, who is also no ordinary mortal being but a celestial entertainer of Śiva who cursed for negligence, is now born on the earth. The boy Śrīmanta is insulted by his teacher over the absence of his father and is jeered at as a bastard. Śrīmanta's mother tells him the story of his father and his trip to Ceylon and shows him his father's written instructions. Śrīmanta immediately gets ready to go, and at the age of twelve, in spite of his mother's and the king's prohibition, sets sail for Ceylon. He too sees the miracle of the floating and elephant-swallowing girl. Events then take the same course for him as they did for his father, and father and son are united in prison. Śrīmanta abjectly worships and prays to Caṇḍī and meditates using the same form of acrostic hymn, *cautiśā,* as did Kālaketu in a similar situation. Pleased, the Goddess comes to their rescue. The king of Ceylon is suitably punished and intimidated; contrite, he releases Dhanapati, Śrīmanta and the crew, and returns all their treasures and merchandise. Not only that: at Caṇḍī's bidding the king gives his daughter, Suśīlā, to Śrīmanta in marriage. At last Śrīmanta returns home with his father and wife. The local king is so impressed by Śrīmanta's prowess that he too gives his daughter to Śrīmanta in marriage and so Khullanā welcomes not only her husband and son but also two daughters-in-law.

The two legends have several points in common as well as some repetition of individual religious themes. In both we get a song of twelve months (*bāramāsyā*).[14] Kālaketu's salamander changes into a richly decorated beautiful woman. Phullarā coming home sees her there while her husband is absent. Convinced that her husband has taken a mistress, Phullarā becomes scared of losing her husband's affection and tries to dissuade her rival by vividly recounting her poverty. Each month of the year brings new misery to crush the poor family. Suśīlā, the princess of Ceylon, also sings a *bāramāsyā* when her husband proposes to return home, telling her mother how her future life will be an unrelieved tale of misery, each month of the year bringing a fresh misfortune. In both, the heroes are imprisoned and on the verge of death at the hands of the enemy and in the darkest moment of life they pray and meditate on the Goddess, throwing themselves on her mercy, and she immediately arrives to save them. This indicates how the concept of *bhakti*, which emphasizes the saviour aspect of the divine, that had in turn developed into the idea of *prapatti*, abject surrender of the devotee to the Divine mercy and protection, came to be recognized even by the Śākta groups. The theory of *prapatti*, a specific South Indian contribution to Hinduism, had travelled to the North mainly through the spread of Vaiṣṇava theology. The normal Śākta emphasis on *pūjā* and *upāsanā* is abandoned in the above-mentioned emergencies.

It is also interesting to note how Caṇḍī, who is definitely Durgā, when she appears for the punishing of the enemies of Her special devotee resembles Kālī more than she does Durgā, and is surrounded by a grotesque host who are usually followers of Kālī. Thus Kālī, the goddess of Death, first merges into Durgā and through her into Pārvatī, the cosmic Mother. This synthesis of different goddesses converging in one Śakti ideal who as Mother can be brought into a close emotional relationship was convenient for incorporating devotionalism into the Śākta Tantric religion. The influence of Vaiṣṇava religion and religious literature is decisive in moulding the religious attitude of late Śākta Tantrics. The authors of the Caṇḍīmaṅgalas added songs with clear Vaiṣṇava themes whenever they needed to express tender emotions. This may be the direct channel through which Vaiṣṇava emotional *bhakti* and its medium of expression in Bengal, viz., Vaiṣṇava lyrics, found their way to the śākta Tantric poets of a century later. By that time the literary form had become a poetic tradition and could be utilized by any poet, like the writers of the Śākta, *mālsī* songs and the purely *bhakti* songs of the Śāktapadāvalī.[15]

The *Kālikāmaṅgalas* as a genre are of late origin. Although Tantrism was practised in Bengal from at least the beginning of the fourteenth century[16] and great Tantrics like Sarvānanda (c. 1580) and Kṛṣṇānanda Āgamavāgīśa (c. 1500) composed important Sanskrit tracts on Tantric ritual and theology, nothing was written on Kālī in the vernacular. But in the seventeenth and eighteenth centuries several poets, both Tantric and non-Tantric, wrote versions of the *Kālikāmaṅgala.* The earliest of them is Kṛṣṇarām Dās, who lived near Calcutta. The succeeding authors are Balarāon Cakravartī, Govinda Dās, Bhāratcandra Ray (eighteenth century) and Rāmprasād Sen. The work of Bhāratcandra is called *Annadāmaṅgala* and emphasizes Pārvatī's Annapūrṇā (bestower of grain) aspect; it was written at the order of the poet's patron Kṛṣṇacandra, the king of Navadvīpa. The poet was not a Śākta Tantric. He actually adds a new legend to the story of Pārvatī to connect her to his patron king, who was by all accounts an enthusiastic devotee of Kālī.

In general the Kālikāmaṅgalas follow the pattern of the Caṇḍīmaṅgalas. But there is only one legend peculiar to the Kālikāmaṅgalas, and it is quite different from the two in the Caṇḍīmaṅgalas. It is about the clandestine love of a princess and a foreign visitor to her land. The dominant deity here is Kālī, who appears as the bestower of magic power to aid thieves and bandits. It seems that such criminals used to propitiate Kālī with proper Tantric rites.[17]

The story as it now stands resembles a story prevalent in the Deccan plateau and North-west India, and at a certain point was connected with the Kashmiri poet Bilhaṇa, author of the Caurapañcāśikā. In that context the princess's love affair is with a foreign poet, who while staying at the court accidentally sees her, falls in love with her and marries her in secret. But in the end the poet is caught, and he is about to be executed when through the Goddess's blessing he utters such bewitching poetry that the king succumbs to aesthetic enjoyment and pardons him. Needless to say, the clandestine marriage too was made possible by the Goddess's magic power.

In the Kālīkāmaṅgala, the heroine and hero are respectively called Vidyā and Sundara. The names suggest that the story may have been based on an allegory depicting the fact that in human society men eagerly pursue *vidyā*–knowledge, whether conceptualized as scientific skill or as magic and hence miraculous power – while women seek the beautiful, *sundara*. The story is both secular and sophisticated, and lacks the gothic flavour of the stories of the *Caṇḍīmaṅgala*, yet the poets of the Kālikāmaṅgala tried to maintain the outward form of the *maṅgala* poems. There is the usual cosmogony, and stories of Pārvatī–her former existence as Satī, Satī's death, Pārvatī's marriage to Śiva, etc. – are faithfully repeated. The basic theme of divine interference in ordinary life in order to popularize the worship of a particular form of the Goddess–here Kālī–is also present. Individual motifs like the heroine's description of her plight round the year (*bāramāsya*) and the all-important hymn of praise to the goddess delivered by the hero at the point of climax in abject surrender to Goddess's mercy are features which follow the *maṅgala* tradition. But the story itself is more like a literary romance than an old folk-legend. Nor is any special ritual occasion associated with the Kālikāmaṅgala or its recitation.

The story runs thus: Sundara and Vidyā are both actually celestial beings and are born on this planet to propagate the Goddess's popularity. Vidyā has been born as the princess of Vardhamāna and grows up an extremely beautiful and accomplished young woman. Her father is very concerned to find for her a husband of even greater learning and accomplishments. Sundara, a learned and very handsome prince, the son of one of Vidyā's father's esteemed royal friends, is chosen as Vidyā's husband, and her father sends a message to Sundara's father. Meanwhile Sundara hears about Vidyā and determines to marry her. He is a Tantric and a devotee of Kālī, the goddess of magic power (*vidyā*), and his natural talent is enhanced to a miraculous level by Her favour. The adventurous prince starts on his quest in disguise and rides from his home in secret. Through the favour of the Goddess a journey which would otherwise have been long and strenuous is miraculously rendered easy and comfortable. Sundara arrives in the town where Vidyā lives and finds a go-between in a woman gardener who supplies flowers to the royal family. By her aid Vidyā and Sundara meet, and Vidyā falls in love with Sundara at the first sight of his handsome form. After their introduction she is also impressed by his learning and poetic ability. This last quality Sundara has acquired through Tantric *sādhanā*, which has brought him the favour of Kālī, his chosen deity. Soon after first meeting they secretly marry, and in due course Vidyā becomes pregnant. Her parents are very upset as they know nothing of Sundara, who remains in hiding. However, through his clever town sheriff Vidyā's father finds him, and he orders his execution. At the crucial moment Sundara prays abjectly to Kālī for mercy and protection. Kālī responds: she appears in her terrible form and threatens the king. At this point a friend reveals Sundara's identity and the intimidated king is vastly relieved. He relents, releases Sundara and accepts him as his son-in-law. Sundara stays for some years and then returns home with his wife and son to rule his own country and to propagate Kālī's worship among his people. Finally, his mission accomplished, Sundara and his wife ascend to heaven.

It is obvious that this is not an ancient legend. The very name of the heroine recalls the Tantric science of the preternatural, and the story makes its hero an adept of the lore. Not only does he obtain his great poetic capacity through *sādhanā*, but also when he wants to dig a tunnel from the gardener's house to Vidyā's bed chamber he gets a magically empowered tool from the Goddess with a *mantra* to galvanize it, and thus succeeds in his aspiration. Both poetic ability and the power to overcome physical obstacles are well known as *siddhis*, supernormal accomplishments obtainable through Tantric *sādhanā*.[18]

By the end of the seventeenth century *maṅgalas* were becoming rather strained, artificial creations, and gradually they went out of literary vogue. In the eighteenth century the lyric poems (*pada*) of the great Vaiṣṇava poets became overwhelmingly influential in Bengal. Among Tantrics too, devotional songs about the Goddess took the place of ballads as the preferred literary genre, and these songs were eagerly accepted by the common people. The leading figure in the new movement was the Tantric poet Rāmprasād Sen.

Rāmprasād Sen (c. 1720-81) was a Śākta Tantric and an adept in Tantric yoga, the Tantric system of meditation.[19] Following tradition, he composed a ballad on Kālī, his chosen Goddess (*iṣṭadevatā*), called the *Kālī-kīrtana*, on the usual pattern of the *maṅgalas*. But it is second-rate poetry. His main achievement was to introduce a new style into Śākta poetic literature. He revived the early lyric tradition of the Caryā songs and combined it with Vaiṣṇava emotional *bhakti* and their doctrine of grace. This innovation went straight to the heart of the masses. Rāmprasād himself composed countless short hymns in this *pada* form and innumerable poet *sādhakas* (Tantric adepts) have been following in his footsteps ever since. To be fair, one must agree with D. Zbavitel[20] that, although they reflect the influence of contemporary Bengali Vaiṣṇava lyrics, most of these poems display little literary quality. Rāmprasād Sen and other Śākta poets primarily wanted to express their religious experiences, which differed fundamentally from the Vaiṣṇava experience of the Bengal of their times. Vaiṣṇavas gradually built up an aesthetic religion which drew on the classical literary aesthetics propounded by Abhinavagupta.[21] Such a development was slow to come in Śākta Tantrism. Hence the Tantric poet had to curb his poetic imagination to remain loyal to his religious doctrine. The Tantric path of the *sādhaka* is rather a grim method of religious development. The Tantric way of life is, by Tantric definition, a life of tension and contradiction — *vāmamārga*, i.e. the perverse path, the unfriendly way. The joy and ecstasy of Tantric religious experience are more rugged than tender. So it was difficult to introduce into the Tantric ideal the Vaiṣṇava ideology of tender *bhakti* and the divine's spontaneous grace; and even more difficult was it to conceive of a relationship conducive to the tender emotion of *bhakti* with a goddess like Durgā, the belligerent warrior goddess of power, or like Kālī the terrifying goddess of death and destruction. On the other hand, those are the two forms of the Goddess most commonly present to the Bengali mind. Nevertheless, by the end of the 17th century the doctrine of tender *bhakti* became influential enough in the Eastern region of India[22] to give a new flavour even to the non-Vaiṣṇava religions. This produced among the Tantrics the literary genre of Śākta lyric poetry (*śāktapadāvlī*).

The poems of this type can be divided into two categories: (1) *sādhanā* songs, which primarily describe the poet's experiences during his own Tantric practice or deal with different aspects of Tantric ideology, including the poet's personal views on life and religion; (2) *līlā* songs, which depict the Goddess in myth as Umā, on the one hand the beloved daughter of Himālaya and Menakā and on the other the wife and partner of the cosmic god Śiva. The two categories, however, often overlap, in that the *līlā* songs are in fact symbolic expressions of the *sādhaka's* emotional involvement with the Goddess, his chosen deity.

The *līlā* songs tend to show more Vaiṣṇava influence than do the *sādhanā* songs, because in them the Tantric poet could introduce the new theme of tender *bhakti* more freely than he could in the latter, which stood in a tradition going back to the Caryā songs. Seen as a daughter or as a submissive wife, the Goddess no longer seems majestically remote but much more approachable, and this paves the way for a more intimate relationship between Her and Her devotee.

These songs are commonly known as *āgamanī* and *vijayā* songs. The two group respectively treat of the Goddess's arrival at and departure from Her divine parents' home, events which mark the opening and closing dates of Her annual festival in the autumn. In these songs She is always seen as Umā, the young wife of Śiva, the yogin and world renouncer, and consequently subject to extreme poverty. For Her royal parents this is a source of constant pain. Compared with their own affluence their daughter's wretchedly poor household seems an unbearable place to live. The autumnal Durgā festival is for Bengalis the time for family reunion and happiness, and it is envisaged that Umā too then pays her parents a visit. The festival starts on the sixth day of the "bright" fortnight (fortnight of the waxing moon) at the beginning of autumn and ends four days later; thus the tenth day of that fortnight is when the Goddess returns from Her parents' to Her husband's home. The rites on that final day are called *vijayā,* and in this context the word is considered to denote the Goddess's leave-taking:[23] Her devotees bid her farewell and she supposedly takes leave of Her parents. The desperate wait of Menakā, Umā's mother, for the whole year, her boundless joy at receiving her only daughter at the advent of the festive season, her anxiety for Umā's well-being, her pang at the separation and her reluctance to let Umā go back to Her poor and inconsiderate husband–all these highly emotional motifs are incorporated in the *līlā* songs. Obviously, these songs are permeated by the emotion of maternal love. Superficially this resembles the anxious, protective and yet helpless love of Yaśodā for her baby Kṛṣṇa; it looks as if the Tantric poets have unoriginally exploited the Vaiṣṇava source. But a close scrutiny reveals a difference. Here the maternal love is depicted not only in its anxious protectiveness, but also in combination with the emotion of love in separation, an element most important for expressing the religious feelings of the devotee. In the middle-class society of contemporary Bengal, a young married daughter was totally out of reach of her mother. A housewife was effectively shut off from the outside world. Neither mother nor daughter could go out alone to visit the other, even when they lived nearby. The mother's isolation served as an excellent metaphor for the isolation of the individual from his beloved God. When the Mother-goddess is conceived to guard her devotees with unwavering protective love, Her majestic and indomitable divine power affords them a sense of solace and security, but tends not to arouse vivid religious sentiments: with such a figure the poet finds it hard to establish a reciprocal relationship. Moreover, in the 17th and 18th centuries ethical convention made it impossible for a poet-devotee to indicate his feelings for the Goddess by using erotic motifs. Nevertheless, the poets felt a strong urge to reciprocate the Goddess's love by actively serving and protecting Her. They could do so by conceiving Her not as the majestic Power of Kālī or Durgā but as the very young Umā, a paragon of dutiful and submissive womanhood. Imagining Her as a charming young wife, the poet could actively adore his Goddess and give vivid expression to the joy of his religious experiences.

There are many legends current in Bengal and elsewhere of how the Goddess appears as a young daughter to Her devotee. It is said that Rāmprasād Sen once had a direct vision of Kālī, who appeared before him as his daughter and helped him to mend his garden fence. But the little girl in a Hindu family does not live long with her parents; soon she is given in marriage and is lost to them. The poignancy of a doting, longing parent's now unfulfilled love for the absent daughter is an apt allegory for the devotee's yearning for the beloved deity. From this point of view the *līlā* songs too can be considered *sādhanā* songs.

The ecstatic pleasure of Her mother at Umā's short, rare visits expresses the joy of love in union:

> "The city's all excitement, Queen; up and away, thy daughter comes to thee.
> Away and welcome her and bring her home; come, I say, come with me."
> "Jayā, so happy is the news that thou hast brought, that thou hast made me thy purchased slave;
> All that I have ye maidens may command; come to me, and I will give my life to pay my debt to you."
> With quickening steps the queen has gone, her hair all loose about her.
> Love bears her on, as water one who swims. All who approach she questions thus:
> "How far off now is Gaurī, canst thou say?" On and on she goes, when in her path the chariot appears.
> She looks on Umā's face and says to her, "Thou art come, thou art come, little mother.
> Hast thou, who art mother to me, forgotten me who am thy mother? Surely that could not be, my love!
> Śaṃkarī steps from the chariot, bowing before her mother, and hastens in oft-repeated ways to bring her consolation.
> Says Kavirañjana Dāsa in tender tones: whoever else has known a day so fortunate?[24]

On the other hand Menakā's gloom and despair after Umā's departure show the depth of pain at separation from the beloved:

> "O Mountain! My Gaurī did come.
> But, appearing in my dream and making me wakeful, where has she disappeared, she whose form is consciousness?"
> Says the Mountain's wife: "O Static One! What shall I do now?
> I can move no more and have become still.

My life, transient like the goddess of wealth, has lost its treasure, which was knotted into my dress.
Why does she play such a trick, appearing and then vanishing?
Has Mahāmāyā no pity on me?
But again it occurs to me, why should I blame Abhayā? It is the father's fault if the daughter is hard."

The poet, Dāśarathī Rāy (1806-1857), plays on words like *acala* (hill, immovable, motionless), *māyā* (magic, trick, pity), *pāṣāṇa* (stone, hardhearted), and presents a compact but lively picture of a grieving, longing mother who typically blames her husband for her misfortune.[25]

Although Rāmprasād Sen practically started the genre of Bengali Śākta lyric poetry, *āgamanī* and *vijayā* songs mainly flourished in the hands of poets who came after. He himself wrote mostly *sādhanā* songs. He composed a great number of them and dealt with various themes of religious consciousness. He even tried to describe in simple terms complicated Tantric practices such as *śavasādhanā* and *kuṇḍalinī yoga.*[26] Like the poets of the Caryā songs, he drew his similes and metaphors from the familiar life of the village. Agriculture and boating, rivers and the dark and dangerous ocean provide motifs for the songs. On the value of concentrating in meditation on Kālī he writes:

My mind, you don't know how to cultivate.
So fertile a field as human existence you have kept fallow;
If cultivated, it would have yielded gold.
Fence it in the name of Kālī;
Nobody will succeed in swindling you.
That fence of the dishevelled lady is very hard, O my mind;
Death dare not come near it;
Even in a hundred years it will not be confiscated.
Now knowing it your personal property
Harvest it completely.
My preceptor has sown the seed;
Please irrigate it with the water of devotion.
O my mind, if you feel lonely and inadequate,
Please call Rāmprasād to be your partner.

The fence is the method of introverting the mind; the dishevelled lady is Kālī.[27]

Another song uses the motif of diving for pearls in the sea:

Crying Kālī's name, plunge deep, my mind,
Down in the unfathomed shining sea of thy heart.
Never empty of gems is that sea, though diving once or twice thou gainest nought, .
Conquer thy passionate heart, and plunge.
Make way to the very depths of the essential well that is thyself.
In the water of knowledge fruits the pearl of Śākti, my mind.
By devotion thou shalt obtain it, if thou keep the word of Śiva in memory.
Like crocodiles the six passions lurk, greedy for prey they wander ever.
Smear they body with the turmeric of good conscience, the scent will keep them far from thee.
Countless gems and jewels lie in those waters.[28]

Tantric yoga is practised in conjunction with the appropriate devotional attitude. The fourth line refers to the yogic art of breath control (*prāṇāyāma*). The adept plunges into the depths of his mystical body, which contains six centres of concentration imagined to exist in a vertical line down the centre; the bottom centre is the usual locus of the Kuṇḍalinīśakti, where the individual self too exists, and it is here called the essential well.[29]

He who practises Tantric methods of liberation treads a perilous path:

Beware, beware, the boat is sinking!
Ah, my careless mind, the days are passing,
And thou hast not adored the spouse of Hara.
Thou hast weighed down thy boat with vain goods of thy traffic, thy buying and selling.
All day thou hast waited at the quay and now with evening thou wouldst cross the stream.
Thou hast made thine old boat heavy with sins.

If thou wouldst pass over the ocean of the world,
Make Śrīnātha thy helmsman.
Seeing the leaping waves the six boatmen have fled.
Mind, now trust thine all with thy preceptor, the Absolute (Brahman),
He will be thy helmsman.[30]

Life is here seen as a great turbulent river, dangerous in the gathering darkness of the poet's advancing years, in which he has started his *sādhanā*. But his guru Śrīnātha can ensure safe crossing. The foolish poet has filled up his boat, i.e. life, with useless heavy goods and failed to propitiate Kālī with proper adoration. Kālī is wife of Hara ("who takes all"), meaning that through Kālī's grace the poet might have got rid of his burden of sins. But his spiritual teacher can still save him, because his guru is the Absolute, i.e. the Absolute divine. In the last analysis, according to Tantric ideology, guru deity and devotee are one.

Rāmprasād Sen and other Śākta poets of his period belonged to an age which witnessed an important change of religious attitude among Hindus, especially in and around Bengal. Very slowly the sectarian bigotry of the middle ages, which had been rife in this area, was being replaced by a religious syncretism in which the Godhead of one sect was not necessarily relegated to a position subordinate to the Godhead of another. In the two sects predominant in the Bengal of that time Vaiṣṇava and Śākta, Kṛṣṇa occupied the highest position in the former, Kālī in the latter. These were two utterly different gods, whose only common characteristic was a dark (*śyāma*) complexion. But the playful Kṛṣṇa so imbued the social life of Bengal that almost every delicate emotion depended on a Kṛṣṇa theme for its expression, and contemporary religious literature reflects this phenomenon. This development of a common Bengali literary culture started in the 17th century and is expressed in the *maṅgala* literature, where Vaiṣṇava songs irrelevant to the plot are introduced to demonstrate delicate emotion.[31]

Rāmaprasād boldly declared that there is no difference between Kālī and Kṛṣṇa; and by that he did not mean in the traditional way to indicate that Kālī as the highest Divinity subsumed every other divine being. He on the contrary emphasized the equal greatness of both deities:

> O my mind, you are still deluded.
> You remain engrossed in the reality of Śakti,
> But you fail to discern in Hari and Hara One Reality.
> You have not grasped the essence of Vṛndāvana and sacred Kāśī.
> Through your self-deception
> You only go round the cycle of life.
> You do not accept the identity between Yamunā and Gaṅgā.
> You are unable to realize the meaning of Kṛṣṇa's flute, which is the self, and thus cannot react properly.
> Says Prasāda, under such confusion all your religious endeavours are in vain.
> You differentiate between Śyāma and Śyāmā; hence, though you have eyes, indeed you are blind.[32]

The poet equates Vṛndāvana, where Kṛṣṇa lived and played, with Kāśī (Varanasi), a place blessed by Śiva's presence. The Yamunā is always associated with Kṛṣṇa, the Gaṅgā with Śiva, and yet the poet denies any difference in their religious value. For him Śyāma and Śyāmā, Kṛṣṇa and Kālī, are but the male and female forms of one and the same Dark (*śyāma*) God.

The overall sense of harmony achieved by Rāmprasād was maintained in the Tantric poems of his younger contemporaries. The need to press this point appeared to Śākta poets and spiritual people the more urgent since from the middle of the 18th century a new custom of worshipping Kālī publicly with great pomp provoked the Vaiṣṇavas and caused serious sectarian conflict between them and the Śāktas. The Tantric poet-philosophers tried to remove the cause of these conflicts by preaching the doctrine of one transcendent Personal Deity who is sometimes a woman, the Goddess, and sometimes a man (Puruṣa), Kṛṣṇa, Viṣṇu or

Śiva. The new concept is clearly presented in a song by Kamalākānta Bhaṭṭācārya, who lived in the last quarter of that century:

> O my mind, don't you know that Kālī, the supreme source, is not just a girl?
> Sometimes, adopting the colour of the clouds, She appears as a man.
> Again, dishevelled, sword in hand, she frightens the sons of Danu.
> Sometimes, descending in Braja, the same One steals the hearts of the milkmaids.
> Sometimes, Her three *guṇas* in full display, She creates, sustains and destroys.
> Voluntarily accepting the bondage of Her own illusion, sometimes She shares the pain of human existence.
> In the minds of Her devotees She appears in the forms of their choice.
> In the lake of Kamalākānta's heart She appears within the lotus there afloat.[33]

Kālī, the cosmic deity, is not confined to a single sex. As the warrior Goddess She control the demons (Danu's sons), and as the playful Kṛṣṇa the same Divinity bestows grace on the milkmaids. As the Creatrix She weaves the creation out of Her essential strands (*guṇa*).

This neo-Śākta movement of 18th century Bengal, characterized by doctrinal synthesis and harmony, in which the Tantric emphasis on esoteric ritual and meditation was blended with emotional *bhakti* and a monotheistic religion of grace, culminated in the person of a great 19th century figure Rāmakṛṣṇa Paramahaṃsa (1836-86). A traditional Śākta Tantric adept and a priest of a rich Kālī temple near Calcutta, he preached and practised this neo-Śāktism. He was not an educated person; all his teachings were oral and were recorded by his disciples. The five volumes of his discourses collected by Mahendra Nath Gupta[34] ("Ma") are a valuable document of Rāmakṛṣṇa's brand of eirenic Śāktism.

A large body of Bengali Tantric literature is by Vaiṣṇava Sahajiyās, Bāuls and Nātha *siddha yogins.*[35] All three groups followed comparable systems of esoteric rites and meditation. Besides works of a purely literary character, like devotional and *sādhanā* songs, the first group has produced a vast number of treatises on their doctrines and sexual yogic practices. Broadly speaking, what they have to say on these topics is much the same as what is in early Hindu and Buddhist Tantras.[36] Though the three cults have a basic resemblance, only the Vaiṣṇava Sahajiyā sect worships the Divinity in female form. But their adored Goddess is Rādhā, the eternal beloved of Kṛṣṇa. These Bengali Tantras, composed between the 17th and 19th centuries, take the form of dialogues between Śiva and Pārvatī. M.M. Bose has edited two of them, the *Āgamagrantha* and the *Ānanda-bhairava.* He also has published a bibliography of seventy-nine Bengali Vaiṣṇava Sahajiyā Tantras.[37] However, the spirit of these texts differs considerably from that of the Sanskrit Tantras. Influenced by Caitanya and his followers, they depict a form of religious aesthetics alien to the Sanskrit-Śākta Tantras. But their doctrine influenced some Śākta practice, and the above-mentioned poet Kamalākānta compares the rising of *kuṇḍalinī* to the highest centre with Rādhā's clandestine visit to Kṛṣṇa.[38]

III. Tantric Literature in Hindi and Related Languages

Before considering Śākta literature in Hindi, I must note that I shall treat Maithilī, Rājasthānī, Brajbhāṣā and Panjābī literature separately. My main reasons are both cultural and literary. Both Maithilī and Rājasthānī Śākta literature enjoyed patronage of royal courts belonging to Śākta kings and princes. Both are highly cultivated literary languages and have produced considerable bodies of literature. Śākta literature in Brajbhāṣā presents just the opposite situation. As to Panjābī literature, I have indeed very little material on Śākta themes. Panjab and Haryana possess several important Devī shrines which are still very popular. Devī occupies an important position in the religious practices of the Hindus and the Sikhs of the region. So presumably there exists a body of Śākta literature here both on the folk level and on the high literary level. I have only handled the latter.

By comparison with its profusion on the themes of Kṛṣṇa, Rāma or God unqualified (*nirguṇa*), Hindi literature offers little on Tantric Śāktism. Tantrism in its broader sense, which embraces both the Nātha cult and the Siddha cult, was (and to some extent still is) widespread in the parts of India where Hindi and languages close to Hindi are used. The difference between the Nāthas (popularly known in North India as the *avadhūta*) and the Siddhas is often tenuous; but the former lay more stress on purely meditative practices while the latter are inclined to Kaula religious practices using sex, alcohol and non-vegetarian food. Poets belonging to these two groups have produced considerable literature depicting their religious ideals and experiences. But these are not Śākta in spirit.

On the other hand, ballads and hymns on the Goddess in different local dialects of Hindi exist in considerable number. One such popular form of hymn on the Goddess (Śakti) is the group of forty verses (*cālisā*). These praise the Goddess in Her various manifestations, extolling the majesty of Her various aspects. There are *cālisās* on Durgā, Kālikā and Vindhyeśvarī. The last named is the presiding deity of a village called Vindhyācal, which is situated at the foot of the Vindhya range, not very far from Varanasi (Benares). Vindhyeśvarī is worshipped in the temple at the foot of the hill; on its top is the temple of Durgā, and in a nearby wood stands a temple of Kālī. The cult of Vindhyeśvarī is influential in the neighbouring region and has a long tradition behind it. It is a very sacred place (*pīṭha*) for Tantrics and devotees of the Goddess. However, popular though She is locally, She has left no mark on literary Hindi. The simple hymns composed by Her devotees are in local dialect and bear no sign of poetic or mystic power. Nevertheless, pious Śāktas feel it their duty daily to recite one of the *cālisās* in praise of Durgā or Kālikā or Vindhyeśvarī.

> I salute Thee, Durgā, bestower of all happiness!
> I salute Thee, Mother, remover of all misery!
> Thy flawless glory covers the three worlds.
> Thy forehead is like the moon, Thine eyes are wide and red,[2]
> Thy frown fearsome.
> To see Mother's beauty is blissful, those who witness it feel great pleasure.
> Thou hast made the world, which is Thy power, and givest food and wealth for sustenance.
> As Annapūrṇā Thou art the world's sustainer; Thou indeed art Sundarī and Bālā;
> Thou art the destroyer of all in the final cataclysm; Thou art Gaurī Śiva's beloved.
> The yogin Śiva sings Thy praise, Brahmā and Śiva ever meditate on Thee...[3]

This Durgā-cālisā goes on to complete the required number of verses without adding anything of great ideological value. But it nonetheless shows the dedication of the devotee to his Goddess, who stands above all other deities. In these simple eulogistic poems, Durgā or Kālī or Vindhyeśvarī is in fact the Mother, Ambikā, the source of all.

> In the morning, drums are beaten at the Mother's door;
> Gods, men, sages and others stand with their palms together in veneration.
> The four Vedas cannot tell all Her glory,
> Even great pundits like Śeṣa[4] are inadequate in telling Her glory.
> On the head of the Lord of the Universe[5] be pleased to place Thy protective hand;
> His sole duty is to sing Thy praise.
> Desire, anger, conceit, delusion, greed – these great warriors,
> Buckling on the weapon of courage, I shall fight.

Another such folksong equates Vindhyeśvarī with Mahāmāyā or Viṣṇumāyā, who took birth as the real daughter of Nanda and Yaśodā, Kṛṣṇa's foster-parents, and who was murdered by Kaṃsa's men when Vasudeva, Kṛṣṇa's real father, swapped her for Kṛṣṇa and laid her by the side of his wife Devakī.

> Hail Mother Vindhyācal, O hail Mother Vindhyācal!
> Mother, Thine abode is on the range of Vindhya under which flows Gaṅgā.
> Taking birth in the house of Nanda the cowherd, Thou didst appear in Mathurā.
> When the king Kaṃsa hurled Thee, Thou flewest up through the sky and Thy voice was heard.
> With folded hands I propitiate Thee; be pleased to listen to me;
> I am Thy little son, who meditating on Thy feet sings Thy glory.
> Thou art my mother, bearer of the crescent moon.

These few examples show that on the folk level Hindi hymns to the Goddess convey the same fervour and dedication as do those in Bengali and Maithilī. These hymns have not been anthologized, as have the Bengali devotional hymns to the Goddess (Śākta padāvalī).

In literary Hindi Tulsī Dās (1532-1623) occupies a special position as the foremost poet of devotion to a qualified God (*saguṇa bhakti*). Although he was a great devotee of Rāma, an *avatāra* of Viṣṇu, one can discern a strong Śākta undercurrent in his epic, the Rāmacaritmānas.[6] The narrator of this Rāma epic is Śiva, and Umā is the sole audience. Tulsī Dās grafts several Śaiva myths onto the Rāmāyaṇa story, for instance the story of the marriage of Śiva and Pārvatī.

A ballad called *Pārvatīmaṅgala*[7] (the marriage of Pārvatī) is also ascribed to Tulsī Dās. This work gives much the same account of Pārvatī's marriage as is found in the Bengali Caṇḍīmaṅgalas. Nārada comes to the house of Himālaya and Menakā and at their request examines Pārvatī's palm to predict her future. He tells them that she will marry a madman. Pārvatī consoles her parents, and leaves her home to embark on a great penance. She gets Śiva as her husband, but at the wedding her mother is shocked at the sight of the bridegroom. The target of Menakā's wrath is Nārada, whom she accuses of bamboozling them into accepting Śiva as Pārvati's husband. However, the marriage ceremony is completed. At the time of the couple's departure, the usual pathos haunts the poetry.

There are a few stray poems by Tulsī Dās on Śākta themes. In all humility and faith he dedicates himself to the Goddess, asking Her to save him from the misery of the bottomless desire that besets all creatures. The Goddess of death and annihilation is the final absorber of all and is above all cosmic gods. She indeed is the last resort of all beings. The poet in one poem describes the Goddess's exquisite beauty, even though it defies description. Perfect in every part and dazzling as if She contained the lightning, the Goddess, decked in celestial dress and ornament, with Her beautiful dancing gazelle eyes and moon-like face puts to shame millions of Ratis. (Rati, pleasure personified, is the wife of the god of love.) In another poem he addresses Kālikā, who dispels fear from the world and is served by gods, men, sages and demons, and asks Her to bestow devotion and liberation. The poet propitiates the Goddess, beseeching Her to grant him total devotion to Rāma.[8]

Guru Govind Singh, the tenth religious leader of the Sikhs (1866-1708), composed in Hindi a poem called *Durgācaritrauktivilās* on the model of the *Durgā-saptaśatī*, the last part of the *Mārkaṇḍeya Purāṇa.* In 1702 Dalapati Miśra wrote a small poem in Hindi called the *Kālikāṣṭaka*, notable for its adroit handling of metre and the devotional ardour it expresses. In 1718 Śrīkṛṣṇa Bhaṭṭa composed the *Durgābhaktitaraṅgiṇī*, which is again a free rendering in Hindi of the *Durgāsaptaśatī.* In 1786 Rāmacandra of Balia (Uttar Pradesh) wrote a beautiful poem about the feet of Pārvatī, the cosmic Mother. Its title is *Caraṇacandrikā* and it is the only poem on Devī written in literary Brajbhāṣā that has come to my notice.[9]

There was a tradition of making Hindi metrical translations of the *Durgā-saptaśatī* in order to illustrate Hindi prosody. The basic Sanskrit text on prosody is ascribed to Piṅgala, and this type of work is accordingly called Piṅgala poetry. In 1735 Ananya Kavi composed such a work, and in 1791 Hari Ānanda Dibai another, the *Devīvilāsa.*[10]

Even in the time of Tulsī Dās, there existed a vast body of magic formulae considered to be Tantric.[11] Collectively these are called the Sāṃvarī Tantra. The formulae are often accompanied by magic diagrams. They are mainly used, even nowadays,[12] to cure various diseases and misfortunes such as possession by an evil spirit, or to find lost property or to trace a lost person.

Maithilī literature is closely related to Bengali both linguistically and culturally; this is especially true when it comes to Tantra. During the fifteenth century the worship of Kāli obtained a new vigour in Bengal through the direct influence of Mithila or Tirhut. The *Śakti-saṃgama Tantra* (sixteenth century)[13] makes it clear that Mithila was a great centre of Śakti worship. So it is natural that a considerable literature on this theme has been composed in Maithilī, the regional language.

As early as the fourteenth century, Vidyāpati composed a few poems on Devī, the Goddess. At the request of his royal patron he wrote a handbook for the ritual worship of Durgā, the *Durgā-bhakti-taraṅgiṇī.* He also composed popular songs about Pārvatī mainly on her marriage with Śiva and the couple's honeymoon and later conjugal life. Several collection have been made of these songs. The story of Umā's marriage follows the purāṇic tradition recorded above, with only small local variations. Thus, in one song Umā's mother Menakā confronts Śiva, who has come to win her daughter dressed as a mendicant. Vexed, she exclaims:

> "How has this monk entered here? Gaurī (the fair one, i.e. Umā) is engaged in penance. My daughter the princess will be scared at the snakes (which adorn Śiva's body). I shall dishevel his matted locks and rip open his bag of alms. If the monk should refuse to leave even when repulsed, I shall insult him. Hara (the destroyer) has three eyes; (in the third) there burns a terrible fire–let my delicate Umā not behold it." Says Vidyāpati: "Listen, mother of the world, that man is not just a madman; He is the Giver of the three worlds."

One of Vidyāpati's many contributions to the literature of the vernacular languages of Eastern India is the *nācāri* form of lyric poetry. In recounting the source of this type of poetry Ramanath Jha says that in the play Vikramorvaśīyam Kālidāsa used the lyric form called *carcarī*, a kind of melody sung to accompany a dance. In the twelfth century Jayadeva further developed this style in his Gītagovindam, in which each lyric is set to a melody and is presumably to be sung as accompaniment to the dance drama. Though ostensibly describing the milkmaids' love for Kṛṣṇa, these songs are primarily devotional. As we have already seen, the Buddhist Tantric poets adopted this type of lyric poetry set to popular tunes to depict the poet's emotional experiences of his deity. The poet would sign such a poem by including his name in the refrain. Vidyāpati's *nācāris* are of this character. They are devotional songs recounting myths of Śiva or the Goddess. Many are more descriptive than devotional and therefore have always been used at such social events as weddings or festivals on the birth of a son. But some more emotional ones are used by devotees for pouring out their own emotions before the deity. Ramanath Jha reports that in some cases the devotee singing these songs begins to dance and even reaches ecstasy.[14] Here is a typical such hymn to the Goddess:

> Glory, glory be to you, Bhairavī, who frighten the demons, the beloved of Śiva, Māyā!
> O Goddess,[15] give us the boon of natural honesty and grant that we may ever follow your feet.

> Your feet decorate the corpse of Śiva, whose crest-jewel is the moon.
> You have killed the demons and some are devoured and some disgorged.
> Your black eyes, reddened, resemble a cloud decorated with red *koka* flowers.
> Your gruesome lips are foaming with blood.
> In your wild dance of destruction your anklets jangle madly while your sword destroys life.
> The poet Vidyāpati is your servant. O mother, do not forget your son.[16]

In about 1643 Haridās wrote *nācāri* songs about Devī of which only one is now available:

> Go and look, O mother, Gaurī is roaming about with this ascetic and playing. His horn pours out sweet music. The ascetic does not want any alms but begs for Bhavānī. Where ever Gaurī goes playing with her friends, the ascetic appears dancing and beating his drum. The wily ascetic comes every day and asks for Gauri. Says Haridās, he is the great God. The supreme Lord, the beloved of Gaṅgā is Gaurī's destined husband.[17]

The kings of Mithila were worshippers of Devī and several of them were good poets. Maheśa Ṭhākur (1536-69) composed many hymns on Gaṅgā and Tārā. Mahīnāth Ṭhākur composed in 1601 a song on Kālī and its similarity to Bengali Śākta songs is striking.

> Her face is formidable; She wears corpses as earnings and Her teeth are fearsome;
> Her hair is dishevelled; Her complexion is dark as a cloud;
> In two hands She carries a severed head and a sharp sword; the other two make the signs protecting from fear and bestowing boons; the Mother is naked;
> Her firm high breasts are adorned with a garland of severed heads still shedding blood;
> Her waist is girdled with severed hands from corpses; from the corner of lips blood oozes down;
> Seated on a corpse in the cremation ground She meditates surrounded by Yoginīs.
> O Mistress of the universe, King Mahīnāth prays to You. Hail.[18]

Locana, author of the *Rāgataraṅgiṇī*, composed several hymns of Śakti (c. 1681). They too describe Kālī as the terrible Goddess, grotesque, mysterious and yet of aetherial beauty.

Not all composers of such hymns were Tantrics. It was the overall atmosphere of the country that inspired devotional songs on the Goddess, whether as Kālī or as Umā/Durgā. Most people, including the king, were Śaivas or Śāktas. Thus a vast number of popular devotional songs, often anonymous, were collected in family song-books.[19] The poet's signature (*bhaṇitā*) at the end of a song is not always proof of authorship. One song with Vidyāpati's *bhaṇitā* contains distinctive Tantric ritual concepts. It addresses the Goddess as Chinnamastā (She of Severed Head):

> Victory to the light of world, giver of a good ending to the universe, to Her Whose forehead is lovely with charming locks. O high-breasted maiden, to those in Your service even the impossible becomes possible. In the heart of the lotus diagram with the sun's orb in its centre are three triangles. Above them Rati, a veritable river of gracefulness, is lying on top of her husband Madana. On her are placed Your feet, and their anklets (?—*padalasa*) appear as if the moon were lining the sun.

The mystical value of the number three in Tantric theology is underlined in the following song:

> I shall worship Gaurī with three ingredients: vermilion, flowers and the leaf of the *bel* tree.
> I shall offer her three foods: banana, coconut and pomegranate.
> I shall worship Her with three kinds of incense:[20] *agaru, guggula* and camphor lamp.
> I shall ask Her to grant me three favours: upright character, steadfast performance of my religious duties and good luck.

Some of the songs, again like their Bengali parallels, stress self-surrender:

O saviour of the world, when will You remove my pain?
Saviour of life, when will you remove my pain?
My boat is capsized on the ocean of life.
Do not delay a moment or I shall be drowned.
O Mother, only when You come and take up the oar,
Mother, then and then only shall I dare to hope for safety.
O Mother, I have thrown myself completely upon Your care;
Mother, how can You keep Your eyes shut and stay reclining?

Many of these songs were composed in the area which lies within the modern boundaries of Nepal. The downfall of Hindu royal dominance shifted the centre of gravity of Maithilī literary activity to Nepal, where the courts had come to patronize Maithila culture. Thus after 1527 hardly any literature was produced in Mithila proper for about fifty years, till Locana, author of the *Rāgataraṅgiṇī,* flourished at the court of King Mahīnāth Ṭhākur in the last quarter of the seventeenth century.

Among the poets of Nepal, King Bhūpatīndra (1695-1722) is important for his Śākta devotional songs:

O Goddess Bhavānī, grant me protection.
Whatever I do with my mind, speech or body
Is all dedicated to your feet.
I am a poor and humble person
. . .
I long to make my mind a bee
Devoted to your lotus feet in each of my births.
King Bhūpatīndra sings this song of devotional sentiment.
Glory be to the speech of the Husband of Pārvatī.[21]

Noteworthy is the Vaiṣṇava influence expressed in the concept of *bhakti rasa,* here translated "devotional sentiment". The same image of a bee at the lotus feet of the Goddess occurs in the Kālī songs of later eighteenth-century Bengal; the metaphor of nectar in turn suggests *bhakti rasa.*

The intensive Śaiva/Śākta affiliation of some Maithila poets was also expressed in another literary area: drama. Lala Kavi[22] (1744–61) wrote a play entitled *Gaurī-svayaṃvara.* It is in Sanskrit, Prakrit and Maithilī, though the former two languages are used extremely sparsely, just to give the play a Sanskrit framework and to accommodate stage directions and means of advancing the action. Otherwise the play is written entirely in Maithilī lyrics set to various melodies, similar to the ballad songs (*kīrtana*) of Bengal and Assam. It is interesting to note, however, that in Bengal and Assam there is no parallel use of the *kīrtana* to create a Śaiva/Śākta devotional opera. The form of this play is that of minor Sanskrit plays of operatic type known as *nāṭya-rāsaka*, a form also found in the Rājasthānī ballad poems called *rāso.* The devotional mood of the *Gaurī-svayaṃvara* is set in the opening prayer to Gaurī, the Fair Goddess. The theme is Her marriage to Śiva, following the same purāṇic story as Kālidāsa's *Kumāra-sambhava,* starting from the burning of Madana, the god of love, by Śiva. The play ends happily with the wedding.

Śivadatta (fl. c. 1800) wrote a play entitled *Gaurī-pariṇaya* on the same theme. Unlike the earlier play, this starts with Gauri's falling in love with Śiva. The episode of the burning of Madana only comes after Śiva has agreed to marry Her: after the betrothal Śiva unaccountably becomes lost in meditation and when Madana tries to upset his concentration Śiva burns him in an outburst of peevishness. However, through the good offices of Nārada the marriage is finally accomplished.

The literature of Rajasthan, "the land of princes", does not go much further back than the sixteenth century. The early literature was mainly bardic and religious. The geographical area of Rajasthan was from the early medieval period divided into several princedoms. The rulers were mainly Śaiva/Śākta, though some of them were influenced by Vaiṣṇavism and the monistic devotionalism of Dādū, Kabīr and the Nātha yogins.

Although most of this literature consists of heroic bardic compositions, a considerable corpus of devotional literature has also come down to us. One of the earliest Rājasthānī works of this type is Śrīdhara's *Saptaśatī rā chanda*, composed around the fifteenth century. The poem describes the battles of the Goddess against the Buffalo Demon and other fiends. As is evident from the title the theme comes from the Sanskrit *Saptaśatī*. This ballad is in effect a prayer in 121 verses.

Īśvaradāsa Vārahatta of Jaipur was one of the most respected bardic poets of Rajasthan and was famous for his devotion. He was respected and patronized by many kings of mediaeval Rajasthan;[23] his holiness earned him so much respect that people called him the great God.[24] He wrote several long religious poems, among them one on the Goddess as the personification of cosmic energy (*śakti*) called the *Deviyāna*. Though by temperament he was a devotee, it seems that he conceived the highest deity not as a personal god but as Brahman, the Unqualified (*nirguṇa*). It is said that his guru, Pītāmbara Bhaṭṭa, initiated him into the yogic tradition of the *siddhas* and that he successfully completed the course of Tantric practice called the *ajapā sādhanā*, a very high level yogic practice.[25] He had the experience of union with the Ultimate Reality and thus became a *siddha*. As a devotee he believed in the efficacy of using divine names as mystic formulae (*nāma-mantra*). He composed panegyrics on various deities.

The *Deviyāna*[26] is a panegyric on the Goddess consisting of 85 verses in *Adal* metre with three verses at the end in *Chappaya* metre. The Goddess is addressed by all possible names in all her aspects. The poem starts with a profusion of the letter "ka" (*Kartā hartā śrīṃ hrīṃkārī, Kālī Kālarayana kaumārī*), which is the first letter of Kālī's seed-*mantra, krīṃ*. The poet uses this form of alliteration quite often, thereby hinting at the Goddess's mystic form as the *varṇamātṛkā* (the primal alphabet), the wellspring of all *mantras*. The exact Sanskrit parallel is the afore-mentioned *Kakārādi-Kālīsahasranāma-stava*.[27] From time to time the poet begs the

Goddess to protect him from sickness and other calamities and to grant him liberation:

> O Goddess, You who remove all fear of sickness, protect me. O Goddess, please to liberate me. O Goddess, liberate me.

Another ancient type of Rājasthānī poetry is the *Veli.* This form was widely used by both Jaina and non-Jaina Rājasthānī devotional poets. Poems in this genre have been written ever since the fifteenth century.

Mahādev Pārvatī rī veli or *Hara Pārvatī rī veli* was probably composed in the latter half of the seventeenth century. It has 381 verses. Its theme is the marriage of the cosmic couple Śiva and Pārvatī. In the last verse the poet gives his name: Kisanau. The poem contains the usual story of Śiva's married life with Satī, his first wife, and her final disastrous encounter with her father Dakṣa, which leads to her death. There follows a rousing account of the destruction of Dakṣa by Śiva. The poem ends with a delightful description of Śiva's courting and marrying Pārvatī.

In the manuscript library of Bikaner there is a manuscript dated A.D. 1585 of a short work called *Tripurā rī veli* composed by a certain Jasavant about twenty years before the *Hara Pārvatī rī veli.* The work consists of nine short poems of *dohā* type and two of *kuṇḍalī* type containing thirty lines each. It is a eulogy of the Goddess, Who is cosmic Energy, as Tripurasundarī, a form in which She rides a lion:

> O Mother, the flame of sacrificial butter is reaching You; please listen to one supplication... You are the bestower of perfection, of discriminating knowledge; You always grant the enjoyment one longs for. By the favour of Tripurā one obtains prosperity and increase of one's treasury. She is the giver of elephants, vehicles, horses, and all desired property.[28]

The Śākta Tantric literature in Brajbhāṣā, the language of the Mathura region, is quite different in character from that in Rājasthānī: that was polished 'high' literature, while this is folk literature. Worship of the Goddess has been important round Mathura since antiquity, but, as in the

Vindhyācal region, hymns and ballads to Her were popular literature, never elaborated into complex forms. In this region the popular form of the Goddess is Gaurī, the fair young wife of Śiva who is completely identified with Durgā. As Gaurī She is worshipped by young women for obtaining a good husband and fulfilment in married life. She combines in herself the three aspects of Devī as the daughter, as the wife and as the mother.[29] She is envisaged as a very young girl, *kumārī*, yet she is identified with Bhagavatī and Bhavānī, the supreme Goddess initiating and controlling creation, the cosmic Mother. The annual spring festival of Gaurī, Nauratā, has long tradition behind it and is mainly observed by women. Important features of it are feeding and giving gifts to very young girls[30] and songs sung in praise of the Goddess:

> Today I see Bhavānī as a little girl. My Mother! goodness is before You and behind You; I have seen the sacred fig-tree, the gateway to righteousness; a barren woman begs at my Mother's door for a fertile body; a blind man implores for recovery of his sight; a poor man asks for food. O my Mother! I constantly mediate on You and sing Your praise.....

Visiting temples and pilgrim centres is important for Her devotees and the area has many ancient Devī-shrines. There are many songs describing such pilgrimages, popularly known as *yātrā*. The devotee is impatient to start his pilgrimage in his eagerness to meet the Goddess. In a fine poem this is expressed in terms of a son's impatient longing for his tender mother; the devotee accuses her of not showing enough eagerness to receive him:

> My Mother! why do You not force me to go to You by pulling me with a rope? I have climbed a hill and sighted my tender Mother; my mind is already with You; but my father delays to give me money for the journey, my brother delays to bring the horse; mother delays in preparing food; and aunt delays to give sweetmeats for the trip; my sister wastes my time in singing auspicious songs for me; aunty takes her time to put auspicious marks on my forehead; my wife procrastinates in making my way free; thus I am held back.

The Goddess is indeed supreme over all other divinities and is worshipped by all gods:

> Your immense divine form has brought confidence to the minds of those who propitiate You; Nārada is engaged in meditating on You; Brahmā recites to You the Vedas; Indra worships and praises You. To You the weapons are but toys for the mind and the lion is harmless as a cow. O You who possess twenty arms and the crescent moon, I fail to describe Your beauty!

Jagdev kā pamvādā is a ballad about a devotee of the Goddess Bhavānī called Jagdev. It consists of ten short narrative poems each describing a heroic adventure undertaken by Jagdev in the cause of Bhavānī. The ballad is written in the first person; whether such a person really existed is still unclear. The Goddess is variously addressed as Bhavānī of Himlāj, Kaṅkālī of Jalpā, the Mother of the universe and Durgā of Nagarkoṭ, and the poems express deep religious feelings.[31]

As has been pointed out, literary Hindi has virtually neglected the Goddess until very recent times, when her image as a slayer of demons has become the subject of allegory.[32] The story of the birth of Durgā, the concentrated form of the divine power of the gods born to subjugate evil, embodied in the Buffalo Demon, has been used since the early modern period as an allegory to justify warfare and to stimulate the fight against immoral non-believer oppressors.

This allegorical treatment was anticipated in Panjābī literature. Sikhs venerate Bhavānī or Bhagavatī, the demon-destroying goddess Durgā. Guru Govind Singh,[33] the activist leader of the Sikhs, who turned the religious community into a warlike sect of iron discipline and patriotic fervour, was a devotee of Durgā. He wrote a panegyric of Caṇḍī, the *Caṇḍī di Var* or *Var Śrībhagautijī ki.* This text is considered one of the major mystical texts of the Sikh scripture.[34] Although the basic story is taken from the *Saptaśatī,* the author introduced new themes. In this version the Buffalo demon Mahakhasur (Mahiṣāsura) was in the first place sent to humble the gods, who in their conceit and lust for power had forgotten their duties (*dharma*). The demon defeated the gods and usurped their power but forgot that he was but a vessel of God's will and purpose. He plunged into self-deception, became arrogant and tyrannical. Thus he forfeited God's protection. The gods in despair and humility became penitent and propitiated Śakti, the divine Power, manifest in Durgā, the goddess at once terrifying to the evil and benevolent to the righteous and meek. It is obvious that in this allegorical narrative lay a message relevant to Guru Govind's time. By their own fault the rulers of India were defeated by aggressive Muslim invaders, who are non-believers. But the Muslims did not follow the laws of justice and turned into great tyrants. The time was then ripe for the subjugated to rise and purge themselves of their immorality. Then in God's name, under divine tutelage as God's servants, with the active aid of God's divine Power they would destroy the tyrants.

Caṇḍī di Var is a poem of medium length. Var is the name of the literary genre of the poems of heroic tenor. The poet invokes the supreme Goddess, Bhagavatī, and recalls all Sikh leaders preceding him. Then he starts narrating the glories of the Goddess, who is the creatrix of the universe. This work has been translated by Mrs. Aviar Kaur and I give here just the opening few lines.

> Let us invoke Bhagauti and meditate on Guru Nanak,
> That Guru Aṅgad, Amardas and Ramdas be our support.
> Let us remember Arjan, Hargoviṇd and Sri Har Rae.
> Let us think of Sri Har Krishan whose sight eradicates all miseries.
> Let us contemplate on Teg Bahadur who is the source of Nine Nidhis, May they shield us ever.
> First of all You created the Khanda and established this universe.

With the advent of Brahma, Bishan and Mahesh, the spectacle of Nature was stretched.
Then followed oceans, mountains, earth and the sky that stands without support.
And then You created demons and gods and infused conflict amongst them.
It is You who brought forth Durgā for the destruction of the demons.
It is from You that Rāma derived power and destroyed Rāvaṇa.
It is from You that Krishna got strength to hold Kansa by his hair and slew him.[35]
Great Munis and gods did penance for ages, none could perceive Your mystery!

The Goddess is the primordial Divine Power and every single display of justifiable heroism is a manifestation of that Power.

NOTES

I

1 Mircea Eliade, *Yoga: Immortality and Freedom,* pp. 37, 171, 361. See also Dietrich Langen Archaische Ekstase und Asiatische Meditation, p. 47, Dieser auf der letzten Stufe des Yoga-wegs (*samādhi*) erreichte Zustand ist verschieden übersetzt worden: Enstase . . . (Eliade), Einfaltung . . . (Hauer), Trance . . . (Monier-Williams), meditative absorption . . . (H. Müller), Superconsciousness . . . (S. Vivekananda), Ausgewogenheit . . . (Wood).

2 For a detail discussion see S.B. Das Gupta, *Obscure Religious Cults,* pp. 413-424; Per Kvaerne, *An Anthology of Buddhist Tantric Songs,* pp. 37-60; and Zbavitel, Bengali lit., p. 120 ff.

3 Hevajra Tantra, I, pp. 99-100; II, pp. 60-62.

4 Zvelebil, in *Handbuch,* pp 130-165; K.A. Nilkant Sastri, *Development. . .,* pp. 41-43.

5 Sukumar Sen, *Bāṃgla Sāhityer Itihās,* p. 186.

6 C. A. Menon, *Kali-worship in Kerala,* passim.

7 Per Kvaerne, op. cit., p. 8.

8 Nityotsava, pp. 57, 121, 143 and 151.

9 Lālan-gītikā (an anthology of the songs of Lālan Sāh Fakīr) edited by Dr. Matilal Das and Srī Pijuskant Mahapatra, song no. 141, p. 96. *kibā rūper jhalak dicche dvidale / se rūp dekhle nayan yāy bhule // phaṇī-maṇi-saudāminī jini e rūp ujjvale //*; compare also the Tamil Siddha Songs: Zvelebil, *The Poets of the Powers;* and the same *Tamil Literature,* pp. 237-243.

10 Thompson and Spencer, *Bengali Religious Lyrics,* p. 48.

11 Zvelebil, *The Poets of the Powers,* passim; *Tamil Literature,* Leiden pp. 111-17 and 135-37; *Tamil Literature,* Wiesbaden, pp. 207-10; 132-34 and 190.

12 See C.A. Menon, *Kali Worship in Kērala.*

13 See pp. 198-268.

14 Bagchi, *The Kaulajñānanirṇaya,* Introduction, see Part I, ch. II, footnote 74.

15 Das Gupta, *Obscure Religious Cults,* pp. 211-255, 345-354.

16 H.V. Guenther, *The Royal Song of Saraha,* p. 7.

17 Munidatta, the commentator, has explained all these symbols in the Sanskrit commentary on this song; see Per Kvaerne, pp. 113-117.

18 Locana Śarmā of c. 17th century A.D. wrote a music treatise, *Rāgataraṅginī.* In this text he records that Jayata, a hereditary musician, was employed by king Śiva Siṃha Deva to set to music the text of Vidyāpati.

II

1 Abhinavagupta, Abhinava-bhāratī on Nāṭyaśāstra V.

2 In the Dharma Maṅgala, Dharma, the Absolute ineffable God, is the supreme creator and his cosmic spouse is Ketakā, the Original Goddess (Ādyā Devī). But the cosmogonic section of the Manasā Maṅgala is really only concerned with the birth of Manasā.

3 S. Sen, *Bāṃglā Sāhityer Itihās* II, p. 144.

4 See *Abhayāmaṅgala.*

5 S. Sen, op. cit., p. 503.

6 Bṛhaddarma Purāṇa, quoted by S. Sen, op. cit., p. 507.

7 Cf. T.A. Gopinath Rao, *Hindu Iconography* I, p. 373.

8 Op. cit. I. 2; II. 13.

9 Zbavitel, p. 165; Ashutosh Bhattacharya, Bāṃglā . . . Itihās, 466 ff.

10 *Ākheṭi* or *Ākṣeṭi* is the name of a certain hunting tribe living at the fringe of Hindu society.

11 Mukundarām Cakravarti, *Caṇḍīmaṅgala,* part I, pp. 418-26.

12 E.g. Pūrṇānanda, *Kakārādi-kālī-sahasranāma.*

13 Dvija Rāmadev, *Abhayāmaṅgala* pp. 104-6.

14 Charlotte Vaudeville *Bārahmāsā;* see the author's introduction.

15 *Mālsī* songs are songs about Pārvatī seen in intimate domestic light as daughter of Himālaya and Menakā, wife of Śiva and mother of Skanda and Gaṇeśa. These and the *padāvalīs* or *bhakti* songs on Kālī are described later in this chapter.

16 See S.C. Banerji, *Tantra in Bengal,* pp. 74-78.

17 S.C. Banerji, op. cit., p. 219.

18 See *Saundaryalaharī,* ed. N.S. Veṅkaṭanāthācārya, pp. 216-248.

19 Gupta Hoens and Goudriaan, HT, p. 163 ff.

20 Zbavitel, *Beng. Lit.,* p. 203

21 Umā Ray, *Gauḍīya Vaiṣṇavīya Raser Alaukikatva,* p. 95 ff.

22 Actually this vast region covers present-day W. Bengal, Bangladesh, Assam, Bihar, and parts of Orissa and Nepal. See S.B. Das Gupta, *Obscure Religious Cults.* p. 7. also, S.B. Das Gupta *Bhārater Śaktisādhanā o Śākta Sāhitya,* pp. 206-278.

23 *Vijayā* normally means "victory" or "victorious" and relates to the old Indian custom that in autumn warrior princes marched out for conquests. To worship Durgā, the war goddess, when setting out for war would be appropriate.

24 Translation: Thompson and Spencer, 95.

25 Arun Kumar Basu, *Śaktigīti Padāvalī*, p. 259.

26 Shibaprasad Bhattacharya, *Bhāratcandra o Rāmprasād*, p. 310.

27 Ibid.

28 Transl. Thompsom and Spencer, p. 50.

29 Gupta et al., *Index*, p. 200, s.v.

30 Trans. Thompson and Spencer, p. 52.

31 E.G. Dvija Rāmdev, *Abhayāmaṅgala*, p. 140.

32 Shibaprasad Bhattacharya, op. cit., p. 372.

33 Amarendranāth Rāy, *Śākta Padāvali*, p. 101.

34 Śrī "Ma", *Rāmakṛṣṇa-kathāmṛta*, A translation.

35 See Gonda, Religionen Indiens, II, pp. 154; 161; 224; 330; 171 f.; 179; 219 ff.

36 Dasgupta, *Obscure Religious Cults*, p. 117 ff.

37 Manidra Mohan Bose, *Post Caitanya Sahajiyā Cult of Bengal*, passim.

38 Dasgupta, *Obscure Religious Cults*, p. 129.

III

1 E.g. Dr. Hajarīprasād Dvivedī: *Hindi sāhitya uskā udbhav aur vikās*, pp. 27-69.

2 Wide and red eyes are considered in India to be majestically beautiful.

3 Das Gupta, *Bhārater Śaktisādhanā o Śākta Sāhitya*, p. 383.

4 Śeṣa is the cosmic serpent on which Viṣṇu lies. In the Vaiṣṇava tradition he is Saṃkarṣaṇa, the propagator of the Vedas and hence of wisdom.

5 Jagannātha is Viṣṇu.

6 Das Gupta, *Bhārater Śaktisādhanā o Śākta Sāhitya*, pp. 386-8.

7 Ed. Rāmcandra Śukl, *Bhagavāndīn and Brajratndās, Tulsī-granthāvalī*, II, p. 25.

8 Das Gupta, op. cit. pp. 388-93; *Tulsī-granthāvalī*, p. 387.

9 It was published in 1802 by the Bharat Press, Varanasi.

10 Dr. Dindayal Gupta *Hindi sāhitya kā Bṛhat Itihās*, part V.

11 *kali viloki jagahita hara girijā / sāvaramantrajāla jinha sirajā. Rāmacaritmānas, Bālakāṇḍa.*

12 This work is available in popular publication at Dehātī Pustak Bhandar, Delhi. This edition is supervised by Santrām 'Sant': the title as *Sāṃvarī Tantra* (Serḍe ka Jādu).

13 Tean Goudriaan and Sanjukta Gupta, *Hindu Tantric and Śākta Literature*, p. 68f.

14 Ramanath Jha, *Vidyāpati*, pp. 39-46.

15 "Gosauni" –literally: "revered lady".

16 Deśrajsiṃha Bhāṭī, *Vidyāpati kī kāvya-sādhanā*, p. 172.

17 A. Jayakanta Mishra, *Maithili Literature*, I, p. 226.

18 Ibid.

19 Ramnath Jha, op. cit., p. 43.

20 This refers to the rite of *ārati*, waving a lamp and incense in front of the image.

21 Jayakanta Misra, *Maithili Literature*, I, p. 246.

22 Ibid., p. 318

23 Hirālāl Maheśvarī, *Rājasthānī Sāhitya*, pp. 70-126. *Rāso* is a major type of bardic poetry, ibid, pp. 232-37.

24 Hirālāl Maheśvarī, op. cit., p. 189; "*isara so parmesara*".

25 Gupta et al., p. 180.

26 Ed. Sankardān Jethībhāi Kavi, Limbī, saṃvat 1948.

27 See p. 339 and the note 12 thereon.

28 Hiṛālāl Maheśvarī, op. cit., pp. 177, 193.

29 Pushpendra Kumar Sharma, *Śakti Cult in Ancient India*, p. 73

30 Das Gupta, *Bhārater Śaktisādhanā o Śākta Sāhitya*, pp. 409-18; Dr. Satyendra, *Braj-lok-sāhitya kā Adhyayan*, pp. 249-61.

31 Ibid.

32 Puspendra Kumar Sharma, op. cit., v. 112 of Maithiliśaran Gupta, *Caṇḍī*, Sahitya Sadan, Chirgaon (Jhansi) 1948; Himmat Singh, *Mahiṣāsur-badh*, Indian Press Ltd., Prayāg, 1932.

33 Serebryakov, *Punjabi Literature*, pp. 33-35.

34 See the editor's introduction to the translation of the poem: Panha Sanjam, vol. V., Special Number, Punjabi University, Patiala, 1972.

35 Ibid., pp. 2-3.

10. Women in the Śaiva/Śākta Ethos

INTRODUCTION

You can confiscate
money in hand;
can you confiscate
the body's glory?
Or peel away every strip
you wear,
but can you peel
the Nothing, the Nakedness
that covers and veils?
To the shameless girl
wearing the White Jasmine Lord's
light of morning,
you fool,
where's the need for cover and jewel?
(Ramanujan 1973:129)

Thus Mahādevī of Karnataka, the Vīraśaiva[1] poetess-saint of the twelfth century CE, challenged her critics. Whence came such boldness, so unusual in a Hindu woman? That is the question I wish to investigate in this chapter.

In his article, "On Women Saints" (1982), A.K. Ramanujan has made some excellent points to help analyse the lives of women saints in Hindu devotional (*bhakti*) tradition. He shows how the lives of these saints can be divided into five or six stages and sets them out in a chart as follows: early dedication to God, denial of marriage, defying societal norms, initiation, and marrying the Lord. From the second stage, as Ramanujan demonstrates, various options were open to these women devotees, all of whom had from childhood chosen God exclusively as their beloved. Some of them were married nevertheless, while others somehow escaped marriage.

The religious path which all these women chose is known as *prapattibhakti*; that is, single-minded devotion to God and total dedication to God's service.[2] And it was at exactly this point that the struggle started. In the normative Hindu tradition, which is dominated by lawgivers like Manu, woman is utterly subservient to her guardian, the male head of the family. After her marriage, her husband is for her in the position of God. A woman is not allowed a separate identity. In marriage, she must totally submerge herself in the identity of her god-husband. A husbandless woman is a social anomaly. So parents did not keep their daughters long unmarried, for fear of losing face and social position. Sonless widows too were a social burden and, in noble families, they were encouraged to perform sati.

In the theology of *prapattibhakti*, the devotee's single-minded love of God and ecstasy on seeing God – be it in a temple image or in her or his mind – and the depression ensuing in the absence of that experience, are all described in terms of erotic love. In Sanskrit, God is called *pati*, a word meaning 'lord', 'master' and 'husband'. As emotional *bhakti* spread through India, this erotic symbolism became pan-Indian. Therefore, as Ramanujan points out, women saints of the devotional movements had no existential problem in changing their social or biological roles (1982:316-17, 324). The husband of a married woman is her 'lord' and 'master' (*pati*) and, ideally, should be her sole object of devotion. The problem was to replace one's mortal husband with God.

By the brahminical norms of the lawbooks, which affected most of the higher castes, a woman was not supposed to take any independent decision about herself.[3] A late medieval book on the duties of women declares that the ideal wife should busy herself with the affairs of her husband and his family and should not even visit a temple.[4] Unlike men, women were not free to renounce social life and its attachments. This prohibition was especially strict for a married woman whose husband was alive and around. Thus even though, according to devotional theology, a woman saint of the devotional path (*bhaktimārga*) should have been free of the problem of role reversal which confronted an upper-caste male devotee, she had to overcome tremendous social opposition if she rejected her husband's claims. It needed great courage to declare one's lawfully wedded husband to be a mere sneaking lover, as Mahādevī does in this poem:

> Husband inside
> lover outside,
> I can't manage them both.
> This world
> and that other,
> cannot manage them both.
> O lord white as jasmine
> I cannot hold in one hand
> both the round nut
> and the long bow. (Ramanujan 1973:127)

Ramanujan bases his analysis of the lives of women saints on the biographies of devotees from both Vaiṣṇava and Śaiva movements from widely-separated regions of India. Both sectarian tenets and regional differences influenced the option available to the saints and played major parts in shaping their lives. Admittedly, much of the biographies of these saints from medieval India is legendary. Very few facts are now available to us about their lives. I want to argue that Śaiva poetess-saints were able to subvert their social roles and so achieve self-determination and spiritual fulfillment because the Śaivas – influenced by the *śakti* theology of the *tantras* – were apt to revere women's spirituality and to respect the autonomy of women saints. This attitude is by contrast totally lacking in the theology of the important Vaiṣṇava sects. Unlike Śiva's *śakti*, Viṣṇu's *śakti* has no autonomous power. Iconographically, Viṣṇu's *śakti* (Lakṣmī) is almost never depicted alone or in a terrifying form. She is the idealization of the model Hindu wife. Even in non-sectarian circles, Lakṣmī appears as the ideal, loving and serving wife as, for example, in the popular depiction of Viṣṇu floating on the cosmic waters asleep on his serpent-couch, eternally tended by his wife. I shall return to this subject in my discussion of the notion of *śakti*.

I have chosen six poetess-saints belonging to the medieval to early modern period. They all wrote in their vernacular. I shall deal first with the three Śaivas in chronological order and then with the three Vaiṣṇavas. The first Śaiva poetess is Kāraikkāl Ammaiyār of the sixth century, the earliest Tamil Nāyanār, who wrote in Tamil. The second is Akkā ('elder sister') Mahādevī of the twelfth century from Karnataka, who wrote in Kannada (Canarese).[5] She belonged to the group of close associates of Basava, the founder of the Vīraśaiva sect, the headquarters of which were at Kalyani. Her biography is recorded in the *Śūnyasaṃpādane*, the Vīraśaiva sectarian compendium of the sixteenth century. The third is Lallā Dēd ('granny' Lallā), who by her own account belonged to the Kashmir Śaiva tradition founded by Vasugupta (Temple 19247ff.). She flourished in the fourteenth century and her teachings are recorded in collections of her poems known as "The Sayings of Lallā" (*lallāvākyāni*), written in the Kashmiri language. The three Vaiṣṇavas are: Āṇṭāḷ of the ninth-century Tamil country; Mīrā Bāī of fifteenth-century Rajasthan; and Bahiṇā Bāī of seventeenth-century Maharashtra. Āṇṭāḷ wrote in Tamil, Mīrā Bāī in Rajasthani, and Bahiṇā Bāī Marathi.

Three Śaiva Poetess-Saints

Kāraikkāl Ammaiyār of the Tamils

Kāraikkāl Ammaiyā ("the lady of Kāraikkāl") is the earliest saint-poetess of the devotional (*bhakti*) tradition. Cekkilar gave an account of her life in his *Periyāpurāṇam*, written in the twelfth century CE. She herself lived in the sixth century CE. In the intervening period, she was warmly and respectfully praised by other great Śaiva poet-devotees, but nobody chronicled her life (Zvelebi 1975:135-7; Nilakanta Sastri 1966:368). Only four of her compositions have come down to us, of which the two containing her unique description of Śiva's dance competition with his wife Kālī at the forest of Tiruvalaṅkāṭu are the most famous. Here she describes how she herself witnessed this celestial incident as a female ghost in the retinue of Kālī. Kāraikkāl Ammaiyār's poems vividly demonstrate her great devotion for Śiva, a burning emotion of filial – not erotic – love (Karavelane 1956:16-41). Most probably, the emotional love of God experienced by devotees was not yet expressed in erotic terms at the time when she was composing her poems.

Plate 1: Kāraikkāl Ammaiyār sings with other spirit companions of Kālī to accompany Śiva's dance at Tiruvalaṅkāṭu. This photograph was taken by David Smith at the temple in Gangaikondacolapuram, Tamilnadu.

It was her husband who abandoned her, according to tradition, while she was prepared to live with him. He was scared of her miraculous abilities, taking her to be a manifestation of the goddess. Accordingly, he removed himself to a distant place, married again and named his newborn daughter after her. Tradition also says that being thus rejected by her husband, Kāraikkāl Ammaiyār now totally dedicated herself to Śiva in single-minded devotion and finally obtained his grace.

She left home to practise her devotion in the seclusion of the forest. It is said that she asked and obtained two boons from Śiva: one was to become ugly like a ghost, so that people would avoid her; and the other was to witness in person Śiva's famous dance. It was for her that Śiva danced at Tiruvalaṅkāṭu, a desolate place, surrounded by the hosts of ghosts and demons. In her poem describing this cosmic dance, Kāraikkāl Ammaiyār refers to herself as the ghost of Kāraikkāl (*kāraikkarpēy*). In iconography, she is depicted as an emaciated figure with dangling breasts like a demoness and often with long dishevelled hair. Some of her extant images strongly remind one of the goddess Cāmuṇḍā, while in others she is presented as part of the demonic musical ensemble of the dancing Kālī (see Plate 1).[6]

Thus, according to tradition, she defied the genteel society of the rich merchants of Kāraikkāl and deliberately chose the extreme life of a skull-bearing Śaiva ascetic (*kāpālika*) in the wilderness. Yet she was paid homage by great poet-devotees like Campantār, Cuntarār and Mānikkavācakar, some of whom lived not long after her (Zvelebil 1975:137). Obviously, Kāraikkāl Ammaiyār found it natural to identify herself with one of the divine members of Kālī's entourage and the Śaiva community found no problem in accepting her as such, her husband being the first to do so. Since little is known of the true facts of her life, I shall not discuss them in any detail.

Akkā Mahādevī of Karnataka

Akkā Mahādevī was born in Udutadi, a small village in Karnataka, into an upper-class family. She was beautiful and had very long hair. The local king, charmed by her beauty, brought a proposal of marriage to her parents. The king was a Jain, whereas they were practising Śaivas, they assented to the marriage on the condition that he became a Śaiva. But he did not keep his promise after the marriage. At this Mahādevī, who was extremely devout, became so angry and frustrated that she left the conjugal home and discarded everything she possessed, including her clothes. She wandered alone and naked, her long dishevelled hair covering her nudity. Did she want to emulate Kālī, the fierce goddess, a benign mother to her devotees but the killer of her enemies?[7] Kāraikkāl Ammaiyār imitated Kālī's companion-demonesses as she wished to be a serving-maid to Śiva. Mahādevī, on the other hand, chose as her husband the image of Śiva in a temple on a sacred hill (*śrīśaila*) in Karnataka called Srisailam.

She headed for the Vīraśaiva headquarters at Kalyani, in quest of spiritual guidance. When she finally arrived there, her mad appearance and behaviour evoked a lot of criticism. But she gave the Vīraśaivas satisfactory answers, and they were impressed by her spiritual wisdom and her command of Śaiva metaphysics. When someone criticized her eccentricity in going naked, she answered:

> People,
> male and female,
> blush when a cloth covering their shame
> comes loose.
> When the lord of lives
> lives drowned without a face
> in the world, how can you be so modest?
> When all the world is the eye of the lord,
> onlooking everywhere, what can you
> cover and conceal? (Ramanujan 1973:131)

Mahādevī always wore her hair in such a way that the tresses effectively concealed her private parts. One of the Vīraśaiva saints pointed out this anomaly in her stance: that she had abandoned clothes as signs of the ignorance (*avidyā*) that lurks in one's mind before it experiences Truth, yet she preserved vestiges of a social sense of modesty. She humbly answered that until she had attained complete union with Śiva, some effects of that ignorance would inevitably remain in her mind – effects also evident in her questioners:

> Till the fruit is ripe inside
> the skin will not fall off.
> I'd a feeling it would hurt you
> if I displayed the body's seal of love.
> O brother, don't tease me
> needlessly, I'm given entire
> into the hands of my lord
> white as jasmine (Ramanujan 1973:112-12)

She was accepted into this group of saints and it seems she took Allammā Prabhu as her teacher (*guru*). The saints gave her the designation Akkā, "elder sister". The Sanskrit equivalent is *jyeṣṭhā*, which is also the name of a goddess, a cosmic emanation of the supreme mother goddess, Śiva's *śakti* (Nijenhuis and Gupta 1987:22).

After staying some time in Kalyani Mahādevī became impatient for complete union with Śiva in her chosen image – Mallikārjuna ('white as jasmine') – in the temple in Srisailam. Eventually she went there, was married to the image, and became united with her god-husband by merging into that image. This last is a common motif in the biographies of devotees who fixed their love on a particular image in a particular temple. Both Āṇṭāḷ and Mīrā Bāī were believed to have merged into temple images in Srirangam and Dvaraka respectively.

Lallā Dēd of Kashmir

Lallā was born into a brahmin family in Kashmir and was married early to a young brahmin who apparently was very much under the influence of his mother. According to tradition, the latter hated her daughter-in-law and was very unkind to her. Not content with torturing Lallā herself, she also managed to poison her son's mind against her. Lallā's deep religiosity and independence of spirit may have triggered this animosity. Another possible cause was the fact that Lallā never had any children. It is said that finally her mother-in-law managed to turn her out of her conjugal home.

Instead of going back to her natal home, Lallā took up the life of female tantric renouncer and ascetic practising yoga (*yoginī*). Turning her back on the pure and sedate brahminical way of life, she roamed about wearing a minimum of clothes and sometimes none at all. Brahmins do not eat meat or drink wine, but Lallā followed the 'Left-hand' tantric tradition (an extreme form of ritual and yogic practice) and used both wine and meat in her religious offerings:

> Arise, O lady, set out to make thine offering,
> Bearing in thy hand wine, flesh and cakes.
> If you know the syllable that is itself the Supreme Place,
> Thou [wilt also know that] if you violate the custom,
> It is all the same. What loss is there therein?
> (Grierson and Barnet 1920:32)

It seems that in her spiritual training, Lallā depended mainly on her own judgement. Her poems never mention any person as her initiating *guru*. Perhaps she studied Śaiva texts under some guidance, or perhaps she simply listened to the religious discourses of contemporary Śaiva religious teachers. Whatever the cause, her understanding of the central tenets of Śaiva nondual (*advaya*) philosophy was sound:

> Lord, that I am Thou I did not know,
> Nor that Thou art I, that One be Twaine.
> Who am I? Is doubt of doubts, and so
> Who art Thou? Shall lead to birth again
> (Temple 1924:171)

Passionate love (*bhakti*) for Śiva drove her out wandering in search of her beloved. But her Tantric Śaiva background prevented her from going to any temple or worshipping any image: 'An idol is but a lump of stone, a temple is but a lump of stone' (Grierson and Barnett 1920:39). She practised a special ascetic technique and method of meditation known as Tantric *kuṇḍalinī yoga* and found both her *guru* and her beloved within her own inner self.

Passionate, with longing in mine eyes,
Searching wide, and seeking night and days,
Lo! I beheld the Truthful One, the Wise
Here in my own House to fill my gaze.
That was the day of my lucky star.
Breathless, I held him my Guide to be.
So my lamp of knowledge blazed afar,
Fanned by slow breath from the throat of me.
Then, my bright soul to my self revealed,
Winnowed I abroad my inner Light,
And with darkness all around me sealed
Did I garner Truth and held him tight.
(Temple 1924:167)

Again

Think not on the things that are without;
Fix upon thy inner Self thy thought:
So shalt thou be freed from let or doubt.
Precepts these that my Preceptor taught.
Dance then Lallā, clothed but by the air;
Sing then, Lallā, clad but in the sky.
Air and sky: what garment is more fair?
'Cloth,' saith custom; 'cloth that sanctify?'
(Temple 1924:173)

Thus it seems that Lallā led a life much like that of an *avadhūta*; that is, the life of a tantric 'master' (*siddha*) who has realized the true nature of Reality and who has thus reached salvation. For such a person is indifferent to social and religious laws and norms.

Not only did she command great respect among the Śaivas of Kashmir, but (allegedly) the great sufis of that time also revered her (Temple 1924: introduction; Parimoo 1978:88-106). Her title, *dēd* ('Granny'), reflects the affection and respect with which people regarded her; they treasured her sayings (*vākyāni*) for their prophetic wisdom. Her solitary and antisocial way of life may at first have brought her criticism, even abuse, and in some of her poems she refers to this fact; but in the end she was able to overcome such criticism and win trust and respect for her spirituality. There is no record of any strong family disapproval or restriction once she left home as a renouncer. There is also no record of her being molested as a helpless woman roaming alone, just as there is no record that Mahādevī was ever molested. As a Śaiva tantric, Lallā had the option of renouncing social life and following the ways of a renouncer and contemplative saint (*yoginī*), or even of emulating the stance of the more witch-like *ḍākinī*,[8] All she had to do was to win people's trust through her honest religiosity.

Three Vaiśṇava Poetess-Saints

Āṇṭāḷ of the Tamils

The first Vaiṣṇava saint I shall mention is Āṇṭāḷ, the famous Āḻvār saint of the ninth century. She is said to have been found under a plant and brought up by the brahmin Āḻvār, Viṣṇucitta. The Āḻvārs were the great Tamil Vaiṣṇava poet-saints who through their exquisite poetry introduced *prapattibhakti* to the Vaiṣṇava religion. Viṣṇucitta is recognized as the greatest among them.

Āṇṭāḷ chose as her husband the image of Viṣṇu in the temple at Srirangam. As the marriage was being organized, she is said to have disappeared into the image. In the longer of the two poems assigned to her, Āṇṭāḷ describes this marriage arrangement and the advent of the bridegroom to claim her. Both these poems are extremely beautiful and very popular among Tamil Vaiṣṇavas.

Āṇṭāḷ died very young. She was later elevated to the position of a wedded wife of Nārāyaṇa (Viṣṇu), and is still worshipped as such.

As in the case of Kāraikkāl Ammaiyār, very few facts are known about Āṇṭāḷ (Zvelebil 1975:158-9). We do not know if marriage to a temple image, in other words, being dedicated to an image in a temple, was a common custom at that time. In later times, such girls were called "servants of god" (*devadāsī*), or temple dancers. Āṇṭāḷ was after all an adopted daughter of her brahmin parents. It is possible that they finally agreed to her being dedicated to the service of the temple god.

Mīrā Bāī of Rajasthan

Although she was born into a famous royal house, and then married into the most famous royal house of Chitor (Chittaur), Mīrā Bāī's life remains little known to us. According to the consensus of Mīrā's historians, she was born at the end of the fifteenth century. Her father was Ratna Singh Rathor. Like Āṇṭāḷ, Mīrā was born into a Vaiṣṇava family and she grew up as an ardent devotee of Kṛṣṇa in the fortress city of Merta. She was married at the age of 18 to Rana Sanga's son, Bhoj Raj. But he died not long afterwards and there was no child born of the marriage.

Until the death of Rana Sanga, Mīrā was allowed to follow her own way of worshipping Kṛṣṇa. She spent most of her time in the temple singing the devotional songs she composed herself and she often danced to these songs. She obviously refused to follow the sedate life of a royal widow. She also loved to discourse with others Vaiṣṇava devotees and mixed with them freely. She publicly declared herself to be madly and ecstatically in love with Kṛṣṇa.

After Rana Sanga's death, Bhoj Raj's stepbrother inherited the throne. He was then still a teenager and his mother became very powerful. As a result of his mother's instigations, the young Rana started disapproving of Mīrā's way of life and asked her to reform and follow convention. Although Mīrā had strong political connections, tradition has it that the Rana more than once attempted to kill her but she was miraculously saved. Probably after these attempts, Mīrā went back to her parental home at Merta. After the fall of Merta, she went on a pilgrimage to Dvaraka in western India and stayed there in the temple of Kṛṣṇa, Ranchorji, until her death. This later part of her life is most obscure.

One thing is sure: although Mīrā was a princess with considerable political power and position, she could not escape prolonged persecution from her husband's family, even though the Chitor royal family had been Vaiṣṇavas from the time of Rana Kumbha (Alston 1980:3). While it is now difficult to know for sure which of her innumerable lyrics are authentic, many of them describe the opposition she met with amongst her conjugal family:

> I donned anklets and danced.
> The people said "Mīrā is mad."
> My mother-in-law declared
> That I had ruined the family's reputation.
> The King sent me a cup of poison
> Which I drank with a smile.
> I have offered body and mind
> To the feet of Hari,
> And will drink the nectar of His holy sight.
> Mīrā's Lord is the courtly Giridhara:
> My Lord, to Thee will I go for refuge.
> (Alston 1980:48-9)

Thus Mīrā Bāī took refuge in the protection of her god and husband, Kṛṣṇa, the courtly lover. She dedicated herself to pleasing, entertaining and serving him. She wanted to spend all her time in Kṛṣṇa's temple, a public place open to all devotees. But donning a dancer's costume and singing in rapturous devotion was not how a princely widow should normally behave. Nor was her keen longing to spend all her spare time in the company of other devotees – discoursing on the meaning of *prapattibhakti* and other theological matter – acceptable to her royal relatives. Objections were raised and, to some extent, Mīrā had to yield.

It seems that the legend of Mīrā going to Vrindaban (Vṛndāvana) is not true. Under the impact of the two great Vaiṣṇava leaders of that period, Vallabhācārya and Śrī Caitanya, Vrindaban became a flourishing place of pilgrimage and religious centre. Even though Mīrā wanted to go there to follow the lifestyle of the hundreds of other devotees who had renounced everything to serve Kṛṣṇa it is very doubtful that she ever made it. She did spend her later life in Dvaraka, a much quieter place, probably, supported by her brothers and cousins of the Merta royal house (political rivals of the Chitor royal house). However, it is clear that Mīrā could not totally disregard her social responsibilities. She had to compromise.

Bahiṇā Bāī of Maharashtra

Bahiṇā Bāī was born into a brahmin family in Devgao in northern Maharashtra. Her life coincided with a period in the history of Maharashtra which was significant both politically and theologically; it is the latter that concerns us here. In the seventeenth century, there was a great florescence of Vaiṣṇava devotionalism (*bhakti*) in Maharashtra. Saint Rāmdās – said to be the preceptor of King Śivājī – preached devotional theology within the cult of Rāma and established many temples and monasteries (*maṭha*) to consolidate his movement. Even more important was Tukārām, the saint, poet and singer from the farmer caste. Tukārām revitalized the Vaiṣṇava emotional *bhakti* movement through his marvellous hymns in Marathi, hymns composed in the style of an ancient popular lyric genre called *ābhāṃ*. The main object of his devotion was the image of Viṣṇu called Viṭhobā (or Viṭṭhalanātha) in the famous temple at Pandharpur.

From Bahiṇā Bāī's autobiographical writings (also in *ābhāṃ* style), we get a glimpse of her early married life. She was but a child when she was married and she started living with her husband in very adverse circumstances: her entire natal family depended on her husband's earnings and lived with him. He was an orthodox brahmin who followed the vocation of a traditional priest and astrologer; he was also a reciter of traditional lore. When for some reason Bahiṇā's parents had to flee from their home, her husband was obliged to escort them, travelling further and further away from Devgao until they finally settled for some time at Kolhapur.

There Bahiṇā, hardly 13 years old, acquired a taste for the hymns of Tukārām and started attending the congregations where they were sung. Extraordinary things happened to her there, bringing her to public attention. People thought that she was having religious trances and many came to visit her at her home. This upset her husband who thought that a wife who had broken the rules laid down for a brahmin wife brought shame on his family. He treated Bahiṇā harshly, while her parents and others felt they could not interfere. They told her that a husband's right over his wife is supreme. Her husband did not hold with the devotional cult of Viṭhobā: he declared that, for a wife, her husband is the only god. Bahiṇā was forbidden to attend any congregation and to go to any temple.

At this point, Bahiṇā's religious propensities hardened into conviction. She solved the outward clash with her husband – in which she had no support from any of her close relatives or friends – by totally internalizing her religious activities. She dreamt that Tukārām came and initiated her with the six-syllable Vaiṣṇava mantra (*rāma-kṛṣṇa-hari*). As a result, she was able to reconcile herself to staying home as a humble wife and to curbing her desire to visit temples and so on she played the role of a dutiful wife while mentally renouncing all attachment to life. She became a mother, but strangely enough did not accept her son as a son but treated him as a fellow religious aspirant and a friend (*kalyāṇabandhu*). Her mental rejection of her husband was complete. She made that clear in her songs, which narrated her present and previous lives to her son (Abbott 1985:52-7).

Bahiṇā's rebellion against society's unfairness towards women was expressed solely in her songs. By being docile, she could at least see and hear Tukārām from a distance. For her, Tukārām the saint and Viṭhobā the god became one entity and she loved them with intense devotion. But, in her position, outward rebellion was impossible. The only religious models available to her were those of Sītā and Lakṣmī, ideals of conjugal fidelity and meek docility.[9] Therefore Bahiṇā's religious fulfillment had to be internal. It was a compromise between her chosen exclusive path of devotion (*bhaktimārga*) and the will of society with its orthodox traditions; for, throughout its history, Vaiṣṇavism has always accepted the brahminical ethos so far as social life is concerned. Hence the popular tantric dictum regarding the secrecy of the left-hand path of *śakti* worship (*kaula*):

> Keep your *kaula* identity secret, outwardly
> behave like a Śaiva, but when in society
> behave like a Vaiṣṇava.[10]

The Notion of Divine Power

Let me now add a few words about the Tantric theology of divine power (*śakti*). I believe that these ideas, at the time relevant to us, were widely diffused in brahminical society throughout India, and especially among Śaivas. On the other hand, the theology subsumed many local cults of mother goddesses.

What is *śakti*? The term means literally 'power', 'potency', 'potential'. It denotes God's power, his indomitable energy and at the same time his conscious thought. Personified as a goddess, Śakti is described as being created from God's blazing consciousness, symbolically taken to be his sacrificial fire (*cidagnikuṇḍasambhūta; Lalitāsahasranāmastotra* 2.1).

God's act of creation is described in *Ṛgveda* 10.90 in terms of a sacrifice in which he sacrifices himself and out of which creation emerges. The Tantric monotheists took the upaniṣadic concept of *brahman* for their concept of God. To maintain the ultimacy of God, they separated and concretized God's creative thought and action as his *śakti.* This concept is then mythologized as a divine person, Śakti, the Goddess, and her close relationship to God is emphasized by taking her to be his wife. She inheres in God and yet is a separate entity. As believers in the ultimacy and transcendence of God on the one hand, and in the reality of his created world on the other, the Tantrics used the concept of *śakti* to explain the process of creation.

It is important to understand that Tantric theology combines a great many symbol systems and conflates different levels of understanding: what is merely metaphorical to advanced initiates may be understood literally by outsiders or beginners. From the viewpoint of the enlightened, *śakti* is an abstraction, the aspect of godhead accessible to human thought. As one moves down the scale of sophistication *śakti* becomes something one can talk about as an entity in its own right; an object endowed with visual and phonic form; a mythological character, a goddess. All these levels are present in Tantric worship and meditation.

God is manifest in this world through the medium of his *śakti,* the Goddess (Śakti). She is both the agent and the material cause of creation. The universe is *śakti:* unconscious matter and all material objects as well as conscious souls are nothing but limited manifestations of her. As the world is both created from within her and held in her, she is looked upon as the cosmic Mother who has created the world as if from her womb (often symbolized by a triangle) and who nurtures it herself. From the simple unity of the central Śakti, the world is created – like rays from the central energy – as various limited aspects of her: creation is refractions of Śakti. God's cosmic functions, of which the first is self-concealment of the creator, are assigned to Śakti by his divine authority. Thus she has dual characteristics, being both transcendent and empirical. This is not the only pair of opposites present in her personality. However, she conceals her transcendent nature, which is identical with God, and manifests herself limited by time, space, and other features of the empirical world. Creation starts from the creation of these limitations and the conscious entities limited by them. As the process of creation progresses, the central conscious, subtle and simple entity - *śakti* - gradually congeals into gross, unconscious and complex phenomena. Looking from the cosmic creative *śakti* downwards, we see three co-ordinate ranges of creation: from subtle to gross, from conscious to unconscious, and from simple to complex. In this range, human beings (especially those who are enlightened) are nearer than other phenomena to the central simplicity of *śakti.* Gods and goddesses are closer to the cosmic *śakti* than human beings are. Interestingly, on the strength of their potentiality to be mothers, women are considered closer to *śakti* than men. Many Śākta religious texts stipulate kind and respectful treatment of women, consigning the breakers of this law to hell (see, for example, *Kulacuḍāmanitantra* 3.46-57). Although Tantrics see the entire phenomenal world as mere manifestations of *śakti,* they worship virgins (*kumārī*; see Plate 2) and married women (*suvāsinī*) both as symbols of the Goddess, and as beings in which *śakti* is manifest with the least self-concealment. Such gestures instil a sense of self-respect and confidence in those and other women of the community and also teach men new ways to look at their womenfolk.

Plate 2: A girl of under eight years of age (kumārī) is worshipped. This photograph was taken in Coventry in 1988 by Eleanor Nesbitt (Research for Ṛeligious Education and Community, Department of Arts Education, University of Warwick).

Moreover, theology explains Śakti as the efficient agent of the act of creation in the following way. Śakti is Śiva's creative impulse and thus represents the divine agency (*kartṛtva*), and as such she is irresistible and enjoys autonomy (*svātantrya*). She alone carries the authority (*ājñā*) of Śiva. As the supreme divine contemplation (*vimarśa*), she manifests herself in three aspects: the divine sovereign will; the divine knowledge, to which all created phenomena are distinctly revealed even before their creation; and the irresistible divine activity, which translates all divine desires into deeds.

Thus the cosmic functions of God which are common to the Indian monotheistic religions are assigned to Śakti. This accounts for the oppositions in her character: she is both benign and terrible, at once nurturant and destructive (see David Wulf 1982). She is the delusive Māyā ('illusion') who conceals the true experience of God from his creatures. She is the cause of their transience. As the supreme divine will, she has the universe under her control. She is the cosmic sovereign power which rules the created world as the sole representation of divine authority. In this position, she dispenses rewards and punishments according to her law.

Finally, she also grants God's grace; in fact, she is God's grace. To be close to her is to be close to grace. To be a woman is thus considered a blessing in itself, since women are closer to her than anyone else. Śakti is indeed God's personality; and personality does not exist without the person – here, God. So, wherever Śakti is manifest, God is manifest through her. To worship her is to worship God; to insult her is to insult God.

Conclusions

Religion is not only a model of society but also a model for it (Geertz 1975:93-5). Whether consciously or unconsciously, both Mahādevī and Lallā emulated Kālī, the dangerous and destructive goddess of death, while Kāraikkāl Ammaiyār emulated one of Kālī's close associates. As they were Śaivas, this choice was natural to them for they had left the protection of home and family for a life of renunciation and the lonely quest for God. Through the devotional (*bhakti*) tradition, they were also clear about their attitude to God. They were his lonely lovers or bondmaids, yearing for their beloved (husband or master) Śiva. They were poets of considerable power and expressed their inmost thoughts in clear, poetic, and yet popular language. The tradition of Śakti worship in turn enabled the people to understand these women and to accept them. For women *gurus* are familiar and even preferred in *tantra.*[11]

By contrast, Vaiṣṇava theology never presented such opportunities for women. In the Pāñcarātra cosmogony, Nārāyaṇa, the supreme transcendent God (Viṣṇu), through his divine capacity (*viṣṇumāyā*) splits his own self and so disturbs the primal unity and simplicity.[12] Although present, Śakti is deprived of her explicit dynamism and her nature as God's energy. Following the Vedic concept expressed in the *puruṣasūkta* (*Ṛgveda* 10.90), God, in this system, himself descends to the empirical level, manifest as the creation. As one early Vaiṣṇava text puts it, God Viṣṇu divides himself into four primary forms depicting various aspects of divine sovereignty, potency, knowledge, and power (*Sāttvatasaṃhitā*, chapter 2). Through these forms, he gradually manifests himself as the diverse and pragmatic creation, while the nurturing goddess, God's *śakti*, always remains under his active control. Unlike Śiva, the indifferent and passive renouncer, Viṣṇu is viewed as the archetypal sovereign, ruling his own creation according to his cosmic law. With the aid of his power (*śakti*), Viṣṇu maintains cosmic justice and order. The role of his *śakti* gradually became confined in Vaiṣṇava scriptures to the intercessory power of his consort, Lakṣmī, whose prayers God grants because of his special love for her as his meek and caring, perfect wife.

Thus, while all three Śaiva saints I have discussed here were able to leave their homes when their religious objectives clashed with their roles in the family, the Vaiṣṇava saints were unable to do the same. In the absence of a religious model and of a sympathetic environment, Princess Mīrā Bāī had to compromise and Bahiṇā could only blame the fate which had made her a woman. But then she was able to accept that fate and to channel her religious impulse so as to avoid open conflict with her family and society. This she records in the following poignant lines:

> Possessing a woman's body, and myself being
> subject to others, I was not able to carry
> out my desire to discard all worldly things
> (*vairāgya*). And yet a change took place through the power of right-thinking. What a wonderful thing God (Rāghobā) worked!
> (Abbott 1985:38; 60.1-2)

That wonderful thing, God's 'miracle', was her final acceptance of her fate and her compromise with circumstances.

NOTES

1 Vīraśaiva (or Liṅgāyat) is the name of the Śaiva sect founded by Basava (or Basavaṇṇa) in 1156 CE in South India.

2 See Hardy 1983; Gupta 1986. From the beginning, the emotional *bhakti* movement was associated with poet-saints: the Āḷvārs and the Nāyṉārs. The emotional love that the devotees of both sexes experienced was poured out in wonderful spontaneous poetry. The love of God expressed in terms of erotic poetry by women devotees was first found in the lovely poems of Āṇṭāḷ, one of the twelve Āḷvārs.

3 *na strī svātantryam arhati* (Manu 9.3). Cf. Raghavan 1962:353-5.

4 See Leslie's introduction to her analysis and partial translation of Tryambakayajvan's *Strīdharmapaddhati* (1989:1-25). This restriction on the independence of women, and their total dependence on their husband's will as enjoined by the lawbooks, enabled Bahiṇā's husband to impede seriously her religious aspirations.

5 See Rāmanujan 1973:111-14; Menezes and Angadi 1973:v-x.

6 *Periyapurāṇam*, stanzas 1764-5. See also Sasivalli 1984:25, 31.

7 Cf. Gondriaan and Gupta 1981:178-9; Wadley 1977:134; Gross 1985:225.

8 In Tantric technical terms, *ḍākinīs* are minor emanations of *śakti*/Śakti. They are prominent in Himalayan Tantric Buddhism (see Beyer 1973:45-7).

9 Cf. Sri Satymurthi Swami's glossary on Pillai Lokācārya's *Śrīvacanabhuṣaṇam* (1972:1.5-22).

10 *antaḥ kaula bahiḥ śaivo janamadhye tu vaiṣṇavaḥ// Kulārṇavatantra* 11.83 (my translation).

11 Cf. *Prāṇatoṣaṇītantra*, chapter 2. Even today there are hereditary Śākta families in Mithila who follow the tradition that the primary initiation must be given by a woman, preferably one's own mother.

12 See Gupta 1971. In some Pāñcarātra texts, women came to be regarded as so low in status that they were allowed only the general initiation available to all castes (Gupta 1983:89-90).

11. The Goddess, Women, and Their Rituals in Hinduism

The *Mārkaṇḍeya purāṇa (MP)* narrates the story of Saraṇyū just before its famous description of the Great Goddess's repeated triumphs over the powerful demons. Saraṇyū was a daughter of the god Tvaṣṭṛ, and she married god Sun (Vivasvat), who in this myth was considered to be a mortal–that is, part of the created world, which is ultimately transient. Their son Vaivasvata Manu, who is thus half god and half mortal, is the forefather of humankind. As Wendy Doniger has pointed out, Saraṇyū was never venerated as a goddess or as the original mother of humankind.[1]

Her refusal to behave like a good wife or a good mother may have offended the traditional image of a good woman. She took recourse to deception to sneak away from her home, husband, and children and left behind a look-alike woman to act out her wifely and motherly duties. Moreover, she lacked power and was afraid of her husband's concentrated energy. In fact, her father, Tvaṣṭṛ, to persuade her to go back to her husband, had to cut out most of god Sun's energy, leaving him only one-sixteenth of his original energy.[2]

Thus the mother of humankind, Saraṇyū, because of her unwifely and unmotherly behavior, was ignored as a goddess while the *MP* narrated the glory of the Great Goddess, the divine energy, Mahāmāyā (cosmic illusion), who from that time onward gradually rose to eminence as the mother of the universe.[3] In the *purāṇas,* she transcends the social roles of both mother and wife and often functions autonomously. Therefore, she cannot be a role model for women in the broader Hindu society, even though some Hindu community worship very young girls in the family as the image of the goddess, and sometimes women become possessed by a goddess and turn into oracles.[4] However, generally speaking, the paramount importance of the roles of wife and mother for Hindu women cannot be exaggerated. Hence, while the Great Goddess is supremely important in Hindu theology, women's position in society is still rather uncertain in a basically patriarchal and caste-oriented society, where caste is transmitted through the male line of a family. A woman certainly does not possess the goddess's sovereign authority or her divine power. In this society, the role models for women are such epic and *purāṇic* characters as Sītā, who followed her husband to his forest exile, leaving behind the luxury of the palace of Ayodhyā, and Sāvitrī, who followed her dead husband when the god of death was taking him to the land of the dead and tricked the god into returning her husband alive and well.[5]

In this essay, I examine how Hindu women, by employing the means they find in Hindu religious systems, are able to transcend the restricted position in the family hierarchy and the passive role in Hindu religions that are seemingly accorded them by the law books of Hindu dharma—for example, the *Manusmṛiti.* First, I discuss the image of women in Hindu society; second, I briefly sketch the theology of a divine power who is feminine and its effects on the social position of women; third, I show how, in spite of her adverse situation in society and her ambivalent position in theology, the Hindu woman has created for herself a gloriously important position in society through her special religious practices (*vrata*).[6]

Dharma

Broadly speaking, every religious-minded Hindu has some idea of dharma, both social and personal, and the doctrines of karma and *saṃsāra*—the transience of life and the endless transmigration of individual selves from life to life. Popular mythology and philosophical thought current among Hindu women try to give structure and a coherent exposition of dharma, and undoubtedly every person within the religion possesses a basic grasp of it. In its various contexts and applications, this dharma has at least three basically different functions and dimensions: dharma is (1) a principle of causal explanation (of factual events),(2) a guideline to ethical orientation and (3) the counterpart and stepping stone to final liberation attained by renunciation and asceticism. These three functions are balanced, reconciled, and integrated in various manners; they do not form a simple and unquestioned unity. Historically, it is possible to see changes, differences, and tensions between older and later levels of thought and also processes of adjustment of prekarmic and extrakarmic ways of thinking to the theory of karma and *saṁsāra.* As official Hinduism explains, the causality of human station in society and its ranking in the social hierarchy and notions of karma and their retributive effects of good or bad fortune seem to make sense.

Dharma enjoins each person to follow a set of social and religious duties appropriate to that person's individuality (*sva-dharma*)[7] and social station that is usually in harmony with his or her religious and social duties (*jāti-dharma*) as a member of a particular *jāti*—that is, natal community. This dual meaning of dharma is crucial in understanding Hindu social religion. The meaning and scope of dharma have been elaborately discussed in ancient brahmanical law books. All members of brahmanical society must model their actions according to the injunctions of these law books so that the results accrued should be universally beneficial and elevating for active people. A woman's dharma is designated as *strī-dharma.* Note that the universal law of ethics known as the truth (*ṛtam* or *satyam*) transcends both types of dharma and is often referred to simply as dharma. Yudhiṣṭhira, the hero of the *Mahabhārata,* was a paragon of this third and universal type of dharma and is distinguished by the epithet *dharmarāja,* king of dharma.

Dharma, Strī-dharma, and Ritual Acts

Ritual acts can counterbalance the bad results of one's karma. These rituals give the ritualist certain powers even to remedy some previous wrongdoing that has resulted in some calamity in this life. Sāvitrī rebelled against karma and released Satyavān from the noose of death, Yama, but before that she rigidly followed the dharma of a loyal wife. Thus, she established her personal integrity and purity. She chose her husband without knowing that his fate was to die within a year of their marriage, yet, when informed about his fate, she remained firm in her conviction that, once she had decided to give herself to Satyavān, it would be a breach of her dharma not to keep her promise, even though it had never been uttered. In this instance, she followed the third type of dharma (i.e. *satya-dharma*, dharma which is the truth) and paved her way to winning Yama's approval. Yama is the lord of dharma and is called by that name.

As each individual has a special basic nature (*sva-bhāva*) that determines that person's duties, a woman has to determine her basic nature (*strī-dharma*).[8] Ideally, Hindu dharma advises all people to follow their own (*sva*) dharmas. By strictly adhering to her preordained nature and duties, a woman can function in the socially sanctioned dharmic way. She is the mistress of the house and plays a great supporting role as the custodian of the family dharma; she knows the rituals, teaches her children the basic dharma, and is thus responsible for the dharmic structure of the next generation. Accepting the *śāstras*' criticism of the naturally fickle nature of women and the pollution inherent in the female body, women make themselves utterly subservient to the voice of family authority and frequently engage in acts of ritual purification. I shall soon make this point clear.

Enjoined by God, the cosmic ruler, the prime mover, karma functions as the principle of causal relations of factual happenings. For instance, it explains the causality of human station in society and also supplies a guideline for ethical orientation, the concept of individual responsibility for every intentional act and its future result, ensuring the inevitability of *saṁsāra,* even when a person carefully follows both *sva-dharma* and *jāti-dharma.* Nevertheless, ancient brahmanical religion has taught individuals how to transcend their *sva-bhāva* and thus reduce the importance of their *sva-dharma* by (1) meticulous adherence to religious duties, coupled with strict self-control, which is sometimes close to ascetism; (2) total renunciation of attachment and greed, together with removal of all physical, emotional, and moral weakness, thereby leading to purity of body and mind, followed by deep meditation on the real nature of oneself and the phenomenal world; and (3) reception of God's grace through perfect devotion.

The first of these ways really means the correct performance of all the rituals prescribed by the religious system. It associates such rituals with a program of self-restraint and certain ascetic practices whose main purpose is to purify a person's physical, mental, and emotional flaws.[9]

The second way—that is, the way of yoga—is universally accepted by all Hindu religious systems to be the basic of all religious endeavour. The preliminary step for practicing yoga is to control emotion and passion by cultivating calmness (*śama*) and self-restraint (*dama*). The practice of calmness and self-restraint leads a person to renounce the attractions of greed and passion. People are not always required to really renounce their station in life, but the spirit of renunciation (*vairāgya*), going hand in hand with deep meditation on the chosen deity, is highly valued as the basic moral and spiritual requirement for anybody who is seeking God's favor through devotion.

The third way is what underscores all such sects and religious systems that, together with traditional Brahminism, have been called Hinduism. God is supreme and the ultimate authority, whose grace alone can save a person from *saṁsāra.*

God's pleasure, then, forms the main goal of all religious practices. People can aspire to it through selfless devotion and constant loyal service to God.

In the real world of the believers in the religions collectively called the Hindu religions, however, these ways are not at all exclusive. There are countless permutations and combinations of these ways to produce a multitude of religious systems and sects. Every pious and religious-minded Hindu believes in the existence of a supreme god, who subsumes all other deities, including a specially chosen beloved deity (*iṣṭadevatā*). Thus, the paradox of monotheism and polytheism functioning simultaneously in Hinduism poses no problem in a Hindu's religious awareness. Sectarian theology amalgamates all three ways mentioned of escaping karma and its result, *saṁsāra*.

In the patrifocal brahmanical tradition, women were systematically excluded from ritualistic religious duties because they were deemed unclean and impure. Hence, they were classed alongside the other impure social group, *śūdra*. This impurity is inherent in women because of their basic capacity to bear children, which sounds paradoxical, especially in the context of *jāti*-dominated Hindus. Let me expand on it. *Jāti* is determined by birth as a son to a man who belongs to a specific *jāti*. The transmission of *jāti* is from father to son. It is the most important factor in arranged marriage and inheritance. Women may belong to a lineage (*kula*) but cannot transmit it. A man needs a wife to beget children to prepetuate his *jāti* and lineage (*kula*). Obviously, a man has to be sure of his own paternity. Hence, early lawgivers betrayed their anxiety on this point by setting up an elaborate system of manipulating women's sexuality. *Manusmṛti*, the most famous ancient Indian treatise on ritual, social and ethical laws, and the system of penalties, did not consider women fit to be free individuals; they should be under the control of their male protectors—that is, their fathers, husbands, and sons. Note that these lawgivers, who were male and of the Brahman *jāti*, indicated only the spirit of the social values rather than the actual situation.[10]

Not only did the age of marriage for women sink lower and lower until it was normal for a female child to be given in marriage before puberty but also her menstrual flow came to be regarded as polluting and dangerous. A woman in her period used to be avoided by all males, and she was treated as virtually untouchable. Because of this recurrent event in their lives, women came to be branded as basically impure and in need of the most elaborate regimen of fasting and other ritual penance to regain their ritual purity. Somehow, the menstrual blood and women's sexuality were held to be violent and dangerous for males. Even though the advent of a girl's puberty was often celebrated as a happy event and she was feasted and decorated, for the first few days she was required to avoid even meeting male members of her family. The mistrust of a woman's menstrual blood, which established her fertility and hence her usefulness to family and society as a future mother, influenced even childbirth. Like death, birth was associated with blood, destruction, and violence, and so it inflicted impurity on those associated with the event. The mother, the midwife, and everything else associated with childbirth were considered polluting. The special birth chamber was a temporary hut outside the residential area, where the new mother had to spend her period of isolation (six days) with only the midwife looking after her. Other female relatives could visit her but had to ritually purify themselves before entering the household, and all rites of passage were postponed in the family to counteract the effects of pollution during those days. This association of women, blood, and danger is an ancient idea to be found even in the earliest Vedic scriptures. In a myth related in the *Taittirīya Saṁhitā* (*TS*), Indra cut off the heads of Viśvarūpa, the son of Tvaṣṭṛ.[11] Indra thus incurred the great sin of brahminicide. He transferred one-third of his sin to women, and they got their menstruation cycle. Because of this myth, a woman was systematically barred from her ritual duties. Vedic rituals were mostly for progeny and increased grain and cattle, but the principal source of fecundity was banished from the rituals. More and more officiating priests usurped the women's position. It appears almost certain that, as the caste system grew in rigidity, women became the focus of male mistrust as a source of danger for their social status, and hence male domination increased.

The *strī-dharma* enumerated by the lawgivers also lists the elements of a woman's innate nature and clearly reflects society's mistrust of female sexuality and its apprehension of a woman's disloyalty to her husband.[12] In one calendrical Vedic sacrifice, there is a ritual in which the wife of the sacrifice is required to publicly confess the names of her lovers. If she lies, the noose of Varuṇa, the cosmic protector of the universal moral order, would punish her.[13] By contrast, a woman's power of childbearing was always highly valued. As the nurturing female, she not only bore and nurtured her own children but also nurtured her husband. His health, wealth, and longevity depended on her auspicious power derived from her abiding loyalty to her husband. The outward evidence of a woman's chastity and loyalty to her husband was demonstrated by her total submission to her husband's authority. She must accept her husband to be her only deity and spiritual teacher; her greatest virtue lay in serving him with her body and mind. She needed nothing else to secure a position in heaven and to redeem herself. The power of an unequivocally loyal wife was taken to be immense, as expressed in numerous legends. For example, a virtuous wife could stop the natural movements of the sun and the moon or, like Sāvitrī, conquer death.[14]

Just as the Vedic ritualists' gradual removal of women's participation led to the pattern of later Hindu rituals, so also the ancient mythological role model of a virtuous, faithful wife fixed her social position in the Hindu family. Her value in the family depended on her having a socially and economically prosperous husband blessed with health, who lived long after her own demise. Her most important function was to produce and nurture healthy sons to perpetuate her husband's lineage. The welfare of the family depended on her virtue and religiosity.

Thus, women's ritual activities became confined to some locally practiced rites observed during life cycle rituals such as birth and marriage, which were exclusively performed by women. But these rites were not in the same category as other brahmanical religious rites, in which women's participation was seriously undermined.[15] Here, local religious tradition came to women's rescue in the form of an entire corpus of women's rites (*vrata*). I shall presently focus my attention on this form of religious practice.

Now let me turn to the topic of the worship of the Great Goddess and its effect on the social position of Hindu women. Of the two most important roles of women in society–wife and mother–the highest respect and appreciation are reserved for the mother. Mothers are more sacred. In motherhood, women achieve symbiosis with the earth and nature on the one hand and with the Great Goddess, the cosmic mother on the other. The greatest respect that can be shown to a woman is to call her "mother". A young married woman as a potential mother is deemed to be greatly auspicious, as her controlled sexuality promises to bring great prosperity to the family. If she is also the mother of a male child, she is marked as the luckiest woman. Marriage is the main event in a woman's life. A wife is welcomed in her marital family as an embodiment of their future prosperity. Marriage is her only major life cycle rite. A widow has no position in this society. Daughters are treated as beloved temporary members of their natal family but are most unwelcome as permanent members. In her marital family, unless she has mature male children, a widow's position is unenviable. She is held responsible for her husband's death by failing to secure his long life. Her sexuality becomes once again a source of danger. Because a woman is married into the husband's family, if she commits adultery, it brings sin upon the whole family. Hence, as a social safeguard, a widow must remain in a permanent state of mourning, observing strict asceticism to expiate the sin that took her husband from her. Ancient Hindu law did not allow women to inherit any significant patrimony, and often a widow could not inherit from her husband if she had no male child. No provision was made for her to follow any profession except that of servant. Thus, high-caste Hindus, following traditional brahmanical religion, did not show much kindness to a woman as an individual in her own right. Respite came from the bhakti movement and from tantric religion.[16]

The majority of pious Hindus worship some goddess or goddesses as protecting, nourishing, wealth-giving, and motherly deities, though some of them may also be awe-inspiring and destructive, punishing and wielding divine powers, violent and gruesome. The idea of a divine mother who is the source of creation is an ancient notion, found in various contexts in the early scriptures of India, the Vedas (1500-300 B.C.E.). Although at Mohenjo-Daro and other ancient cities archaeologists have discovered indications of goddess worship in an even earlier period of Indian civilization (circa 2000 B.C.E.), the lack of recorded evidence makes it impossible to know the nature of that religion. During the fourth and fifth centuries C.E., a number of religious texts known as the *purāṇas* and *āgamas* glorified the Great Goddess. Foremost among them was the *Mārkaṇḍeya purāṇa.*[17] Thereafter, the cult of the Great Goddess developed its theology and rituals in a great number of exegeses. This written tradition is backed up by a rich tradition of plastic art and cult objects. Thus, it is not difficult to achieve an understanding of the nature and ideology of the worship of the Great Goddess since the early medieval period.

What difference did it make to Hindu social concepts and the Hindu worldview if the Supreme Reality, the ultimate divine, is female and not male? Did it change the character of their faith, their attitude toward the divine, or their attitude and conduct toward their fellow human beings, both male and female? Was it an anomaly that Hindu theology—a theology basically oriented to masculinity—developed a feminine theology? Other questions include when the transition occurred, how Hindu society adjusted its attitude toward its women—a daughter, wife, or mother—in the patrifocal family system, and how the women reacted. These and many other questions confront us as students of Hindu ideas of gender and Hindu religions.[18]

During the second quarter of the first millennium C.E., India saw the rise of various religious systems that developed a theology of what I will call inclusive monotheism. The supreme deity is seen as the creator and the savior and as possessing divine indomitable power and potentiality, the cosmic creative energy. However, this Supreme Divine, who is usually identified with either Śiva or Viṣṇu, both male gods, is also regarded—because of the influence of the monistic idealism of the *Upaniṣad*—as totally transcendent, such that nothing can be predicated of him. The *Upaniṣad* (circa 800-300 B.C.E.) speculated on the existence of a unitary, unique, and transcendental truth or reality, which is the essence of all phenomena (*brahman*) and at the same time the irreducible center or self (*ātman*) of all living beings. For theologians, the supreme god is this transcendental reality, eternal and unchangeable, yet he is the creator and sovereign controller of the cosmos as well as of living beings. Although unique and impersonal, this divine entity can be conceived as Śiva, Viṣṇu or any of their various manifestations.

To relate the divine with the creation within the sphere of epistemology, one needs *Śakti*, the feminine principle. *Śakti* cannot be adequately translated by a single word. The concept of power, potency, and potentiality are all present. God has the potentiality to be everything in the world, the power to do everything in the world—if he did not, he would not be God. At the same time, *Śakti* represents sovereign, divine authority. She is seen as the concentration of divine and human prowess the embodiment of glorious victory and of righteousness in the world arena of the struggle between good and evil. She is also the divine consciousness and wisdom. The divine will is expressed through her, and at the same time that will is translated into action by her. Although she carried out the divine will, on the cosmic level she is autonomous and rules creation through the multifaceted powers or energies that emanate from her. Everything in the world, from souls to stones, is an aspect of *śakti* because it is a manifestation and effect of divine power, and just as *śakti* is a hypostatization of the divine essence, an adjective made noun, and an attribute regarded as principle, so everything else can be referred to as if it were a separate entity. Thus, she is the supreme active godhead and wields her divine power through a myriad of secondary powers or goddesses, each of whom represents one special divine area of cosmic activity. It is always the autonomous power, *śakti*, that is the only true agent, as no one can tell her what to do. Here we come to two distinct philosophical ideas—power and authority. Ultimately, *śakti*'s power and potency are derived from the authority of the supreme divine. There is still no paradox here, only personification, because *śakti* is the divine authority and can be regarded as the divine personality. To move to the still more concrete level of myth, *śakti* is God's wife. Because she is related to God as personality is related to a person, their inextricable connection is symbolized by her being half the body of God. The goddess can be one or many, but the local names or forms of the divine feminine principle make no difference to its function as the repository of power and embodiment of God's cosmic force, potency, power, and energy.

This is, in fact, a form of idealism, in that the world is the content of God's thought and the divine power is the thought of God at the primal moment of creation. God's thought is the moment when the plenum of God's pure and contentless awareness is disturbed by God's will to create, which moves divine awareness to the condition of differentiated apperception of experience and its content. This slip from pure self-awareness to will and knowledge and its content is the vibrating point of primal creation. *Śakti* is both God's will and God's omniscience, as well as the content of that knowledge. It is thus the divine feminine principle that is deemed to be the creatrix. She embodies all empirical experience, being both the components of such experience—that is, the signifier and the signified (*vācya* and *vācaka*). Creation is simultaneously both a limitation of the ultimately transcendent awareness and the transformation of the pure spirit into gross material things. The progressive creation is seen in three ranges or gamuts: from conscious to unconscious, subtle to gross, and simple to complex. All three are coordinate and in reality just aspects of *śakti.* Deluded by *śakti's māyā* dimension, human being take the end result of these processes as absolutely real. Salvation lies in the knowledge or realization penetrating these processes and understanding the basic unity of all experiences, all objects, and all awarenesses. Then the delusion (*māyā*) is gone, establishing a lasting realization of the essential unity between the microcosm and the macrocosm. There are five divine acts on the cosmic level: creation; sustenance; destruction or involution, taking creation to be a process of evolution; delusion; and grace leading to salvation. Delusion is the situation when the microcosm is experienced as totally limited by time, space, and karma, making them fragmented and suffering from transience. This, too, is an act of *śakti* concealing the true nature of human beings. Gross matter is seen as the source of creation both in the biological model and in the evolutionary model. It is matter (*prakṛti*) that evolves into all gross objects, all forms. *Prakṛti* also means Mother Nature.

But in tantric theology there also developed the idea of the cosmic feminine principle as Goddess and sexual partner of God, giving birth to creation. This divine sexuality of the Goddess is equated with divine power. This divine power that carried out the divine will is the beneficial power, the nurturing Mother Goddess. But as Māyā the deluder, she is also the great divine aggressive force, which represents divine righteous anger bringing justice and punishing the unjust, the transgressor against cosmic moral laws. Māyā is also called the seducer, here recalling the aspect of her feminine uncontrolled sexuality. She seduces humankind into the bondage of transitoriness, but side by side with her seductive personality is her natural motherly aspect. Full of love for her children, she provides them with the ways and means of receiving her grace, which is the only way to salvation and bliss. This is her fifth cosmic function. The path is expressed in the scriptures, liturgy, and exegeses. All she demands is total faith in her and dedication to her.

Thus, we see that the paradigm of femaleness is reflected on all the different levels of the cosmic principle of *śakti.* Her nature is motherly[19] and wifely.[20] She performs cosmic functions on the authority of God, seen as her husband, and she procreates as the cosmic mother, but her sexuality has the dangerous quality of seduction and even deception. She not only dims humankind's proper awareness of reality and truth, thereby creating the world of complex diversities, but also could at any moment delude their intelligence and derail them from the path of righteousness. At the same time, she is seen as the nemesis that brings down divine punishment.

The concept of the Goddess reveals the central understanding of feminine nature in a society dominated by the brahmanical idea of a caste-oriented community. She is *prakṛti*, the mother or source of all; *śakti*, the indomitable potency and fecundity; and finally *māyā*, the seductress. All three aspects of the Goddess deal with her sexuality and reflect the two accepted roles of women in society– namely, wife and mother. A virtuous wife is she who is sexually loyal to her husband as long as he lives and even after his death. Once married, her sexuality is under the total control of her husband, and any breach of it drives her out of the status of wifehood forever. In Brahmanism, there are strictures against the remarriage of women. This is normal in a society where caste membership is entirely dependent on patrilineality. Motherhood within this normative condition is highly extolled as the fulfillment of a woman's social life. She is the nurturing *prakṛti*. In fact, a sexually active woman as a married wife is considered to be the source of all good fortune, and she is deemed to be immensely auspicious (*sumaṅgalī*). A girl is groomed from her childhood to be a good wife and mother. All social life cycle rites for women overtly deal with her sexuality. As a child, she is often worshipped as an image of the goddess, her purity then unbroken by puberty. At puberty, a symbolic marriagelike ritual is often held to provide her with a surrogate bridgeroom, often an affine girl or a divine image, and she is made aware of her loss of purity and taught caution in relationships with male members of the family. She is then married as soon as possible to bring her sexuality under her husband's control. Finally, her motherhood is greeted with several rites.

Her widowhood, by contrast, is stamped on her by her dress, demeanor, and lifestyle. She is the most inauspicious human being. She has the potency but no proper way of fulfillment, no controller. Uncontrolled potency is like uncontrolled divine potency, dangerous and violent, like Bhadrakālī. The harsh treatment of widows stems from this fear and the desire to control her by other, cruel means.

The reason for Hindu women's subsidiary position in the family should be evident from the material presented so far. I have also made clear that the fact that certain sections of Hindu society worship the Goddess as the active creatrix and even as the saving godhead did not radically change women's position in the Hindu social structure. In fact, as noted before, the feminine paradigm conditioned the view of the devotees about their adored Goddess.[21] The same can be said about the view of the followers of devotional Hinduism concerning their womenfolk although the situation of women in the bhakti movements varies considerably in different parts of South Asia and at different strata of society.[22]

Vratas of Hindu Women

Having given two somewhat pessimistic accounts of the position of women in the Hindu worldview, I shall now give an account of their position in the same society that suggests they are far more powerful in real life than they would appear to be from the religious records. In a real sense, the control of the family usually remains in the hands of the mistress of the house. In the family, little girls get lessons in social behavior that enable them to improve their position in their own society. It is her impurity that makes a woman dangerous to a society in which male ideology prevails. In the case of the Goddess, her sexuality is inseparably entwined with her divine spouse, whose *śakti* she is. But in women such sexuality is viewed as dangerous, and women are taught from childhood to be modest and to suppress their sexuality. Moreover, perfect chastity and loyalty to her husband accords a woman moral superiority over other members of her family.

However, the most important means to derive real moral superiority lies in conducting a spotless religious life and thereby acquiring spiritual power and efficacy, which remove women's impurity. From the teachings of her religions, as outlined earlier, a woman learns how to remove all negative elements from her innate nature (*sva-bhāva*) and overcome her alleged impurity by intensively practicing religious acts (*vratas*) available to her. It is not easy. Living within the family and fulfilling their social duties, women have little opportunity for ostentatious spirituality. Moreover, traditional *vratas* prescribed in brahmanical religious literature are not always available to women.[23] What has evolved out of the utter necessity for self-assertion is a huge parallel religious culture specially followed by women. They are collectively called religious vows (*vratas*) of women.[24] From early girlhood, a woman is encouraged to take up several vows aimed at producing a desirable husband, an affectionate mother-in-law, or long life and prosperity for her brothers. As soon as she is married, vows are taken up for the prosperity of her marital home and family, a good harvest, long life for her husband and children, and safety for her marital and natal families. As soon as she becomes a mother, the welfare of her children is to be safeguarded by taking up yet another vow.

These vows have certain common features: total or partial fasting for the period, voluntary restriction of certain daily habits of food and dress, rigorous purificatory rites, and abstention from sexual acts. We can group them as ascetic abstention, self-mortification, and meticulous physical purity. In these aspects, women's *vratas* do not much differ from the general religious *vratas* mentioned in brahmanical sacred treatises. Instead of the mantras or religious formulas in Sanskrit that are uttered in brahmanical practice, there are metrical compositions in the vernacular that tell the name of the deity and the purpose of the vow, together with recitation of a balladlike narrative in which the deity of the *vrata* rescues her devotees from dangerous situations and bestows on them great prosperity and fulfillment of their wishes. Women who observe these vows often get together and perform them collectively, which develops a certain feminine solidarity. The freehand drawings of diagrams and symbols and the compulsory requirement that participants attentively recite and listen to the narration reveal the underlying element of magic in these rites. The narrative always emphasizes the power of the deity in whose name the vow is taken and who is worshipped. The story emphasizes the efficacy of the ritual practice to fulfill the wishes of the performer, and most important of all, no male priest is needed—in fact, no officiating ritual agent is allowed in. It is entirely a women's affair. In traditional families, women members undertake vast numbers of such vows, and clearly these women are dedicating a great part of their lives to these auspicious religious observances. Because the prayers are always for the longevity and prosperity of their menfolk, in the latter's eyes, the purity and auspicious nature of these women are greatly enhanced. By the constant practice of *vrata,* which combines both the first and second method of redeeming *karmaphala,* women in traditional Hindu families become great ritual specialists; in fact, the religious duties of male Hindus often totally depend on their wives' active assistance. Far from being a hindrance to male religiosity and a source of danger because of her impure nature, a woman in the family is held–thanks to her voluntary ascetic practice–to be morally, ritually, and spiritually pure. Instead of being cast out of religious practices, women in this sphere of religious activity are the principal actors. All the rites revolve around women as the center of gravity.

To illustrate my point, let me describe a few *vratas.*[25] First a married woman commonly observes the Lakṣmī *vrata.* Lakṣmī is the benign and compassionate goddess of wealth, grains, and beauty. As soon as a woman is married, her mother-in-law teaches her to perform the Lakṣmī *vrata* every Thursday or Friday. She fasts on that day, takes her morning bath and wets her hair, and then worships Lakṣmī, whose presence is invoked in a full water pot that is covered with a five-leaf spray of mango. A banana is placed on the leaves, and the water pot is placed on a metal plate that holds a few cowries (an older form of money). A pān leaf, a whole areca nut, fruits, and sweets are offered. The worshipper purifies every object of offering by marking it with the sacred red *sindur* (vermilion) paste. Then she and other married women of the family, who have all fasted, take part in the worship. They offer flowers, *vilva* leaves and *kuśa* grass,[26] a lamp, and incense to Lakṣmī in the water pot. After worshipping the deity with lamp (*ārati*), all the women sit in a circle around the chief worshipper, who recites the story (*kathā*) of the *vrata*. On completion of these steps, the women are free to eat their normal meal.

The *vrata-kathā* usually follows a set pattern: some person falls into adversity and then meets either the deity whose *vrata* story is being recounted or worshippers of that deity. The suffering person undertakes the *vrata*, overcomes the misfortune, fully recovers a former happy life, and gains material prosperity. Some relative or friend witnesses the *pūjā* and derides it and its deity. The latter punishes the scoffer by calling down great calamities. Finally, at the request of a close relative (daughter, wife, or mother-in-law) or as a result of the deity's appearance in disguise or in a dream, this person repents and humbly worships the deity in the proper manner. The person's sins are forgiven, reparation of losses is made, and great prosperity is bestowed. Honesty, faith, and humility are the qualities extolled. Above all, an unflinching faith in the deity's power and the efficacy of the meticulously performed *vrata* are strongly advocated.

A married woman usually takes the weekly Lakṣmī *vrata* for life. The annual Lakṣmī *vrata*, also taken for life, is a very important event, especially in the eastern rice-growing areas of Bengal. It occurs on the first full-moon evening after Durgā's annual worship in early autumn. The goddess is clearly related to the rice grain, and this is the time when, after the monsoon, the rice grain ripens in the fields and the peasants' and farmers' wives worship the grain goddess in anticipation of a good harvest. She is primarily represented by a new terra-cotta plate filled with rice, fruit, and other products of the land that is covered by a round, convex earthen plate. This second plate is painted with figures in red, green, yellow, blue, and black. The figures include the goddess Lakṣmī, her attendants, her vehicle the owl, and ears of rice grain. On the day of the annual *vrata* performance, all performers must fast the whole day and prepare as much food as possible as an offering. They must observe strict purity rules. The house is cleaned and then decorated with line drawings made with thin rice paste. The designs consist of lotus diagrams, rice plants with ears of rice, and small footprints on which Lakṣmī steps to enter the house. The altar, a low table, is decorated with drawings of small lotuses, a comb and a mirror, ornaments, and a pair of small footprints in the middle of the front border. The sacred water pot is placed in the center.[27] The Lakṣmī plate is set just behind it. Sometimes a small mock boat is made of the outer casing of the banana plant, containing little cylinders made of the same, which are filled with various lentils and beans to indicate the later event of the harvest coming home.

After the evening worship and the recitation of the *vrata* story, the worshippers break their fast (*pāraṇa*) by taking a little bit of the offered food, but they do not take rice. Then all of the adult women keep vigil the entire night, by playing dice or card games, awaiting Lakṣmī's arrival. The day before, the worshippers must observe celibacy and eat only once, at noon, rice and vegetables boiled together. On the following day, they must observe the same restrictions, breaking their fast only at noon. This is called keeping the *vāra*,[28] which is essential for all annual *vratas*. The main purpose of the Lakṣmī *vrata* is to keep the family economy in good shape.

Another *vrata* for life is that of Vipattāriṇī, she who removes all calamities. This annual event is observed on any day between the third and the ninth day of the bright fortnight of Āṣāḍha (June-July) to remove bad luck and sudden calamity. It must be observed on a Saturday or a Tuesday. The deity is Durgā or Caṇḍi, who is very popular in Bengal as the remover of all life's dangers and misfortunes. Besides the ordinary ingredients of the offering, the worshipper must get thirteen types of fruit, thirteen types of flowers, thirteen leaves of pān and areca nuts, and thirteen threads bracelets, each consisting of thirteen strands of red thread bunched together with thirteen knots, each knot being stuck with a *kuśa* tip. Thirteen little baskets are offered, each containing one of the special offerings. Apparently, thirteen is a magic number. From the day before the ceremony, the worshipper starts keeping the *vāra.* She must fast completely on the day of the *vrata.* After the worship of the goddess, she recites or listens to the recitation of the *vrata-kathā.* Then, having prostrated herself before the goddess, she puts on one of the red thread bracelets on her own right hand and ties others on the right hands of other family members. She completes her *pāraṇa* the next day at noon by taking a fruit, after which she can eat her usual meal of rice

Although the *Śivarātri vrata* is observed by all devout Hindus, it has special significance for unmarried girls. The *vrata* brings them merit in the form of a suitable husband. Girls under the guidance of older women of the family fast the whole day. They observe *vāra* the day before. Later at night on the *Śivarātri* (the fourteenth of the dark fortnight of Māgha, i.e., January-February), the girls start preparing Śiva *liṅgas* (the phallic symbol of Śiva) with clay collected the day before from a pond or lake. Then they put four *liṅgas* on a metal plate and worship one of these with flowers, fruits, 108 *vilva* leaves, the juice of *vilva* fruit, milk, and coconut milk. The important rite is to pour milk, water, and *vilva* fruit juice on top of the *liṅga,* which has a drop-shaped clay bead on it. They keep a vigil, and at the start of each of the remaining three watches of the night, one of the

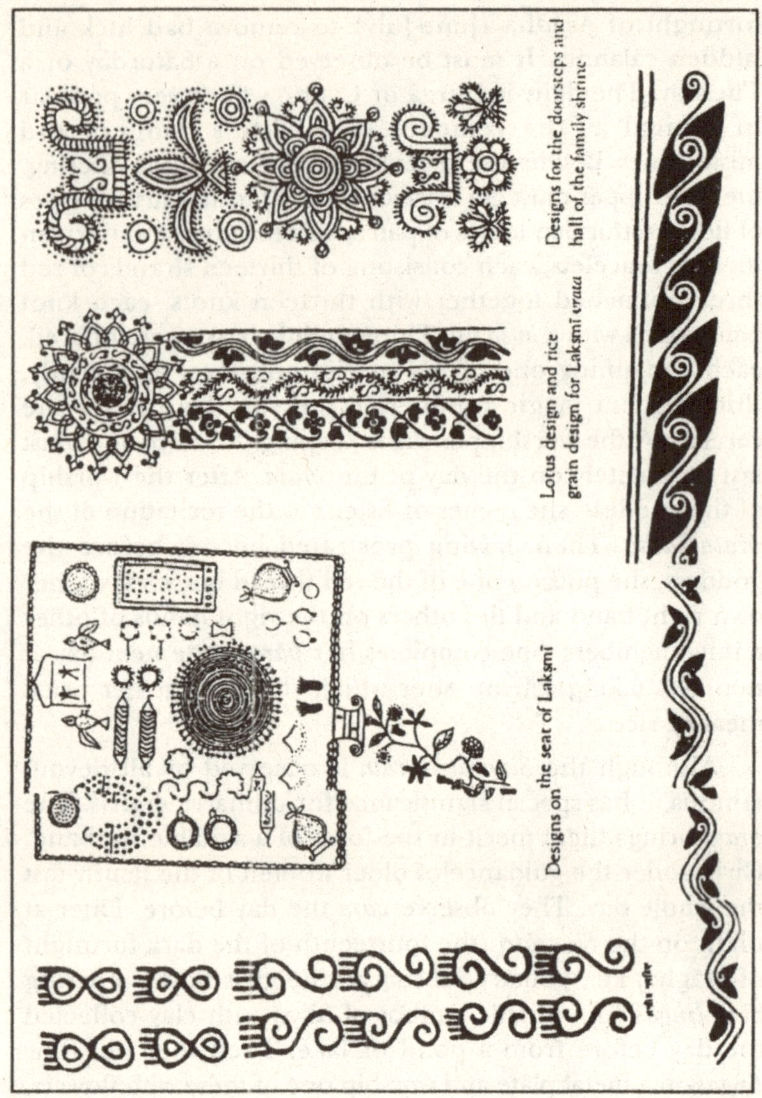

Figure 1: Decorative motifs and designs for women's rituals.

remaining Śiva *liṅgas* is worshipped in the same way as before. The worship of the last *liṅga* finishes with the reciting of the *vrata-kathā*. In the early morning, sacred water is poured over the *liṅgas*, which breaks their form. Then the clay and most of the *pūjā* ingredients, except the food, are thrown into a river. The worshippers then take a bath and break their fast (*pāraṇa*) by drinking *vilva* fruit juice.

What are the important features of these *vratas*?

1. *Vratas* are undertaken either for a limited period or for life. They are not compulsory rituals, but for women in traditional families some *vratas* are so normal that they have become almost compulsory. It is quite normal for married women to observe two weekly *vratas*. If a woman is menstruating, she can still observe the fast while another suitable family member performs the actual *pūjā*.
2. The sense of group solidarity is really noteworthy. Women living in the same neighborhood tend to perform *vratas* together. Older women or experienced women not only teach other women how to perform a *vrata* but also perform it together, often crossing their caste threshold. There are many *vrata* stories in which Brahmin and cowherd women are great friends and observe the same *vratas;* even an outcaste woman may see the power of a *vrata* and undertake it, or sometimes an outcaste woman performs a *vrata* and teaches a higher-caste woman in distress how to perform it. It is also a requirement of a *vrata* ritual that the recitation of its story must have an audience, and even a friend from a low caste may help a *vrata* observer by listening to the recitation. In the world of *vrata* stories, women seem to join in each other's lives without bothering about caste or class barriers.
3. Bathing, donning freshly washed clothes, and then fetching pure water in the water pot are important features. The goddess, who is worshipped in most *vratas*

in some form or other, is always worshipped in the water of the water pot (*ghaṭa*). In some cases, the performers must go to a body of water, but *vratas* are usually performed at home, either on specially consecrated ground or inside the family shrine.

4. These rituals are almost entirely outside the domain of men. If the invoked deity belongs to the official Hindu pantheon, a priest may be employed for the central *pūjā* rites, but for the majority of the *vratas* male priests are not needed, and women perform all the rites themselves. Nevertheless, in almost all casts, the beneficiaries of the *vrata* are the male members of the family. There are, of course, *vratas* observed for the benefit of the worshipper, for instance, to get a suitable bridegroom or to obtain a husband's love and attention.
5. The paraphernalia (*upakaraṇa*) of worship (*pūjā*) often involve magical symbolism. Diagrams are drawn with special materials, such as rice powder, red *sindur*, and cow dung, to ensure the purity of the auspicious site of the ritual and to safeguard it. Sacred designs like the lotus or conch shell are employed to enhance the purity of sacred space. Objects within the boundary of a diagram acquire magical value. For example, a performer may draw some jewelry inside the diagram in the hope that the deity will give them to her. Sometimes important points of the *vrata* story are drawn inside the diagram.[29] Magical numbers, special sorts of fruit and flowers for specific deities, and compulsory attendance for all women to some *vrata* performance to listen to the narration of myths attached to the *vrata*, point toward the use of magic to propitiate a deity who has power to manipulate human destiny.
6. *Vratas* for a husband's protection and prosperity are almost always finalized by inviting, decorating, and feeding a married woman, often a Brahmin, and giving her presents and money. In some special *vratas*, often

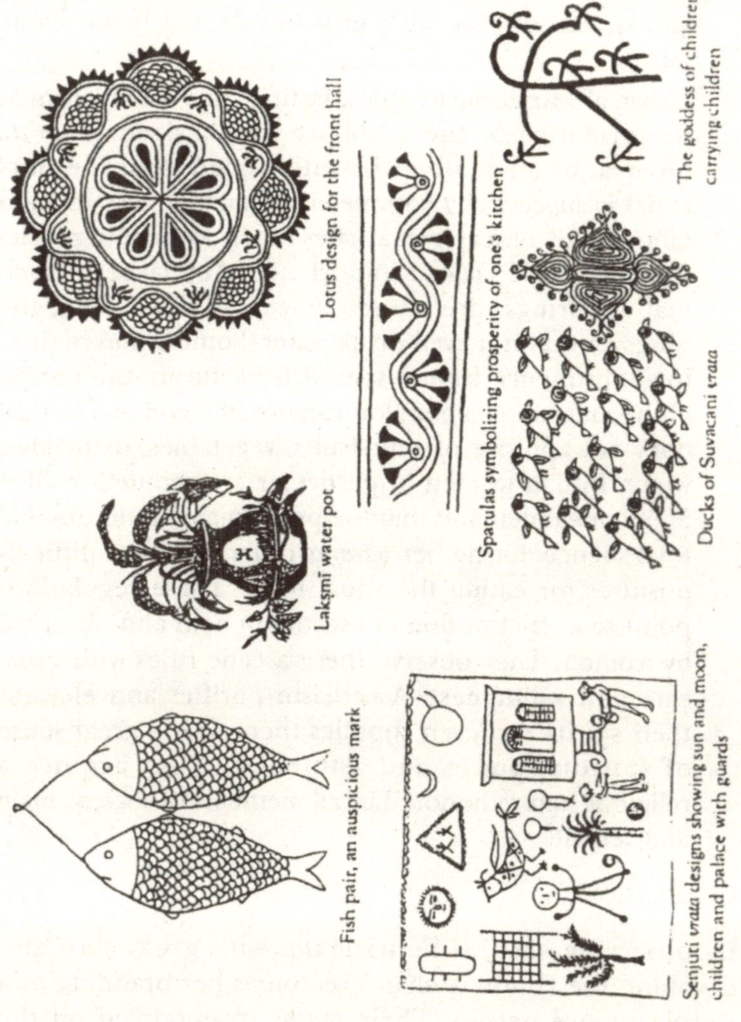

Figure 2: More decorative motifs and designs for women's rituals.

related to the goddess Gaurī, the daughter of Himālaya and spouse of Śiva, little girls are treated in the same way.

7. Above all, strict purity rules, fasting, and uninterrupted performance of the *vrata* are emphasized. A *vrata* observation must never be interrupted until the final ritual is successfully completed. Similarly, certain food taboos and other special rites, such as keeping strict silence, are of crucial importance. Any lapse in such matters brings dire consequences. When fasting, the observer may not even drink water. Some *vratas* require total abstinence from a special fruit during the period of the *vrata* observation; for instance, the goddess Santoṣī does not approve of sour fruits, vegetables, or pickles, which Indian women in particular are reputed to like. Some *vratas* demand that the performer should observe total silence during her *pāraṇa*; others stipulate difficult postures for eating the ritual meal. These regulations point to a strict notion of asceticism held and observed by women. They observe these ascetic rules with great care and willingness. Asceticism purifies and elevates their spirits and even supplies them with a great sense of spiritual power and astuteness. They acquire a religious stature honored by all members of society, male and female.

Conclusion

By observing such arduous *vratas* with great care and devotion, the Hindu woman overcomes her branding as a sinful, impure person. Their *vratas* are modeled on the brahmanical religious rites and sectarian rituals and follow the general Hindu religious value system. Women also follow the ethos and practices of the renouncer yogins. On top of all these, their natural affinity for the value of the religion of bhakti has helped them to follow their own ways with confidence. The ecstatic bhakti religion does not condemn passion–even sexual passion. In that religion, women have found religious freedom and dignity. Historically, with the help of that religion, they rose above their debilitating "innate nature" and became spiritual equals to the best of the religious personalities in the ancient and modern history of the Hindu religions. Instead of being a source of danger and degradation to her family, a woman is looked on as the repository of family welfare and spirituality. The equal of Sāvitrī and Sītā, she is endowed with the beneficial feminine power of the goddess, which commands both respect and awe.

The mythological role models present few options for women. They can be virtuous and suffer like Sītā, the virtuous wife of the righteous King Rāma of the epic *Rāmayaṇa*, and mutely or perhaps not so mutely accept their destiny. Innumerable *vrata* legends narrate how a virtuous and uncomplaining sufferer finally triumphs; that is, indeed, a bhakti concept that shows total dependence on God's will. They can be virtuous but assertive and aggressive, like the dangerous goddesses, as in the story of Kaṇṇaki-Paṭṭini in Cilappatikāram,[30] or the wife of the leper.[31] Virtuous elderly widows also follow that pattern and obtain respect. The third option is to turn to religion and leave one's family. I have shown why this is not an easy option.[32] It is available in some Śaiva sects, and, at their inception, many great women saints adorn the Nayannārs, Vīraśaivas, and Tantric Śaivas. In eastern India, the Tantric Śaivas have continued to uphold the special position of women saints and spiritual leaders. Sometimes the status of a woman guru is higher than that of men.[33] In some esoteric sects of Bāuls, for instance, a woman is considered the most suitable of all gurus. Their strict sectarian ethics requires the Tantric Śaivas to show special respect to women.

For ordinary women in Hindu families, however, the practice of *vrata* and the strict maintenance of the purity and honor of the family enable a woman to enhance not only the family's prosperity and social respectability but also her own spiritual progress. It enhances her power as well. For women who stay in family life, *vratas* are the most important religious practices for redemption, spiritual elevation and even release from *saṃsāra*. What the renouncers achieve by leaving family life, women achieve within the family by practicing austerity and the self-restraint required for the observance of the rituals of countless *vratas*.

NOTES

1 Doniger (1996), pp. 157ff.

2 *Markaṇḍeya purāṇa,* ch. 80-81, describing the reigns of Vaivasvata Manu and of Sāvarṇi Manu, when the goddess appeared to kill the buffalo demon.

3 Coburn (1991); Brown (1974).

4 Gupta (1991), pp. 193-209; Erndl (1996), pp. 173-94.

5 *Mahābhārata* Vanaparva, 3.277-83; *Rāmāyaṇa,* passim.

6 *Vrata* consists of a corpus of female religious practices that exist parallel to traditional brahmanical and sectarian religious practices. See McGee (1991), pp. 71-88; Robinson (1985), passim.

7 One's *sva-dharma* is determined by one's innate nature, *sva-bhāva.*

8 Leslie (1989), passim. See also Gupta (1991). A woman is by nature (*sva-bhāva*) not only polluted but also potentially dangerous because of her excessive sexuality. Therefore, in her family her sexuality should always be controlled, and she should always be subservient to male authority. Her sexuality is a source of prosperity when it is active but controlled by her husband; in any other situation, she must totally repress it.

9 Most important Hindu ritual acts for rectifying one's bad *karma-phala* are called *vratas.* The performer of a *vrata* declares an intention to follow a special ritual program of a certain deity or deities over a fixed span of time. The period can be any

length of time. The program includes elements of austerity and ritual expiatory acts meant to purify the performer's body, mind, and spirit.

10 Leslie (1989), p. 328.

11 Smith (1991), pp. 23-26, 42-45; Viśvarūpa had three heads (TS, 2.5.1).

12 Leslie (1989), pp. 246-49, 318-21.

13 Kane (1941), ch. 31, pp. 1091-1106.

14 *Mārkaṇḍeya purāṇa*, xvi, 14-90.

15 For example, in the *Bṛhaddharma Purāṇa* (Uttarkhaṇḍa, ch. 8. 7), married women are prohibited from observing religious rites involving fasting and the like because their only religious rite is to act in accordance with their husbands' wishes. See also Robinson (1985), pp. 190-93.

16 Gupta (1991). See also McGee (1991), pp. 74-76. In sectarian religions, a great number of rites called *vrata* are prescribed for sect members, which are often performed by both sexes. See also Robinson (1985), pp. 1950-99.

17 Agarwala (1963), preface, pp. iv-xii; Gupta (1979), pp. 8-10, 159-60.

18 McDermott (1996), pp. 294-304.

19 As indicated by the idea of *mātṛkā* and the epithet *jagajjananī*—that is, the mother of the universe.

20 As seen in the conception of Umā-Pārvatī and Lakṣmī.

21 In all visual representations of Viṣṇu lying on the couch, made by the body of Anata, the cosmic serpent, the goddess Lakṣmī is portrayed as massaging the feet of her divine spouse, Viṣṇu. In Bengal, the most popular form of Umā-Pārvatī is the mother of Gaṇeśa.

22 Gupta (1991).

23 Robinson (1985), p. 192; see also Gupta (1991).

24 McGee (1991), pp. 71-88; Robinson (1985), pp. 195-211.

25 For a fuller description, see Kayal (1969), pp. 177-200; and Tiwari (1991), passim.

26 Pān is betel leaf; vilva is *Aegle* marmelos, a tree whose fruit and leaves both possess medicinal value; *kuśa* grass is always used in ritual worship as a purifying object.

27 See figures 1 and 2; and Thakur (1956).

28 *Vāra* is a Bengali term meaning restriction of food and drink, observed by the performers of a *vrata* on the day(s) before and after the *vrata*.

29 See figures 1 and 2.

30 Zvelebil (1975), p. 112.

31 *Mārkaṇḍeya purāṇa*, ch. 80-81.

32 Gupta (1990), pp. 50-59; (1991), passim.

33 Personal discussion with a Bāul lineage head. See also Vidyālaṅkāra (1820).

12. Lālan Fakir: The Confluence of Islam and Hindu Popular Mysticism

The history of Bengal's literature as well as its religions would be incomplete without a thorough study of the Bengali lyrics composed and sung by generations of *fakirs* and *bāuls* of rural Bengal. It is well known that Rabindranath Thakur was greatly influenced by *bāul* mysticism and by their lyric idiom. This latter has been reflected in many of his poems.[1] Whether his understanding of *bāul* mysticism was correct is not relevant to this paper, which is a short introduction to the mystic religion of a famous *bāul* of Kusthiya, now in Bangladesh. One reason for his fame in Bengal is the great admiration Rabindranath felt for his particular mystical experiences and his philosophy of life. These he expressed in marvellously lyrical and picturesque language in countless songs.

He was called Lālan Fakir and belonged to a sect which could be loosely said to follow a form of Darveshī mysticism.[2] To his followers he was known as Lālan Sāi.[3] It becomes evident from his songs that Lālan was an intelligent, alert and fairly educated man. According to the tradition of his sect, Lālan was born towards the end of the 18th century, of high caste; his *kāyastha* parents belonged to the rural Hindu middle class community. He lost his father early and was brought up by his mother. As was the contemporary custom, he married as a boy. Obviously, he was very religious and was a Vaiṣṇava by choice. In his early teens he joined a group of pilgrims to Puri. But soon after starting, he came down with a virulent attack of smallpox and was abandoned by the road side by his companions. They took him for dead and on their return told his family so. Meanwhile, Lālan was rescued by a poor Muslim man who, together with his wife, nursed him back to health. This childless couple adopted Lālan as their son and he lived with them for quite some time. During this period he met and became a follower of Sirāj Shāh, who subsequently initiated Lālan into his religion. Tradition also says that before becoming a disciple of Sirāj, Lālan did pay a visit to his mother and wife, who declined to accept him back home, since he had lost caste by staying and eating with a Muslim family. Probably the village of his adoptive parents was far away from his home, preventing him from going back earlier. Nothing more is known about him except that he died in 1890 at a very ripe age.[4] One of his disciples, Duddu Shāh, in the second half of the 19th century made some of Lālan's religious ideas clearer, in a number of songs composed in a more modern Bengali than that used by Lālan Shāh.[5] Lālan's headquarter (akhāṛā) was in Kusthiya district. This place was remembered by his followers long after his death. But it never became a sacred place like a *dargāh*, nor was his death anniversary observed by his followers at this place as is customary for Sufi saints.

THE BĀULS

Bāṅglār bāul o bāul gān, by Upendranath Bhattacharya is still the only comprehensive study on the *bāuls* and their songs. Earlier studies of note are those by S.B. Das Gupta and K.M. Sen.[6] K.M. Sen was the pioneer in trying to bring the *bāuls* to the notice of scholars. According to Bhattacharya, the *bāul* movement started in the middle of the 17th century. The 18th and 19th centuries were the most productive period of the movement. The present century has witnessed a gradual decline of the *bāuls*, who now at the end of the century most probably face extinction.

Who were these *bāuls*? *Bāuls* were a heterogeneous group of sects, both Muslim and Hindu, mainly drawn from agricultural and other labourers. The Muslims were generally called *fakirs* and their songs are often called *murśida* and *marifati* songs;[7] the Hindus are generally called *bāuls* and they are often overtly Vaiṣṇava in their inclinations and behaviour. However, both followed more or less the same type of secret ritual practice, *sādhanā*, based on a simplified interpretation of the ancient Buddhist *sahaja yāna sādhanā* and the *Haṭhayoga* practices of the Nātha yogins.[8]

It is well known that in medieval India various traditions of religious thought and practice, both Hindu and Muslim, came together to form a broad movement of mystical devotionalism. Kabīr, Dādu, Rāmdās and Caitanya all contributed to the development of this syncretistic religious ideology, which became immensely popular among the people of northern India. Lālan, like other *bāuls*, was aware of this movement and often responded in his songs to the same ideology:

> "My master is imprisoned at the doorstep of His devotee.
> He does not discriminate between Hindus and Muslims.
> Intoxicated by his pure devotion
> Kabīr, who is a Muslim weaver,
> Has chosen Kṛṣṇa of Braja
> To dedicate himself and everything he possessed."[9]

In Bengal the independent Sultans encouraged Hindu-Muslim harmonization. It is said that Hussain Shah (1493-1519) introduced into Bengal the worship of Satya Pīr, a curious Sufi-cum-Vaiṣṇava divinity. The two senior theologians of Bengal Vaisnavism, Rupa and Sanātana Gosvāmī, held very high positions in the court of Hussain Shah.

The Muslim community in Bengal had always been large and consisted predominantly of peasants and fishermen. The overwhelming majority were those of converts. It has been suggested that the success of Islamization of Bengal was due to the undercurrent of Buddhist *Vajra yāna/sahaja yāna* practitioners who were diffused among the rural poor in pre-Islamic Bengal. Under the Sena kings, who were orthodox Hindus from South India, Bengal experienced a great revival of the Hindu caste system and Brahmanical fundamentalism.

Under this pressure, the Hindu lower castes and the Buddhists suffered a great deal of indignity and social injustice. The early Sufi religious leaders who converted so many peasants, fishermen, and other poor working people, were pious, fair-minded, sympathetic and permissive in dealing with the new converts. These virtues appealed to the socially oppressed individuals and induced them to become Muslims.[10]

How far this suggestion is correct is difficult to ascertain in the present state of our knowledge of the history of Islam in Bengal.

One point may be mentioned here. The scholars who proposed the above-mentioned theory took as their model Geertz's study of the Indonesian Muslims — another case of mass conversion of a rice-growing peasant community. The comparison seems to be logical.

The tolerant behaviour of the early *Pīrs* and *fakirs* resulted in a great variety of unorthodox practices. Later the radical Sufis were having a further unorthodox influence. The secret practices of mystic sects both Muslim and non-Muslim interacted quite freely.[11] For men of simple piety subtle theological and ideological differences did not mean much. For the unlettered poor of rural Bengal, written traditions, whether Sanskrit, Arabic or Persian (much Sufi ideology was recorded in Persian), were completely inaccessible. They depended entirely on the oral tradition of the line of pupillary succession of the same saintly *guru* or *Pīr*, a line usually no more than a few generations in depth. Religious equality and the freedom of every individual sect-member to practise secret rituals were the social keynotes of the Buddhist *Vajra yāna* religion, and this also was characteristic of Sufi ideology. Under Caitanya's influence the new form of devotion (*bhakti*) to God, heavily charged with passionate love and yearning for Him, spread among all mystic sects whether Muslim or Non-Muslim. This passionate love for God gave a new meaning to the human body, in that it enables a person to experience such deep emotions. In this idea one may detect strong influence of the Sufi concept that God created man in his own image to enjoy man's love for His own glory. Thus man is glorified as God's mirror-image and as the seat of God.

It is against the background of all these concepts and ideologies, as they filtered down to the often uneducated village holy men that one should understand the *bāuls*. The three most important characteristics of a *bāul* are his simple piety, his universal sympathy for human beings, and his love and yearning for God. Lālan sang,

"The man of my heart is not in this country.
How can I remain here?
How can I stay in this land?
Oh my beloved, these people are not good.
They won't let me talk about Kṛṣṇa.
If I am always weeping how can I please any one?
It is my own bad luck.
Don't you know that, dear Kṛṣṇa?
I can't breathe here.
Lālan says, Oh! what shall I do?
I shall leave my home and live in the forest."[12]

The *bāuls* do not make much of the differences between Muslims and Hindus. A *guru* or a *murśida*, respectively the Hindu and Muslim names of religious teachers, may and does take disciple from both religious communities. The Muslims take the title of *fakir* and their teachers are entitled *Shāh*, which is a known Sufi custom. The non-Muslim *bāuls* are almost always outwardly Vaiṣṇavas and hence often take up the title Dās, servant (of God). They are generally referred to as *bāul*. The word *bāul* means a crazy man; in this case, a God-crazy man. The Sufi equivalent of *bāul* is *divānā*, one who is mad for divine love. *Bāuls* wear the standard dress of a Sufi *fakir* and carry similar accessories: rosary necklace, staff, a hanging shoulder bag, etc.

SĀDHANĀ

All *bāuls* practise a type of secret ritual programme closely resembling the practises of *Haṭha yoga* and the sexual practises of the Vaiṣṇava *sahajiyās*. They follow the yogic exercise of breath control, *prāṇāyāma*, and certain yogic postures to control the muscles of the abdomen, rectum and sex organs. The yogic process they follow is a version of the *kuṇḍalini yoga.*[13] The secret rites are called the piercing or controlling of the four 'moons'. These 'moons' are semen and menstrual flow, which are the important ones, and urine and faeces, which are of secondary importance. The yogic training is called *kāya sādhanā* meaning the practice of controlling one's physical functions. A *bāul* learns to control his semen and other physical waste.

For a *bāul* a woman partner is essential. His main *sādhanā* for the direct experience of God is not mental but physical. Although they admit the transcendence of a God who is at the same time inherent in all, their goal is to enjoy communion with God as the enjoyer of His female principle, *prakṛti.*[14] This aspect of God is termed '*sahaja mānuṣa*'. This is the primordial polarized form of God when He passionately enjoys the ecstasy of union with His *prakṛti.* In this aspect He is the enjoyer of perfect bliss, and a *bāul* aims to be united with Him in this aspect to experience the same bliss, which is a step forward to their main goal. This experience is only possible when the *bāul* can, through *sādhanā,* identify his essential self, manifest in his semen, with the cosmic *prakṛti.* As the cosmic male principle is manifest in the semen so also the female principle is manifest in the menstrual flow. These are the concrete forms (*rūpa*) that the abstract God assumes in the polarized state of the created world. But at the same time He abides in every person as his essence, in his transcendental form (*svarūpa*), which can be experienced in the *ājñā cakra,* the sixth yogic centre of the human body, as just a mass of light. *Sahaja mānuṣa* is the plenitude of aesthetic delight, *rasa*:

"What beauty pervades the two-petalled (lotus, i.e. *ajñā cakra*)
Its enchanting form is glittering.
How can I describe that form?
It is superior to countless artificial lights all together (gas light?).
Even the brilliance of the crest-jewel of a snake or the moon-light.
Cannot be compared to it.
The root of divine love
Is surrounded by the well of *Rasa* (i.e. *sahaja manuṣa*).
By the rays (of this *Rasa*) the quicksilver gushes out.
(And) covers the two-petalled (lotus).
He who sees this form,
What use has he for studying the Vedas?
Lālan, the slave of the poorest says, only a connoisseur can enjoy it."[15]

One may notice how the tantric concept of the transcendent God as pure consciousness, the light, *prakāśa*, and the Sufi concept of *nūr*, the divine light, and the primordial emanation of God, all coincide in the above concept of God's own *svarñpa.*

In ritual practices, a *bāul's* aim is to reach God, the *sahaja manuṣa* who lives in the seventh *cakra, sahasrāra,* above his head, perpetually united in coitus with His *prakṛti.* This a *bāul* can only endeavour to achieve through sexual union with his own female partner, while practising *prāṇāyāma* and thereby suspending the normal circulation of respiratory air and forcing it into the yogic *suṣumṇā* channel. This channel connects the male sex organ to his seventh *cakra.* During a woman's menstrual period, the cosmic *prakṛti* appears in concrete form in the woman's body. *Sahaja mānuṣa,* who cannot stay separated from His *prakrit,* follows her there.

This happens on the first three days of the woman's period. A *bāul* must try to utilize this opportunity to unite with the *sahaja mānuṣa.* He has coitus with his partner all three days. But there are moments when it is best to have coitus. He must not ejaculate, but must bring his woman to orgasm, while himself being on the verge of it. At that moment the *bāul*, through his penis, sucks in the woman's orgiastic fluid and menstrual blood, by a special *Haṭha yogic* muscular process and with the aid of *prāṇāyāma* sends these and his own semen into the *suṣumṇā* and up towards the *dājñā cakra*. This is what is called the controlling of the secret 'moons'. In another equation these four 'moons' are the four elements: semen = air; menstrual blood = fire; urine =water and faeces = earth.[16] Bhattacharya drew the above information from two texts which he found to be used by the *bāuls* themselves. These are the *Vivartavilāsa* by Akiñcana Das and the *Bṛhat nigama* by Locana Dās. Lālan refers to this secret *sādhanā* in a characteristic oblique way:

> "The two resplendent ones are always floating together inside the human frame.
> They appear regularly at the end of the aeon at the wharf of the cascade.
> One male and one female,
> They are floating in the same way forever.
> The high master who appears in the audience hall joins them.
> At the end of a month between these two.
> A meeting of passion takes place.
> By rare luck some know this rite of worship.
> He who knows these two resplendent ones.
> Will achieve perfection in wakeful *yoga*.
> Lālan Fakir misses his chance through hesitation."[17]

This is a brief summary of *bāul* secret practice. There are endless variations of these practices. The *Nātha siddhas* have similar practices, so do some radical Sufi sects. Several Bengali texts of the 15th to 18th centuries show how various types of synthesis of mystical esoteric practices achieved in rural Bengal in that period by many radical sects.[18] *Bāuls* call the state of their god-experience, *fanā*, a Sufi term.

Theology: Heterodoxy

On the ideological side too, this synthesis is evident. But the salient characteristic of *bāul* religion is its total rejection of all orthodoxy and religious systematization. The *bāuls* are rebels against the Hindu caste system and worship of many gods. But they equally rebel against the orthodox Muslim *śariat.* They also rebel against all sectarianism both Hindu and Muslim. Thus even Sufi sects cannot bring them into their folds. Their religious preceptors, *guru* or *murśid* or simply *sā̃i* (master), do not at their death leave any mystic power (*Baraka*) behind. The only tradition that remains is the remembered songs composed and sung by these preceptors to express their theology and *sādhanā.*

This is expressed in the following lines from a song of Lālan:

> "(The learned) recorded (four) religious ways,
> *Shariat, tarikat, hakikat* and *maraphat.*[19]
> But there are other ways besides these four.
> Only Darvish and fakir know those ways."[20]

Guru

The *guru* or *sā̃i* is the most important factor in the *bāul's* religious life. Without a *guru* the secret *sādhanā* is absolutely unattainable. Nor can anybody besides the *sā̃i,* transmit the religious experience of God. Like the Sufi *pīr,* he is the perfect manifestation of God in this world. And he is often identified with God. A *bāul* often addresses God as *sā̃i.* Lālan frequently addresses God, *murśid.* Although the *guru* in the state of *fanā* is totally immersed in God (in *bāul* terms, *fanā* is living death *jyāntemarā*), yet God sends him back to the living beings to save them by teaching divine love.

Love for God is the only way of attaining God. The *guru* possesses this love which exists between *sahaja mānuṣa* and His *prakṛti.* This engrossing love leads the *guru* to his *fanā.* Thus he alone can show his pupil the true way of divine love, *surāga.* This is a consummate love and a *bāul* yearns only for God. Being truly in love with God a *bāul* also loves all that are dear to God, viz. His creation. Love for fellow beings, complete non-aggressiveness, humility and mildness are hallmarks of a *bāul*. *Bāuls* are almost always vegetarians and tolerant of human weaknesses.

Importance of the Body

In the discussion of the *bāul* secret *sādhanā*, I have explained how the body acts as the only instrument with which to attain *fanā* or *samādhi*. This system, too, is based on the yogic tradition of the equation of the microcosm with the macrocosm. All pilgrimages, all holy places, in fact the entire creation is in the microcosm.

God manifests Himself in creation in three aspects: the enjoyer, *puruṣa*; the object of enjoyment, *prakṛti*; and the union of these two, the bliss which is non-dual existence (*advaya sattā*). But there is another explanation of these three basic manifestations of God, inspired by the theology of love of Caitanya's Vaiṣṇavism. There, these are the *ātmatattva* (i.e. the person), *paratattva* (i.e. *śakti*) and *prematattva* (i.e. experience of the unification of the first two, symbolized in the divine forms of Kṛṣṇa and Rādhā respectively). The third reality is represented by the *guru*. Sometimes the latter is replaced by the personality of Caitanya, who is considered to be the embodiment of the union of Rādhā and Kṛṣṇa.

God Himself is manifest inside this body. It is in the *ajñā cakra* within the human body that one can have a glimpse of God's immutable form (*aṭala mānuṣa*); that is why the *ajña cakra* is called "His chamber of audience (*barāmkhānā*)". Therefore Lālan sang:

"Could I ever again acquire human form?
O my mind, make haste to achieve your goal in this life.
Sā̃i created innumerable forms,
But I have heard that none is better than man,
Even gods pray to be born as a man.
......
......
In the human frame (God) would enjoy the sweet passion of love.

Therefore God, the pure one created the human form.
Lālan the servant (of God) ponders.
If (he) fails this time there is no way out."[21]

Again:

"Open your eyes and see where within your body
Mecca and Medina are situated. If you fail to know the secret of your own body
You will never be a wise man.
Says Sirāj Sāi, O Lālan, why are you roaming around without knowing *rupa* (concrete form)?"[22]

Rūpa and Svarūpa: Man and His Essence

Rūpa is the human form of the person, *jīva* wherein God abides as the transcendent reality and the essence, *svarūpa. Svarūpa* is pure consciousness, the light. As the absolute, God is beyond all experience; but still He sometimes appears to the adept in his *ajñā cakra.* This is an appearance of the transcendent in his plenitude and immutable state, *aṭala rūpa.* The paradox lies in the fact that both *rūpa* and *svarūpa* are one and the same. Lālan often replaced these terms with the Urdu words *khod* and *khodā* respectively. It is through his *guru*, a *bāul* obtains the discriminating knowledge of the basic unity between the pragmatic concept of self as the worldly and limited person and the unconditioned absolute quintessential Self. Cf.

"The *rūpa* finds its simile in the (divine) form.
Which is (brilliant) like the crest-jewel of a snake or the moon light.
He who has experienced that *aṭala rūpa*
Has lost his power of speech and has become silent;
He has crossed the abyss of becoming (*bhāva*),
Repeating the name of (*sva*) *rūpa* in his heart like a rosary.;
Says Sirāj Sāi, Lālan, simply find that (*sva*) *rūpa* in your own form."[23]

In another song Lālan concluded,

"The boat of form containing both *svarūpa* and *rūpa*
Is dancing on the (water) of the three worlds.

Says Fakir Lālan, listen my deluded mind,
You are embracing darkness to your bosom.[21]

God, The Beloved, Maner-Mānuṣa

The path to attain unity with God is on the other hand not at all a gnostic or intellectual one. It is a path of highly emotional *bhakti*. The absolute reality is not only one's essential being: who is the inner controller of each person. He is the unique beloved as well. To address his beloved God, the *bāul* coined the term '*maner-mānuṣa*', the person of one's heart's desire. He resides deep in the human heart. But men remain unconscious of that fact and the lovelorn *bāul* pines after his *maner-mānuṣa*. Often in Lālan's songs this *maner-mānuṣa* is said to be very close but nevertheless beyond one's comprehension:

"I have not beheld Him even for a day.
Close to my house is the mirror city (i.e. mind or heart),
And there lives a neighbour.
......
......
If my neighbour touched me,
My pain of death would have disappeared.
But although He and Lālan live at the same place,
There is a gap of millions of miles (between them)."[25]

He may be close but it is not easy to know this *maner-mānuṣa* directly. In ordinary life a thousand distractions hamper the *bāul* to concentrate on his beloved God who is also called *Rasa*, the repository of aesthetic pleasure. Cf.

"I cannot achieve that desired state of mind.
How can I learn the way of divine Love?
Distracted by the guiles of my enemies, the senses and their objects,
My mind travels from one branch (of the tree of life) to another.
Now, if I can concentrate on the One, I can avoid death.
Those who are connoisseurs (*rasika*) and devotees,
They attain the great Jewel.

How can I overpower the snake (*kuṇḍalinī*)?
When shall I supplicate the ambrosial *Rasa*?
Darvīsh Sirāj Sāi warns, Lālan you will be destroyed by its poison."[26]

God is absolute and inaccessible. Yet to His devotee He does manifest Himself fleetingly. he is like Kṛṣṇa the ever elusive lover. In his heart of hearts the *bāul* suddenly gets a glimpse of Him, yet fails to perpetuate this supreme moment. God's transcendence makes Him difficult to capture within the limited scope of human experience.

"In the case of mind, I do not know how that unknown bird comes in and flies away.
Had I been able to catch Him I would have put the shackle of my mind round His feet.
......
Lālan asks (please tell me) how does the bird open the cage and flies off?"[27]

The yearning of desire deepens the steadfast love of the *bāul* and through this self-effacing love he aspires to attain divine union, *fanā*. The technical term of this emotional devotion is *rāgabhakti*. *Rāga* means attachment. *Bāuls* call their loving devotion *surāga*, perfect attachment, as against the imperfect wordly attachments. In this form of devotion the devotee and his devotion become one and the same. God greatly enjoys such devotion and comes of His own account to enjoy such devotion. This is the characteristic of the *sahaja mānuṣa* who is the perfect lover. The *bāul* takes the advantage of this nature of the *sahaja manuṣa* and feels confident of the ultimate fulfilment of his love and attachment.

"Just behold, in the room of *rūpa* sports *aṭala rūpa*
Whose beauty surpasses that of the crest-jewel of a snake,
And who is revealed in the mutual love (of the devotee and his God).
He who is in love goes to the realm of love.
Unlocking the (door of) love, he beholds that beauty.
At the threshold of the abode of (*sva*) *rūpa*

Stands the divine form (of love)
(And) he has the key to the door.
He who can be identified with this divine form would get the passage.
Lālan says these people will get the unattainable."[28]

Love is the single path to attain the immutable and quiescent God of the *ājñā cakra.* This love is sustained by an active desire to communicate or to relate with Him who forever sports with His *prakṛti,* and revels in ecstacy of love. This *līlā* aspect of God has been greatly emphasized by the Vaiṣṇava of Bengal. But unlike the Vaiṣṇavas, Lālan and many other *bāuls* kept their mind fixed on the absolute God and aimed to attain this *aṭala rupa* and not the *līlā rūpa.* In the middle of the song just quoted above, Lālan warns his listeners not to wave from their ultimate goal, *aṭala rūpa,* and fall in the quagmire of the *līlā rūpa* and get lost in the secret practices of the five elements (*pañcatattva*), viz. meat, fish, snacks/ woman, alcohol and sex.

"The means to attain pure love is the unorthodox practice,
(But) the vision of love is fixed above this ceaseless sport (*līlā*).
Meditate on the Master *aṭala rūpa.*
In that aspect there is no *līlā.*
He who sinks in the *līlā rūpa*
While practising five elements,
Never realizes the character of *aṭala rūpa.*"[29]

Here in this poem Lālan conveyed the *bāul* attitude towards their secret practices. The *bāul* is not interested in the *prakṛti* (the cosmic female element) except in its use as a means to get close to God, albeit to His *līlā rūpa.* But the *līlā rūpa* helps one finally to attain the *aṭala rūpa.* The *bāul's manermānuṣa,* his beloved God, is within the human body, where He is completely undistinguishable from His *prakṛti.* These dual and yet inseparable realities, the polarized God, inhere in all creation. A *bāul* must learn to distinguish between these two polar points and find the undifferentiated absolute God in his own self. Cf.

"Listen my mind, in this person exists
He who is called the jewel-man;
Lālan exclaims, even when I have got the jewel,
Alas, I fail to recognise Him."[30]

This distress and despair felt by the *bāul* is the central point of the emotional *bhakti* introduced by the Vaiṣṇavas. The intensity of *bhakti* grows as the devotee-lover feels more and more the acute pain of separation from his beloved God. The tradition of Sufi also enriched this concept. *Mahabba* (affection) for God is an all-consuming passion which makes a person a constant sufferer until he attains his *fanā*.[31]

Lālan, the devotee, was the yearning lover of God. But Lālan, the religious teacher, was sober in his confidence in his religious path and ideology.

"The *sādhanā* reaches its goal when the adept realizes his self.
The meaning of self (ego, 'I') is very deep; Me! he is not my self.
In endless cities and markets
Cacophony rises in the sound of 'I'.
But I do not know me and so read the Vedas like a crazy man.
When there were no heaven and earth, only self was the Reality,
Then started the wheel of creation (and there appeared)
The form of 'you' out of the Self.
Manṣur Hallāj, the fakir said 'I am the Truth'.
That statement was made about the law of the Master.
Can sharī'a fathom its meaning?
'Rise by my order', 'rise by the creator's order';
These are two orders of the Master, I am only His mouthpiece.
Says Lālan, only *murśid* knows how to unravel the difference of meaning of these two (orders)."[32]

It is interesting to see how Lālan arrives at a complete synthesis of ideas, both Hindu Vedantic and Sufi ideologies. In another song he declares:

"My mind! without the knowledge of self (*ātma-tattva*)
You will fall in your *sādhanā* and become confused.
First get the meaning of God's world (*qawl allah*) right;

Ana 'l-haqq Allah, who is called man.[33]
My mind! do not study so much and become spiritless.
Just open your eyes full of love and behold (the truth).
The master Himself is the fakir, and the means of (knowing) Him is none other than himself.
It is His *līlā* that He forgets His own self and floats on the water of His love.
"There is no god' (this formula) is the body, 'but Allah' (this formula) is its self and these two are related through love.[34]
Is that self me? If you know the answer all evil will depart.
Lālan says, in that case I would not have to travel in this abysmal cycle of life."[35]

THE IDEAS OF ŚAKTI, THE DIVINE POWER AND UNIVERSAL MOTHER AND NŪR OF ALLAH

The same type of ideological synthesis is evident in Lālan's attempt to accommodate the tantric concepts of *puruṣa* and *prakṛti*[36] in the mystical cosmogony of *nūr* of the Muslims.[37] For him Fatima, the daughter of the Prophet Muhammad and wife of Ali bin Abi Talib, the fourth Caliph, is *prakṛti*. Ali was regarded by Sufis as their Shaikh[38] (leader and teacher). Hence for Lālan, a Bengali Muslim, it was Fatima rather than A'isha, the Prophet's wife who was chosen for the role of the cosmic mother. Cf.

"Who may answer my question about the sacred love?
What love was that in which Allah and Muhammad communed in *mi'raj*?
Mi'raj is the land of ideas.
Where the unmanifest discourses with the manifest.
How can one prove which of the two there, is the *puruṣa* and which *prakṛti*?
What type of love led Fatima, the loving one,
To serve the Master as husband?
And urged by what type of love did the Master call Fatima His mother?
What love is that which makes the teacher a boat (to cross the ocean of life)?

And again what love inspires the pupil to be the helmsman?
Lālan, it is useless to cultivate love without knowing its inspiration."[39]

This enigmatic song seems a total confusion of ideas. Yet Lālan was most probably trying to understand the unity lying behind the specific roles of a woman as wife and mother, by blending them in the figure of Fatima and identifying her with *prakṛti*. All manifest forms are emanations of *śakti*, which Lālan equated with the Sufi concepts of divine light and beauty, *nūr*. Muhammad was the first and perfect manifestation of this *nūr*. He during his ascension, *mi'raj* came in direct contact with Allah and He lovingly chose Muhammad to be His messenger to bring back to mankind His message. According to some Muslim mystics, God is in love with His *nūr* and created the first man Adam in His image out of His *nūr*, so that He could enjoy His love.[40] Therefore, all forms of love are ways in which the divine love for *nūr* fulfils itself. For Lālan, the Muslim *bāul*, *prakṛti* and *nūr* being the same, the love of *puruṣa*, and *prakṛti* is model of the love between God and His messenger, Muhammad.

Lālan did not feel that his adherence to Islam prevented him from accepting the tantric doctrine of *puruṣa* and *prakṛti*; so he is reconciled to the necessity of the secret sexual rites of worship.

"A strange *rasika* is floating on the (lake of) *rasa*[41]
He has no hands and feet yet he rushes in at high speed.
That lake of *rasa*, O Mother, gets denser bit by bit;
And somebody controls its ebbs and tides.
If one plunges into (this lake of) passion,
One comes to know the *līlā* of that *rasa*;
And then one's purpose in being born as a man is fulfilled by His touch.
On his left side is the *kuṇḍalinī*[42]
Who is called Yogamāyā.
Says Lālan, constantly recite her name and she will take you back to your home."[43]

This song with its oblique references to the sexual practice, declares that Yogamāyā, the primordial manifestation, to be the only means to attain the goal of being merged in God. This is a fundamental Hindu tantric position. She is dormant in every person as the *kulakuṇḍalinī*. When roused from her slumber through the yogic process known as *kuṇḍalinī yoga,* she lifts the *yogin* to the realm of the absolute to be merged in it. Lālan did not stop there. Instead he boldly proceeded to identify Yogamāyā with Fatima.

"Worship the messenger Muhammad in your heart,
After having realized his nature.
What price should you pay?
To attain your real self?
If you recall Fatima (in your *dhikr*)[44]
Then you must follow the secret practice;
Because such is the ruling of the Master.
....
....
I have heard my mother is possessed by God.
Yogeśvarī (Fatima)! be always my mother.
Just because men fail to grasp the right moment (for sexual acts),
They indulge in it at wrong moments and hence perish in the storm (of life).'[45]

Lālan Fakir freely used ideas from all the forms of mysticism available to him. *Bāuls* inherited a long Indian tradition of religious eclecticism and bold innovation. The innovation of *bāuls* lay in their adjusting the diverse concepts they inherited, especially the Muslim ones, to provide ideological justification for their sexual rites of worship.

Such adjustment of ideology to practice has happened many times in the history of Indian mysticism. Caitanya introduced rapturous singing and dancing for attaining a religious ecstatic state very much like the Sufi practice of *samā'*. Among the common villagers, mysticism did not observe any communal barrier and despite stern treatment from the custodians of orthodoxy, religious radicalism flourished. Lālan was himself little educated and his interpretations were often simplistic. The subtle tantric concept of non-dualism of God and His *śakti* was as difficult for Lālan as was the great theological interpretation of the Sufi of the Quranic Islām. Yet the basic doctrine of unity of all phenomena in God and the theology of love he understood perfectly.

In the nineteenth century, Muslim revivalist movements were very active in India. In Bengal orthodox Muslim activists, both non-Sufi and Sufi, were busy persecuting the followers of folk Islamic mystics.[46] Lālan had to confront and react to these activities. Sometimes he declared his allegiance to the orthodox Islamic laws and the code of ethical conduct. But he was far too involved in the syncretistic mysticism of the *bāuls* to keep the stance of orthodoxy up for long. He had to ask himself the question that if the Islamic laws could bring perfection to the followers then why people have to bother to attain mystical gnosis, *ma'rifa'*.[47] Some of his songs predominate in Vaiṣṇava concepts and show great reverence to Caitanya as divine love incarnate. Others show a preponderance of Sufi ideas. But everywhere the syncretism of various mystic concepts is perfect and presented with great feeling and beauty of expression. As Dimock says, the *bāuls* reached the perfection of harmonizing many relevant mystical concepts: "While not quite Sahajiyās, the Bāuls are fitting hybrids; the Vaiṣṇava, Sahajiyā and Sufi strains yield beauty, sympathy and strength. From the Vaiṣṇavas, and from the Sufis, comes the Bāul vision of warmth and humaneness and love of God. From the Sahajiyās comes their conviction of His compelling immediacy.... In the songs of the Bāuls the power of divine love is felt, graced with human dignity."[48]

NOTES

1 See Tagore, *passim*; Rabindranath was the first to collect Lālan's songs, of which twenty he published in the Bengali monthly magazine *Pravāśī* edited by Ramananda Ray. These were published in 1916. Dasgupta, S.B. 186-187.

2 Haq. 397-422.

3 *Sā̃i* = Sānskrit *Svāmin*, master.

4 *Lālan Gītikā*, Introduction by Dasgupta, S.B.; Bhattacharya, Upendranath, 535-545.

5 Ibid. 807-837.

6 Dasgupta, S.B., 157-187; Sen, 46-59.

7 Jassīmuddin, 1-2 and *passim*.

8 Briggs, 258-283.

9 *Lālan Gītikā*, 37; Vaudeville, Introduction; Rizvi, 322-396.

10 Chowdhury, Abdul Momin, 10-14; Geertz, *passim;* Eaton, *passim*.

11 Ahmed, 32-34; Haq, 297-316; Rizvi, 301 ff.

12 Dasgupta, A and Ann, M, 72. Lālan calls his God Kṛṣṇa. But Kṛṣṇa here is not the mythological figure of the Hindu *Purāṇas*. He is merged into the figure of the beloved but hard to attain God of the mystic. See Dasgupta's article in Bhattacharya, Jatindrāmohan, 153-172.

13 Dimock, *passim*.

14 Gupta, Hoens and Goudariaan, 170-179. Lālan was not the only Bengali Muslim mystic to equate to the Tantric Goddess, Roy, 94-95.

15 *Lālan Gītikā*, 83.

16 Bhattacharya, Upendranath, 369-481.

17 *Lālan Gītikā*, 81.

18 Haq, 368-396; Rizvi, 301-302.

19 A Sufi is called a *sālik*, wayfarer, and the path he follows is the way (*tarāqā*) of reaching one's goal of perfection. This path is divided into stages and stations, *maqām*. These latter are four: *nāsūt, malakūt, jabarūt* and *lāhūt*. On the basis of these stations the stages are often divided into four: *shari'at, tariqat, haqiqat*

and *ma'rifat.* The first is the orthodox Muslim ecclesiastical law and hence the way of the orthodox Islam. The second is the way of the Sufi sectarian laws. The third is the way of the Truth, *ḥaqīqa,* and the last is real gnosis. In his book, Haq gives a chart depicting the late Bengal development of these concepts in the hands of the syncretistic Muslim mystics. Schimmel. 98-99, 109-130; Haq, 97-99 and 416,

20 *Lālan Gītikā,* 154.

21 Ibid. 286.

22 Ibid. 200.

23 Ibid. 12.

24 Ibid. 14

25 Ibid. 12-13.

26 Ibid 19–20.

27 Ibid 202-203

28 Ibid. 93.

29 Ibid 93.

30 Ibid. 101

31 See Hardy, *passim;* Bhattacharya, Jatindramohan, Introduction; Valiuddin 18-24 and *passim.* "*Mahabba* and *ma'rifat* are the last station of the way to God" Schimmel. 130.

32 *Lālan Gītikā,* 171-172.

33 Manṣūr al-Hallaj, the famous Sufi of the ninth century. His most famous statement is 'I am the absolute Truth' which means that he declared himself to be God: '*Anā'l-Haqq*'. The essence of God is that He is *al-Haqq,* absolute Truth. Schimmel, 66-67.

34 Haq, 81. Islam profession of faith runs in two parts: *la ilāha ilia Allah* (there is no god but God) and *Muhammad rasul Allah* (Muhammad is God's messenger). Sufis are more concerned with the first rather than the second part. Schimmel, 99.

35 *Lālan Gītikā,* 170-171.

36 Gupta et al, *loc. cit.*

37 Haq, 56-62 and 402-403.

38 Rizvi, 25; Schimmel, 27.

39 *Lālan Gītikā,* 163-164. *Mi'raj* is the mystical ascension of Muhammad through the heavens to the presence of God. This became a prototype of the mystic's spiritual ascension to the intimate presence of God in rapturous ecstacy. As Rūmī expressed it:

"Love is ascension toward the roof of the Prince of Beauty. Read the story of ascension from the cheek of the beloved." Schimmel 1219.

40 Haq, 402-403.

41 The lake of *rasa* refers to the menstrual blood.

42 Gupta et al, 45, 171-179.

43 *Lālan Gitikā,* 89-90.

44 "But the distinctive worship of the sufi is the *dhikr* ... the remembrance or recollection of God ... that can be performed either silently or aloud." This is considered to be the first phase of love. Schimmel, 167-168. In a *Hadīth, umm al mu'minīm,* i.e. mother of all faithful, a title was designated for the Prophet's wife. The Sufis adopted it for Fatima, Ali's wife instead.

45 *Lālan Gītikā,* 165.

46 Ahmed, 33.

47 *Lālan Gītikā,* 143.

48 Dimock, 270.

Bibliography

PRIMARY TEXTS; CANONICAL AND EXEGETICAL

Āgamaprāmāṇyam, by Yāmuna Muni, ed. Dr. M. Narasimhachary, GOS no. 160, Baroda, 1976.

Abhayāmaṅgala, by Dvija Rāmdev, ed. Āśutoṣ Dās, Calcutta University, Calcutta, 1957.

Ahirbudhnya Saṃhitā, ed. Rāmānujācārya, Adyar, 1916, 2nd edn. revised by V. Krishnamacharya, 2 vols, Adyar, 1966 (ALS 4).

Ānandalaharī, ed. and transl. by Arthur Avalon "Wave of Bliss", Madras, 1961.

Brahmāṇḍa Purāṇam, ed. Prof. J.L. Shastri, Motilal Banarsidas, Delhi, 1973.

Brāhmaṇasarvasva by Halāyudha, ed. D. Bhattacharyya, Calcutta, 1960.

Bhāvanā Upaniṣad, ed. Sītārāma Shāstrī, in *Kaula and Other Upaniṣads*, Calcutta, London, 1922 (Tantrik Texts XI), pp. 37-65.

Bṛhat Tantrasāra, Kṛṣṇānanda āgamavāgīsa, ed. Rasik Mohan Chattopadhyāya, Nabobhārat, reprint, Calcutta, 1996.

Bṛhaddharma Purāṇa. Bibliotheka Indica Series, Asiatic Society of Bengal, Calcutta, 1888-97.

Brahmasūtra with Śaṃkara's commentary.

Devī-bhāgavata, ed. Śrī Pañcānana Tarkaratna, 2nd edn, Calcutta, 1832 (Śakābda).

Devī-māhātmyam, (DM), edited with an introduction, translation and critical notes, Vāsudeva S. Agrawala, All India Kashiraj Trust Varanasi, 1963.

Devī Purāṇam, ed. Śrī Pañcānana Tarkaratna, Calcutta, 1892.

Devī Upaniṣad, ed. A. Mahadeva Shastri, in *The Śakta Upaniṣads*, Adyar, 1950 (ALS 10), pp.71-92; A. Danielou, ALS, Vol. 19, 1955, pp.77-84; transl. A. G. Krishna Warrier, *The Śākta Upaniṣads*, Adyar, 1967 (ALS 10).

Deviyāna, by Īśvaradāsa Bārahaṭṭa, ed. Śaṅkar Jetibhāi, Limbri, 1946.

Dhvanyāloka by Ānandavardhana with Abhinavagupta's Commentary, ed. J. Pathak, Vidyabhavan Granthamala 97, Varanasi, 1965.

Jayākhya Saṃhitā (JS), GOS No. 54. ed. Ember Krishnamācārya, Oriental Institute, Baroda, 1967 (2nd edn.).

Kādambarī by Bāṇabhaṭṭa, ed. and transl. by M. R. Kale, Bombay, 1968.

Kālikāpurāṇam, Chowkhamba Sanskrit series 5, Varanasi, 1972.

Kāmakalāvilāsa by Puṇyānanda, ed. and transl by Arthur Avalon, Madras, 1953.

Karpurādistotra, ed. and transl by A. Avalon, *Hymns to Kalī*, Madras, 1953.

Kaulajñānanirṇaya, ed. P. Ch. Bagchi, in *Kaulajñānanirṇaya and Some Minor Texts of the School of Matsyendra Nātha*, Calcutta, 1934.

Kavikaṃkana-caṇdī by Mukundarām Cakravartī, ed. Śrīkumār Bandyopādhyāya and Viśvapati Chaudhurī, Calcutta University (new edn), Calcutta, 1962.

Kāvyādarśa, by Dandin, BORI, 1938.

Kulārṇava Tantra, edited with a Bengali translation and notes by Upendra Kumar Das, Nabobhārat, Calcutta, 1977.

Lakṣmī Tantra, ed. V. Krishnamacharya, Madras, 1959 (ALS 87).

Lālan-gītikā by Fakir Lālan Śhāh, ed. Matilal Das and Pijuskanti Mahapatra, Calcutta University, Calcutta,1958.

Lalitā-sahasranāma-stotram, translated with Bhāskararāya's Commentary by R. Ananthakrishna Sastry, Theosophical Publishing House, Adyar, Madras, 1951.

Layayoga Saṃhitā, ed. Association of Publishers of Mahāmaṇḍalaśāstra,Varanasi, VS 1970 (1914 CE).

Mahābhārata (MBh), ed. V. S. Sukthankar and others, Bhandarkar Oriental Research Institute, Poona, 1933-66.

Mantramahodadhi, by Mahīdhara, ed. Kh. Śrīkrṣṇadās, Bombay, 1962; *with the Author's own Commentary Naukā*, ed. by a Board of Scholars, Volumes I & II (Bound in one), Sri Satguru Publications, Delhi, 1981.

Manu Smṛti/Mānava Dharma-sūtra, Manu Smṛti/Mānava Dharma-sūtra, ed. with Commentaries of Medhātithi, Sarvajñanārāyaṇa, Kulluka, Rāghavānanda, Nandana, Rāmacandra, Maṇirāma, Govindarāja and Bhāruci, by J. H. Dave, 6 vols, Bhāratiya Vidya Bhavan, Bombay. 1972 – 84.

Nityaṣoḍaśikārṇava Tantra with Commentaries of Śivānanda and Vidyānanda (ed. with an Introduction) Vrajavallabha Dviveda, Varanaseya Sanskrit University, Yoga Tantra Books Series No.1, Varanasi, 1968.

Nityotsava of Umanandanātha (Supplement of *Paraśurāma-kalpa-sūtra*), ed. Late Mahadev Sastri and Late Swami Trivikrama Tirtha, GOS, no. 23, Vadodara, 2000.

Nīla Tantram, ed. Jyotirlal Das, Navabhārat Press, Calcutta, 1388 Beng. Era (1981).

Paraśurāmakalpasūtra with Rāmeśvara's Commentary, ed. Late Mahadev Sastri and Late Sakarlal Yajneswar Sastry Dave, GOS, no. 22, Vadodara, 1999.

Pauṣkara Saṃhitā (PS), ed. by His Holiness Sree Yatiraja Sampathkumara Ramanuja Muni of Melkote, Published by A. Srinivasa Aiyangar and M.C. Thirumalachariar, 9th Main Road, Malleswaram, Bangalore, 1934.

Prāṇatoṣinī, by Ramatoṣaṇa Vidyālaṃkāra, ed. J. Vidyasagar, Vasumatī Sahityamandir, Calcutta, 1898.

Pratyabhijñāhṛdayam by Kṣemarāja, ed. Jaydev Singh, Varanasi, 1961.

Prapañcasāra Tantra, ed. Arthur Avalon, Tantrik Text 3, Calcutta, 1914.

Pūjātattva, by Pūrṇānanda Sarasvatī, ed. G. Kaviraj, Varanasi V.S. 2014 (1957-58 C.E.).

Pūjāvidhinirūpaṇa, by Trimalla, ed. and transl. by F. Nowotny, in *Indo-Iranian Journal*, I, 1957, pp.109 – 154.

Rāmcaritmānas by Tulsīdās in *Tulsī-granthāvalī*, part I, ed. Mātāprasad Gupta Allahabad (undated); *Tulsī-granthāvalī*, part II, ed. Rāmchandra Śukul, Bhagavāndīn and Brajratndās, Varanasi, 1957.

Rāmapūrvatapanī Upaniṣad, ed. N. R. Acharya, in Īśādiviṃśatyuttaraśatopaniṣadaḥ, No. 57, Bombay, 1948.

Rāmayaṇa, ed. G.H. Bhatt, BORI, 1960.

Rudrayāmala Tantra (*Uttara Tantra*), ed. J. Vidyasagar, Calcutta, 1937.

Saṃvitprakāśa by Vāmana Datta, edited with English Introduction by Mark S.G. Dyczkowski, Ratna Printing Works, Kamaccha, Varanasi, 1990.

Śakti-gīti Padāvalī (A Collection of Hymns on Śakti), Arun Kumar Basu, Calcutta, 1964.

Śākta-padāvalī, ed. Amarendranāth Rāy, Calcutta University, Calcutta, 1971.

Śaktisaṃgama Tantra, ed. in 3 volumes by B. Bhattacharya, GOS, 661, 91, 104, and 166, Vol. I Kālīkhaṇḍa, Vol. II Tārākhaṇḍa, Vol. III Sundarīkhaṇḍa and Vol. IV, *Chinnamastākhaṇḍa*, ed. Vraja Vallava Dviveda, Baroda 1932 - 1947 and 1978.

Śāradātilakam by Lakṣaṇa Deśika, ed. M.M. Pandit Śri Mukunda Jha Bakshi, Chowkhamba Sanskrit Series, Varanasi 1963.

Sāttvata Saṃhitā (SS), Published by L.N.Tiwari, Librarian, Sarasvati Bhavana Library Sampurnanand Sanskrit University Varanasi with a Commentary by Alaśiğabhaṭṭa, ed. VrajaVallabha Dviveda, 1982.

Saundaryalaharī by Śaṅkarācārya, ed. Vidvan N. S. Venkatacharya, Oriental Series 114, Mysore, 1969.

Śrī Pāñcarātrarakṣā, Vedānta ḍesika, ed. Pandit M. Duraiswami Aiyagar and Pandit T. Venugopalacharya, Adyar Library Series no. 36, 2nd edn, Madras, 1967.

Śrīvidyārṇava Tantra (2 vols), Vidyāraṇya Yati, Kalyaṇamandir Prayāg, Allahabad, 2023 Vikramābda.

Śvetāśvatara Upaniṣad, (Śv.U), ed. Patrick Ollivelle, in *The Early Upaniṣads: Annotated Text and Translation*, OUP, New York, 1998, pp. 413 - 433.

Taittirīya Āraṇyaka, (TA), with Commentary by Bhaṭṭa Bhāskara Miśra, ed. A Mahadeva Sastri and K. Rangacarya, Motilal Banarsidass, Delhi.

Tantrarāja Tantra, pt. I (chs 1 - 18), ed. Lakśmana Śāstrī, Tan.Texts VIII, London 1918, pt II (chs. 19 -36), ed. Sadāshiva Mishra, Tan. Texts XII, Calcutta/London, 1926.

Tantrasamuccaya by Nārāyaṇa, ed. V.A.R. Sastri and K.S.M. Sastri, Trv. Skt. Ser, Vols 151 and 169.

Tārābhaktisudhārṇava by Narasiṃha, ed. Pañcanana Bhaṭṭācarya, Tan. Texts XXI, Calcutta/London, 1940.

Toḍala Tantra, ed. Bhadraśīla Śarmā, Allahabad, 2010 VS (1961-62 CE), ed. Gopinath Kaviraj in *Tantrasaṃgraha*, Vol. II, Varanasi, 1970, pp.53 - 94.

Tripuratāpanī Upaniṣad, ed. A Mahadev Sastri, trans. A.G. Krishna Warrier, in *The Śākta Upaniṣads*, ALS 89, Adyar, 1967.

Tripurārahasyam (*Jñana-khaṇḍam*) with a Commentary by Draviḍa Śrīnivāsa (1831), ed. With an Introduction by Gopi Nath Kaviraj, Sarasvatībhavanagranthamālā Series no. 15, 2nd edn, Varanasi, 1965.

Vākyapadīya by Bhartṛhari, cantos 1 and 2, ed. K. Raghavan Pillai, Delhi, 1971.

Varivasyārahasyam by Bhāskararāya, ed. S. Subrahmanya Sastri, Adyar Library Series 28, Madras, 1934.

Viṣṇu Purāṇa (VP), ed. H.H.Wilson, *The Visṇu Puraṇa: A System of Hindu Mythology and Tradition*, reprinted by Punthi Pustak, Calcutta, 1967.

Yoginī Hṛdayam with Commentaries by Amṛtānanda and Bhāskararāya, (ed with Preface and Introduction) Ma. Ma. Śrī Gopīnātha Kavirāj, Sarasvatībhavangranthamālā Series no. 7, 2nd edn, Varanasi, 1963.

Yoginī Hṛdayam with the Commentary by Amṛtānanda (ed with a Hindi Introduction and translation), Vrajavallabha Dviveda, Motilal Banarsidas, Delhi, 1988.

SECONDARY LITERATURE

Avalon, A. *Principles of Tantra*, by Śrīyukta Śiva Chandra Vidyārṇava, Madras, 3rd edn, 1960.

-------*The Serpent Power being the Śaṭcakranīrūpaṇa and the Pādukāpañcaka*, Tantric Texts II, Madras, 6th edn, 1958.

——& E. Avalon, *Hymns to the Goddess*, Madras, 1952.

Ahmed, Rafiuddin. *The Bengal Muslims 1871-1906 : A Quest For Identity*, OUP, Delhi, 1981.

Awasthi Shastri, S. S. *Mantra aur mātṛkāon kā rahasya*, Varanasi, 1966.

Babb, Lawrence A. *Indigenous Feminism in a Modern Hindu Sect*, in ed. Rehana Ghadially, *Women in Indian Society: A Reader*, Sage, New Delhi, 1988.

Bagchi, P. Ch. *Studies in the Tantras*, Vol. I, Calcutta, 1939.

Banerjea, J. N. *The Development of Hindu Iconography*, Calcutta, 1956.

Banerji, S. C. *Tantra in Bengali ... A Śtudy in Its Origin, Development and Influence*, Calcutta, 1978.

Beane, W. C. *Myth, Cult and Symbols in Śākta Hinduism... A Study of the Indian Mother Goddess*, Leiden, 1977.

Bennett, Lynn. *Dangerous Wives and Sacred Sisters: Social and Symbolic Roles of High-caste Women in Nepal*, Columbia University Press, New York, 1983.

Bharati, A. *The Tantric Tradition*, London, 1965, 4th edn, 1975.

Bhattacharya, Ashutosh. *Bāṃlā Maṃgal Kāvyer Itihās*, Calcutta, 3rd edn, 1958.

Bhattacharya, Shibprasad, *Bhāratachandra o Rāmaprasada*, Calcutta, 2nd edn, 1967.

Bhattacharya, H. *Tantrik Religion in the Age of Imperial Kanauj*, in *History and Culture of the Indian People*, IV, Bombay, 1955, pp. 314–326.

Bhattacharya, Upendranath. *Bāṃglār bāul o bāulgān* (new edn), Calcutta, 1981.

Bhattacharya, Jatindramohan, *Bāṃglār Vaiṣṇava-bhāvāpanna Musalmān Kavir padamañjuṣā*, 2nd edn, in the appendix an article by Dasgupta, S. B., *Bāṃglār Musalmān Vaiṣava-kavi*, is added. Calcutta University, 2nd edn, Calcutta, 1962.

Bose, Mandakranta, ed., *Faces of the Feminine in Ancient, Medieval and Modern India*, OUP, New York, 2000.

Bose, Manindra Mohan. *The Post-Catanya Sahajiyā Cult of Bengal*, Calcutta University, Calcutta, 1930.

Briggs, G. W. *Gorakhnāth and Kānphaṭa Yogīs*, Calcutta, 1938.

Brown, Cheever Mackenzie. *God as Mother: A Feminine Theology of India*, Hartford, VT: C. Stark, 1974.

——*The Triumph of the Goddess: The Canonical Models and Theological Vision of the Devī-Bhāgavata Purāṇa*, SUNY Press, Albany, 1990.

——*Kālī the Mad Mother,* in ed. Olson, Carl, *The Book of Goddess: Past and Present,* The Cross Road Publishing Company, New York, 1985, pp. 110 – 123.

Brown, Norman. *Theories of Creation in Ṛg Veda, JAOS,* 85 (1965).

Brunner -Lachaux, H. *Somaśambhupaddhati. Lev rituel quotidian dans la Tradition śivaite de l'Inde du Sud selonSomaśambhu,* 3 vols, Pondichery, 1963, 1968 and 1977.

Brubaker, Richard L. *The Untamed Goddesses of Village India,* in ed. Carl Olson, *The Book of Goddess,* pp. 145 – 160.

Bühnemann, Gudrun. *The Iconography of Hindu Tantric Deities,* Vol. 1, *The Pantheon of the Mantramahodadhi,* Gonda Indological Studies, Vol. IX, Groningen, 2000.

——*The Iconography of Hindu Tantric Deities,* Vol. II, *The Pantheons of the Prapañcasāra and the Śāradātilaka;* Gonda Indological Studies, Vol. IX. Groningen, 2001.

Carlstedt, G. *Studier I Kulārṇava-Tantra,* SURIU 14, Upsala, 1974.

Cashin, David, *The Ocean of Love: Middle Bengali Sufi Literature and the Fakirs of Bengal,* Skrifter utgivna av Foreningen for Orientaliska Studier no. 27, Stockholm, 1995.

Chakravarti, Ch. *The Tantra: Studies on Religion and Literature,* Calcutta, 1963.

Chowdhury, Abdul Momim. *Conversion to Islam in Bengal: An Exploration,* in ed., Ahmed, Rafiuddin, *Islam in Bangladesh: Society, Culture and Politics,* Bangla Itihas Samiti, Dhaka, 1983.

Chari, S. M. Srinivasa. *Vaiṣṇavism: Its Philosophy, Theology and Religious Discipline,* Motilal Banarsidass, Delhi, 1994.

Coburn, Thomas B. *The Devī-Mahātmya: Crystalization of the Goddess Tradition,* Motilal Banarsidass, Delhi, 1985.

——*The Structural Interplay of Tantra, Vedānta, and Bhakti: Nondualistic Commentary on the Goddess,* in *The Roots of Tantra* ed. by Katherine Anne Harper and Robert L. Brown, SUNY Press. Albany, 2002, pp. 77 – 89.

——*Encountering the Goddess,* SUNY Press, Albany, 1991.

Das, U. K. *Śāstramūlaka Bhāratīya Śaktisādhanā,* Vols. I and II,Visvabharati, Shantiniketan, 1373 Bengali era.

Das Gupta, S. B. *Bhārater Śaktisādhanā O Śākta Sahitya,* Calcutta, 2nd edn,1966.

——*Obscure Religious Cults as Background of Bengali Literature,* Calcutta, 2nd edn, 1962.

Dasgupta, Alokranjan and Mary Ann, *Roots in the Void: Bāul Songs of Bengal,* Calcutta, 1977.

De, S.K. *The Early History of the Vaiṣṇava Faith and Movements in Bengal,* Calcutta, 3rd edn, 1969.

Dimock, E. C. *The Place of the Hidden Moon. Erotic Mysticism in the Vaiṣṇava Sahajjīyā Cult of Bengal,* Chicago and London, 1966.

Doniger, Wendy, *Saraṇyu/Sajñā: The Sun and the Shadow,* in John Stratton Hawley and Donna Marie Wulff, ed., *Devī: Goddess of India,* University of California Press, Berkeley and Los Angeles, 1996.

——O'Flaherty, transl. *Rig Veda: An Anthology,* Penguin Classics, 1981.

Dumont, Louis. *The Conception of Kingship in Ancient India,* in *Religion, Politics and History in India,* Paris and The Hague, 1970.

Dvivedi, Hazariprasad. *Hindi Sāhitya: uska Udbhav aur Vikaś,* Delhi, 1952.

Dviveda, Vraja Vallabha. *Tantra Yātrā, Ratna,* Varanasi, 1982.

Eaton, Richard Maxwell. "The Growth of Muslim Identity in Eighteenth Century Bengal" paper read at the International Colloquium on *Eighteenth Century Renewal and Reform Movements in Islam,* Institute for Advanced Studies, Jerusalem University, 1985.

Eliade Mircea. *Yoga: Immortality and Freedom,* tr. Willard R. Trask, Routledge & Kegan Paul, London, 1969 (2nd edn).

Erndle, Kathleen. *The Goddess and Women's Power: A Hindu Case Study,* in ed. Karen L. King, *Women and Goddess Tradition in Antiquity and Today,* Fortress Press, Minneapolis, 1997, pp. 17 - 38.

——*Victory to the Mother: The Hindu Goddess of Northwest India,* in *Myth, Ritual, and Symbol,* OUP, New York, 1993.

——*Serāṁvālī,* in ed. Hawley and Wulff, *Devi,* 1996.

Fell McDermott, Rachel. *Mother of My Heart, Daughter of My Dream: Kalī and Umā in the Devotional Poetry of Bengal*, OUP, New York, 2001.

——ed. with Jeffrey J. Kripal, *Encountering Kālī in the Margins, at the Center, in the West*, University of California Press, 2003.

——ed. with Cynthia Ann Humes, *Breaking Boundaries with the Goddess: New Directions in the Study of Śāktism*, Manohar, Delhi, 2009.

Gayatri Devi and Shanta Rama Rau. *A Princess Remembers: The Memoirs of the Maharani of Jaipur*, New Delhi, 5th edn, first published in London, 1976.

Geertz, Clifford. *Negara: The Theatre State in Nineteen-century Bali*, Princeton, 1980.

——*Islam Observed. Religious Development in Morocco and Indonesia*, Chicago, 1971.

Gombrich, E. H. *Four Theories of Artistic Expression*, in *Architectural Association Quarterly*, XII, 4, 1980.

Gonda, Jan. *Aspects of Early Viṣṇuism*; V.A.Oosthoek's Uitgevers Mij. Utrecht, 1954.

——*The Sacred Character of Ancient Indian Kingship, Studies in the History of Religion* (supplement to Numen) 4, Leiden, 1959, pp.172-180

——*The Indian Mantra*, in *Oriens* 16, 1963, reprinted in J. Gonda's *Selected Studies*, IV, Leiden, 1975, pp. 248 - 301.

——*Puṣan and Sarasvatī*, North Holland Publishing Company, Amsterdam, Oxford, New York, 1985.

——*Vedic Literature* (*Saṃhitās and Brāhmaṇas*), *A History of Indian Literature*, Vol. I, Otto Harrassovitz, Wiesbaden, 1981.

——*Vedic Cosmogony and Viṣṇuite Bhakti, Indologica Taurinensia* 1977, pp 85-111.

Goswami B. B. and S. G. Morab. *Chamundesvari Temple in Mysore*, with a Foreword by Surajit Chandra Sinha, Anthropological Survey of India, Calcutta, 1975.

Goudriaan, Teun, *Kubjikā's Samayamantra and its Manipulation in the Kubjikamata* in ed. Andre Padoux CNRS, Paris, 1986, see especially the discussion on this paper.

Gross, Rita M. *Hindu Female Deities as a Resource for the Contemporary Rediscovery of The Goddess,* in ed. Car Olson, *The Book of Goddess,* New York, 1985, pp. 217 – 230.

Guenther, H.V. *The Royal Songs of Saraha: A Study in the History of Buddhist Thought,* Translation and Annotation, Seattle and London, 1969.

Gupta, Parameshwari Lal. *Coins,* National Book Trust, 3rd edn, 1979.

Gupta, Sanjukta. *Lakṣmī Tantra: A Pāñcarātra Text,* Indian Edn, Motilal Banarsidass, Delhi, 2000.

——*The Changing Pattern of Pāncarātra initiation: A Case Study in the Reinterpretation of Ritual,* in *Selected Studies on Ritual in the Indian Religions: Essays to D. J. Hoens,* ed. Ria Kloppenborg, Leiden, 1983.

——*Yoga and Antaryāga in Pañcaratra,* in *Ritual and Speculation in Early Tantrism: Studies in Honor of Andre Padoux,* ed. Teun Goudriaan, SUNY Press, Albany,1992. pp. 175-208.

——*The Caturvyūha and The Viśākha-yūpa in The Pāñcarātra,* The Adyar Library Bulletin, Vol. XXXV, parts 3-4. Madras, 1971. pp. 189-204.

Halbfass, Wilhelm. *Tradition and Reflection: Exploration in Indian Thought,* SUNY Press, Albany, 1991.

Harper, Katherine Anne and Brown Robert L, eds. *The Roots of Tantra,* SUNY Press, Albany, 2002.

Hawley, John Stratton and Donna Marie Wulff, eds. *The Divine Consort Radhā and the Goddesses of India,* Beacon Press, Boston,1986.

——*Devī Goddesses of India,* University of California Press, Berkeley, 1996.

Humes, Cynthia Ann. *Is the Devi Mahatmya a Feminist Scriptur?* In Alf Hiltebeitel and Kathleen M. Erndl, eds, *Is the Goddess a Feminist? The Politics of South Asian Goddesses,* Sheffield Academic Press, Sheffield, 2000.

Haq, Muhammad Enamul. *A History of Sufiism in Bengal,* Asiatic Society of Bangladesh, Dacca, 1975.

Jagadeesan, Dr. N. *History of Sri Vaishnavism in the Tamil Country,* Kendal Publishers, Madurai, 1977.

Jasīmuddīn, *Murśidā Gān*, Bamla Academy, Dhaka, 1977. Nicholson, Reynold Alleyne, *Studies in Islamic Mysticism*, Cambridge, 1921.

Joseph, Allison, ed. *Through the Devil's Gateway: Women, Religion and Taboo*, SPCK, London, 1990.

Jurewicz, Joanna. *Playing with Fire: The Pratītyasamutpāda from the Perspective of Vedic Thought*, in *Journal of the Pali Text Society*, vol. XXVI, 2000.

Kane, P. V. *History of Dharmaśāstra* (*Ancient and Mediaeval Religious and Civil Law in India*), 2nd edn, 5 vols, Poona, 1968 - 77.

Kayal, Akshay Kumar. *Women in the Folklore of West Bengal*, in Sengupta, Shankar, ed., *Women in Indian Folklore*, Calcutta, 1969.

Kinsley, David. *Hindu Goddesses: Vision of the Divine Feminine in the Hidu Religious Tradition*, University of California Press, Berkeley, 1986.

——*Tantric Visions of the Divine Feminine: The Ten Mahāvidyas*, University of California Press, Berkeley, 1997.

Kumar, P.Pratap. *The Goddess Lakṣmī: The Divine Consort in South Indian Vaiṣṇava Tradition*, American Academy of Religion, Series No. 95, Atlanta, Georgia, 1997.

Kunjunni Raja K. *Indian Theories of Meaning*, Adyar Library Series 91, Madras, 1963.

Kvaerne, Per. *An Anthology of Buddhist Tantric Songs: A Study of the Caryāgīti*, Universitetvorlaget, Oslo, 1977.

Lupsa, Michele. *Chants 'a Kālī de Rāmprasād: Introduction, Traduction et Notes*, Pondichery (PIFI), 1967.

Lalye, P.G. *Studies in Devī Bhāgavata*, Popular Prakashan, Bombay, 1973.

Leslie, Julia. *The Perfect Wife: The Orthodox Hindu Woman according to the Strīdharmapaddhati of Tryambakayajvan*, OUP, 1989.

——ed. *Roles and Rituals for Hindu Women*, Pinter Publishers, London, 1991.

Malamoud, Ch. *La Brique Percee: sur le jeu du vide et du plein dans l'Inde brahmanique, Figure du vide, Nouvelle Revue de Psycoanalyse, XI*, Spring, Paris, 1975.

Mani, Lata. *Contentious Tradition*, in Sangari and Vaid, *Recasting Women*, New Delhi, 1989.

Marglin, Frederique Apffel. *Kings and Wives: The Separation of Status and Royal Power*, and Adrian C. Mayer, *Perception of Princely Rule: Perspective from a Biography*, in ed. T. Madan, *Way of Life: King, Householder, Renouncer: Essays in Honour of Louis Dumont*, New Delhi, 2nd edn, 1982.

Matsubara, Mitsunori. *Pāñcarātra Saṃhitās and Early Vaiṣṇava Theology With a Translation and Critical Notes from Chapters on Theology in the Ahirbudhnya Saṃhitā*, Motilal Banarsidass, Delhi, 1994.

Maxwell, T.S. *Viśvarūpa*; Oxford University Thesis (1981), Oxford University South Asian Studies Series, OUP, Delhi, 1988.

McGee, Mary. *Desired Fruits: Motive and Intention in the Votive Rites of Hindu Women*, in ed. Leslie, London, 1991.

Narasimhachary, M., ed, Āgamaprāmāṇyam by Yāmunācārya, GOS, No. 160, Baroda, 1976.

——*Contribution of Yāmunācārya to Viśiṣṭādvaita*, Sri Jayalakshmi Publications, Hyderabad, 1998.

Olivelle, Patrick, *Upaniṣads: A New Translation*, The World's Classics, Oxford University Press, New York, 1996, pp. 253-265, 384-395.

O'Hanlon, Rosalind. *Issues of Widowhood*, in *Recasting Women*, 1989.

Padoux, André, transl. Jaqcues, *Vāc: The Concept of the Word in Selected Hindu Tantras*, SUNY, Albany, 1990.

——*Mantra et Diagrammes Rituels dans L'Hinduisme*, CNRS Paris, 1986.

Parikh, Indira, and Pulin K. Garg, eds. *Indian Women: An Inner Dialogue*, Sage, New Delhi, 1989.

Pintchman, Tracy, I *The Rise of Goddess in the Hindu Tradition*, SUNY Press, Albany, 1994.

Preston, J.J. *Cult of the Goddess: Social and Religious Change in a Hindu Temple*, New Delhi, 1980.

Qureshi, M.S. *Poemes Mystiques Bengalis, Anthologie: Chants Bauls, Traduction, Introduction et Commentaires*, Collection Unesco d'oevres represe ntatives (Serie Bangladesh), 1977.

Raghavan, V. *The Integrators: The Saint-singers of India*, Delhi, 1964.

——and P. Ramachandran, *Nottusvarasahityas of Śrī Muttusvāmī Dīkṣitar,* Madras, 1979.

Ramesan, M. *Sri Kamakoti Pitha of Sri Sankaracharya,* in *Sankara and Shanmata,* Souvenir published in connection with the Conference on 'Sankara And Shanmata' held in Madras from June 1-June 9, 1969, Madras. Cf also Sri Anantanandendra Saraswati Swamigal, *Kamakotipuri and the Pitha,* in the same volume.

Rāy, Amarendra. *Śākta Padāvalī,* Calcutta University, Calcutta, 1971.

Raychaudhuri, Hemchandra. *Material for the Study of the Vaishnava Sect,* University of Calcutta, 1936.

Renue, Louis. *Hinduism,* Prentice-Hall International, London, George Braziller Inc. New York, 1961.

Rizvi, Saiyid Athar Abbas, *A History of Sufism in India,* I, Delhi, 1978.

Robinson, Sandra P. *Hindu Paradigms of Women: Images and Values,* in ed. Haddad and Findlay, *Women, Religion and Social Change,* SUNY Press, Albany,1985.

Salomon, Carol Goldberg. *The Baulsongs,* in ed. Donald Lopez Jr, *Religions in India in Practice,* Princeton Readings in Religions, Princeton, 1995, pp. 187 - 208.

——eds. Alan Entwistle and Carol Salomon with Heidi Pouwels and Michael Shapiro, *Literature, Language and Culture,* Manohar, New Delhi, 1999.

——*The Cosmogonic Riddles of Lalan Fakir,* in eds. Arjun Appadurai, Frank Korom and Margaret Mills, *Gender, Genre and Power in South Asian Expressive Tradition,* University of Pennsylvania Press, Philadelphia, 1991, pp. 267 - 304.

Sangari, Kumkum and Sudesh Vaid, eds. *Recasting Women: Essays in Colonial History,* Kali for Women, New Delhi, 1989.

Sanderson, Alexis, *Mandṇala and Agamic Identity in the Trika of Kashmir,* in ed. Padoux, André, *Mantra et Diagrammes Rituel dans L'Hinduisme,* edtion du CNRS, Paris, 1986.

——*The Visualization of the Deities of the Trika,* in ed. Padoux, André, *L'image Divine Culte et Meditation,* edition du SNRS, Paris, 1990.

Sastri, S. B. ed. *Caryāgītikośa of Buddhist Siddhas,* Visva Bharati University, Santiniketan, 1956.

Schimmel, Annemarie, *Mystical Dimensions of Islam*, Chapel Hill, 1975. Sen Gupta, Shankar, ed. *Women in Indian Folklore*, Indian Publication, Calcutta, 1969.

Sen, Nilratan, ed. *Caryāgītikośa* (facsimile), Simla, 1977.

Sen, Kshitimohan, *Bāṃlār Bāul*, Calcutta University Press, Calcutta, 1954

Smith, Frederic M. *Indra's Curse, Varuṇa's Noose and the Suppression of the Women in the Vedic Śrauta Ritual*, in ed. Julia Leslie, *Roles and Rituals*, Pinter Publishers, London, 1991.

Śrī Ma, *Rāmakṛṣṇa-kathāmṛta* (a translation), Ramakrishna Mission, Madras, 1947.

Swami, Sri Satyamurthi. *Śrīvachanabhushanam, by Sri Pillai Lokacharya, and Yatiraja Vimsati, by Srimad Varavara Muni, An English Glossary*, Shri Ram Nam Yogashram, Faizabad, U.P., printed at Sadhana Press, Lohia Bazar, Gwalior, 1 1972.

Tagore, Rabindranath, *The Religion of Man*, London, 1931.

Tambs-Lyche, Harald, ed. *The Feminine Sacred in South Asia*, Manohar, New Delhi, 1999.

Thakur, Abanindra Nath, *Baṃlar Vrata*, Visva Bharati, Calcuta, 1956.

Thompson, E.J. and A.M. Spencer, *Bengali Religious Lyrics: Śākta* (The Heritage of India Series), London, 1923.

Torella, Raffaele, The Iśvarapratyabhijnnākārikā of Utpaladeva with The Author's Vṛtti, Critical edition and annotated translation, Instituto Italiano per il Medio ed Estermo Oriente, Roma, 1994.

Tiwari, Laxmi G. *The Splendour of Worship: Women's Fasts, Rituals, Stories and Art*, Manohar, New Delhi 1991.

Valiuddin, Mir. *Love in its Essence: The Sufi Approach*, Indian Institute of Islamic Studies, New Delhi, 1967.

Vaudeville, Charlotte. *Kabir Granthavali (Doha)*, Publications de L'Institut Francais d'Indologie, No. 12, Pondichery, 1957.

Venkatachari, K.K.A. *The Maṇipravāḷa Literature of the Śrīvaiṣṇava Ācāryas*, Anantahacharya Research Institute Series no. III, Bombay, 1978.

Vidyārṇava, Śivacandra. *Tantratattva*, new edn, Calcutta, 1973.

Wilson, H. H. *Rig-Veda: Translation and Note*, Vol. II, Poona, 1925.

Zvelebil, K. V. *Tamil Literature*, Handbuch Der Orientalistik, Zweite Abteilung, Indien, Zweiter Band, Erster Abschnitt, E.J.Brill, Leiden, 1975.

Zbavitel, D. *Bengali Literature*, Wiesbaden 1976 (A History of Indian Literature, Vol. IX, 3).

Selected Glossary

Ajapā: Japa is the repetition of a mantra for a predetermined number of times. The worshipper often him/herself determines the number of such repetitions and it is a voluntary act. It is part of the tantric yogic practice of dhyāna and dhāraṇā. After long practice, the worshipper becomes perfect in the yogic practice and spiritually reaches the highest state, viz. samādhi, when she/he only practises the japa of the mantra of the identity of him/herself with the supreme Self, known as the Haṃsa-mantra. Eventually the practice of japa becomes automatic just like breathing. Such automatic japa is called ajapā.

Āvaraṇa śaktis of Navāvaraṇa maṇḍala/Śrī-cakra: The goddess Tripurā is worshipped on a graphic design known as Śrī-cakra. This is a cosmogram representing the cosmic goddess. She is the centre/essence of creation, which she created by evolving herself through her projected śaktis. These śaktis encircle her in ever outgoing circles. These circles are called āvaraṇa or cover because they progressively hide the real nature of the essential supreme Śakti. In Śrī-cakra there are nine(nava) such circles or āvaraṇas. These secondary śaktis represent the gradual creation from subtle to gross. The further they are from the central Śakti the grosser they are.

Iṣṭadevatā: A Hindu individual is free to choose a specific divinity from the divine pantheon. As the supreme divine is truly transcendent and unique, all divine forms are just a manifestation of the supreme God in a particular aspect. So a devotee chooses the aspect to which she/he can closely relate in worship. This is why it is termed the wished for (iṣṭa) deity.

Upacāra: ingredients and accessories used for worshipping deities.

Kalā: 16th part of the full moon, hence it means part of a whole. In Tantra it also means Śakti the divine power; ontologically it is the fourth limitation of the Self (atman) which distinguishes it from the supreme Self. Again, kalā is the fourth of the six tāntric paths of soteriological practice, where the practitioner meditates on the six ways (ṣaḍadhvā).

Kuladevatā: The deity traditionally worshipped by a family and often also the clan it belongs to. However, in the tantric religious system kula is the name of a particular sect and its system is called *kaulācāra* with the cult of a special goddess. The followers are called *kaulas.*

Kumārī: Another name of the Goddess. The term really means a girl before her puberty. Many devotees of the Goddess worship such a girl(s) as representing the goddess. The most famous kumārī is worshipped in Kathmandu in Nepal.

Gṛhadevatā: The deity worshipped by the family as the deity of the household.

Guruparamparā: The lineage of a famous guru where succession is strictly determined by pupillary line, which is very important for esoteric sects. In all sectarian esoteric ritual a tāntric must invoke and worship all his/her predecessors in the pupillary line. They are divided into three groups (ogha), viz. divyaugha (the divine gurus), siddhaugha (the liberated gurus) and mānavaugha (human gurus).

Cakra: This is a multivalent term. Cakra may mean a wheel, a circle (of closely related entities like various yoginīs or śaktis, cf. Āvaraṇa śakti), or a circular design, often indicating cosmoses, divine worlds. This cosmic aspect relating to the supreme Goddess is used in Yogic meditation to unite step by step, the creative stages, and finally arriving at the centre which is also the apex of creation. This is the seat of the supreme Śakti (the Goddess) in the state of creation; above that Śakti is transcendent and totally merged in the supreme God. Cf. Śrī-cakra.

Mātṛkā: Literally it means little or adorable mother. But at a certain point it came to refer to warrior goddesses. These goddesses then became a formal group of eight mātṛkā, viz. Māheśvarī, Brahmāṇī, Vaiṣṇavī, Vārāhī, Nārasiṃhī, Kaumārī and Cāṃuṇḍā. Each of these Mātṛkās is regarded as the śakti of the god her name is associated with, viz. Śiva/Maheśvara, Brahmā, Viṣṇu/Nārāyaṇa, Varāha, Narasiṃha and Skanda/Kumāra. But Cāmuṇḍā is not connected with any god. Most probably, Camuṇḍā represents Śakti not in her creatrix stance when She is the evolving, creating prakṛti, but the exhausted unfertile state of Śakti poised for the total dissolution prior to the beginning of a new creation. In iconography she is represented as an old and haggard woman in contrast with the iconography of other śaktis in divine conjugal status, who are young and voluptuous, indicating their fertile state. However, they are part of the divine host helping the Goddess to overcome the seemingly invincible royal demons and their army. They are not independent śaktis but are projections from the Goddess. Mātṛkā also means source, and in tāntric cosmogony it means manifest speech, i.e. varṇa, viz. fifty or fifty-one Sanskrit letters. The usual arrangement of the letters starts with the letter a and ends with the letter *ha.* Sometimes the letter *kṣa* is added. However, these letters are arranged quite differently in different sectarian esoteric systems.

Mudrās of Tripura: During the worship of the goddess Tripurā the practitioner uses ten mudrās or hand gestures and postures. The first, Trikhaṇḍā, is used for invoking Tripurā, the other nine are used for invoking śaktis of each circle. These are also venerated as śaktis in their own right. Each of them should be worshipped within the circle (cakra) each belongs to. The names of these nine śaktis are Kṣobhiṇī, Vidrāviṇī, Ākarṣiṇī, Āveśakarī, Unmādanī, Mahāṃkuśa, Khecarī, Bīja and Yoni. All ten mudrās are represented during worship by a specific hand gesture or body posture.

Prapatti bhakti: Passionate and steadfastly loyal devotion to one's adored god. Mainly relevant in Vaiṣṇava theology, it has been there systematized and requires the devotee to take no steps for self-security, never worship any other deity and never waver from complete trust in god Viṣṇu the only saviour.

Śrauta: Vedic tradition, which defines the traditional system of Hindu ritual as against Tāntrikī, i.e. tantric system of ritual performance.

Ṣaḍaṅga-nyāsa: The body, whether divine or individual, in the tantric ritual system is divided into six parts or limbs. These are heart (hṛt), head (śiras), the sacred tuft of hair (śikhā), torso or, armour protecting it (kavaca), eyes (netra) and weapon (astra). These are regarded as the essence of a full image of a deity and the adept's sacred body. In ritual these are needed to replace the adept's empirical body by the placement of the divine essential body, thus making it divine. Also while invoking a deity to be present at the place of the deity's ritual worship this placement (nyāsa) is needed to create the deity's pragmatic image.

Ṣaḍguṇa: In Pāñcarātra theology God in His creative aspect is defined as having six divine or ideal qualities (guṇa). These are *jñāna, aiśvarya, śakti, bala, vīrya* and *tejas. Jñāna* stands for supreme divine knowledge and omniscience; *aiśvarya* stands for cosmic sovereignty; *kriyā* is indomitable potency and potentiality; *bala* is irresistible strength; *vīrya* is supreme valour and efficacy in creating and evolving without changing the divine integrity; *tejas* is divine energy and brilliance, the divine effulgence.

Ṣaḍadhvā: The Creator God and Śakti have evolved in six(*ṣaḍ*) ways(*adhvā*) into the empirical world. It is actually Śakti who evolves from subtle to gross creation and God is always immanent in all of Śakti's stances. The main divisions of these six ways are two. The first three ways are variations of speech (*vāc*) and the remaining three are stages in which the world evolves into its pragmatic form. The former group are references and the latter referents. A tāntric yogin engaged in his/her spiritual practice must follow this gradual route of divine creation, albeit in the reverse order. These are *varṇa, pada, mantra, kalā, tattva* and *bhuvana.* The system of *ṣadadhva* yoga is somewhat different in the Śaiva tāntric system than the Vaiṣṇava tantric system. Quite possibly the latter borrowed it from the former.

Ṣaṭkarma/ krurakarma: Tantrics use their yogic power not always for beneficial purpose for themselves (salvation) nor for others (*śānti karma*). The purpose of achieving tantric power is also to do harm and other criminal acts. These acts are listed rather differently in different tantras, but the differences are minor. Basically these are: subjugation, causing a person to go somewhere involuntarily, causing paralysis, causing animosity between friends, causing loss of one's home, and causing death. These are considered to be misuse of occult power and performing criminal (*krura*) acts unless performed for social and communal benefit.

Siddhi: Achievement of perfection in tāntric ritual practices and supernatural powers. Besides the soteriological goal of mukti or salvation, in the tantric tradition there are eight this-worldly goals or achievements, viz *aṇimā,* capacity to become extremely minute; *laghimā,* to become almost weightless; *garimā,* to become very heavy, *mahimā,* to enjoy universal respect; *prāpti,* power to obtain anything; prakāmya, irresistible willpower; *īśitva,* supreme lordship; *vaśitva,* supreme control of all; and *kāmāvasāya,* capacity to be anywhere.

Index of Indic Words, Texts and Authors